JACK JONES

A TRUE FRIEND TO CHINA

'THE LOST WRITINGS OF A HEROIC NOBODY'

Collected and edited by

Andrew Hicks

THE FRIENDS AMBULANCE UNIT 'CHINA CONVOY', 1945-1951

Jack Jones, later famous as, 'Jack Reynolds'
Author of "*A Woman of Bangkok*"

A TRUE FRIEND TO CHINA

ISBN-13: 978-988-82730-1-0

Published by Earnshaw Books Ltd. (Hong Kong).

JACK JONES' "CHINA CONVOY"

During the late nineteen forties Jack Jones and his Quaker colleagues of the Friends Ambulance Unit's 'China Convoy' distributed medical and relief supplies across vast areas of 'free China', long devastated by poverty and disorder, as the communists moved towards and entered Chungking.

Jack wrote many contemporary accounts of his experiences in China for the weekly China Convoy newsletters, including how he was captured and beaten by bandits and soon after rolled his loaded truck into a ravine. Recently rediscovered in archives in London and Philadelphia, these regular newsletter articles have the freshness, passion and immediacy of a modern blog and the extracts from them that appear in this book tell a gripping story of remarkable people in remarkable times.

Under the pseudonym, 'Jack Reynolds', Jack later achieved worldwide fame in 1956 with his novel, "*A Woman of Bangkok*", published a year before Richard Mason's "*The World of Suzie Wong*". In 1974, some years after settling in Thailand, his short stories of the local women he treated at his clinic in Chungking were published in Hong Kong under the title, "*Daughters of an Ancient Race*".

Always perceptive, sometimes lyrical and often funny, Jack Jones' newsletter writings, collected here for the first time, are an important perspective on turbulent times as China recovered from war and as the communist liberation swept away the crumbling structures of a feudal society. They also tell the story of a young man finding a role in life as he and his co-workers, both European and Chinese, were swept up in the tide of world events, struggling to do something to alleviate the appalling human suffering that was ever present around them.

CONTENTS

F.A.U.
FAU·116

PREFACE

I first heard how the Friends Ambulance Unit's 'China Convoy' distributed medical supplies to 'free China' under tough wartime conditions when I was a lecturer in law at the University of Hong Kong in the late seventies. Bernard Llewellyn, Oxfam's overseas director, who used to stay with me on his way to plan new development projects in the region, had been on the China Convoy and he told me how, when supplies of petrol could no longer be brought in over the Burma Road, they converted their trucks to run on charcoal gas.

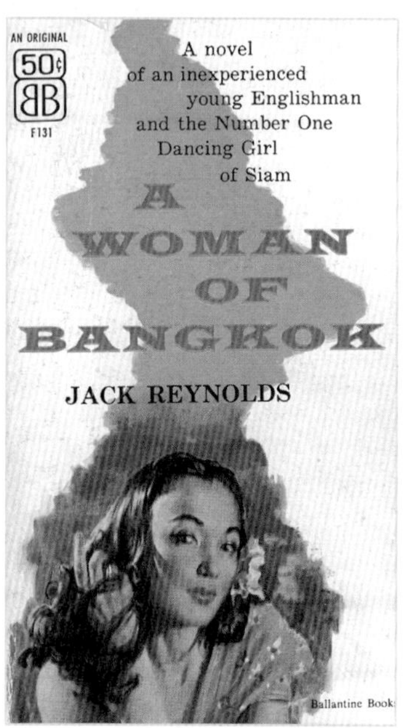

Many years later when living in Thailand I wrote and published a romantic backpacker novel called *Thai Girl*. It sold well but critics would sometimes say that for a cautionary tale about cross-cultural relationships you could never beat *'A Woman of Bangkok'* by Jack Reynolds. It was out of print but I at last found a second hand copy and it quickly drew me in. About a naïve young Englishman who gets romantically entangled with a Bangkok dance hostess, its story line anticipated Richard Mason's, *'The World of Suzie Wong'* but with no happy ending.

It intrigued me that Reynolds had produced so fine a novel, a bestseller published both in New York and London and in print for many years, but had apparently written nothing else, neither before nor since. No one on the internet forums knew who 'Jack Reynolds' was so I started digging.

I discovered that Jack Reynolds was a pseudonym and that he was in fact 'Jack' Jones who had lived from 1913 to 1984, Jack being a long standing nickname. After a time I managed to meet his widow, some of his six surviving children in Thailand and several of his Bangkok friends. His family knew very little of his first four decades before he fetched up in Bangkok and produced no archive of papers for me, so my quest for Jack was to be arduous, a slow and painstaking detective story starting totally from scratch.

To my surprise and delight I learned that Jack had been a leading light in the FAU China Convoy and coincidentally that on meeting Bernard Llewellyn, they had become life long friends. Bernard's son Michael has since produced for me Bernard's copy of Jack's unknown pre-war book of poems, a copy of his book of China stories, *'Daughters of an Ancient Race'*, another book called *'The Utter Shambles'* and many other leads that have helped me learn more about Jack and the FAU.

My forays into the archives of the Bangkok Post then unearthed many articles by Jack including one about China, but the real hidden treasure was to be found in the archives of the Quakers, the 'Religious Society of Friends' in London. There I discovered a hoard of China Convoy news letters, a flimsy weekly distributed to FAU workers scattered around China to which Jack regularly contributed.

In 1946, following cessation of hostilities, control of the China Convoy was transferred to the American Friends Service Committee and their later news letters are deposited in the Friends' archives in Philadelphia. This caused problems of access for me but, with the help of many people, I have now collected from both sides of the Atlantic a substantial selection of Jack's news letter articles, business letters and reports from 1946 to 1951, the most engaging of which I have edited for this book.

Jack was thus writing in China for a tiny news letter audience, bashing away tirelessly on an old typewriter in the hellish heat and humidity at the main transport depot in Chungking. Remarkably efficient, the post office then delivered his typed drafts to headquarters in Chengchow or Shanghai where the news letters were edited and mailed out to all FAU posts around China. Read by a handful of people more than half a century ago, probably destined to be hung up in the latrine and since lost and forgotten, these are a unique contemporary account of the struggle for life in China and of the FAU's gruelling work at that time. His writings thus constitute a vivid contemporary picture that a formal history can describe but can not evoke.

In addition to Jack Jones' China writings the book includes photographs of China, of Jack and his friends and of the activities of the China Convoy which truly speak a thousand words. Many of these have been sent to me in response to several years' work tracing surviving FAU members and their families all over the world and most have not been seen before in print. Because of challenging conditions in China and often printed on tiny scraps of photographic paper their quality is often poor but they do somehow evoke that exciting era.

Few of these pictures can be attributed to a specific photographer, though the fine work of Jack Skeel, Anthony Reynolds, Stanley Betterton, Lindsay Crozier and Robert Reuman among others is well represented. FAU members always freely shared their photos for their friends to send home and the continuation of this generous spirit is gratefully acknowledged.

Finally, I owe an enormous debt of gratitude to all the people who have helped me to assemble Jack's writings and to put this book together. They are far too numerous to mention individually, though in particular I have to thank Ullrich Dennerlein who undertook the overwhelming task of manually transcribing the many scans of fading newsletters that I sent to him in Thailand. I would never have contemplated this book without his enthusiasm for rediscovering Jack's work.

In a special category also, I have to thank Mike Frankton, Howell Jones, Mark Jones, Peter Mason and Dorothy Reuman all of whom served with Jack in Chungking. They have given me their photos and papers and answered my incessant questions with remarkable recall. Great survivors all of them, you will see their names cropping up from time to time as you read Jack's newsletter articles.

A book such as this is, I believe, a justification for preserving huge archives of dusty old papers and without the unstinting help of librarians at the Friends Library in London and at the American Friends Service Committee in Philadelphia and of Elizabeth Douglas, my research assistant there, Jack's own story and writings would have been lost forever. To all of these my collaborators and to so many others, I am eternally grateful.

As the centenary of Jack's birth fell on 19th June 2013, this is a timely opportunity to resurrect these writings that so vividly take us back to those turbulent times and which make him and the characters he describes so human, young, vigorous and alive. They did their work with commitment and passion and it's good now to remember them as they all most certainly were, true friends to China.

Andrew Hicks
Hampshire, UK
January 2015

In Chungking Jack sketches Christ carrying the cross

A Modern Map Of East Asia

China As The FAU Knew It

1. Provinces, 1939, showing the old Sikang province
2. Cities and railways in 1949
3. The Burma Road and main FAU distribution routes
4. The new focus on relief work in Honan, 1947

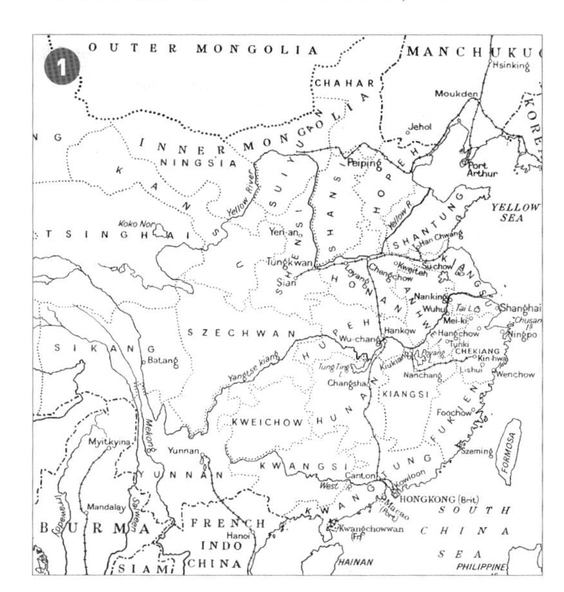

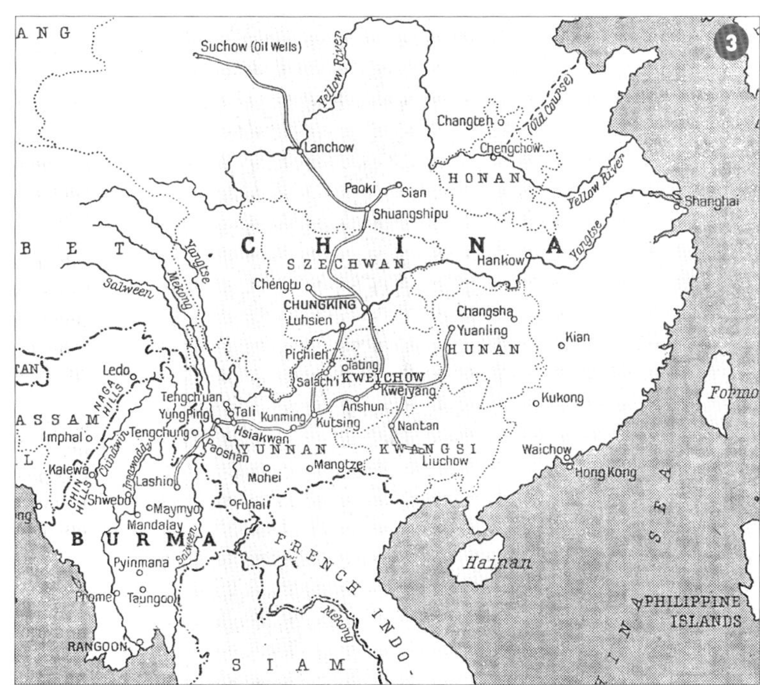

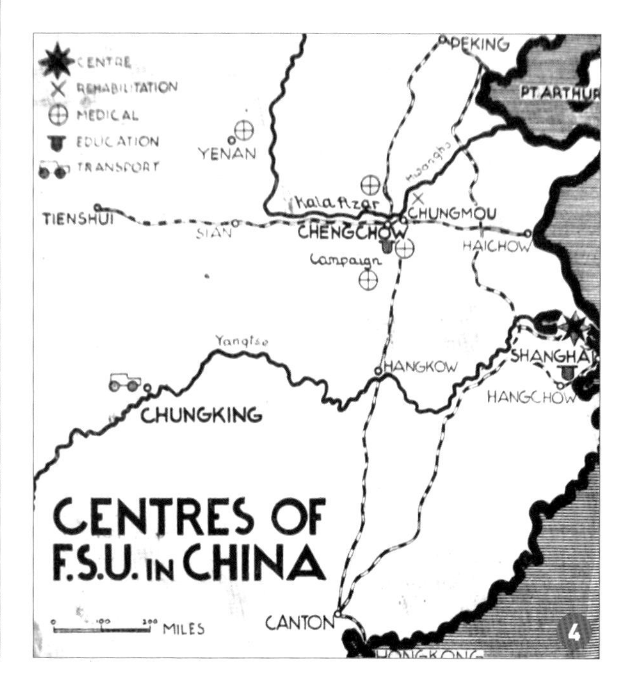

The Burma Road

This map was sketched by Bernard Llewellyn when he was an FAU member in the early nineteen forties. With Burma itself off the map to the left, it shows the Burma Road running through the mountains to the city of Kunming. In response to the Japanese invasion of northern China in 1937 the Burma Road was urgently built as an essential supply route, an achievement of raw manual labour in much the same league as the Great Wall. After it was completed in 1938, military supplies to support the fightback against the Japanese were taken from the port of Rangoon by train to the railhead at Lashio and then by truck over the Burma Road to Kunming and beyond. When the Japanese invaded Burma early in1942 the road was cut and supplies, including medical supplies for distribution by the FAU, had to be flown in to Kunming over the Himalayas.

The map shows the road plunging into the malarial gorge of the Salween River and climbing again to the ancient city of Paoshan where the FAU ran a field hospital and mobile surgical units for soldiers wounded on the Salween front. It then drops down again to the Mekong River and continues its roller coaster ride for many more miles. Past the turn to the lakeside city of Tali it reaches Yunnanyi, where the AVG operated against the Japanese from a nearby airstrip. The American Volunteer Group, nicknamed the Flying Tigers for the shark jaws painted on the front of their Curtis Warhawk fighters gained almost mythological status.

The road then finally reaches Kunming, the once remote capital of Yunnan province, which had become a booming centre for receiving war and relief supplies by air. From there the FAU shipped medical supplies by the narrow gauge railway or by truck to its base at Kutsing (Qujing) from where it was distributed northwards by one of two routes and ultimately to Chungking, the northernmost extension of the Burma Road.

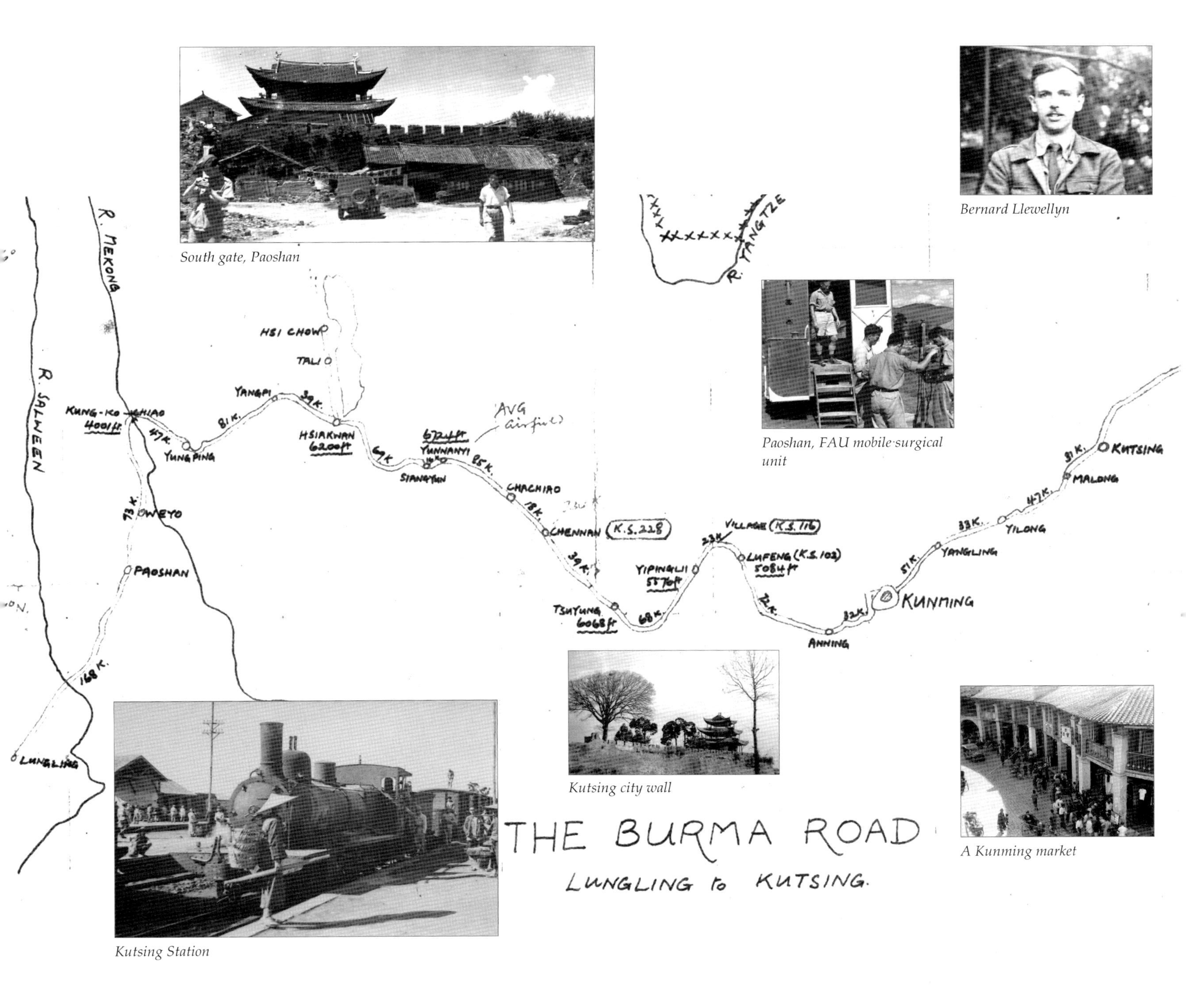

South gate, Paoshan

Bernard Llewellyn

Paoshan, FAU mobile surgical unit

Kutsing city wall

A Kunming market

Kutsing Station

The Road to Chungking

This map shows the extension of the Burma Road running from Kutsing (Qujing) in Kweichow province (Guizhou) northwards along the south west highway built by the Nationalist government to link Yunnan province with Chungking (Chongqing) in Szechuan province. Soon after Kutsing the road passes the left turn onto the mountainous road to Luhsien on the Yangtse River where the FAU had a transport depot. Then it reaches the fabled Twenty Four Bends, an impossible series of hairpin bends constructed by the Nationalists in 1936 and re-engineered by the American army in 1943 that were so tight trucks sometimes had to back up to get round them. Crossing the suspension bridge over the Pan Kiang gorge, the road then passes the dramatic Wong Kuo Shu Falls (Huangguoshu) before reaching Anshun. At Huang Tu Po just outside Kweiyang, the provincial capital of Kweichow, the FAU had its first transport base.

Further north is the major commercial town of Tsun I (Zunyi), well known as the place where Mao Tse Tung was first elected to the leadership of the communist party at a major conference during the Long March. The road then drops down off the mountains onto the hot and fertile plains of Szechuan province, finally reaching the FAU's Chungking garage four and a half kilometres short of the Yangtse River, on the other side the city of Chungking, the Nationalist capital during the Japanese occupation.

The map was drawn in 1944 by Paul Cope, an American member of the China Convoy who preceded Jack Jones as garage manager of the Kweiyang transport depot.

Scrawled on the map are the words, 'Evans/Condick', a reference to the place where Chris Evans and Ron Condick suffered a 'mishap' in June 1944 when the road collapsed under their truck. Condick wrote in a letter, 'Chris jumped out between the truck and the cliff and the truck rolled over him. He remembers looking upwards quite calmly and saying, 'I wonder if the bastard will hit me?'

Pan Kiang gorge north of Annan on SW Highway

Anshun inside the walls

公誼救護隊

FRIENDS' AMBULANCE UNIT : CHINA CONVOY

AFFILIATED TO THE INTERNATIONAL RELIEF COMMITTEE OF CHINA

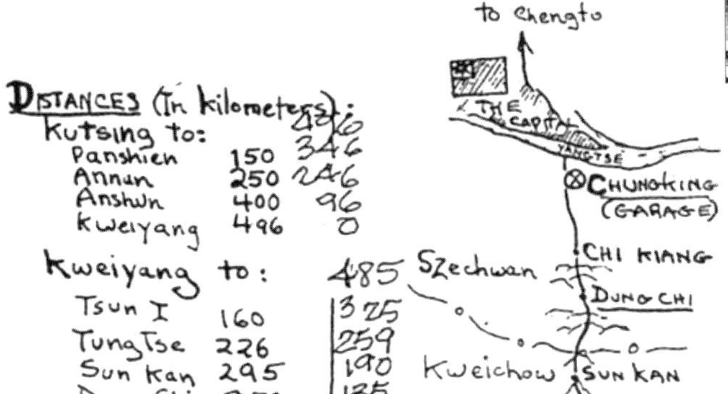

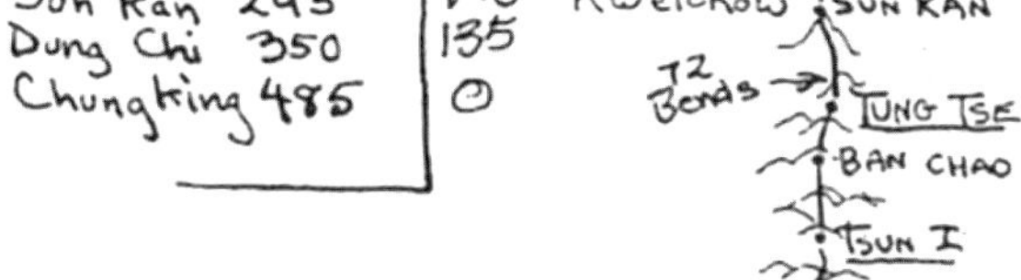

EVANS-CAUDICK

PAUL M. COPE Jr. - 44

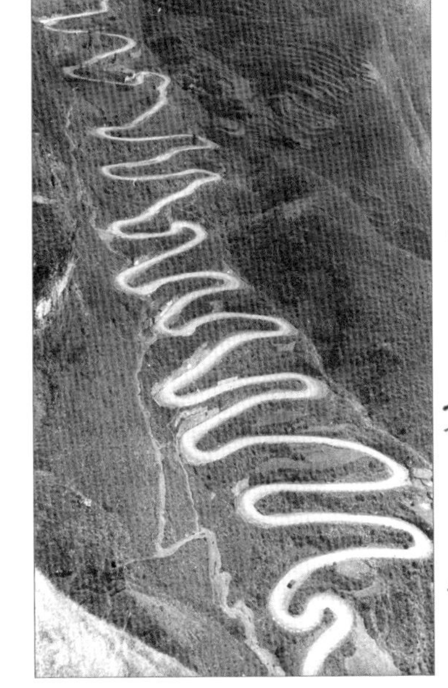

The Twenty Four Bends

Huang Kuo Shu falls, 1945

Fuel Convoys to Suchow

This map, also by Paul Cope and dated June 13, 1945, records his convoy from the Chungking transport depot travelling far beyond Lanchow in Kansu province to the oil wells in Suchow to buy petrol. Beside each place name the distance from Chungking is given in kilometres, Suchow being 2288 kilometers away over appalling roads, a journey of several months.

From Chungking the route crosses over the Yangtse on the vehicle ferry, continuing to Tungliang, Suining and Santai where there were small Quaker missions. The hospital at Suining has recently celebrated its centenary since its Quaker foundation, coinciding with the opening of a fine new hospital campus. At Mienyang a road goes left to Chengtu while to the north are many names that recur in Jack Jones' writings. At Miao Tai Tse was an exotic temple, sometimes visited by FAU members such as Mark Jones. (Fuel convoys were often photographed and some striking images appear below at page 136.)

Shortly after is Shuangshipu where the China Industrial Cooperatives 'Bailie School' was supported by the China Convoy before moving to greater safety at Shantan at 1997 kilometres before Suchow. It was to this school that the remaining Chinese staff, trucks and equipment transferred when the China Convoy was finally wound up in 1951. At Shuangshipu a major route goes east towards Paoki and a few hundred kilometres further on another to Sian.

Paul Cope seems to have been a man of irrepressible energy and optimism with 'a grin that nothing could wipe from his face'. His graphic skills included a nice line in cartoons, such as one of the FAU's newsletter editor feeling the heat in Chungking, skills which led on to a successful career as an architect in Philadelphia.

Dressing for Chungking Reception *The Communicator in Chief* *Morning Start-Up on the Road*

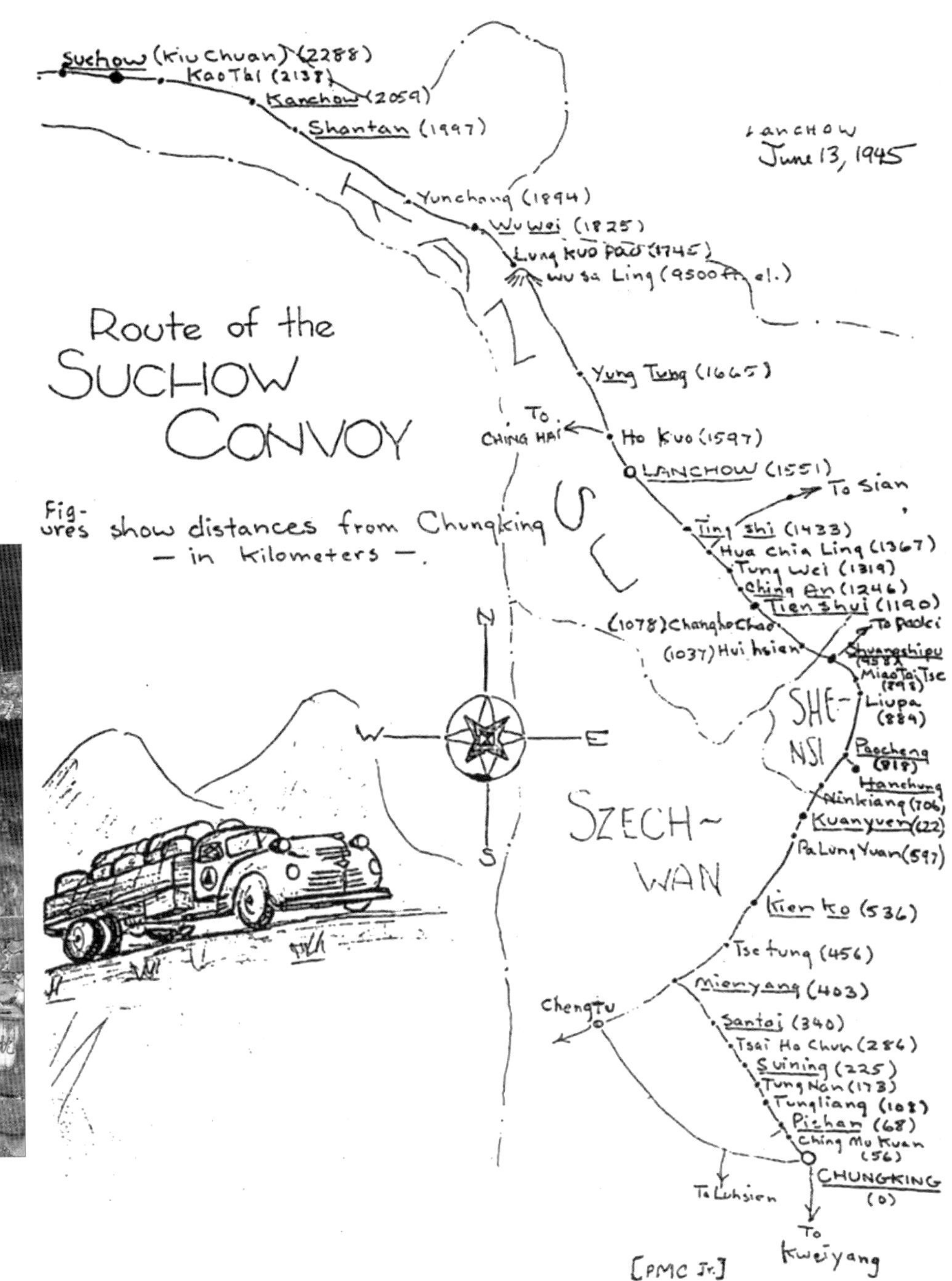
Suchow (Kiu Chuan) (2288)
KaoTai (2138)
Kanchow (2059)
Shantan (1997)
Lanchow
June 13, 1945
Yunchang (1894)
Wu Wei (1825)
Lung Kuo Pao (1745)
Wu sa Ling (9500 ft. el.)
Route of the SUCHOW CONVOY
Yung Tung (1665)
To CHING HAI
Ho Kuo (1597)
LANCHOW (1551)
To Sian
Figures show distances from Chungking — in kilometers —.
Ting Shi (1433)
Hua Chia Ling (1367)
Tung Wei (1319)
Ching An (1246)
Tien Shui (1190)
(1078) Changhochao
(1037) Hui hsien
To Paoki
Shuangshipu (958)
MiaoTaiTse (898)
Liupa (884)
SHE-NSI
Paocheng (818)
Hanchung
Ninkiang (706)
Kuanyuen (622)
PaLungYuan (597)
N
W
E
S
SZECH-WAN
Kien ko (536)
Tse tung (456)
Mienyang (403)
Chengtu
Santai (340)
Tsai Ho Chun (286)
Suining (225)
Tung Nan (173)
Tungliang (108)
Pichan (68)
Ching Mu Kuan (56)
CHUNGKING (0)
To Luhsien
To Kweiyang
[PMC Jr.]

Mark Jones at the Miaot'aitzu temple, Paoki convoy, 17 Dec 1946

Kunming to Chungking

This map is Mark Jones' schematic plan of the south west highway from Kunming to Chungking at the top of the page, via Kutsing and Kweiyang. It covers similar ground to Paul Cope's first map, in addition showing the roads they often travelled eastwards from Kweiyang towards Hunan province to towns such as Changsha, Hengyang and Liuchow.

One of Jack Jones' competent and dependable convoy leaders, Mark Jones arrived in China aged only nineteen having recently left Ackworth, the traditional Quaker boarding school in Yorkshire. His FAU logbook from which this map has been copied, a green Ackworth School notebook, is a methodical record of all of his convoys, including detailed lists of the mechanical problems that plagued them every day and of the distances he drove each month, totalling 15,811 miles in all. The map records the dates when Mark was in each place and gives a scale in both miles and kilometres. Convoys were never less than gruelling and Mark's diary records the exhaustion they experienced on getting back to the depot after a long trip. Yet within a few days, he wrote, they were getting itchy feet and were again longing for the challenge and excitement of the open road.

Mark Jones' convoy pulls in at Hengyang, June 1946

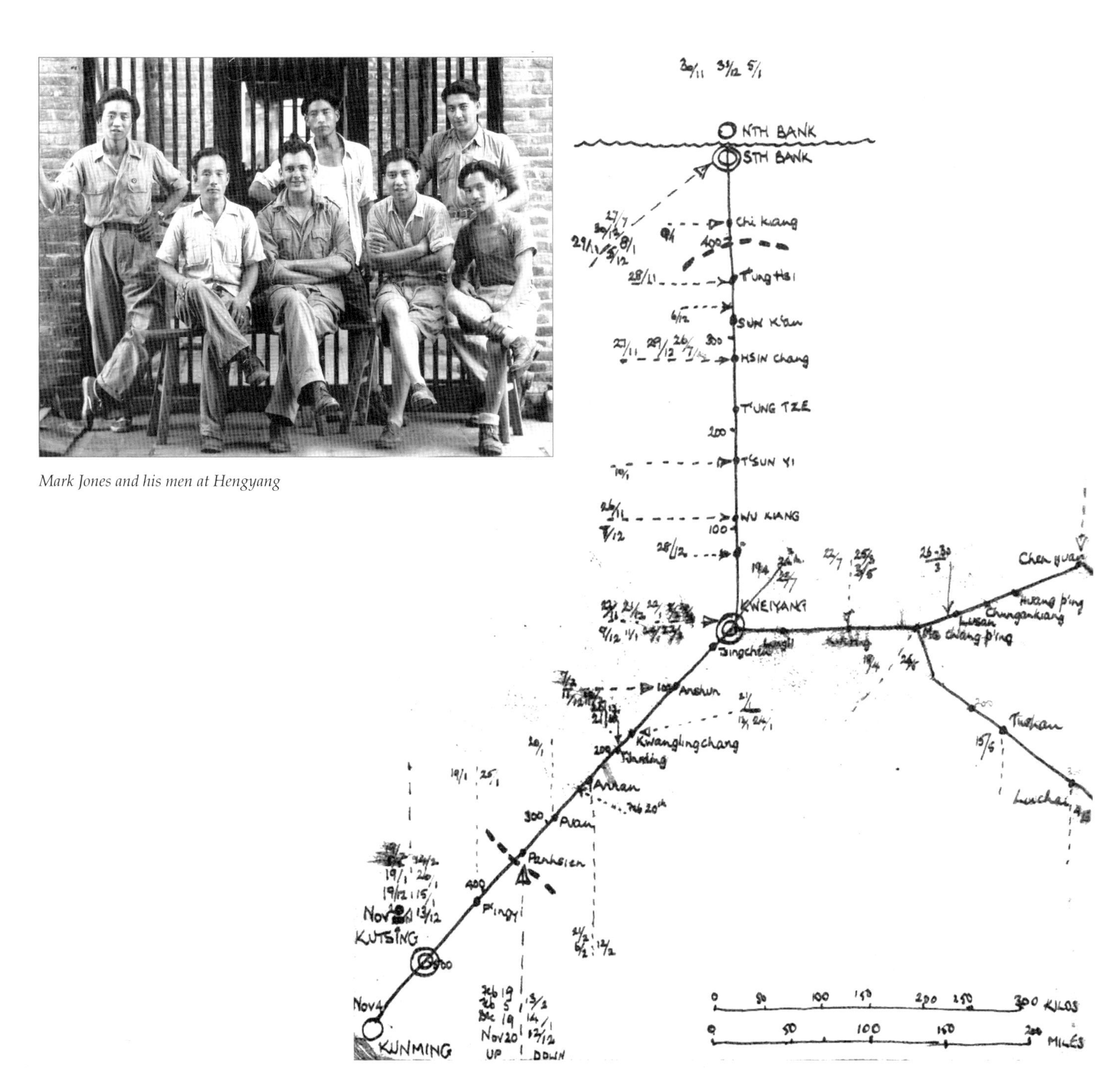

Mark Jones and his men at Hengyang

Mark Jones' Travels in China

This map from Mark Jones' photo album records his journeys with the FAU including his arrival by air in Kunming from Calcutta. It shows the main routes he drove up to Kweiyang and Chungking where he was later based, as well as to destinations eastwards from Kweiyang. It was along the road to Changsha that the truck he was driving on 26 March 1946 slid off the side of a mountain road and fell into the gorge below. While the seven passengers were thrown clear half way down, Mark went all the way to the bottom. Somehow there were no serious injuries and a day or so after his close shave with death he was photographed casually swinging off the wreck of the truck before it was winched back to the top.

The map also shows his convoys further north and there is an arrow pointing far out beyond Lanchow to Urumchi in Xinjiang province to which Mark delivered a truck for the British consul there. His flights from Chungking appear as dotted lines as well as train journeys presumably to a staff meeting at the headquarters in Chengchow. Finally a dotted line shows his departure from Shanghai for home by sea via Hong Kong and Singapore. A tiny map of Wales on the same scale, his country of origin, shows the vastness of China.

Mark Jones' truck is winched back up the cliff face

Mark Jones swinging off his wrecked truck

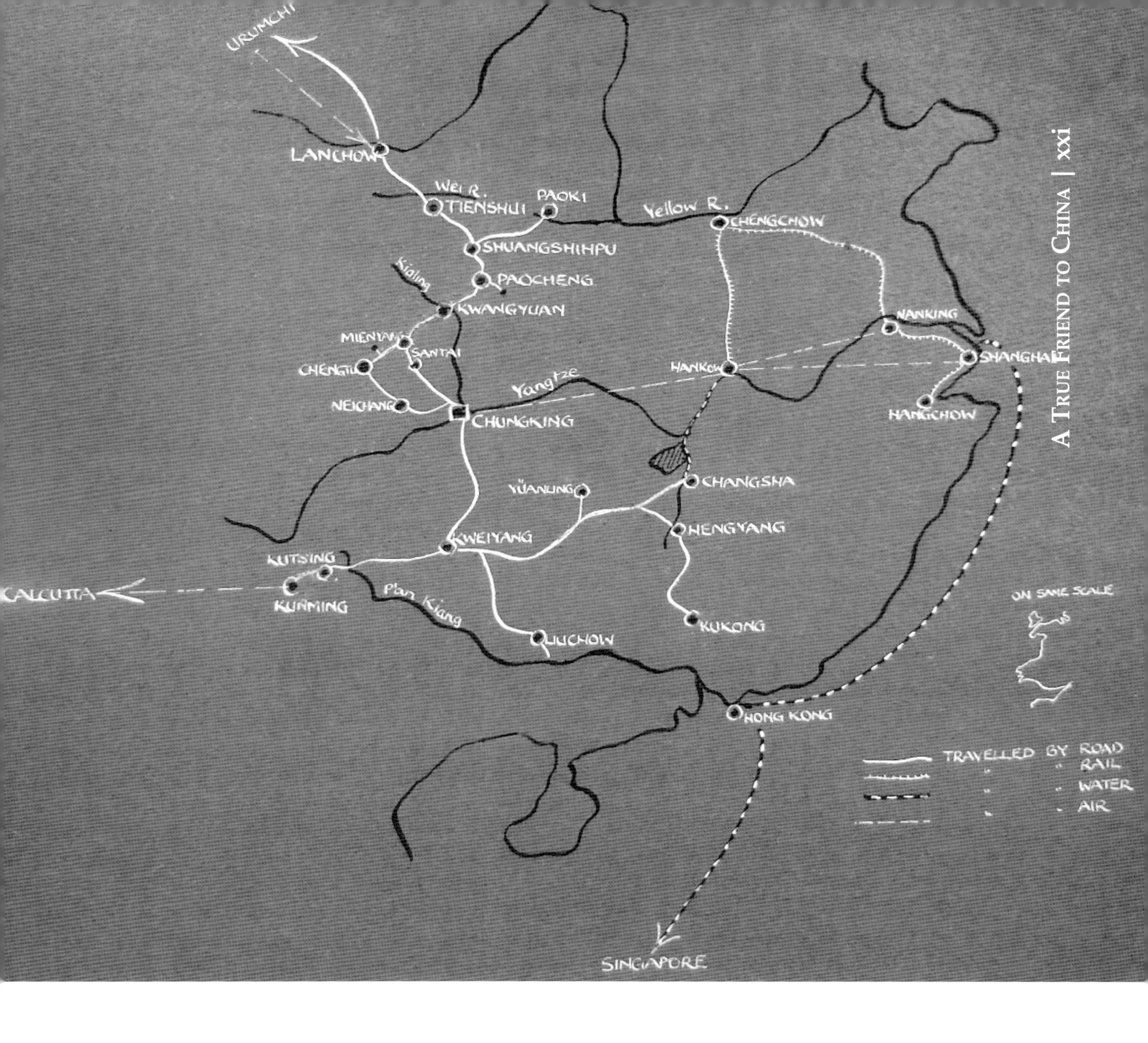

URUMCHI
LANCHOW
Wei R.
TIENSHUI
PAOKI
Yellow R.
CHENGCHOW
SHUANGSHIHPU
PAOCHENG
Kialing
KWANGYUAN
MIENYANG
SANTAI
CHENGTU
NEICHANG
Yangtze
CHUNGKING
HANKOW
NANKING
SHANGHAI
HANGCHOW
YÜANLING
CHANGSHA
HENGYANG
KWEIYANG
KUTSING
CALCUTTA
KUNMING
Pan Kiang
LIUCHOW
KUKONG
ON SAME SCALE
HONG KONG
TRAVELLED BY ROAD
" " RAIL
" " WATER
" " AIR
SINGAPORE

Chungking City in 1938

A convoy leaving the FAU's transport depot on the south bank and going northwards, would drive the four and a half kilometres of dusty road which falls steeply down to the Yangtse River, arriving there along what is marked as the 'Kweichow Highway' at Haitangchi in the bottom right hand corner of this map. Across the wide expanse of the river the city of Chungking confronts you, still enclosed in the ancient walls indicated on the map by the crenellated line around the centre. The city stands high above the river, a cliff of several hundred feet to which clung a chaos of shanties on bamboo stilts, beyond them the more permanent buildings of the city.

The river itself was either a tame winter stream running between shingle banks, its limits shown by the dotted lines or a raging monster. The ferries constantly had to adapt to changing water levels and small shops and shanties appeared everywhere on its winter foreshaw. In spring the water could then rise by eighty feet in a few days, swelled by the Tibetan melt waters, the river becoming a beast of immense power and inundating the seasonal airfield marked on the map. In anticipation of the floods the populace would gather new bamboos and shore up their dwellings high on the banks in the hope that they would not be swept away. To the north the Jialing River falls into the Yangtse creating the strategic peninsular on which the city was founded, secure in its hilltop defence. Access to the city from the south was up the face of the cliff and as there were few water sources at the top, most of the water had to be carried all the way up in buckets, leaving the stone steps constantly wet and slippery.

Pre-war view of Chungking city, the confluence of the Kialing River and the Yangtse to the right

Chungking steps

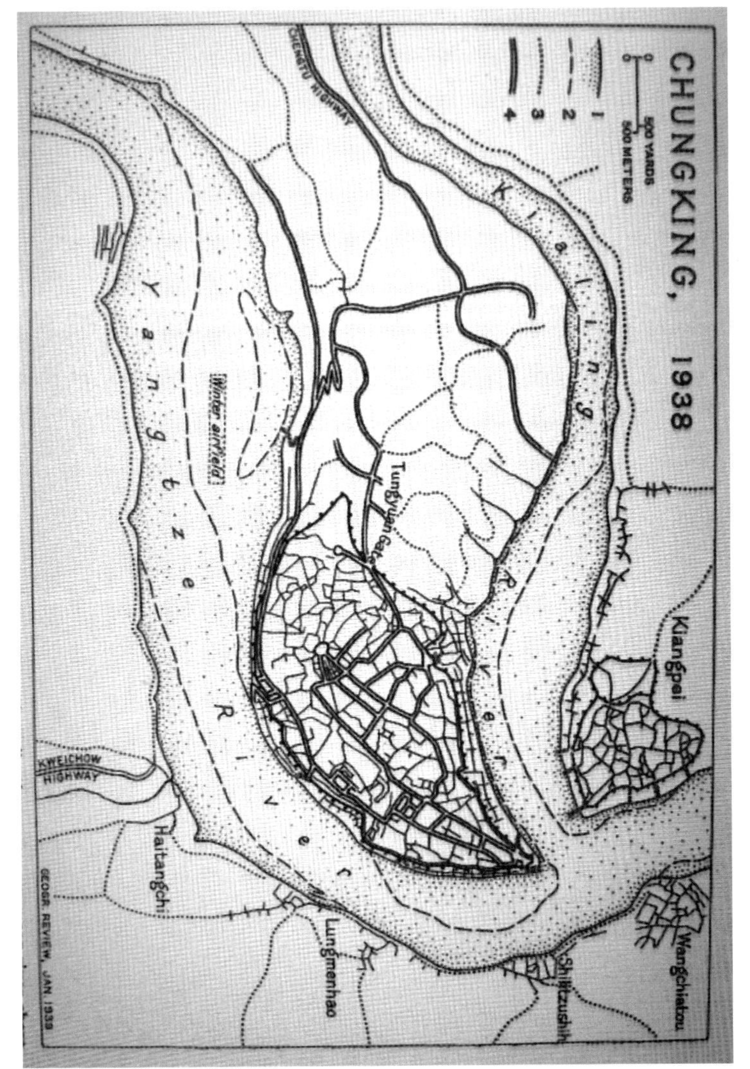

Coolies unloading on the foreshore

'Preparing for the Yangtse to rise in the spring.' Presumably shoring up stilt houses with more bamboo. Early 1950

'Yangtze ferry boarding.' South bank, Chungking, early 1950

'How to Find the FAU in Chungking'

This sketch map was published in the FSU Chronicle on 24 January 1948 as a light-hearted description of how to find the transport depot on the south bank of the Yangtse for those arriving by plane. Sanhupa was a seasonal airstrip on a shoal in the river that floods every spring when the snows melt far up in the mountains. Temporary terminal buildings and mat sheds were either dismantled before being inundated or departed downstream on the flood towards Shanghai. Tony Stickings' diary describes landing there 'on the stone block strip' after a seven hour delay owing to poor weather, adding that three days later the strip was seventy feet under water. Sanhupa was thus only in use over the winter, though unfortunately this was when drizzly rain and mists hang over the river, often causing long delays in takeoffs and landings. Poor visibility made landing treacherous, and coupled with the high cliffs of the city so close by and the shortness of the strip it was a dangerous place for flying. Planes encountered turbulence and a sudden updraft on landing could mean ditching in the river beyond unless the pilot was very skilled. Takeoff was little easier. The universal C47 'Gooneybirds' (Dakotas to us Brits) would sit ready for takeoff, the pilot anxiously gunning the engines to full power, roaring and spitting fire, the airframe shuddering and vibrating fit to burst. Then as he released the brakes she'd lumber off like an angry elephant, thumping and rumbling over the massive stone blocks, the water ahead coming closer, then tail up and not a moment too soon she'd slowly get airborne. Using Sanhupa was, the American pilots said, like flying a heavy transport plane off the deck of an aircraft carrier.

The FSU depot generally didn't know when visitors or new recruits were coming, so new arrivals at the island strip crossed the water towards the city with the dramatic cliffs in their face and phoned from the CNAC office. Peter Mason and Fleda Jones were both lucky on first arrival in Chungking as Jack got into his jeep and came down to the river to meet them. Dr Mary Mostyn was not so fortunate and had to find her own way across the passenger ferry and walk the dusty road to Ssu Kung Li Pan, an experience high on culture shock. On landing from the ferry on the south bank at Hai Tang Chi visitors reached a steep village of steps and shanties, close by the Mai Lee café much enjoyed for its for coffee and ice cream, from where the south west highway led to the transport depot and over many hundreds of miles to Kunming and the Burma Road itself.

As travel by road was appallingly slow and dangerous, flights were sometimes used for redeployment or to get to Chengchow or Shanghai for staff meetings but flying was still a rare and pleasant luxury. Today the shoal in the river is still there, now bisected by vast bridges across the river, and it seems wholly improbable that this was once Chungking's airstrip of preference when not submerged under many meters of water.

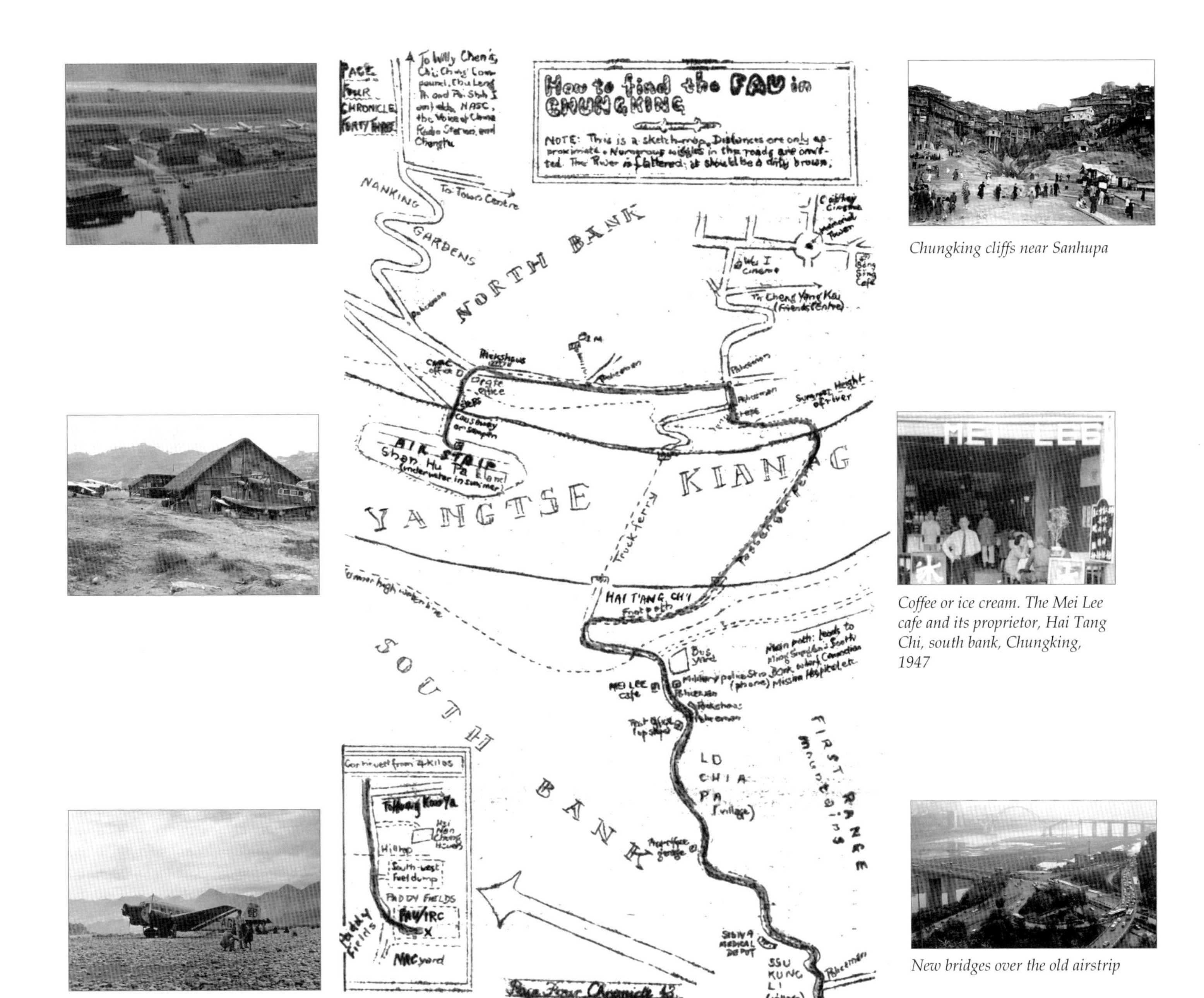

Chungking cliffs near Sanhupa

Coffee or ice cream. The Mei Lee cafe and its proprietor, Hai Tang Chi, south bank, Chungking, 1947

New bridges over the old airstrip

The Yangtse ferry

INTRODUCTION

Jack Jones and the Work of the FAU 'China Convoy'

On 6th October 1945 'Jack' Jones flew over 'the Hump' from India and landed in Kunming in south west China to work with the Friends Ambulance Unit's 'China Convoy'.

For a man in his early thirties who had never before left England the experience must have been both exciting and terrifying, even after long months of training and anticipation. Though the Japanese invaders had recently surrendered, China was still in turmoil. At her lowest ebb after a century exposed to foreign expansionism, to gunboats and superior fire power, she had no real friends in the world.

The western nations had humiliated and dismembered China with unequal treaties, extorting trade and extra-territorial rights and had brought her to her knees, causing widespread disorder and distress. On top of the usual ravages of drought and flood, famine and pestilence were piled political chaos, the continuing armed conflict between the Nationalists and Mao's communists and the incremental invasion of the Japanese, culminating in all-out war in 1937. Caught in the middle between world powers seeking dominance in Asia, China was in a seemingly unending cycle of sorrow and suffering.

By early 1942 both Hong Kong and Singapore, Britain's two great colonial outposts had fallen to the Japanese who were now invading Burma. After entering Rangoon with little or no opposition the Japanese troops advanced northwards and in April took the railhead at Lashio, thus cutting the Burma Road, China's crucial backdoor route for the importation of military and other supplies. This seven hundred mile road over the mountains to Yunnan province and beyond had been supplying China with huge tonnages but now with Japan occupying the coastal ports and the Haiphong to Kunming railway also closed, China was substantially blockaded. There thus began the first great strategic military airlift in which unarmed American transport planes based in India at great risk ferried vast quantities of war supplies over 'the Hump', the hazardous mountain ranges forming a southerly spur of the Himalayas, into the once sleepy but now booming town of Kunming. This material was intended for the Nationalist government's defence of China and later to supply the US air bases under construction for the proposed bombing of Japanese cities. All the while Chiang Kai-shek, the Nationalist leader, constantly campaigned for a greater share of these American Lend Lease supplies to equip his armies and to secure his own future. Much of this war material, however, was hoarded or went missing in a widespread and lucrative black market.

The objective of the Anglo-American allies in providing this support was to keep China in the war. They were constantly urging 'the Generalissimo', as he was called, to engage the Japanese in combat, thus to tie up their military resources and so to deplete their strength in the Pacific war. In contrast the classic Chinese approach was to avoid major conflicts with the Japanese and to await victory simply by outlasting them. Romanticising their role of supporting their gallant Chinese friends, the Americans hoped to win this future world power as an ally in the post-war period. Meanwhile Chiang Kai-shek was keeping his powder dry for the more deadly long-term struggle with the communists of Mao Tse-tung that would be a fight to the death once the Japanese had been defeated. As to the British, they also looked beyond the present conflict to protecting their colonial interests in India and to recovering those they had lost in Hong Kong, Singapore and Burma.

Meanwhile the Friends Ambulance Unit, having been driven out of Burma by the advancing Japanese and over the Burma Road into China, now became solely dependent upon the air route over the Hump. This was their only way for personnel to get into China and for obtaining the essential medical and other supplies that had to compete for precious cargo space on the heavily laden C47 aircraft of the American Transport Command.

China itself was thus in a dreadful state of underdevelopment and chaos, its populace often in abject misery. The Japanese invasion had uprooted many civilians, factories and colleges that fled away from the coast westwards as refugees. By 1941 Chiang Kai-shek had also been displaced from northern China, making the city of Chungking, high up the Yangtse River, his capital. The city endured years of heavy bombing by the Japanese, its primary defence being the swirling clouds that often prevailed during the damp and dismal winter.

As for the ordinary people, they had long endured government by elites who had no concern for the poverty and famines that afflicted them. Much of the energy of these elites was focussed on the political intrigues necessary to cling onto power, on enriching themselves by corrupt means and on manipulating the Americans to allocate them more war supplies. Meanwhile rampant inflation made money almost valueless and public services were in a state of collapse. Thus for example a majority of hospitals, many of them run by Christian missions, were unable to operate or did so with inadequate supplies of drugs and other essentials.

Into this tormented world came the men and women of the Friends Ambulance Unit such as Jack Jones. They came as friends to China, though the lessons of recent history would have made it hard for a Chinese to recognise any foreigner as a friend. In impossible conditions, they thus tried to do the relief and rehabilitation work that was so desperately needed and which they knew could only be a drop in an ocean of need.

Surprisingly the first major project the FAU was asked to run was transporting medical supplies. The distribution of medicines and equipment from the airfield in Kunming and across mountain roads to the far flung hospitals and clinics of 'free China' was of crucial importance, the view being taken that only a body such as this running convoys of trucks, each one led by a foreigner, had a chance of getting through. Thus it was that despite a desperate lack of spare parts and imported fuel the FAU is credited with hauling eighty percent of all medical supplies in Nationalist China over this period. Hence it came to be known as 'the China Convoy', a nickname that had great resonance for those who took part in it.

The Friends Ambulance Unit

The FAU was a charity, set up under the auspices of the Religious Society of Friends, the Quakers, though independent of it. The majority of its members in China were not Quakers and, unlike the missionaries who had long been doing medical work in China, they did not come carrying bibles.

The Quaker church, established in England in the mid-seventeenth century, believed that a relationship with god was not mediated through hired clergy and formal sacraments but was to be found and expressed through inner conviction and by direct experience in day to day life. They practiced the principle that all human beings, rich and poor, male and female are equal, they opposed participation in war and promoted social justice. They campaigned, for example, for the abolition of slavery and when the Cadbury, Fry and Rowntree families were successful in trade, being excluded as non-conformists from public office and the professions, they put their wealth towards improving the living standards of their workers.

The bible taught them that Jesus Christ was a pacifist who told his followers to love his enemies and that worldly wealth is an obstruction to spiritual development. Their work through the FAU in China was thus to live these principles rather than to evangelise. In Jack's writings there is hardly a mention of Christianity and even then it's usually a wry comment about eccentric missionaries or the ponderous collective decision-making of Quaker-style meetings.

The FAU was set up during the First World War as a channel for non-combatant service by Quakers who refused to bear arms and had registered as conscientious objectors. At the beginning of the Second World War it resumed the same role to enable pacifists to contribute to humanitarian and medical services in a way that accorded with their consciences. The FAU was thus active in many spheres including Egypt, Greece, Syria, Ethiopia, continental Europe, India and of course China. With the introduction of conscription for military service, tribunals were established which allowed exemption if the applicant could prove that their conscientious objection was genuine and a real obstacle to bearing arms. Unlike soldiers, they worked as volunteers for no pay and forsook all pension and other family benefits that were available to the military. Furthermore, they often faced the odium of society for refusing to fight and risked discrimination when later applying for jobs. Being a 'conshie' was not a soft option and the alternative service that was required of them was often dangerous and demanding. Indeed Jack saw the deaths of three fellow members of his small transport unit, Pip Rivett dying of polio, Brian Sorensen being killed in a plane crash and Robert Waldie dying from complications following the removal of his appendix.

The Friends Ambulance Unit in China did not in fact operate ambulances as its primary activity. It distributed the medical supplies flown in to Kunming from India and provided medical services, often based in the few mission and other hospitals that were still operating. The Unit took over transport and distribution of medical supplies for the National Health Administration and the International Relief Committee, carrying medical supplies across routes totalling 6,000 kilometres to many hundreds of hospitals and clinics. As such it was the major civilian medical and relief transport organisation working in areas controlled

by the Nationalist government. However, as a strictly neutral agency, at the earliest opportunity supplies were also taken into communist areas with a convoy delivering medical supplies to Mao's headquarters in Yenan as early as February 1946 and a medical team moving there later that year.

The political, financial and practical obstacles to the transport operation were sometimes almost insurmountable. The transport unit handled a huge tonnage of relief supplies in impossible conditions, running heavily loaded trucks on appalling mountain roads, subject to floods and land slides and open to attacks by bandits and

US Army transport plane at Chengchow ready to fly FAU medical staff to the communist headquarters at Yenan, November 1946

harassment by Nationalist soldiers and officials. Crashes and breakdowns were a constant hazard. Tyres and spare parts were hard to get and when the Burma Road, the one remaining supply route, was cut by the Japanese and there was no more fuel, they adapted the trucks to run on charcoal gas. Following the Japanese surrender, new opportunities arose for relief and rehabilitation work further north and while the transport operation based in Chungking run by Jack Jones continued on a smaller scale, it ceased to be the core activity.

A slumbering hoard of historic writings

'Jack' Jones was a key chronicler of the Friends Ambulance Unit 'China Convoy' during the immediate post-war period and until its final closure in early 1951. Sadly his writings have since been lost or forgotten and this book is now an opportunity to preserve them for posterity and for new generations of readers.

Under the pseudonym, 'Home Brew', Jack wrote regular contributions for the FAU Newsletter which came out almost weekly and for its successor, the 'Chronicle' produced by its replacement organisation, the Friends Service Unit, when the American Friends Service Committee (AFSC) took over running of the China Convoy following the surrender of the Japanese. These circular newsletters were produced in the Unit's China headquarters on flimsy paper and passed round members who were scattered widely across vast areas of inhospitable terrain.

I thus discovered these ephemeral newsletter articles slumbering in the archives of The Friends Library in London and of the AFSC in Philadelphia and it became my quest to transcribe them and to find what I could of Jack's other writings about his experiences in China.

It was necessary therefore to photograph hundreds of poorly printed and fading pages, often impossible to capture properly when tightly bound at the spine with metal pins. Far too indistinct to be digitised by scanning, the only way was to type them in by hand, a task that was utterly daunting as each line sometimes had to be peered at for minutes on end to decipher its wording.

These writings thus make up a body of work that paints an authentic day to day picture of how things were for the FAU in China at this critical time in history. They have a style which is both lively and informative and which has an immediacy that a formal history written by a library-based scholar who wasn't actually there can never achieve.

So who was 'Jack' Jones?

Before he went out to China, Jack Jones was a nobody, a drop-out as we might call him today, but he became an important figure in the latter days of the China Convoy. Later when living in Bangkok and working for Unicef, he became known internationally for his novel published in New York in 1956, called, "*A Woman of Bangkok*", soon to be republished in London the same year as, "*A Sort of Beauty*". This story of how a young Englishman fell for a dance hostess and came to grief, an earlier 'Suzie Wong' romance in a Thai setting but without the happy ending, sold in large numbers and gave him a moment of recognition and fame as a writer.

Though writing was a passion for Jack, he only produced one other significant book, "*Daughters of an Ancient Race*", which was published in Hong Kong in 1974. This collection of short stories is about the turbulent lives of the women he treated in his clinic at the FAU garage at Chungking on the south bank of the Yangtze, the history of which is recorded below.

Jack sailed for the East from Liverpool on 3 September 1945, the day following VJ Day when the Japanese formally signed the surrender. He landed in Calcutta and flew over the Hump into Kunming in October. Like most new FAU recruits he probably

spent his first days in this resurgent boom town billetted at the substantial French style house of 'Stamp' Smith, the irascible Old China Hand who was postal commissioner for Yunnan province.

After a few weeks there, he was then sent to the old walled city of Kutsing (Qujing) where he was in training and driving a truck on main routes for a few months. After Kutsing he spent seven months at the FAU's Kweiyang (Guiyang) garage doing mechanical work and running convoys before it was closed, moving to an expanding depot on the south bank of the Yangtse opposite the city of Chungking, the Nationalist's capital, at the beginning of September 1946. Jack stayed behind briefly to do final closure work, before driving the 500 kilometres over the mountains to Chungking in the ex-American weapons carrier they called, 'WC for Relief', a wry reference to relief work in West China. Extracts from his newsletter accounts of this and of the years that follow are transcribed below.

Jack quickly seems to have fallen on his feet on arrival in China. In October 1946 he was appointed West China Agent and soon found himself running the south bank garage outside Chungking city and later its clinic until everything was wound up following the communist 'liberation'. He finally obtained his exit permit and left China, one of the very last FAU

Stamp Smith

The FAU transport depot, Chungking, on the south bank of the Yangtse

members to go, early in 1951. His unbroken service of more than five years is a tribute to a tenacity and dedication which is often apparent from his writings. To take an example of this, among the documents I have transcribed is his pencilled report to the FAU's Shanghai headquarters arguing passionately that his Chungking garage should not be closed. In this he included from memory detailed lists of the Chinese staff and their families, two hundred in all, who depended on the FAU for their livelihoods, all written from his bed in hospital as he recovered from a near fatal attack of typhus. When the doctor told him not to work and refused to give him a pen, he'd had to make do with a pencil. Through the sheer force of a principled and obsessive personality, Jack thus made a success of his work in China, and it is undoubtedly true that his China experiences also made Jack.

The church and manse, Buntingford

Jack was born Emrys Reynolds Jones at Buntingford, Hertfordshire to the north of London in 1913, the son of the Congregational Church minister there. Postcards of the time show a handsome church with the manse alongside, Jack's childhood home.

His father, Joseph, had been born in 1881 into a poor family from Colwyn Bay in North Wales that had moved to Liverpool where work could be found. Joseph was the fourth child but his mother died within a few months of his birth. Joseph's father, Jack's grandfather, was a warehouse man and corn sampler in the docks, and because of his distressed circumstances was unable to keep the child. In a letter written to a niece in 1962 Joseph described how he was given to his late mother's sister and her husband, 'on the strict understanding that I was not to be told later on that I was not really their own child'. These his 'early protectors' then also died and he was 'passed from one aunt to another' on his mother's side, only learning of his true birth parents when in his early teens. It seems that he attended the Blue Coat School, a charitable institution in Liverpool where he must have been an able and ambitious pupil. 'As a poor boy in Liverpool', he wrote, 'I often used to look with awe at the University buildings and wonder if I should ever become a student therein, never believing for one moment that a time would come when I should become a student not of Liverpool but of London University! "God moves in mysterious ways…"'

In 1906 he thus registered as a scholar at New College, London to study for the Congregational ministry. Unfortunately he failed his first year Latin exam and then failed the resit exam, so could not apparently proceed to a Bachelors or full Honours degree course. Nonetheless, he completed his formal training, was ordained in 1911 and was appointed as minister to the prosperous and active Congregational Church at Buntingford. Soon after, on

Village fete, Revd Joseph Jones standing at centre with Jack below the sign

21st September 1912 he married Emily Mary Ellen, another Jones, thereby unduly complicating my genealogical research, and on 19 June 1913 Jack was born as Emrys Reynolds Jones. Jack thus acquired his gentle Hertfordshire accent in this small town where he spent the first decade of his childhood as a son of the Manse. Meanwhile his father held memorial services for the former church choir boys who were being slaughtered on the Western Front and worked in a munitions factory as war service in lieu of call-up.

Buntingford School

Jack has described his father, Joseph, as 'a ferocious man with a ferocious religion', though in his letters written in his early eighties Uncle Joe, as he called himself, comes across as a warm and energetic individual. Joseph pushed hard for Emrys, his only son, to go to university and to follow him into the ministry, perhaps projecting onto him his own unrealised academic ambitions. Now a minister with a new living in north London, he had found his son a good school in Wood Green. There the young Emrys, probably a loner, became known as Jack. 'On your Jack Jones again', I guess they said to him, Cockney rhyming slang from a popular music hall song, meaning 'you're all on your own'.

Jack apparently failed to pass his school leaving exams and to 'matriculate', and, in conflict with his father, suffered what he called a nervous breakdown, leaving home to stay with an uncle at his bakery in Llangollen, North Wales. In these circumstances, it is not hard to see how a father who had escaped the poverty of a broken home would react angrily on seeing his dreamer of a son wasting the chances in life that he was offering him. This was the early thirties, the time of the Great Depression and finding a living and a secure future cannot have been easy, even with a better education than Jack's.

Revd JR Jones

Tracing Jack's chaotic trajectory has proved impossible, but at some time he 'ran away to sea', working on a fishing trawler in the North Sea out of the aptly named Grimsby. He worked as a gardener probably in a stately home in Hertfordshire and in market gardens. He worked in a sugar beet factory, he dug potatoes, worked as a tour guide in the hills of Llangollen and for a business that made grass tennis courts. And he became a speedway rider, chancing his arm weekly on the south east speedway circuits and occasionally coming to grief.

In the late thirties, perhaps remembering the deaths of his father's parishioners in the trenches and now working with a Lincolnshire sculptor and monumental mason called Philip Pape who was a committed pacifist, Jack's pacifist principles took shape. Attending a Friends Meeting House in Hertfordshire, attracted presumably to their pacifism, in 1940 with the war on he applied to be a conscientious objector so as to be exempted from call up for military service. The tribunal duly registered him as such on condition he work on the land or with the Friends Ambulance Unit and thus he became a 'conshie'.

He must then have continued working in food production, a demanding wartime battle front, for a few more years, as it was not until early 1944 that he applied to join the Friends Ambulance Unit, in March presenting himself for the nineteenth FAU training camp at Manor Farm, Northfield, Birmingham. The mugshot on his personnel card shows Jack as bespectacled, with a strong jaw, a weathered face and wary eye. After sixteen tough months

ANDREW JONES,
THE MODEL BAKERY,
Church Street, LLANGOLLEN.
Bronze Medallist 191[illegible] & 1913 for White & Brown Bread.
The production of pure White and Wholemeal Bread and Cakes guaranteed at this bakery under the personal supervision of the proprietor.
Deliveries to any part of Llangollen.

The 'Helios', Jack's trawler

of work and training in hospitals (where 'FAU' was said to mean 'Faeces and Urine'), and in vehicle mechanics and truck driving, he then made his big move and volunteered for deployment to China. With soldiers soon returning from the war to their former jobs and the economy in ruins, the future was uncertain and this was now his chance for a big adventure.

Selection of applicants for China was rigorous, Jack being described by his FAU assessors as 'practical, quiet and slow' and as showing 'strong China concern'. He was prepared to commit to three years' service in China, was versatile because of his 'med/mech training', though he was thought to be most suitable as 'a transport man'. Accordingly the committee approved him for China reinforcements and the die was cast, the course of his life turning on their decision. Jack set sail from Liverpool for India, just as hostilities were finally over and when he would soon be demobilised and free to look for whatever work he chose.

Now in his early thirties, a young man who'd been a rolling stone, a Jack of all trades who had done a lot of things but had stuck at nothing, who'd been a dare-devil speedway rider and had even published a book of his own poems, he was thus something of an enigma. Older than most of the others arriving in China who were generally in their early twenties, despite his lack of experience as a leader, responsibility seems to have come readily to him. Jack soon found a total commitment to the work he was doing and the Chungking garage became his reason for being. Later when the FSU was retrenching for financial reasons and his garage was targeted for closure, he fought his corner passionately, raising funds to keep it running by whatever means he could. While other projects were closing down following the communist victory, Jack was expanding his new clinic that served the poor inhabitants of the local villages on the south bank of the Yangtse. This clinic he writes about in, "*Daughters of an Ancient Race*", a book which is a tribute to the courage of the women he treated and whose lives he came to know so well. 'These poor tormented females', he wrote, 'were condemned forever, as it seemed to me then, to poverty, pain, disease, mistreatment and misery', but, as he portrays in the book, they refused to be crushed by centuries-old discrimination against their sex.

Like so many of his contemporaries sharing similar experiences, China made a huge impression on Jack and he never returned to live in England, spending the rest of his life based in Bangkok. He worked for Unicef in Thailand, later travelling abroad for other UN agencies on numerous foreign contracts and filling the time between contracts with newspaper work and other writing and editorial work in Bangkok.

"Daughters", was published in 1974 some time after the events it describes and is an excellent read that Jack said was his favourite book. However, his contemporary accounts in the Newsletters and Chronicles have an intimacy that is unique and compelling. Today they would most likely be a blog and Jack would attract many hits as a first rate blogger.

Mike Frankton and Jack Jones, Chungking, October 1945, taken at 9.45am by Lindsay Crozier

THE KUTSING GARAGE DEPOT

Jack spent his first few months in China at Kutsing, an ancient walled city, where the FAU had its first purpose-built garage depot. Surrounded by spectacular stone walls, the city inside was a medieval world unchanged for millennia. A day's run north east of Kunming by road or the much slower narrow gauge railway, the city was at the junction of the south west highway towards Szechuan and Chungking and a road running northwards over high mountains to Luhsien on the Yangtse. This secondary road the FAU used for a time as a main distribution route.

A photo of John Briggs wistfully gazing over the rail of his ship en route to China is extremely poignant as John was never to return home. Assigned to supervise building of the new depot in June 1942 he caught typhus fever and died. Only a few days later another member, Douglas Hardy, also died of typhus. Nonetheless, morale was high and the China Convoy was expanding, enjoying its glory days. Pictures show different views of the depot from the outside, including its curious gatehouse. Inside the compound photos were taken of their beloved trucks, of the assembled men, the workshops, the remarkable 'tinwork' made entirely from old oil drums for the front end of a Dodge truck, and of Wilf Jackson and the 'canvas lady' working on the fabric roof of his truck. Departing convoys were also an exciting and auspicious time when the cameras often came out.

55

THE GROUP PHOTO AT THE CHUNGKING SOUTH BANK GARAGE

This photo of FAU staff sitting on the ex-American army weapons carrier they called, "WC for Relief" was taken at the FAU garage depot on the south bank of the Yangtse at the four and a half milestone on the road from Chungking to Kweiyang just past the village of Suu Kung Li Pan. It was probably taken in early October 1946 shortly after the transport unit closed its depot in Kweiyang and moved to the depot in Chungking. Everyone in the picture looks hot, though Chungking should have been cooling by then. Even so, a typical day time high in the upper seventies or eighties with relative humidity of 85% would feel sticky and it is no surprise that Jeanette, the Chinese hostel warden, is busy fanning herself.

The date can be plotted reasonably accurately by following the movements of the men in the picture. Three weeks after the move to Chungking Jack Jones wrote that Brian (Sorensen) was in hospital and Geoff (Bonsall) was down with malaria, but they're both in the picture. A newsletter reports that in mid-October Jack and Howell Jones were flying out of Chungking probably for a meeting in Chengchow. In December Jack went to Chengtu and in early February 1947 he and Hugh Russell were en route to a staff meeting in Shanghai when their truck fell sixty feet into a ravine. Hugh did not return to Chungking but flew back to England, so an early October celebration of the move before all of these events seems to be the most likely reason for the photo.

It has been my quest to identify all the faces in the picture and to try to trace what became of them in later life after they left China, and in this I have had considerable success.

At centre of the group in beard and singlet is **Jack Jones** himself who left China early in 1951 and settled in Bangkok. There he worked as transport manager for Unicef, later taking similar UN contracts in Jordan, Africa and the Far East, interspersed with writing and journalism in Bangkok. He and his Thai wife had seven children and he died in Bangkok aged 71 in 1984.

On his left is **Howell Jones**, born in 1926, who sent me the original tiny print of this photo and whose remarkable memory sixty five years on has enabled all of the British staff slowly to be identified. On leaving China he qualified as a doctor in Hong Kong, spending seven years there. After some time in England, he settled in Canada in 1965 with his English wife where he had a distinguished career as an orthopedic surgeon, retiring in Gander, Newfoundland. In June 2012 I met him off the plane at Heathrow airport and we spent a pleasant few days together at my home and visiting his sister in Hay-on-Wye in the Welsh border country.

On Howell's left with the pipe is **Walter Kirby** who trained in England for the FAU with Jack Jones and who, as aspiring artists, became close friends. Walter met his wife-to-be in Shanghai where she was working for a New Zealand relief agency and they settled in New Zealand. I have spoken on the phone to his son, David and his mother then aged 93. They told me that Walter qualified as a registered nurse in London but as male nurses were not permitted in NZ, he made his living as a plumber, retiring in 1977 in his late fifties to devote himself to painting and pottery. He died aged 77 in the late nineties.

Back row left is **Robert C. Gairns**, a Scot reputed for his great physical strength. In mid-1956 he wrote to Jack that he was not happy in his job in York and was emigrating to Canada where he settled in Montreal. A technical writer for Atomic Energy of Canada, his obituary described him as a 'good old guy, stubborn and independent' and that his passions were Scottish dancing and gliding. In September 1999 he was photographed aged eighty sitting in the vintage glider he had spent a year restoring before its maiden flight. Tragically the glider then crashed after release from the tow plane and he was killed instantly. The funeral was held in the hangar as he was a single man with no relatives and the gliding club was in effect his home.

The fair haired man at the back is **Anthony Owen Stickings** who arrived in Chungking early in 1946, sometimes holding the fort as acting boss when Jack was away. With his wife, Jean, he later worked in Sarawak as a surveyor, returning to England in 1953 before emigrating to Canada in 1957 where he was a surveyor, geography teacher and, with his wife, a church organist. They had five children, three of them adopted and his obituary in 2005 praised him as, 'a teacher, musician, adventurer, pacifist, husband and father'. His two oldest children tell me that their mother is still living and that she has his letters home from China and also his photographs.

To his left, the man in the big hat is **Mark W. Jones**. His career culminated as group personnel director at Rowntrees and on retirement he published a beautifully self-illustrated guide book called, "*A Walk Around the Snickelways of York*", done in the style of Alfred Wainwright. This sold in large numbers and led to further books and a retirement career as a speaker on York country wide. In May 2011 I met him at the China Convoy reunion in London where he gave a talk and sang a ditty penned by him from his China Convoy days. He also loaned me his superb album of China photos, all meticulously captioned.

Mike Frankton

Front row left is **Mike Frankton**, a chartered electrical engineer who retired from ICI to live in Darlington, County Durham. After working with the FAU in Europe at the end of the war in the concentration camps, he was an active photographer in China. He has sent me scans of about fifteen pictures of the Chungking depot including several of Jack. Howell Jones has described him to me as being, 'the epitome of gentle strength, quiet authority and great ability'. In his late fifties he developed his early skills as a clarinetist, formed The Darlington Clarinet Ensemble and with it has traveled the world performing to large audiences. As of early July 2010, he went to Finland to visit family for six weeks.

Seated at the front with the dog is **Geoffrey Bonsall**, son of a China missionary and one of two brothers in the FAU. I met Geoffrey in Hong Kong in the early eighties where he was studying the China coast artist, Chinnery. Having graduated with an MA in Classical Chinese from Cambridge and in Library Studies from Hawaii, he was a librarian at the University of Hong Kong, later becoming director of the Hong Kong University Press. He was most widely known there as a radio broadcaster under the style of 'Charles Weatherill'. In 2010 I met his sister-in-law, Nellie Bonsall, also an FAU member, in London but sadly she told me that Geoffrey had suffered a stroke and died. I have since written an account of his career with the FAU which has been published in the journal of the Royal Asiatic Society, Hong Kong Branch of which he was a leading member and editor.

Brian Sorensen

The tall man at the front is **Lord Hugh Russell**, one of the sons of the twelfth Duke of Bedford, a family whose names are given to a number of prominent London streets and squares that they owned, making them one of Britain's wealthiest families. Before arriving in China Hugh had considerable experience with the FAU in Egypt. He died a few years ago and I have spoken to his son Mark who farms in Cornwall and has a collection of his father's letters home from China.

The man on the extreme right is **Brian J. Sorensen** who, aged twenty three, was killed ten months later on 31 July 1947 when the C47 plane he was travelling in went missing in a remote mountainous region of China on the fringes of the Gobi desert. He had been flying back from delivering a truck to the British consulate in Urumchi on the trip of a lifetime during his pre-repatriation leave. Only after three weeks was it learned that the plane had, in his father's words, "flown through the mist into the mountains - and beyond". Brian's ashes were scattered from the cockpit window of a plane over Honan province by FAU photographer, Lindsay Crozier, and a memorial service was held in Chungmou to coincide with an FAU staff meeting, at which Lewis Hoskins and Jack Jones gave spoken messages about him. Brian had a brother, Michael, also in the FAU, and they were brought up as sons of a non-conformist minister in Walthamstow, just like Jack whose family lived nearby. Their father, Revd. Reginald Sorenson, became Labour MP for Leyton and was later elevated to the Lords as Lord Sorenson. In 1947, Colin Sorensen, a cousin who served with the FAU Post-War service, saw a news stand in London with the headline, 'MP's son lost in China'. With a feeling of dread, he just knew it had to be Brian.

I have recently been in touch with several members of the Sorensen family who tell me they mourned Brian for years, but that they knew little of the recovery of the body and the rites that followed.

The girl with the fan is **Jeannette Lee Ching-hsing** who was the hostel warden at

Chungking. She married **David Shek Yu-hwa**, (the Chinese man on the extreme left) in Hong Kong on 9 October 1948. Howell Jones later visited them at their home in Hong Kong and Jeanette, who had two children, used to baby sit for Bernard Llewellyn's children when he was there working with Oxfam. Nellie Bonsall tells me her brother-in-law, Geoffrey, had heard they have both since died.

The Chinese man standing at the back is probably **Wang Hsiao Hsin**, while the one sitting next to Jack with a dog but no shirt is unidentified. However, the said dog on his lap is '**Phoebe the Fecund**', the number one dog and champion producer of puppies who often features in Jack's writings in the FAU Newsletter.

This group photo is a striking image and although it would have been much copied and sent home to families and friends and while the camera must have clicked more than once, Howell Jones' tiny copy is one of only two prints that have surfaced in family collections despite my lengthy researches.

FAU garage depot and workshops at Chungking

JACK'S FAU 'CHINA CONVOY' NEWSLETTER ARTICLES, LETTERS AND REPORTS

What follows are transcripts of articles by Jack Jones that were published in the Friends Ambulance Unit 'China Convoy' news letters and its successor, the Friends Service Unit 'Chronicles' from 1946 to 1951, together with some of his letters and reports to staff at headquarters in China and abroad.

These accounts are engaging on a personal level but also are an important anecdotal record of the latter years of the China Convoy and of its changing role as the advance of communism swept away the old feudal order. They have a wry contemporary flavour, though Jack's robust reportage was probably tempered by his obligation to be positive and to boost morale in the Unit. He also makes relatively few references to wider political events in China perhaps because news sources were few and as self-censorship may have been necessary to avoid giving offence either to the current regime or its impending successor. What he writes is, nonetheless, frank and open and at times controversial. In one piece he challenges the desirability of having married women within the Unit and in another debates whether tensions exist between Friends and non-believers within their ranks.

His news letter articles, written for a small audience of insiders are full of ephemeral contemporary references, in-jokes, pseudonyms and nick-names and so they sometimes can be difficult for twenty first century readers to follow. When reading about the Chungking garage on the south bank of the Yangtze, who would know that Mary is the generator, Celery Stalks and Jumbo are jeeps and that Cuthbert, attending a meeting at the university in Chengdu, is a dog. The organisational and financial background of the Unit, often referred to, is also complex and confusing, not to mention the many transitory relief agencies

Chiao Tien Men, Chunking's main port, offloading IRC medical supplies, Nov 1946

that invariably are known by their initials. I have therefore tried to shed light on some of these by inserting short explanatory notes in square brackets within his texts which I hope are less irritating than footnotes, and by providing a *Glossary of Abbreviations*. Words that appear in round brackets are Jack's while those in square brackets are thus my own inserted notes.

If these notes or my introductions and comments are sometimes a little repetitious, this is intentional as I assume readers will probably dip into the book rather than read it straight through. I hope these occasional reminders about the many names and other details that recur in the documents will thus allow my various commentaries to be understood independently of earlier ones.

One set of initials that will keep cropping up needs to be explained at the outset. The IRC, was the 'International Relief Committee' for whom the FAU's transport unit distributed drugs and medical supplies. In the words of FAU member, David Morris in his book of 1948, *China Changed My Mind*, 'this body was formed by a group of mission hospitals to buy drugs abroad, ship them to China and distribute them to the hospitals inside China. The personnel who ran it were all medical missionaries, drawn from different mission hospitals'. At first the IRC relied on commercial trucking firms for distribution but when this proved unsatisfactory the IRC started its own small transport organisation in Kweiyang (Guiyang).

The FAU then set up a transport unit and took over the IRC's trucks and depot and all distribution of drugs within China on behalf of the IRC and other agencies.

Mike Fox and Dr Bob McClure inspecting an engine

A small mystery is that at first the letters IRC stood for International Red Cross, a name which was evidently misleading. On 6th September 1941 Dr Robert McClure, signing himself off as Commandant, Friends Ambulance Unit China Convoy, Chungking, wrote to Madame Chiang Kai Shek, Generalissimo's Headquarters, Chungking. He started by politely regretting that, 'your health is far from good and knowing the strain of work that has been put upon you at this time'. He then told her that, 'the inclusion of the words, "Red Cross" in our title has been irritating to the National Red Cross of China and also to the American Red Cross', and therefore the name was being changed to the International Relief Committee.

The FAU developed a partnership with the International Relief Committee that was so close that Jack and all members of the FAU's transport unit in Chungking were formally seconded to the IRC which was accordingly responsible for their maintenance. Jack's writings therefore regularly refer to the IRC, at times with greater affection than others.

Finally, both in Jack's handwritten and self-typed articles and letters, he was adept at writing a correct and well-edited draft first time with very few changes or deletions. I have therefore been sparing as an editor and have made minimal corrections. However, the poorly printed documents that languish in the archives have often been more than challenging to decipher and in a few places a little guess work has been necessary.

Jack also spatters his writing with Chinese terms. These are sometimes followed by my translation in square brackets and I have also provided a *Glossary of Chinese Terms*. Finally, Jack's original spelling of Chinese place names has been retained and I have used the same spellings in my notes and commentaries. However, a table of romanised place names lists

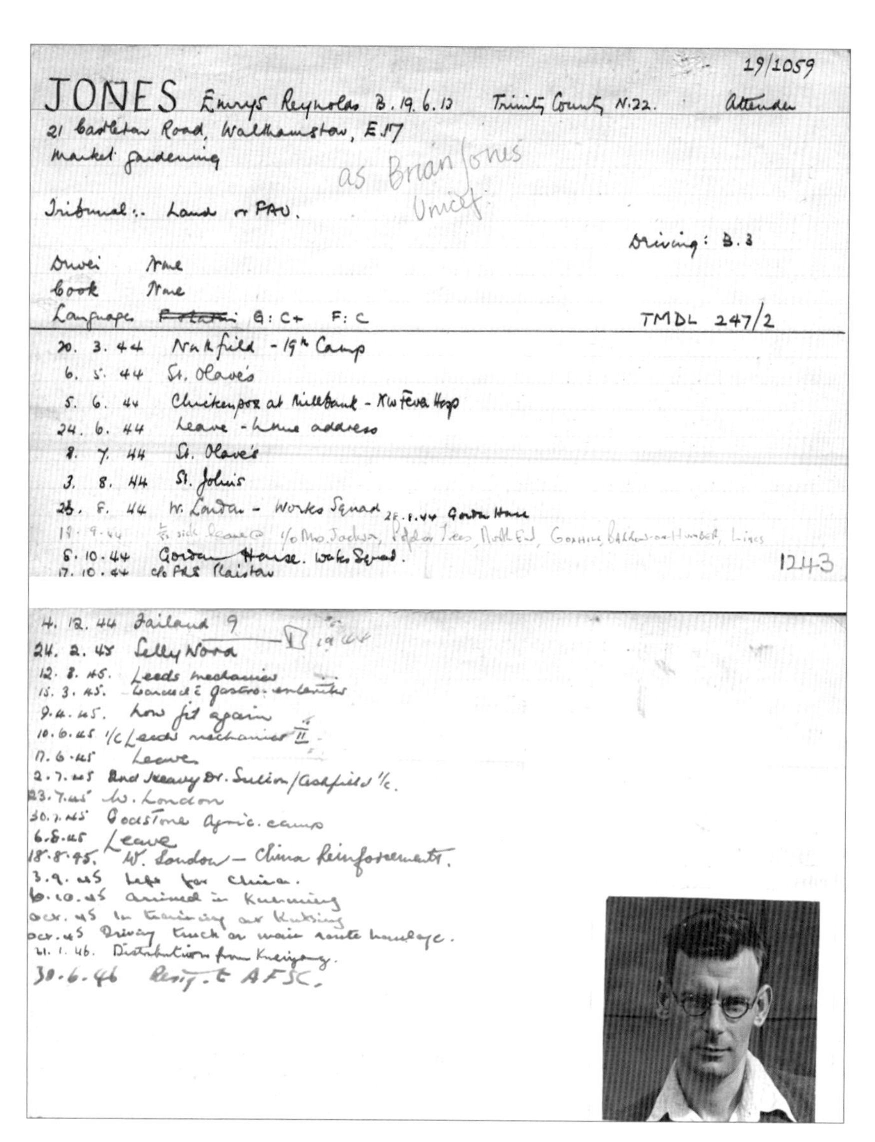

19/1059

JONES Emrys Reynolds B. 19. 6. 13 Trinity County N.22. Attender
21 Castleton Road, Walthamstow, E.17
Market gardening
as Brian Jones
Unicef

Tribunal:. Land or FAU.

Driving: B.3

Driver None
Cook None
Language G: C+ F: C TMDL 247/2

20. 3. 44 Northfield - 19th Camp
6. 5. 44 St. Olave's
5. 6. 44 Chickenpox at Millbank - NW Fever Hosp
24. 6. 44 Leave - home address
8. 7. 44 St. Olave's
3. 8. 44 St. John's
28. 8. 44 W. London - Works Squad 28. 8. 44 Gordon House
18. 9. 44 [illegible] sick leave @ c/o Mrs. Jackson, Poplar Trees, North End, Goxhill, Barrow-on-Humber, Lincs
8. 10. 44 Gordon House. Works Squad.
17. 10. 44 c/o FRS Plaistow
1243

4. 12. 44 Failand 9
24. 2. 45 Selly Nora 19 [illegible]
12. 3. 45. Leeds mechanics
15. 3. 45. [illegible] gastro-enteritis
9. 4. 45. Now fit again
10. 6. 45 i/c Leeds mechanics II
17. 6. 45 Leave
2. 7. 45 And Heavy Dr. [illegible]/Ashfield i/c.
23. 7. 45 W. London
30. 7. 45 Godstone Agric. camp
6. 8. 45 Leave
18. 8. 45. W. London – China Reinforcements.
3. 9. 45 Left for China.
6. 10. 45 Arrived in Kunming
Oct. 45 In training at Kutsing
Oct. 45 Driving truck on main route haulage.
21. 1. 46. Distribution from Kweiyang.
30. 6. 46 Resig. to AFSC.

Jack's personnel card, the only record of his FAU service, ends in 1946 after which time the project was run from Philadelphia

the most common names both in their Wade-Giles and later Pinyin versions.

Jack's first article in the China Convoy newsletter that I have found was written six months after he arrived in China and appeared a couple of weeks after he was transferred from Kutsing (Qujing) to the garage in Kweiyang (Guiyang). This expresses his thoughts about an approaching famine in Hunan to the east of Kweiyang, one of the grain baskets of China whose provincial capital is Changsha, where Mao Tse-tung went to school. On the 430 mile long route from Kweiyang over which Jack drove to deliver medical supplies to Changsha and Hengyang the road crosses the provincial border about half way there, dropping down from the mountains of Kweichow onto the more fertile plains of Hunan, and passes through Ankiang and Tunkou and finally Hsiangtang shortly before reaching Changsha.

1 TRANSPORT WORK AT THE KWEIYANG GARAGE – MARCH TO SEPTEMBER 1946

Famine in Hunan – Jack pleads for a new approach

FAU News Letter, Number 199
Information Office, Chungking, 2 March 1946

The Rice Bowl is Empty

After Tun K'ou the country's character alters. No more mountains to speak of. No more Miao folk. Turbans and pale blue rags give place to bare close-shaven heads and darker blues: Kweichow is for Cambridge: Hunan, apparently favours Oxford. Constantly the roads are fringed with trotting files of men: you see more smiles and fewer harelips, more trees and temples, but fewer ponies, and no goitres at all. At nights in the towns and villages pandemonium reigns, for it is the Chinese New Year: the air is grey with the smoke of fire crackers, shaken by drums and gongs and explosions: softly luminous lanterns wave gently on long poles, like flowers on slender stalks. Mounds of oranges and fat yellow pomelos are still stacked in the brightly-lit shops of Ankiang. A crowd gathers to hear the wai ko jen [foreigners] engaged in chaffer. He feels like Bob Hope in a Technicolor film. He forgets the desolation – Paoching, for instance, two long streets of brand-new shops stretched across acres of broken bricks and rubbish; the blown-up bridges along the road; the horde of carpenters making pews in the fire-blackened chapel; women, infants, old men, herded in dismal, smelly dens called Refugee Centres.

What if the price of rice is going up daily fifty-thousand for one tang (150lbs) in Heng-yang today? (16.2.46) The girls in the rickshaws of Changsha have plump red cheeks, happy eyes, magnificent

Chinese soldiers clearing rubble in bombed temple, Paoshan

legs. Even in Hsiangt'ang, that sombre, soldier-ridden city the sun is shining, and the bustle continues; a squad of Japs loll on a heap of rubble, self-possessed and comfortable [presumably prisoners of war still awaiting repatriation]; the children, who know not Ting Hao, accost you with "Abcdefg...", which they rattle off like the children of North Wales reciting "Llanfairpwllgwngyllgogerychryndro bwll-llantisiliogogogoch" [the longest Welsh place name]. Nobody shows any fear.

Yet there is plenty to be afraid of. The little old Bishop of Hengyang said so. Sitting behind his enormous desk, looking like Charlie Chaplin in 'The Great Dictator', he slowly faltered out: "Zere is no raina. Forty yiss in Funan such a dry vinter I remember cannot." The Hungarian father, bouncing beside me in the cab, shouting to make himself heard above the music of a Dodge in motion, had a theory. "I zink it is ze atomic bomb. Ze Bope brotest at ze time. It fill ze air wiz calories – dry up also ze clouze." Father Fidelio was more explicit. Never have the rivers been so low. Ponds have dried up. For the first time in the history of the Catholic Orphanage for Girls in Hengyang – that is, for three hundred years – their spring has failed them. The ground is too hard to plough. And anyway there are no buffalo left to plough it. Like some of the orphans, they did not survive the occupation. There is going to be a famine. Even if it rains within the next month there is bound to be a famine. If it doesn't rain soon....

We walked across the fields with Father Fidelio. Fields? They were more like a desert. Parched, yellow, cracked, they stretched for miles in all directions. Here and there an attempt had been made to plough; a few shallow furrows had been scratched; then the farmer had given up in despair. One field had been laboriously worked with a Chinese hoe, but no frost had come to break up the soil and kill the pests in it; nature "wouldn't play ball." In all that vastness not one man was at work. Here was desolation worse than that of the towns and cities.

What is being done to meet this situation? Not much, it seems. The great mass of the people isn't bothered. Rice is expensive, but is still procurable. Few people realise how small the stocks are, or how slim now the chances of replenishment. The missionaries are anxious and at present have only meagre premises and resources, and no money. The hospitals are piling up stocks of pills and tablets; they will be ready when the crisis comes; it is not their job to try to prevent it.

UNRRA? [United Nations Relief and Rehabilitation Administration.] They have a magnificent office in Changsha, containing a number of massive, shining desks; it may just be coincidence that the only person I have ever seen at work there is the boy who daily dusts and polishes the said desks. And anyhow even UNRRA can't make it rain. Nor can they breed buffalo faster than buffalo breed – which is too slowly to meet the present emergency. Yet it seems to me to be a case of putting the horse after the cart for relief organisations to wait for the famine to start before they do much about it. That is the usual method, of course. Nobody ever hears of a famine until a few thousand people advertise it by dying. But here is a famine that so far has only been prophesied – reliably, I imagine, by people who know what they are talking about – and relief workers could start to attack now, instead of the effects of malnutrition, its causes.

The obvious thing to do is to import food. But there is a larger issue. It was grievous to me to see those vast agricultural areas lying sterile now, when, if ever, they should be productive. The farmer is going to wait until it rains; if it doesn't rain soon he will wait till next year. His methods are not flexible enough: with his plough immobilised, his ground too hard for the hoe, and too hard to grow rice anyway, he is helpless. If only he had a spade! The average Chinese field could be turned over in a day or two. Shock troops of diggers could work the whole of China's Rice Bowl in a few weeks? Less thirsty crops than rice could be planted... But there are no spades, no iron stirrups for the farmer to protect his sole with if he had a spade, no seed, no desire to try out anything new, and the only crop that flourishes between Paoching and Changsha is mustard. Meanwhile the refugees are crowding back to their ruined homes in thousands. Three times I have visited the district during the last three months; on each return the situation has grown more ominous. It is time to do something vital and decisive. The FAU has trucks and drivers galore: could we not do something for Hunan besides cart in IRC drugs?

Jack Jones.

Terraced fields on road to Luhsien

THE KWEIYANG GARAGE DEPOT

About 500 kilometres further up the road towards Chunking, the FAU's depot was just outside the Kweichow provincial capital of Kweiyang at Huang Tu P'o. The FAU had originally taken over the trucks and premises in Kweiyang of the IRC, but Kutsing became the more important base and the HQ was shifted to Kutsing in August 1942. However, the centre of gravity later moved towards Chungking and it was Kutsing that was the first to close.

Every day from their Kweiyang hostel building the men walked away from town over what they called the 'stinking brook' towards the rural setting of the garage, nestled beneath a range of curious round hills. Here the men, Jack and Bernard included, went climbing, taking a camera with them if they could to snap the garage from above. On their reunion visit in 1996 a group of elderly FAU members struggled to find their old haunts or even to recognise the once familiar hills. As Nellie Bonsall's photos show, the 'stinking brook' was still apparent but the open rice fields were now submerged deep beneath ugly grey concrete buildings.

1944
1996
1944
1996

Goodbye to Bernard, Mrs White and Sam

Jack moved from Kutsing (Qujing) to the garage at Kweiyang (Guiyang) at the end of January 1946 where he wrote the following article. He was quickly promoted to garage manager in Kweiyang in place of Paul Cope and, when the Kweiyang depot was also closed, he moved on to the garage on the south bank of the Yangtse at Chungking (Chongqing) at the beginning of September 1946. The news letter was now edited at the new headquarters in Chengchow (Zhengzhou) and Jack was a major contributor to it. Under the style of 'Farthest West' by 'Home Brew', he sent in regular news items about the West China-based transport unit.

The following article hints at his anxiety that since the FAU's ambitious new 'Honan Area Project' had moved the focus to the desperately poor Yellow River region of China, in particular working on the rehabilitation of the devastated village of Chungmou, the original core activity of transport was becoming a thing of the past. It also makes one of the last references to the charcoal burning trucks that had been the mainstay of transport during the war years.

After the flood, Chungmou

FAU News Letter Number 204, Information Office,
Chengchow. 20 April 1946

FARTHEST WEST

News Letter 201 reached Kweiyang last night. As one man we flung ourselves upon it. What were the brave lads on the convoy doing? And what did it say about us? We soon found the answer to the second question. Far from forgetting ourselves we are, as far as Chengchow is concerned, by the world forgot. Not a word about us. Isn't it possible, O distant twinkling Starr, that thy thoughts never turn in our direction? Nor thine, immortal Johnson? We feel they must and, to satisfy the curiosity, if only of a few, I type this - er - sheet. [At least the editors ran Jack's jibes at their expense!]

Boys, I'm sorry to have to say it, but Kweiyang ain't what it used to be. [Chris] Evans got the hell out of here for the last time last Wednesday morning. With him went [Paul] Cope. Now only very ordinary oaths disturb the quiet airs of Huang T'u P'o. Lionel Hampden, deprived of his doughtiest champion, Paul, has retired to the darkest corner of the record cupboard and left the field to Haydn, Mozart and Beethoven, the classical boys. The same day which bereft us of these two men bereft us also of [Jack's close friend, Bernard] Llewellyn. No longer is the divine Rita [Hayworth] extolled at the supper table in noble and eloquently moving periods. If you prefer Alice Faye or Esther Williams – or even poor, derided Lucille Ball – you can say so now and nobody bothers. The entire section turned out the other night to see "Thousand Cheers", [a patriotic morale boosting movie of 1943] and when they returned it was clear they had gone after strange gods – or rather, goddesses. St. Bernard would have corrected them sternly, and brought them back to worship of the only true celluloid deity; but he has departed, and apostasy is rampant in Kweiyang. Farewell, Evans, Cope, Llewellyn!

Mike Frankton and Alice Faye

And farewell to Mrs. White. [Walter] Kirby got her here at last after twenty-eight days on the road. She arrived in pretty bad shape. In fact, [Doug] Turner towed her in from Kuanglingchang. Mr. Turner has a theory about towing. He says if the tow-ee has poor brakes it is up to the tow-er to go faster and faster, so that there will be less chance of the tow-ee hitting the tow-er in the rear. The theory did not work out too well in practice, and Mrs. White arrived with her face pretty well bashed in. Beauty, however is only skin deep, and there is something about Mrs. White that gets people. Suitors swarmed about her. When five million was offered for her and her spares we closed at once. They took her just as she stood, brakeless, clutchless, radiatorless. Our boys manhandled her out of the gate. And then Mrs. White suddenly realised what was happening. In a paroxysm of grief at leaving the Unit she broke

Wilfred Jackson's charcoal burner

away from the boys and flung herself on her side in a field of cabbages. You know the one, boys: on the left as you come out of the gates at Sze Chih Shan. There she lay all afternoon while her wrecked bodywork was taken off her. She was salvaged by teatime and led away, a travesty of her former sturdy self. Truly, the China Convoy is breaking up.

But we still have our moments. A mighty roaring and snorting of engines outside our door one night proclaimed the arrival of Messrs. Jones (G.) [Geoff], [Mike] Frankton, and [Dave] Tanner, in the charcoal burners. They too had had a rough trip – nine days – ditchings, pao mao's [breakdowns], even bandit scares. A few days later a brand new member, Roy Lucas, dropped off a China Dodge after what he called an easy trip from Kutsing – two and a half days and no troubles. The China Dodge was continuing to Changsha, so it seemed sensible to let Roy carry on in her, as he desired; by the time the coal-carts arrive in Chengchow [Zhengzhou] he'll be an Old China Hand. Turner and Henry Liu have gone to Kutsing: theirs is positively the last truck to go there (unless some more do). [David] Thawley should be back from Chungking soon, ready and willing to lead the new boys to Changsha and points east. No sign of [Bill] Skurr yet. The other Jones boys [Mark and Howell], undaunted by their three and a half somersaults [their truck fell into a ravine] – one more than made the thousands cheer the trapeze artist in that film – are proceeding Changshawards under the fatherly guidance of Wilf [Jackson]. Russ Beck will be off in the same direction any day now.

Other items. Poor old Sam the handsomest dog in Kweichow, perished under the wheels of a six-by... First job for the new ch'ang chang [Jack as garage manager] was to get a woman out of clink: her husband had bought some GMC spares from us, and she was impounded with them, possibly on the assumption that she also might have been pinched from the U.S. Army... Michael's mao ping [breakdown] book has really gone this time: he left it on the bonnet of a Chev., and along came a gust of wind and whipped the current entries over the hills and far away. They are now probably being studied with interest by the police in Hua Hsi... Jeanette [the young Chinese hostel warden] has been ill, but is now, we are glad to report, recovered... Phoebe [the dog] sends her love to you all... So does Na Li [the cat], but what the hell do you care about Na Li, any of you... I thought as much!

HOME BREW.

Americans training for China. Next to the instructor, Paul Cope, Rhoads Murphey, Ted Mills, Wesley Chin, David Stafford and A.M. McMillan, seated centre, all looking so very clean

Comings and goings... Rhoads Murphey

FAU News Letter Number 208, 21 May 1946

FARTHEST WEST - II

One day not long ago a nautical-looking figure in a blue guernsey and seaboots rolled into Shih Tse Shan and began spinning yarns about how he had been shanghai'd (also Chengchow'd and Hankow'd), how he had jumped no less than ten ships on the voyage down from Chungking, and how he was on his way to Kunming to offer his services to Admirals Cope and Evans who in the South of China, were even then planning an American invasion of the British Isles (the second in a lifetime). [Paul Cope and Chris

Evans were returning home to the USA via the UK.] For seventeen hours and a quarter this sailor talked with amazing eloquence and rapidity, pausing only now and again to give vent to a high hysterical laugh; and next morning, still furiously talking, (about how he was going to fly the Atlantic every year to be Philadelphia representative at the Annual Dinner of the China Convoy in London,) he bowled out of port, leaving a wake of dust behind him.

It was observed that he had a piratical-looking ruffian named Wei Fu Lin [one of the employees] in the wheelhouse with him, and another fairly desperate-looking character, Doug Turner (with a fresh beard) in the launch astern... Happy voyage, Rhoads! [Rhoads Murphey later became Professor of History at the University of Michigan, specializing in modern Chinese history and his book of memoirs about the FAU, *Fifty Years of China to Me* was published in 1994.] ....

Rhoads Murphey

Those who are acquainted with Shih Tse Shan and its personnel will be interested to hear that China's gift to the F.A.U., Joe Jerk, has been promoted from kitchen boy to garage hand. This is not because he has had a sudden rush of brains to the head, but because he has developed what in my young days used to be called 'a certain disease', and it is no longer desirable to have him picking our tea glasses up by the brims, as his habit was. Ten minutes after his translation Chang Chih Ping, the cook, sprang indignantly into the room, averring with much emphasis that it was impossible for one man to keep the ch'ang chang supplied with tea and at the same time to feed the boys. Rather than attempt the impossible he would resign, and this he did, removing his overalls and badge there and then, and leaping out of the office, this time for ever, with a final defiant toss of his copious mane. It looked as though the boys would go supperless to bed that night, but there is one man in Kweiyang who

Wei Fu Lin

can be relied on in any emergency, our prop and staff, buyer, seller, liaison officer, advisor on strategy, chief translator and guide, mentor and friend, the redoubtable Chien Lo Tien. He was last seen that night with an apron tied round his middle, his brown woollen cap on his head, a pan of bubbling fat in his hand, and he looked as though he could do that job better than anyone else, too.

HOME BREW

A breech birth, cat fights and a break-in

FAU News Letter Number 209, 25 May 1946

FARTHEST WEST - III

Man is born to trouble as the sparks fly upwards; and as for poor old Woman... Chang Min Sang's missus, lovely ex-leading lady of the Kweiyang Windmill Theatre, [who merits a whole chapter in Jack's book, *Daughters of an Ancient Race* and a long article below] has a dark patch on her right lung; yesterday Sam's missus had her right ovary removed; and as for Mrs. Wei Fu Lin, she is about to have a child for the fifth time in five years, but this time the baby is coming backwards, or something extraordinary – my Chinese is so vague...

Rear spring top-leaves and other missiles were flying in a cheery free-for-all the other day, the cause of the fracas being an alleged mis-distribution of overalls. During the proceedings carpenter Yu Tse Lin hit fuel-coolie Chen Yu Wu over the head with a rice-bowl; this is the surest method yet devised of shattering rice-bowls. Peace was not restored until the ch'ang chang [Jack] had offered to fight everybody himself; this did not cow the contestants, as was intended, it made them laugh: the employees, instead of staggering back to work with black eyes and bloody noses, staggered away helpless with laughter – a touch of bathos, I'm afraid.

One day somebody knocked a hole in the wall of the boy's hostel at Shih Tse Shan and got away with all Chang Yuin's and Tsen Fu Chiao's belongings. The same night we had an unauthorized visitor in what we like to think of as our compound at Huang T'u P'o. The heroine of this occasion was a certain buxom wench named Na Li [the cat], who went for the intruder in no uncertain manner and frightened him so much that he fell off the wall, but unfortunately on the far side and without breaking his neck. Two seconds later the ch'ang chang, leaping out of his narrow crib, fell over Phoebe, who was standing in his doorway feebly wagging her tail and looking as dazed as females usually do when they are rudely awakened at three in the morning. (As I should imagine. I protest that is a pure speculation. Gentlemen, gentlemen, please resume your seats)....

HOME BREW

Female company and falling off the top bunk

FAU News Letter Number 218, 3 August 1946

FARTHEST WEST VII

Well, it's been quite like old times lately. Twelve people in for meals, snores from the convoy room – we even had to open up a special ladies' dormitory, Mike being the chivalrous chap this time. Cause of the crush was the arrival of the Yunnan rearguard – David Johnston and Emma Yang in the Ford pick-up, followed a few hours later by Dr. Fong and Miss Pan of the Kutsing Huei Tien [hospital] with the Thawley convoy. For a few days Jeanette had a little feminine company which was more to her liking than Phoebe and Na Li. Howell is suspected of having shaved twice a day, Mike changed his trousers on weekdays. Then on Tuesday, July 9th the visitors departed with the Thawley-Kirby convoy to Changsha. Amongst other things we are sadly missing is the Kutsing gramophone which is now on its way to Chengchow with six tons of QM supplies.

We had just got into bed the other night when there was the squeal of Dodge brakes outside and a violent crash as Mr. Frankton got out of bed without remembering that he was in a top bunk. It was Bob Gairns and Wei Fu Lin weighed down with yellow fish [passengers] (the only cargo they could get in Pichieh), the passengers of the Pichieh bus (which had pao-mao'd) and the casualties of an overturned six-by [a six wheel drive truck]. One of these was a bloke with a fractured femur. Bob had done a good job with a chiao pole, his belt and a spare shirt. Owing to this and that trucks aren't allowed into the city at night, we had to transfer

John Johnson crashed out at the Chungking depot

the injured man to the weapons carrier in which we drove up to the Medical College at midnight. Two doctors then gave us an excellent insight into medical procedure, waggling the limb about until unmistakable sounds of crepitus [the grinding together of broken bones] confirmed Bob's diagnosis of a simple fracture of the femur. Strong coffee was partaken of in the small hours and nobody missed the "workman's special" in the morning.

Mark is still in Hunan and in twelve more days will have equaled Skurr's record for a stay in those parts… Thawley and Jones H. have been infected by Kirby and are now collecting pipes: you can't walk across the room now without tripping over either Mao Tai [Howell's dog], or a bamboo pipe anything up to two yards long…

HOME BREW

Phoebe's pups and big plans afoot

FAU Newsletter Number 223, 31 August 1946

All other news of course pales into insignificance beside the fact that… Phoebe, having bitten the postman at 5.10 p.m. on Monday, August 5th, was delivered of a fine boy about ten minutes later, and she went on delivering boys (and girls) about as quickly as the postman was delivering letters, until there was the grand, and in Phoebe's history, unparalleled total of NINE of the little blighters in the tyre store. Not to be outdone, Na Li [the cat] (in medical lingo a primipara), [ie pregnant for the first time] had a fight with Phoebe one day, and then retired under Lao Lin's bed and did her best with a total of four. With Mao Tai, Mimi and the three kittens, the total number of our far-from-dumb, indubitably four-footed friends at Huang T'u P'o is now, therefore twenty – which will produce some headaches for transport at the end of the month.

John Peter and the dogs

For the rest of us, life is pursuing a perhaps less sensational course. Our whole fleet of trucks is at present in the yard, and our plans are that Walter Kirby shall take three to Pichieh on Monday, Bill Jordan, two to Chungking on Tuesday, Bob Gairns or David Thawley (whichever is the fitter), two to Changsha the following Monday, and then on about the 28th of the month, a mammoth convoy consisting of the remaining seven trucks (and the three Pichieh ones, if they have got back in time) will pull out for Chungking and our new home. Left behind will be Home Brew who will tie the final knots and then see if he can drive all the way to Chungking in that lovable vehicle [the ex-American army weapons carrier] "W.C. for Relief". We have made plans like this before though, and we know what happens to them. However, if it is humanly possible etc, etc, etc.

HOME BREW

Up high on the Pichieh road

The last days of the Kweiyang garage

FAU News Letter Number 227, 28 September 1946

END OF A SECTION

For the last time I sit me down to write these notes. Kweiyang is dead – long live Kweiyang. The Section died, according to plan during the last days of August. I am glad to say there was nothing Eliotesque about the demise – we went out, not with a whimper but with several loud bangs, like a V2. There was for instance, a farewell feast to the boys, at which the Rev. Mr. Thawley [David Thawley had been a theology student] proved himself a distinct credit to the cloth – but getting rapidly more indistinct as the evening advanced. There was a superb feast thrown by Mrs. Ho, who had bought the garage building: [Walter] Kirby, who had been losing at the finger-game all evening (some say deliberately) subsequently worked himself into a passion about a tiny hand which was frozen. [The finger game is a noisy Chinese drinking game in which the contestants both fling out some of the fingers of one hand, at the same time loudly guessing the total number of fingers. The objective is to get your opponent drunk. In one version, a correct guess means a penalty for the other who then has to down a tot of a strong drink.]

The next night we had another farewell feast, this time to Kirby himself and his boys, who had been pounding the roads of China when the first one had been held: Kirby must have played even worse that night, for not only did he combine his aria with the Dying Swan pas seul, but he also did a volatile Don Quixote act tilting at the windmills of an electric light shade with a bamboo lance, and with far more success than attended the famous Manchian in his battles.

There was a farewell trip to Hua Hsi, [a local beauty spot with a lake], all the boys in a truck managed by Mike [Frankton] and his willing road-boy Howell [Jones], all their wives and other womanfolk in the weapons-carrier – driven of course by Home Brew [Jack] (but the damn thing wouldn't

Hua Hsi, Kweiyang

'WC for Relief' driven by Brian Sorensen

break down). In the interests of truth I must also admit that there was a small number of squabbles over repatriation and things [severance payments to enable local staff to travel home]; and at the very last moment one of the boys drove at top revs in second into the rear of another truck which had an old chassis poking over the tailboard; and one or two things disappeared unaccountably, and so on; but on the whole, and taking it by and large, the famous spirit of Kweiyang endured to the end. And it was, I believe, with genuine regret that members and employees alike went out of the gates for the last time.

On the 26th [David] Thawley took the last two trucks of IRC goods to Changsha and points west. On the 29th and 30th ten trucks with Kirby, Frankton, H. Jones, and [Robert] Gairns, pulled out for Chungking, leaving the world to darkness and to me. (For [William] Jordan had gone previously with three trucks). For a few days I stayed on at Huang T'u P'o with the new owners, Sam (Yin Chao Chen) and his charming wife, finishing off reports, accounts and sales. Then on Monday September 2nd I too left, with Tien Lo Chien and Liu Shao Yin in the "W.C. for Relief." As I drove up Huang T'u P'o between the cavalcades of charcoal ponies in the brilliant sunshine, I had, for once in my callous life, some sentimental thoughts.

Never more, I thought, to back out over the ditch and practically into the front door of the handsome semi-detached villa (a truck body) which harbours the girl with the million-dollar legs. Never more to roar up Huang T'u P'o with its jingling ma chih [horse carts], half-naked blacksmiths, the forest of thumbs uplifted in reverent salute. Never more to turn into the New Road and see the mountains heaped on the horizon ahead, to spin down between the brick-kiln and paddy fields, steering a course between the pot-holes, bumps and booby-traps: to pause at the bridge to drop the cook with his basket and smile and to pick up a desperate gang of cut-throats – our tame employees: to roar up the Shih Tze Shan amongst the bare-behinded kids, the Miaos [a tribal hill people] descending from the hills, the scampering dogs and the camel-backed pigs, the old woman selling sweets under the blasted oak, the grinning sentry at the barracks gate, the special lady in the red-and-white check knickers who often had such a delirious effect on a crucial gear-change: never more to swirl through the gates of the garage under a fusillade of stones and imprecations from Jimmy [the monkey], and draw up under the stern of a majestic Dodge.

Never more – jumping to the other end of the day – to sprawl at ease in the lounge of Huang T'u P'o entertaining female missionaries in extraordinary hats, or be entertained by Kirby on the gramophone – never more to be yanked out of lethargy by the squeal of brakes outside the door.

Echoes of the past came to my ears – "Jeezel, Crosfield, let's get the hell out of here boy" – "In my opinion he should be flogged" – "Like walking on a sea of breasts" - "Wo pu tung. Ni pu hoa. [I don't know. You are no good!] Share wa-a-a-a." "Is that Chungking? Can you hear me Chungking? You can't? Oh hell" – "The Bishop's shot hisself." – Oh yes, I know him too. In fact he's a cousin of mine" etc etc. [Chris Barber's cousin was Anglican bishop of Chungking.]

Kweiyang is dead, my friends, but a little of its spirit still lingers in the city: Sam has set up an engine-shop at the ex-Hostel, the profits of which will go into a clothing factory for the poor of Kweichou...And our ex-landlady at the garage has installed in her house an ancient petrol drum "to remember you by" she says.

HOME BREW

Fruit sellers with bound feet at a roadside stall and a bare-behinded boy, Yenfang, north of Kutsing on the Luhsien road

Jack and Mike Crosfield with a five truck convoy

THE CHUNGKING GARAGE DEPOT

Looking at the picture of a bearded Jack celebrating Christmas in 1946 with his staff, it is remarkable that with no previous experience as a leader and having been in China little more than a year he was already Chungking's 'big cheese'. Behind him is David Thawley, later a distinguished Anglican priest in Brisbane and Melbourne and father of an Australian ambassador to the USA. Sitting on the ground are Bernard Smith and Mike Frankton, totally at ease with their Chinese mates. The truck yard was small, the hostel being on the right where the men slept and the workshops beyond. An apparently chaotic jumble of buildings they were in fact built for the purpose in 1944 to carefully drawn blue prints which survive in the Friends' archives in London. Most of these photos of the depot and surrounding scenery were taken a few years later by Bob Reuman in 1950. Taken with colour slide film that was then generally secreted out of the country for processing by anyone returning to the USA, they are a fine record of the countryside he loved so much. Perhaps his most striking photo is the one at the top of this page showing the south west highway heading away from Chungking towards the distant Burma Road, a well-engineered road with the depot standing to the left with trucks in the yard. An odd one out is Wilf Jackson's shot of the surrounding hills taken in 1944, intriguing because it is of the same view as the one taken by Bob Reuman six years later.

FAU

2 CHUNGKING GARAGE-CHEATING THE GRIM REAPER – OCTOBER 1946 TO JUNE 1947

Doggies again, too much sickness and the disappearing bridegroom

FAU News Letter Number 228, 5 Oct 1946

FARTHEST WEST

The ex-Kweiyang and the Chungking sections, after three weeks of married life, are beginning to get used to having each other around, and besides it's a lot cooler now. Each man follows his own bent – Sherving studies English (as exemplified by Punch) [Sherving Po, an associate member and graduate of English literature], Thawley studies algebra, Howell biology and Mike, as ever, truck manuals. Even the dogs are settling down, though Phoebe often makes a completely unprovoked attack on Na Li. And just now and again, perhaps, Na Li makes a little teeny-weeny reprisal raid on Phoebe. Their offspring with a fine impartiality that could well be emulated by humans, patronize either bar whenever opportunity offers. Once there was a movement to eject Phoebe forever from our midst, but Home Brew, with an impartiality equal to the pups' (since he loves Na Li to distraction), pointed out that, a. Phoebe happens to be the oldest member of the Convoy in West China, and b. people who in one breath extol the institution of marriage, and in the next complain that Phoebe the matron is repugnant to them, are displaying so much prejudice and inconsistency that they argue themselves right out of court. All the same she DOES make a hell of a noise at night…

Sherving Po, Joe Awmack and a Honan farmer

There has been rather a lot of ill-health in the Section, Brian having had a spell in hospital with a mysterious temperature, Geoff a few days in bed with malaria, while Bernard and Gerard are both dissatisfied with the state of their insides. I feel a bit groggy myself, but that is due to a wedding we went to last Sunday. The bridegroom was not present, in fact he got taken to hospital on the wedding day, but it is not in the Chinese temperament to let a small hitch like that disturb them, and a jolly good time was had by all the rest of us.

HOME BREW

Weddings of garage employees were important events and Jack even had his account of one of them published in the New Yorker in February 1949. The photo above is of that of Wang En Pei and Lei Ming Cheng on 30 June 1946, the foreigners in attendance being Tony Stickings, Brian Sorensen, Owen Jackson and Bronson Clark, Jack's predecessor as West China Director

Note: Phoebe, the Top Dog

Phoebe had indeed cheated death, life expectancy for China Convoy dogs being pretty short. She had come with the humans from Kutsing days, survived Kweiyang and moved on to Chungking, all the while dropping puppies at regular intervals. In a harsh and perhaps lonely world a fluffy puppy was one of the few comforts available for these young men, isolated and far from home. They often took their dog with them on convoys and one picture shows Mark Jones and Gerard Walmesley in the back of beyond with their puppies, Mark's peeping out from inside his greatcoat.

There was also a darker side to life in general that rarely surfaces but is well expressed in some notes made by a nurse who was a member of the Unit in Kutsing. Describing returning from a walk up to the hill behind the town she wrote as follows in her diary. 'On the way back a man was being tortured by hanging outside a cottage. Part of our ceiling fell down in the night. Phoebe was eating a [human] head on the grass when I went out.'

In his autobiography Eric Shipton, the Himalayan explorer who was British Consul General in Kunming, tells a similar story of how he saw his dog playing with something in the garden. It was the severed head of a baby.

Jack Jones describes the Chungking south bank garage

The following description of the Chungking garage was published in the USA a few months later by the American Friends Service Committee, the Quaker organization based in Philadelphia that in July 1946 had taken over running of the 'China Convoy' from the London based Friends Ambulance Unit. A little bizarrely this article was also published in the July 1947 issue of 'Commercial Motor', the leading British journal for heavy vehicles, presumably rewarding Jack with a useful fee.

The FAU's Chungking garage depot was at Ssu Kung Li Pan, meaning four and a half foreign miles, its officially designated distance from the Yangtse River down the south western highway that ran through Kweichow and Yunnan and ultimately to Burma. An important new route built in the thirties linking Szechuan southwards, this was a dusty strip of unsealed road constructed for motor transport at considerable expense, replacing the ancient pathways used by mules and barrows over many centuries. Today at Sigongli there is an overhead station on the mass rapid transit railway that runs between skyscrapers above a multi-lane highway. No longer a village, it is now a glittering silicon valley with two universities and many industrial estates.

American Friends Service Committee Program in China
Color and Background Material No. 11. April 1947

SSU-KUNG-LI-PAN by JACK JONES
(British member, FSU-China)

The bulk of Chungking lies north of the Yangtse. Here is a network of streets, broad and narrow, wriggling up between cliffs on which the town is built and switch-backing over their tops.

But on the South bank too there is a considerable town – a tangled skein of streets few of which are broad; indeed they are scarcely streets at all in the Western sense of the word, for they consist for the most part of narrow stone staircases which zigzag illogically amongst the crowded, leaning houses. There is only one real road,

Down to the river at Hai Tang Chi, Chungking, early 1950

as we should call it, on the South bank; it begins at the ferry called Hai Tang Chi, and it ends a thousand kilos away at Kunming, in Yunnan; there it joins the Burma Road. This Kunming Road, for its first few miles, is rough and bumpy even by Chinese standards; it is white with dust after three days in the sun, ankle deep with mud after less than three hours of rain; it clings to the mountainsides and tortuously follows their contours, like a thin line of embroidery on a crumpled crinoline. If you are driving a loaded truck, you do not get a chance to use top gear till you reach a village called Ssu-Kung-Li. The name means "Four Foreign Miles," and the village is in fact just over four kilos from the ferry. Half a kilo further on, after a dip and a rise, you come upon the brink of a tiny valley, with paddy-fields in the lower slopes and cabbages on the higher; this used to be called T'u Miao Tzu—"Earth Temple" – but the name, like the temple, has disappeared: It is now called Ssu-Kung-Li-Pan, "4½ kilos." Half way up to the opposite slope, on the left of the road, is a

yard with a jumble of buildings – the FAU Garage.

It is not an impressive looking place. Your eye is more likely to be held by the hills on the left, with their jagged limestone crests, or by the water-buffalo toiling below, urged on by a bawling bronze-limbed ploughman in huge yellow parasol hat; or by the coolies trotting along the road's edge, bearing the rich and powerful in bouncing chairs on their calloused shoulders. The yard is in fact rather small – so small that we have to park some of our thirty-three trucks in another yard not far distant. The buildings look far from substantial: they cling precariously to impossible slopes, with whitewashed mud-and-wattle walls, rickety-looking tiled roofs, windows of torn oiled-paper. A pile of red petrol drums and the week's washing crown the highest point; trees, thin and small, but graceful, lean over the buildings. You notice that all the level places have been dug out of the hillside and that the yard falls into a paddy-field, where two snow-white storks, straight from an Egyptian frieze, are standing among the village's ducks.

Entering the yard (there are two impressive stone gate-posts, but no gates), you find yourself in the midst of a scene which could be duplicated, in this motoring age, in almost any part of the world. Several trucks will be standing around, having things done to them. You will notice that they are all '44 Dodges, sturdy three-ton trucks, with grey-green tinwork and neat brown canvases. Every one of these trucks has now done at least 12,000 miles, over some of the worst roads in the world; but it is a matter of pride with us that they still look smarter and better cared-for than any other trucks on the West China roads, with the exception of the very newest.

To be sure, some of the tyres look a bit queer, and examining one more closely, you will see that the cover has blown out at some time, and been repaired by having another piece of old tyre bolted inside it. This does not surprise you when you hear that new 34 x 7 tyres cost over a million Chinese dollars in Chungking (more than US$150) – if you can get them. Tyres are in fact one of our biggest problems always, for when the hot weather comes, they pop like corks on the rough, burning roads; speeds are reduced to 18 m.p.h., pressure checked every few kilos, water from road-side paddy-fields poured on the treads, but still the rubber and canvas fail to bear the strain. We are exploring the possibility of having tyres flown up to us from Shanghai – but, in Shanghai too, there is a great shortage of tyres.

At the far end of the yard you will find the workshop. If you are interested in mechanics, you will soon perceive that our garage is quite fully equipped. It has to be. Everything that must be done on our trucks we do ourselves, acting on the principle, which is confirmed by bitter experience in China, that if you want a job to be done well, you had better do it yourself. We even have our own boring bars, for no engine can stand more than about 9,000 miles of these gruelling, mountainous roads without wearing itself out; and every one of our fifty-odd engines have now been rebored at least once. We have lathes and our own generator to drive them, and a fully-equipped test bench on which the rebored engines are run in. The reboring is done by a foreigner, an amateur as we all are, but the chief mechanic is Chinese, a man named Wang Wen Pei.

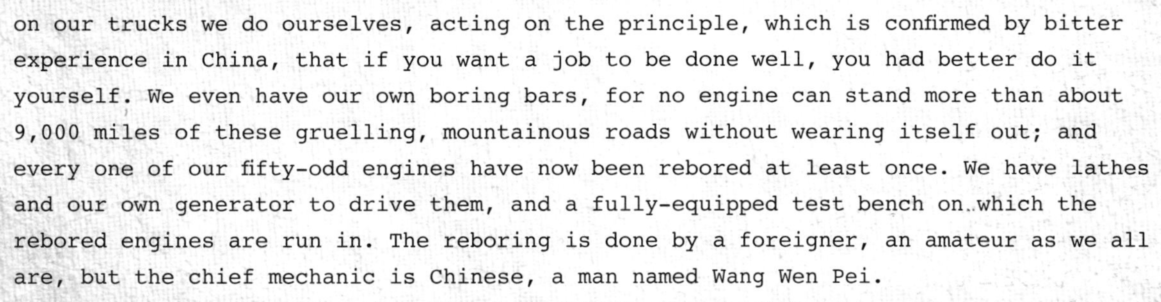

There are fifty employees in all, what with the blacksmiths, tinsmiths, carpenters, the turner, the electricians, the apprentice-mechanics and the road-boys. There is plenty of work for them all too, for whenever a truck comes in it will have some "mao ping" great or small. Here is the turner making a new jet, because jets of the size we want are unobtainable in Chungking. There is the welder mending a chassis, cracked on a bumpy stretch of road in the North. The tinsmiths are busy repairing

radiators and tin work. Two of the carpenters are sawing industriously at a balk of timber while the third, old Tseng Yu Shan, is repairing a bed-board. (For the drivers sleep on their trucks when on the road, spreading their "p'u kais" [quilts or bed rolls] on a board which fits on the cab-roof, and pulling the canvas over their heads to protect them from the rain). Part of the yard is covered in, and under this shelter a dozen mechanics and boys are busy overhauling gear boxes, brake systems (another constant source of trouble), axles, water pumps and the like. Everybody looks very busy, but the garage staff have learned not to judge by appearances in this matter, for mechanics are the same all the world over, and have a genius for looking busy when they aren't!

Suddenly a gong sounds (it is an old tyre-rim actually, struck with a small bar of iron), and with whoops of joy the employees rush off to eat. Many of them, who have wives and families, live in the villages round about: but rather more than twenty, men and boys, live in our own Employees' Hostel. They sleep in dormitories above the workshops, and eat their three meals a day in a small shed clinging to the hill above. They receive the same wages as the men who live outside, but a certain part

Wei Fu Lin still at Chungking in 1950

thereof (which varies from month to month), is deducted for food. They buy the food themselves taking it in turns, and have their own cook. The wages of all employees are based on the cost of living, which is worked out by the Garage Manager every month; it is going up by leaps and bounds, rising on an average slightly more than 10% per month. Married men receive a family allowance, and all employees are issued with overalls twice a year, and with mosquito nets in the summer and overcoats on the winter. After certain periods these articles become their own.

It is worth going into the dining room when they are eating, if only to see the amazing rapidity with which the bowls of rice and the three or four "dishes," most of them blazing hot with red pepper, disappear. Some of these men and boys have been with Transport for four or five years : for example, Wei Fu Lin, the fat and jolly driver, who looks more like Charly Chan [the fictional Honolulu detective of the silver screen] than any other Chinese I ever saw; Chang Min Sang, whose beautiful wife is a famous Chungking actress; Tien Shih Wu (known as "Tulip" to us), who joined the unit as a very small boy, and now, grown big and strong, drives a truck of his own with the usual Chinese dash and verve. Many of the boys are known to us by nicknames, --

Yen Kwan Yen (Old Tobacco) and T'ien Shur Wu (Tulip)

The verandah in front of the hostel

Sugar Bean, Old Tobacco, The Drip, Sam, Rufus, and so on; and the boys reciprocate with Chinese names for us, not all of them polite. One member used to be called "Mien Pao," (Steamed Dough), because, I was told, "there was a lot of him but it was no good:" This was a rice-eater's comment on bread and foreigner combined; and both comments were unjust, in my opinion! Generally speaking, the relations between the boys and the foreigners are very cordial, especially between the foreign convoy leaders and their own particular drivers and road-boys. Living so much together on the road, they get to know each other as well as it is possible for members of two nations to do, when neither is very proficient in the other's language.

We members have a Hostel of our own. It is by no means a commodious building. It is made on the usual style, a frame of slender logs, filled in with walls of mud-and-wattle; the tile roof often leaks, and dogs and rats constantly break through the walls; but we have a Western-style fireplace in the living room, and a thatched verandah to foil the sun and the rain. There are three rooms in all, two filled with bunks and all our belongings; the third is the room in which we eat, read, write, talk, play games, and spend most of our spare time. At the present moment our full strength is twelve, but we never have the full complement in residence at once, even at Christmas time. At the moment of writing five members are absent: two took a convoy of six trucks to Paochi, a 1000 kilos to the north, two weeks ago: two more have taken a convoy to Chengtu; while another was last heard of in Kweiyang, on its way to Kunming, about a week ago. In fact only the office and garage staff are here today, plus two Chinese members who are on their way to Shanghai, after getting married a fortnight ago in Chengtu. I should not forget the dogs -- I think there are seven now; the doyen of the pack is Phoebe, who has been in Transport for years, and is as much of a Transport institution as our midday Chinese-style meal.

You would think that living so much on top of each other, and cut off so completely from the rest of the Unit, we would always be getting on each other's nerves, as people who live in lonely outposts are supposed to do, at least in novels and travel-books. That we do not do so is due perhaps to the fact that we are all enthusiasts.

The trucks, the boys and our reminiscences of the road keep us going with food for talking during the long winter nights. We have a radio, and by switching off the village for half an hour (for we provide them with light), we can manage to hear "Itma" relayed from Radio SEAC Ceylon, once a week. [Itma was a BBC radio comedy, 'It's That Man Again', referring to Adolf Hitler. SEAC was South East Asian Command.] We play bridge, mahjong and poker. We can go to a movie on the other side of the river at the weekends. The postman calls once a day, raising everybody's hope at least once, and sometimes gratifying them. And there is always the possibility that the roar of engines and the squeal of brakes will herald the return of a convoy.

Then we members and dogs all rush out of our hostel while the employees pour out of theirs. There is a great slamming of cab doors and revving up of engines before they are finally switched off. Unshaven, dirty, tousle-headed, wearing strange mixtures of Chinese and Western civilian and military garb, the drivers, foreign and Chinese, climb stiffly out of the cabs. There is much shaking of hands, slapping of backs, and punching of ribs. The Convoy leader is besieged with questions: What sort of a trip did you have? Any trouble? How many tyres have you bust? Did you get a return cargo? Did you bring us any oranges? Did you get held up at the ferries at all? The drivers answer as best they can. Maybe it was a trip full of trouble: water in the petrol, three or four flats or blow-outs, leaking radiators, slippery roads, trouble with the army, or a bad dose of stomach trouble. Sometimes it is worse: a truck overturned or an engine siezed, by no means infrequent occurrences.

But whatever his story, the Convoy leader is sure of a warm welcome: never mind, you're home now, come and have something to eat, there's some letters for you, you can clean up later, we'll put your trucks away. It is a great moment this, when a convoy gets back home again; another hospital provided with its medical supplies, but that is unimportant to us beside the fact that old So-and-so is back again. For a fortnight perhaps he will be overhauling his trucks and collecting his next cargo, then he will be off into the blue again for another month maybe; but in the meantime he is back at base, to revivify us willing stay-at-homers and perhaps in some measure be refreshed by contact with us......

Preparing a convoy to Honan

Jack suffers an 'affaire acute de coeur'

FAU Newsletter 232, 2 November 1946 reports as follows…

"From Chungking we hear that Bernard Smith was admitted into hospital on October 16 with bacillary dysentery and an amoebic liver abscess. Dave Thawley was down with malaria and Jack Jones rapporte suffrir des affaires acute de coeur. We wish all these sufferers well."

Note: So who was Jack's lady (or ladies) this time?

The same news letter reports Jack leaving for the staff meeting in Chungmou and the next article below tells of his return by air.

Jack is back and Jeanette has a brand-new frock

FAU News Letter Number 234, 16 November 1946

FARTHEST WEST

Never did the sun shine more brightly on Chungking than it was shining that day when no. 111, (not to be confused with our truck of the same number), swept like a gull over the Chialing and Pei Hsi and landed with a bump on the island in the Yangtse. [The Chialing is the river whose confluence with the Yangtse defines the city of Chungking. Pei Hsi was the main airfield some miles out of the city but Jack's plane had landed on the seasonal Sanhupa airstrip on the sandbar that floods every spring when melt water from the Himalayan snows raises the river level.]

Even the coolies who passed my tunghsi [my kit] and me from plane to sampan, sampan to office, office to ferry and ferry to South Bank, seemed benevolent, sunkist men – robbers though they were. Indeed, I was just beginning to learn all about the family affairs of the last of them, when the Station Wagon bounced into view. There was old

Blot with his noble countenance [Mark Jones] wreathed in smiles and Jeanette [the Chinese hostel warden] in a brand-new frock all the way from Hongkong; even the Station Wagon seemed to be cavorting with joy (the springs always were bad). Over tea and cakes I learned that all was well; during my absence there had been

"...No levitations in the sun;
No conversions like St. Paul;
No great happenings at all."

[Slightly misquoted from "Letters from Iceland" by Louis Macneice.]

Walter [Kirby] and David [Shek] and Jeanette had returned to the fold [having gone on leave]. Bob and Hsiao Hsin had left it. Jeanette was already making her presence felt; the bedrooms had been so cataclysmically cleaned up that the Garage rats hold nightly protest meetings, 'Too much living room' being the burden of their squeaks. Tears were shed over the defection of Hsiao Hai Tze, who had allowed the honeyed words of Lewis Hoskins to woo him to Shanghai. There was one other sad piece of news: "Mrs Mop", who will be remembered by every road-man who ever docked at Su Kung Li Pan, died in giving birth to a child (her fourth). The child survives, and has been adopted, with the rest of the family, by Mrs Mop's ko-ko, (also an employee of ours).

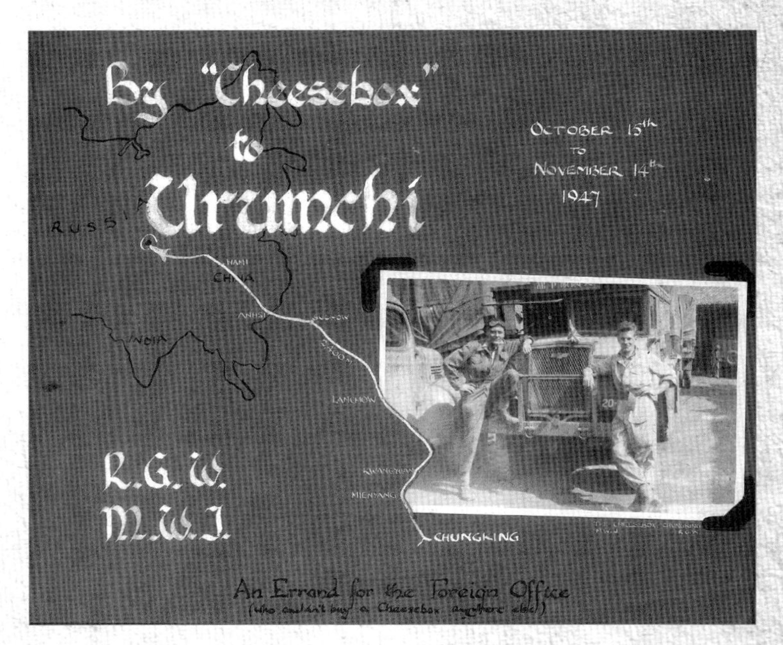

Now, for a few notes on Personnel. Mark [Jones], who for two glorious weeks was the entire office staff here, lost half of his power on the return of David Shek, and the other half when I returned, and has now been hurled into the outer darkness of the store, there to make inventories until Time does him part. Meanwhile he consoles himself with a wild dream about Urumchi. (Mark and Gerard have a scheme to spend their leave taking a station-wagon from Chungking to the British Consulate at Urumchi in Outer Mongolia, a

Friends School, Chungking, Master's residence

'just the job' trip of 2,800 miles – final approval is awaited from the Nanking British Embassy). [Mark told the story of this epic trip at the FAU reunion in London in 2010 and lent me his album which includes a nicely mounted picture of the two of them with their Chevrolet truck set against a sketch map of China.]

Kirby sometimes has a rest from lion-taming [he kept a wild cat as a pet], climbs mountains and crosses wind-swept passes in order to hold Bernard's hand at the hospital. During one of these epic journeys, Walter, who was laughing immoderately at Mike and me because we had just fallen down in the mud, disappeared altogether and was eventually retrieved from a paddy field far below the level of the path; this ought to teach him to treat his betters with respect. Geoff Bonsall calls in at weekends [having been seconded from the garage to teach at the Friends School]: he now lives in such a beautiful bungalow at Huang Kuo Ya, high on a pine-clad peak overlooking about half of Szechuan and several miles of the Yangtse, that it is a wonder that he can ever tear himself away from it to come and see us.

Well, there is nothing more to say, except that for the last two days Mike has been dismembering Mary [the generator that supplied the garage]. As the local power company is in a chronic state of mei yeau tien li [no electricity], this means we sit around all night, in the light of a glorious fire, asking each other such questions as, 'Were you the muse of Erotic Verse?' 'Did you die after eating a surfeit of lampreys?' [As King Henry I so carelessly did.] 'Did you represent the constituency of Upper Tooting in 1907?' etc. etc. etc. Last night we had Cassandra and Aaron in our midst. Come to Chungking and mingle with the Very Best People.

HOME BREW

Geoffrey Bonsall with Stinker, Mike Frankton, Jack Jones and Revd George Wright

Note: The men tended to get bored when stuck in the garage or, even worse the office, for too long. As Hugh Russell commented in a private memoir, "Next I took charge of the garage in Chunking, the least popular of all the jobs since you were tied to the spot, endlessly mending lorries for other people: I had 30 in my care."

Mark Jones and Gerard Walmesley eventually managed to get permission from the Embassy and in November 1947 delivered the Chevrolet truck to Urumchi, way out to the north west on the Silk Road. They got there in one piece, handing the vehicle over to HM Consul for use by Eric Shipton as consul in Kashgar, and returned safely, flying back to Lanchow. Brian Sorensen had earlier in July 1947 done a similar delivery trip but returning to Sian his C47 aircraft was lost with no survivors.

Finally, News Letter Number 237 of 14 December 1946 reports that, "George Wright and Jack Jones returned on the 28th from a tour of Szechuan, and George has now gone off to Kweichow with Mike Frankton." Jack carried a heavy administrative load in the office but welcomed any excuse to get back on the road.

Jack's near-death experience

Driving a truck to Shanghai for the annual staff meeting towards the end of February, on the road from Kweiyang to Changsha, Jack came close to killing himself, Hugh Russell, the son of the Duke of Bedford, and several others besides. Admittedly he was far from home and from his typewriter for some weeks, but what follows seems to be his sole account of the accident and for Jack it is unusually short, perhaps reflecting its true horror.

FAU News Letter Number 248, 8 March 1947.

FARTHEST WEST

Jack Jones writes from Chihkiang, Hunan, Feb. 12, 1947

My valiant attempts to attend Staff Meeting in spite of the grounding of planes ended in disaster yesterday morning about 20 kilos from here. I was trying to pass a stationary truck on a very wet road when we slid down off the crown of the road and shot over the side. We bounced once I am told, and finished up, upside down in the river Yuan a good 60 ft below the road. It is an absolute miracle that Hugh Russell, Jeanette and Lin Chen Wen who were riding on top, weren't killed outright. There were some big boulders underwater, the truck perched on these, and the passengers fell between them into the water. Hugh came nearest to being drowned. An army truck took these three, and Michael Yih and his wife, who were in the cab with me, back to the CIM mission [China Inland Mission] and were very kind to them: one soldier gave Hugh his coat and wouldn't take it back. They are all in bed today but nobody is really seriously injured. Jeanette has bruises and strained stomach muscles, Hugh's face is badly bashed about, and he has had seven stitches in it; Lin Chen Wen's legs are cut and swollen; Michael has a few bruises; his wife has hurt her back and has petrol blisters on her sit-upon; and I look like a Sheik of Araby with a turban of bandages and my beard, Allah be praised, intact... We have lost a lot of cargo as the crates burst; nine microscopes were fished out of the water and hundreds of stray thermometers... I told all the drivers, foreign and Chinese in Chungking before I left that the next bloke to overturn a truck would get the sack, so I suppose I've had it.

Note: Fear of flying?

Jack and Hugh Russell reached Shanghai on 8th March and at the meeting Jack was appointed a member of the Council and as West China Agent. Hugh flew home to London on 20 March via Hong Kong in the luxury of a Sunderland flying boat called "The Huntington". It had three cabins of seven passengers each. Lunch was lobster mayonnaise, peche melba, cheese, fruit and coffee, followed by tea and cakes at Bangkok, tea and cakes in Rangoon and a five course dinner aloft. Meanwhile, back on earth the daily grind continued.

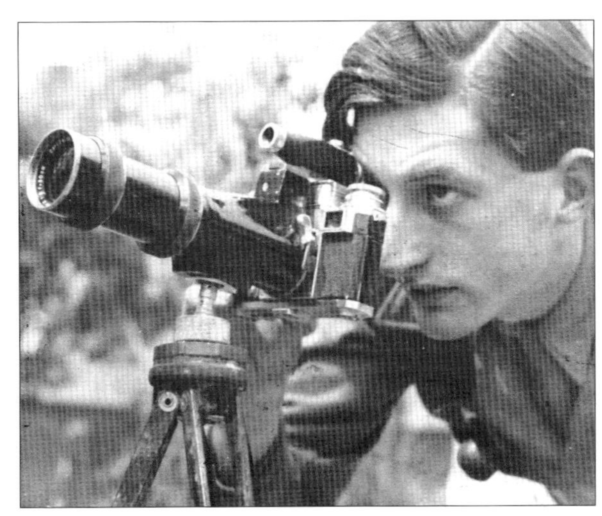

Hugh Russell

Jack, it seems, could have flown back from Shanghai to Chungking but for some reason he returned by road. This ruffled some feathers among the big cheeses as the FAU bosses were called, if cheeses have feathers that is. On 20 March 1947 Brian Jones, secretary to the IRC, wrote from Shanghai to Tony Stickings in Chungking who as acting director was holding the fort there on Jack's behalf. His last paragraph of the third page reads, "I understand Jack Jones leaves Shanghai tomorrow morning to return to Chungking via Honan, Hupeh, Hunan and Kweichow. This surprises me more than a little, now that the air ban has been lifted, as I should have thought it important that he should return to West China just as quickly as possible in order to relieve you of some of the responsibility." At the top of the FSU's carbon copy of this letter are scribbled the following words signed by 'JN', presumably Jack Norton. "I don't know why Jack Jones returned by such an indirect route. IRC claim that he must be superfluous if he can remain away 5-6 weeks and Stickings carries on effectively."

Brian Jones

Tony Stickings reported back to Shanghai that Jack reached Chungking on the 28th apparently after just a week's travel, which was pretty good going. Jack seems to have survived the criticism though and later in 1951 found himself working for UNICEF in Bangkok with none other than Brian Jones as his new boss.

A year earlier on 26 March 1946 a similar accident befell Mark Jones when his truck came off the road and rolled into a ravine, ending up fifty feet below the road. The truck did three and a half turns on the way down, but Howell Jones and a number of other passengers were thrown clear onto a ledge. Mark went all the way to the bottom, but again the gods were merciful and extraordinarily there were no serious injuries. Mark recently sent me his pictures of the truck being recovered, hauled up the near vertical slope on the end of a hawser; 'three hours work by an ex-US army motor wrecker and its Chinese crew', his photo caption reads.

The ins and outs of life on the south bank, including more pups

F.S.U. Chronicle Number 4, Information Office, Shanghai, 26 April 1947

FARTHEST WEST

In these grim days of budget cuts, economies and shortages, it is truly heartening to be able to report that Transport is in the money. This week we sold eight well-worn trucks, for a total of 102,000,000; not so good as we hoped for, but by no means chicken feed. It is sad to see some of the trucks departing, 65 and 11, for instance, half of which turned three and a half somersaults [piloted by Mark Jones] and caused a couple to fall in love with each other while they sat in a stream, while the rest of it was guided by friend

Disused trucks in the snow, Kutsing depot, c.1945

Turner under the bonnet and cab of a six-by. Then there is 124, which was overturned twice in the same trip by Lin Pen Chin, and 102, a noble truck, the one in which the present writer used to terrify the Hunanese (and occasionally himself) until Len Bonsall made him a garage manager and said "in future the only carriage thou shalt drive shall be that attached to thy typewriter".
The proceeds of these sales are to go towards paying for that luxurious building the Unit inhabits in Shanghai… [A gibe at the luxury and elegance of the wood paneled Friends Centre in Shanghai!]

Friends Centre, Shanghai

To save time, I will tabulate the comings and goings.

OUT, one night a large stock of spares from the store… IN and OUT ever since, numerous suspicious characters whom Gerard runs to earth and finds to be detectives…

OUT, four redundant employees, including the chief electrician, who was a nice old boy who has been in the Unit for years and whose only defect was that he was no damn good as an electrician. It was of him that Elderbee [Len Bonsall] said, in one of his masterly work reports, "Spent all day taking the previous afternoon off". Also, "Nov. 16, tried to blow a horn. Nov. 17, blew it."

OUT, on Easter Monday, two truckloads of employees and their families, to Hot Springs for the day. A good time was had by all, especially our head cook. Easter day was also a red-letter day in the life of Youngerbee [Geoff Bonsall]. He set off for Hot Springs on the DKW [Dampf-Kraft-Wagen motorcycle]. He got there. He set off for home again. He got there too eventually. The bike is a mass of Bonsall pan fa's [improvised repairs such as a paper gasket] and Geoff has every reason to feel proud of himself as he tears along the road flat out at 12 miles per hour…

IN, Tony [Stickings], ex Chengtu loaded down with silk and silver loot. The next day we got a lot of letters that looked hard to answer, so I made old Tony Transport Director. He promptly said, "Take 67 to Hsichang on Friday". So I'm on the road again boys, after a whole damn year in the office… (and, as we'll see, came close to being slaughtered by bandits!)

OUT, eight pups, - yes, Phoebe's done it again. A few days later she used one pup as a pillow "so now we are seven"… OUT, about the same time, one kitten, ex Jemima the cat… The same night, OUT, by theft, Jeanette's pyjamas. Jeanette's pyjamas seem to have a peculiar fascination for thieves; she lost one pair in Kutsing and another in Kweiyang, and now she has got quite a bad cold. We believe that Tsen Yu Shan, the ancient head carpenter, was the culprit this time… I suppose that I could go on like this for hours, but I don't wish anyone to get OUT of patience with me, so I will lay down my typewriter, and the next Farthest West will be from the pen of Adhesions [Tony Stickings], my esteemed contemporary…

I am, in fact, now literally OUT of office.

HOME BREW

Mike Frankton and Jack Jones still at work at 10.10am, Chungking, October 1947

Note: The Americans take over the FAU

At about this time control of the China Convoy, which had been run from the London headquarters of the Friends Ambulance Unit, was transferred to the American Friends Service Committee (AFSC), based in Philadelphia. The FAU provided wartime service for registered conscientious objectors so with hostilities ended its job was now done. The FAU's relationship with the AFSC had always been close and with much funding for China coming from the USA, the handover was a natural progression. The FAU News Letter then became the 'Chronicle' and a new name was adopted, 'Friends Service Unit' (FSU), for the continuing project. On the ground things remained much the same, though the transfer caused considerable administrative and accounting problems, including the regulatory and bureaucratic requirements that in China were always tortuous and labyrinthine. Jack, for example, now had to grapple with the question of whether it was possible to avoid the massive task of rebadging and re-registering with the authorities the whole of his fleet of trucks in the name of the FSU. Administrative hassles of this sort took up a large amount of his time and energy and must have driven him to distraction, though in this case later photos show the trucks retaining the FAU emblem on their doors.

Jack cheats death once again – beaten by bandits

American Friends Services Committee Program in China
Color and Background Material No. 12, 27 May 1947

ENCOUNTER WITH BANDITS

The following account is written by Jack Jones, present director of transport of the Friends Service Unit (China). The convoy was made up of five trucks driven by Jack, Michael Frankton (another Unit Member) and several Chinese employees. While enroute, with a load of International Relief Committee supplies, from Chungking to Sichang (Sikang province) the convoy was bandited. [The town of Xichang, then in Sikang province, 5,000 feet up in the mountains south west of Chungking.]

Mike Frankton and Sam Yen

Sikang Kung Lu, leading up to the Erh-Lang-San Pass, a year earlier in 1946

Fukien bandits

"We flatter ourselves, Michael and the boys and me, that you will all be eager to hear of our encounter with the bandits. It happened at the 171 kilo stone, which is 18 kilos up the Sop Ling pass [probably a misprint for So P'ing] and still around 7 kilos short of the top. You will find that Rupe Stanley in his route guide advises you to 'take it easy, boy' on this stretch, presumably so you can admire the view (for the road is quite good). Unfortunately there was no scenery on view on Friday after about the 167 kilo stone, but only mist. It was an easy second-gear slope and 67 was pulling up it nicely at about 8 m.p.h. As we approached a left-hand hairpin bend I noticed three men on the rocks watching us, but then people always watch trucks go by. We swung round the bend, and thirty yards ahead of us some big stones, too big to drive over, were laid across the road. I pulled up to let Yang Kung Fu get out and move them and at that moment the shooting began.

"Shouting men began to appear all over the place, popping up from rocks and thickets on both sides of the road. Yang Kung Fu got on the bottom of the cab and considerately switched off the engine. I sat wondering what to do for a moment. Then a shot hit the frame of the windscreen bang in front of me, cracking the glass in all directions and knocking out the right-hand dash-light. It is mighty lucky it didn't knock me out too. The next second we were hit again. I found out later it was the left headlamp. I decided to get out and see if a bit of foreign tact would do any good. It didn't. Three chaps armed to the teeth with revolvers and rifles rushed up and felt me all over for guns. Then another bloke arrived and began thrashing me with the flat of his sword. He knocked me down and continued to thrash me while I lay on the ground. Then two others tied my hands behind my back, and tied me to a tree. Meanwhile everything was being hurled off the truck and slashed open with swords and stones.

"Soon I saw Chang Min San and Yang Kung Fu tied together, and shortly afterwards I was tied to them and told to sit down by a fire.

The chief man was quite considerate and told the bandits not to take our clothes, papers or sleeping bags. The bandits were not very obedient. Soon one lot of bandits was firing at another lot, and when the air was thick with bullets I thought the thieves were falling out among themselves with a vengeance: I didn't realize that the other four trucks had arrived and were being attacked. We thought they had broken down further down and heard the shooting and would stay were they were. However, we were soon told to get up and go away with the bandits, and we were quite amazed to find Mike and all the rest of them trussed up and shivering like ourselves.

"The bandits forced us to climb the mountain with them. I like climbing mountains usually, but when your hands are tied to two other blokes with a short rope it is not a very pleasant business. Eventually we prevailed on the bandits, some of whom were reasonable chaps, to untie us, and after that it wasn't so bad, though we had to carry some of the tungshi [kit]. All this time, the boys were pleading with our captors to let us go. They wouldn't, but they seemed a bit vague what to do with us. We reached a ridge, went down it, got off it towards the road again and went along it in the opposite direction. When we were just about knocked, we came on a bandit cheese [big boss]. He looked every inch a bandit, but was quite decent, asked us to rest awhile, and noticing we were wet and shivering, tossed us a hospital pyjama jacket apiece which had been taken from the cargo.

"We sat in the mist and rain for what seemed hours, waiting while they decided what to do with us. Mike and I wondered whether we were to be kept for ransom. Soon we were amazed to hear our trucks (a long way down) being started and moved, then shots. The bandits seemed as concerned as we were. Soon two breathless bandits toiled up out of the mist and announced that soldiers had appeared. The few bandits still around disappeared with their loads in all directions. The biggest gang took us. Our boys argued step by step but you can't argue much with guns and swords. We were taken down the other side of the ridge, which was thick snow, and on a scree slope I got half-crippled by a stone which gave me an awful whack on the back of the leg. I have a scar two inches square there. We went on and on, until it was almost dark, and the bandits consented kindly to let us go back. You can guess what it was like climbing that snow-slope again, going down the other side of the ridge in the rain, soaked and falling over every second, and finally getting lost in a thicket of bamboos. But eventually we reached the road, right by Chang Min San's truck, which had been neatly parked like all the rest. We got a big petrol fire going and found some C-rations [US combat rations] and opened some boxes of pyjamas and pull-overs. Thus clad we spent the night in the cabs.

"Next morning we loaded up the trucks again and went on to Fulin. We were held up again at what looked like a checking station but is actually a bandit's headquarters. Quite illegally, he charges everyone who goes by his set prices: 3,000 per coolie, 80,000 per truck from Sichang, 150,000 per truck from Kiating. He respected our papers and we parted friends. He has 600 men who are better armed than the troops and everybody is sick to death of him. We have been asked here to ask the Chungking FAU to ask the Generalissimo's HQ in Chungking to recover our lost goods, etc. [This last sentence of Jack's letter written in Fulin to Chungking on 27 April 1947, as published in China in FSU Chronicle No. 7, was deleted from the above version published by the AFSC in Philadelphia.]

Michael was beaten too but is all right now. The road to Sichang is washed out in seven places but we hope to go on in three days."

The thing to be kept in mind in regard to the above trip is that this convoy has to return to Chungking over the same route. Let's hope their return trip was made with less difficulty than the trip out!

Later, on 3 May 1947 Jack wrote as follows from Sichang before turning for home, published in FSU Chronicle 7.

"We arrived in Sichang last night after a fairly uneventful three-days trip from Fulin. The decent people in Fulin are sick to death of bandits and they are perturbed because this is the first time foreigners have been molested on the road. (So they say but the French Mother Superior told me this morning she lost everything five years ago, including the clothes she was wearing, when her truck was attacked.)

We reckon the bandits got about one and a half tons of tungshi [cargo]. They got all my personal stuff, including both pairs of glasses and my passport; all I have left is the clothes I had on and my precious umbrella… Also they thrashed us and we still have the marks on our backs. If they catch us on the way back, the price for our ransom is expected to be 200 oz of silver according to present prices."

Sichang from the Bishop's house, April 1946

Traffic movements and a Chinese wedding

F.S.U. Chronicle No. 10, 7 June 1947

FARTHEST WEST

For the first time in many moons every member, every employee, every vehicle, every dog, cat, goose, rat and mosquito, is in residence here this weekend, and this morning we have been celebrating the fact by facing a barrage of cameras. The dogs at least should be easily recognizable, at least to anyone who has ever seen them from the rear. The reason why the garage is full is not that we are doing so little, but that we have been doing so much. Since my last contribution in Mid-April George Kan has returned from his leave in Chengtu and taken a convoy of three trucks to Chaotung and back; Kirby has returned from Changsha with one truck and John Peter, and departed to dare the bombs and bullets in wildest Honan; Don Warrington has returned from Jungshien, accompanied by David Tanner and five trucks, in which, amongst the

Tony Stickings took the first photo, with George Kan at rear left, David Shek, John Peter, Mark Jones, (?), Geoffrey Bonsall, and at front left, (?), Jeanette Lee, David Tanner and a dog's rear, Jack Jones and Mike Frankton, while Stickings is front left on the second photo.

t'ung oil and candle fat was a body in a coffin, and since this Don has made two trips to Chengtu, on the second occasion being accompanied by John Peter; we met them in Chu Chi Ho on a very hot night and it was quite impossible to tell which was which, John being white with dust and Don quite black with oil; Bernard Smith has been to Chaotung and back; and Mike and I have returned from Lololand [a minority tribal area in a loop of the Yangtse] after a really wonderful trip, about which I hope to write a few words in next week's issue.

Mark Mantovani Jones has returned to us from the East and was hoping to get off to Urumchi all the month with Gerard [to deliver a Chevrolet truck to the British Consulate there]; the Blue Peter has been at the masthead of the Chev for days, but it has now regretfully been hauled down, as the authorities have failed to cough up the necessary permits, etc. and the trip has had to be put off until the autumn. Meanwhile Mark and Gerard will join our band of convoy leaders and help to expedite the distribution of medical supplies. Mark is at present limping around with a stick, having attempted an airy entre chat in a moment of joie de vivre and found he is no Robert Helpman, and Bernard [Smith] is also invalid, and we fear may have a recurrence of the liver trouble which sent him to hospital last year. But this is not certain yet, and we hope it isn't true. [An entre chat is a particularly athletic type of leap in ballet and Robert Helpmann was principal dancer at Sadlers Wells from 1933 to 1950. Reggie, Jack's protagonist in "*A Woman of Bangkok*" used to go and sit in the gods at Sadlers Wells so it's safe to assume that Jack did too.]

As for the social whirl, we would have you Easterners know that Shanghai isn't the only place were people are given and taken in marriage. Yesterday Liu Chen Wen got married. Bernard Smith, a debonair go-between, had brought the bride from Suining under the mistaken impression that she was going to marry his boy, Hsia Wu Chu. But two days after arriving she visited our hostel and all the boys were lined up as for a royal inspection and she gave them all the once over and then pointing to Liu Chen Wen said, "I'll have that one please", and that was that. The wedding went off with all the usual hitches. The bridal car, which was driven by Tulip [one of the young Chinese drivers], who had had his hair parted for the occasion, passed the fan t'ien [rice shop] once in order to give Old Tobacco time to get the crackers cracking, but had difficulty turning around, with the result that by the time the bride arrived the cannonade was over. Everybody formed up on the near side to provide a guard of

The wedding of Liu Chen Wen, the chosen one, the foreigners from left being Geoffrey Bonsall, David Tanner, Mike Frankton, Tony Stickings, Jack Jones, (?), and Bernard Smith

honour for the bride and she got out on the far side. However, she looked quite nice in a lemon coloured frock and a veil made of several yards of mosquito net, though at least one of the older members present, tweaking the grey hairs out of his beard, was reminded of a little girl "dressing up" for fun. Adhesions [Anthony Stickings] gave her away, looking much more shy than she did. An attempt was then made to reach the photographers by car, but Tulip, in attempting to take a short cut, ditched himself and we all arrived on foot, including the bride. The arranging of the group took an age and when all was ready we were asked to lean slightly to the left to compensate for a slight inclination, constitutional, of the camera in the other direction. All this time Stickings was wandering around enquiring plaintively. "When do I kiss the bride?" We were all relieved when it was time to go back to the inn and we could all get down to the serious business of getting drunk. A veil is drawn over the next four or five hours, which were much enjoyed by all. Melancholy spirituals were still being sung in the dormitory two at midnight, and at four o'clock in the morning, Huang Chi Feng, the night watchman, keeping his usual vigilant watch and ward outside dormitory one, awoke screaming from a nightmare which brought all the dogs galloping from under the bunks and scared one neurotic member out of his wits. Today all is normal again.

HOME BREW

Note: Tony Stickings' son in Canada has sent me this delightful wedding picture with Tony standing at the back next to the bearded Jack.

At the beginning of the above article Jack mentions that everyone was there the next day and so all the cameras came out. The group photos sent me by the Stickings and Peter families probably show that particular day. Tony Stickings, John Peter and Mark Jones all have their cameras around their necks and the right people appear to be in the picture, along with Stinker the dog. In the background behind the flimsy bamboo fence of the depot can be seen stacks of drums at the government's South West fuel dump.

3 TRANSPORT GRINDS ON BUT CHANGE IS IN THE AIR – JULY TO DECEMBER 1947

Departures and a totally disastrous day

FSU Chronicle Number 15, 11 July 1947

FARTHEST WEST

The departure of Messrs. Bonsall, Smith, Tanner and Stickings will have already been reported in the News Chronicle (China Convoy edition), but it would be invidious for me to let them go without the tribute of a passing tear in this here column. It is almost incredible that we no longer have our little Spanner to rig us gadgets all over the place, that our little Smith will no longer enrich the Chinese tongue with new curses of his own invention, that somebody other than Tanner will be able to drive the jeep when we go "overseas" [across the Yangtse] on Saturday afternoon and that the one and only Adhesions has ceased to adhere to the arm-chair nearest the pencil-sharpener. Those of us who are left, to wit: Jeanette, David, Mike, Gerard, Mark, John Peter, George Kan and myself, are going to miss these West China stalwarts a lot: for the first time we feel it in our bones that the old FAU is breaking up, that the tide is receding, leaving only a few curious crustacea gasping on the shore. (And with the temperature nearer 100 than 90 every day, we certainly do gasp.)…

Monday last, June 30, was a day of calamities. It all started when, having seen Tanner and Stickings off at the CNAC [China National Aviation Corporation office just across

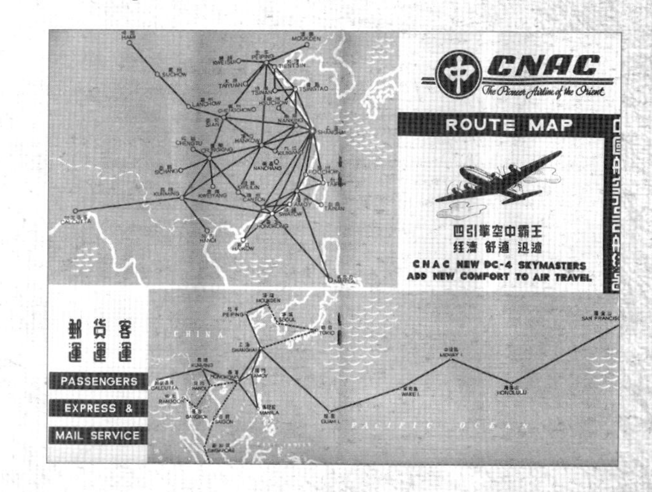

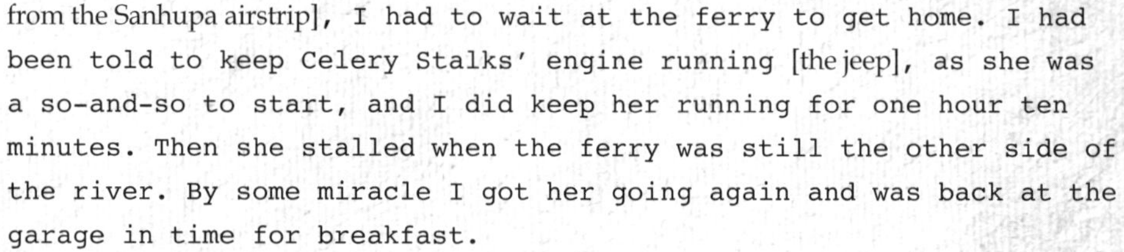

from the Sanhupa airstrip], I had to wait at the ferry to get home. I had been told to keep Celery Stalks' engine running [the jeep], as she was a so-and-so to start, and I did keep her running for one hour ten minutes. Then she stalled when the ferry was still the other side of the river. By some miracle I got her going again and was back at the garage in time for breakfast.

After breakfast I had to take Jeanette [the Chinese hostel warden] over the other side to go to the Bank and she [presumably the jeep] stalled again outside the Bank. After a lot of yao-ing [rocking] by me, to no effect, we did a bit of t'ueing [pushing] together, and she eventually started, only to stall again outside the shoe mender's. But this was on a hill, so it didn't matter.

We got home again that time, to find some telegrams that made it imperative for us to return overseas in the afternoon. This time we took the precaution of taking Yang Kung Fu with us, to assist with the yaoing and the t'ueing. For over an hour we sat by the ferry, fanning ourselves, and then eventually the boat came in. But would Celery Stalks start? Not on your life. In the end an impatient truck driver pushed us on to the ferry, and when we reached the other side, still more impatient, he pushed us off again. Yang Kung Fu and I then undertook a major overhaul, while Jeanette continued to sit fanning herself and giving us useful advice. At the end of two hours we persuaded about fifty kids to t'uei us again and we started. It was now too late to go to the Bank but we thought we might as well send a telegram or two, but the question was, should we have an iced drink first? While we were discussing this point, Celery Stalks gave up the ghost for keeps. We yao'd and t'uei'd until we could yao and t'uei no longer, and then Jeanette phoned for help. Gerard and David [David Shek, her boyfriend] set off [from the garage to rescue them] – in Jumbo! [Another ageing jeep.] Jumbo pao'mao'd [broke down] at the ferry. They yao'd and t'uei'd for about one hour, but Jumbo had had it. Gerard phoned up for Mark to come with a truck to rescue Jumbo, and meanwhile

David came across the river to tell Jeanette and me there was no hope of relief that night.

We then pushed Celery Stalks to Cheng Yang K'ai [the FAU headquarters, several hundred feet up and well into the city centre], Jeanette being driver, with Yang Kung Fu, David and me and some coolies providing the power. It was very hot, although by now it was dark, and I am afraid David overdid it. Coming back on the passenger ferry he was taken very ill with heat cramps and he was soon in terrible convulsions and later unconscious. Luckily there was a good Peiping-trained doctor about a mile away and we soon had David in his hands. It was impossible to get chairs to take us to the hospital, so Jeanette phoned Mark to come with a truck. On the way back we met with a truck p'ao-mao'd in the middle of the road and had to tow it out of the way. This took so long that Mike, (who had just got back from Kunming) and Gerard thought they had better come down and see what was the matter, so, first changing a wheel on the go-able truck in the yard, they set off for the Hai Tang Chi [ferry] too… It was two in the morning when the last of us climbed into bed… David is, of course, still in bed, and is much better, but quite exhausted, and he won't be able to work for quite a time…

We don't want any more days like last Monday, I think.

HOME BREW

Jack gets nostalgic about his old Kweiyang posting

FSU Chronicle Number 16, 19 July 1947

KWEIYANG REVISITED

For a few days it was just like old times in Kweiyang. Mike and I were the first to arrive [at the former transport depot] with five trucks from Chungking. That was at ten o'clock on a typical Kweiyang evening. Rain coruscated on our windscreens, our wheels rustled stickily thru ankle-deep mud. Driving the front truck, I pulled up at Huang T'u P'o with that long low whistle

Dodge convoy on the Luhsien Road, Sept 45

of Dodge brakes which used to act on the members inside the hostel in days gone by, as Romeo's whistle acts on Juliet in that play by what's-his-name. Juliet forthwith appeared in the person of Mrs. Wei Fu Lin.

A handsome rather than a pretty Juliet, with dangling fag and Mae West hips, she seemed indeed,

> "As glorious to this night…
> As is a winged messenger of heaven
> Unto the white upturned wond'ring eyes
> Of mortals, that fell back to gaze on him
> When he bestrides the lazy-pacing clouds
> And sails upon the bosom of the air."

Which, you must admit, is an achievement for a mother of eight, (four still extant). Soon Lao Wei was counting up the survivors, and wailing, "Ai ya, t'ai to, t'ai to," [Ooh, too much!] so we moved on into Sam's quarters [the new owner of the premises]. Here Mike received a hearty welcome from an old friend of his, a famous actress from Kunming, a comedienne I imagine, since she soon had the whole house rocking with a crack about me and goats. [Jack's billy goat beard I guess!] Sam was out, so we drove our trucks into a dangerous bog described as a truckyard, climbed upstairs, and lay listening to the rain as it rattled on the canvas and also to the famous cries of Kweiyang. These, as of yore, went on till two in the morning and started up again at three, and all our old pals turned up to serenade us.

At first sight Kweiyang seems to be quite unaltered. The air is still a-tingle with the bells of ponies bringing panniers of coal-dust into the city. Scores of black fat pigs go by mournfully to their doom, lashed upside down on barrows which out-squeal them mournfully. A new sort of streamlined ma-chih [horse cart] is making its debut, but there are still some hundreds of little green boxes on wheels to recall the good old days. Miao folk wander up and down in the mud, their pleated skirts swinging. The twenty-two peaks still look down on the town, usually through mist or rain, and the girl with the million-dollar legs still lives in the truck-body opposite the hostel. Moreover, her husband's stock-in-trade remains the same, consisting to this day of one second-hand inner tube and a skein of rusty piston rings. I think they must have private means, those two. Mike and I calculated that, what with the inflation and all that, the legs are now worth five million each, at least. Time has not withered them.

That first day was a busy one. I proceeded first to the Catholic mission to unload, and there the representatives of five different nations spent a cheerful couple of hours of misunderstanding each other in three languages, and lapping up excellent coffee. Then we all got into a ma-chih, (except Wei Fu Lin, who was too fat and had to go by rickshaw), and so to the Kweiyang Theatre. The film was the one that our ex-driver, Smiler, used to call "Bath-ing Beauty", [Esther Williams' first Technicolor musical of 1944] pronouncing the first word as if she were busy with the soap in her own back kitchen, and irresistibly reminding me of that classic of modern verse ["Poems and Songs",1939, Gavin Buchanan Ewart.]:

> "Miss Twye was soaping her breasts in the bath,
> When she heard behind her a meaning laugh,
> And looking backwards she discovered
> A wicked man in the linen cupboard."

Every vestige of story had been carefully excised from the film and the sound apparatus remains as aggressive as an under-paid rickshaw boy in Shanghai. Old patrons will be interested to hear that you still get drummed out of the theatre to THAT record… it is still just recognizable. [Presumably the Nationalist anthem.] The power failed once, the film broke twice, and Mike and I emerged in nostalgic mood.

We soon cheered up at Lao Yan Shih. At the next table a women's club was running off its monthly lottery: we saw one dame pocket two million as first prize. While we were waxing merry over our nectar, (for I am sure that what Bacchus on Olympus used to get tight on, was nothing more nor less than what is sold in Kweiyang as sa-li-chou), there entered to us a long file of boys with shaven heads and remarkably tidy suits, followed closely by a file of heavily painted girls in drill-slips. The girls were very little, but so made-up that they reminded me of…

"… a certain young lady of Kutsing
Who said she was fed up with stutsing.
Might well have progressed
If she'd been better dressed
And had gone in for powd'ring and rutsing."

[A very obscure joke! Kutsing, so spelt as transliterated by the Post Office, is actually pronounced 'Chewjing', which then rhymes with 'stooging' and 'rougeing'.]

We found out that these urchins were appearing at the theatre and we naturally went to see them. The theatre as usual was a cross between church and school, with galleries all round and a pot of tea instead of an ink well in the hole in the desk before you. Peanuts, sunflower seeds, and those black seeds you can't eat but just suck the salt off of, kept appearing on the backrest before us; also toffee apples. These are not so good as those they give you in Chengtu, and by the time we had licked a couple to nothing our tongues were glazed. Soon our eyes began to glaze a bit too, for after ten solid minutes of drumming we were subjected to a succession of a dozen women, each of whom sang one interminable solo from Chinese opera. We were reduced to criticizing the ladies' appearance, and it was small wonder when one of us, confronted by a particularly beaten-up-looking and strident soloist, bawled from his seat in the second row, "Thou still unravisht bride of quietness, shut up." Later the show improved, and when the kids came on they were superb. They guyed Chinese opera and they guyed it so well that Mike and I could enjoy the joke too. Some of the dancing and posturing and stylized fighting was as good as any I have seen, and as for jokes… but we must tread warily with a new Editor [presumably David Spillett] around, and I'll tell you about the business with the bun some other time.

Of course, life was just a giddy whirl of pleasure all the time. Mike was buying petrol and I was completely overhauling my brakes. One day I took three tons of salt and seventeen yellow fish [passengers] to Kutsing, which is a place I have some special memories of… ah, those were the days. The next day we came back with three tons of tobacco and no brakes. Mike left for Kunming, and the next night John Peter arrived with four more trucks, also heading for Kunming. The round of feasts, movies, theatres began again. I told John I thought Kweiyang was the nicest town in China. John said he was inclined to agree with me. We ran over its good points… sa-li-chou, the Miaos, sa-li-chou, Hua Hsi [a nearby beauty spot], sa-li-chou, etc.

John Peter

I said, "You can get coffee here now, too. But no milk."

John said, "There was one place in Kweiyang where they used to sell milk."

I said, "Really, where?"

"Just by the monument", said John.

"Oh, that sort of milk," I said. "I wonder if they still sell it?"

"Let's go and see," said John.

We went… and they do.

It is quite the most interesting dairy in the world.

(I am really trying very hard not to upset you, Mr. Editor)

HOME BREW

No romance, a near ship wreck and a plug for Jack's transport unit

FSU Chronicle 16, 19 July 1947

An extract from Jack Jones' letter from Chungking dated July 7th, 1947.

"…Today is the double seventh [a Chinese Valentine festival], and an air of somnolence hangs over the yard. The only workers in sight are Mark wrestling with a gear-box and Mike [Mike Frankton, a keen photographer] padding back and forth to the dark-room. But here in the office the clatter of typewriters never ceases except when we go overseas [across the river to the city] on some errand or other.

"…The only thrills have been provided by the Yangtse, which is going up and down these days like a contralto's

Canadian Mission Hospital, circa 1936

bosom. One day the truck ferry nearly sank under us. (I had a truck full of coke in the stern and the jeep was in the bows, and soon everybody was standing in the bows too, just in case, and the skipper told us they might have to throw the jeep overboard to save the trucks). The next day the float broke away from the launch and Jeanette and I (in the jeep) began to make plans for spending a few days with you in Shanghai, but before long we rammed a junk and our pleasure cruise ended. Yesterday the river rose at phenomenal speed and Mark Jones and I were unable to walk to the Canadian Mission Hospital… we had to cross the river on one ferry and re-cross on the other, and arrived three hours late for afternoon tea. [The path along the south bank was flooded.]

"…Bill's reason for wanting to keep trucks is that commercial transport is still more expensive, less reliable and less convenient than (our) transport, both from the viewpoint of the IRC [International Relief Committee] and of the receiving hospitals and missions. I told Bill that I know of one or two men who had left the Unit and one or two still within the Unit who would be prepared to consider running a small transport organization in China, but there is nothing definite in anybody's plans. I tell you this just to show you how Bill's (Bill Service) mind is running. I think, myself, there is a lot in what he says. [Dr C. William M. Service was acting supervisor of the hospital during the long absence of Dr Stewart Allen on home leave in Canada until early 1948.]

David Shek is up and about again (after heat-stroke and overwork) and has been doing a bit of work today."

Note: In this piece, Jack is taking the chance to oppose the growing move to close the FAU's transport work and to farm out the distribution of medical supplies to commercial truckers.

Many of Jack's contributions, such as this one, were not written specifically for the news letter or chronicle but were extracts from his general reports and letters to headquarters. On some of these original documents in the archives, you can see where the editor has gone through them with a pencil and selected what was of general interest for the Chronicle.

Of major movements, Mary and a good Quakerly monkey

FSU Chronicle Number 17, 26 July 1947

FARTHEST WEST

Only three major movements have to be noted, (for I am told that frequent loose ones, though distressing to the person inside when they occur have little news value). [Details of these convoys then follow.] More disquieting was the news that the [Kuomintang] army is on the move again, and making life difficult for ordinary truck drivers.

On Sunday night five headlightless and battered vehicles came limping into the yard and John Peter's Kunming convoy was back with us again. Amongst John's passengers were our new associate members, Sam Yen and Jimmy. The latter is living, at the moment, outside Mary's room, which means that if you go to see Mary you have to be wary. (It occurs to me that it might be as well to explain at this point, in case I number any low-minded people amongst my readers, that Jimmy is John Peter's monkey and Mary is our generator.)

I recall an occasion in Kweiyang when Jimmy got loose and we had a Reign of Terror in the Garage for two hours, with strong men trembling behind locked doors and not a scrap of work done for all that time, and extensive injuries to Joe Jerk, (who deserved them), and to other employees, and I look forward with interest to the day when Jimmy slips his chain here. The Simon Stylites existence he has been living on top of the water tower at Huang T'u

P'o for the last year has not led him any nearer that ideal of gracious living which he ought to keep ever before him, as a good intelligent Quakerly monkey. [Simon Stylites was a Christian ascetic who is said to have lived for 37 years at the top of a pole.]

The whole garage, fifty employees and the five members at present in residence, are eagerly looking forward to a double wedding next weekend, - Lo Tse Li and Tulip are both going to take the plunge together. The departure of Gerard's convoy to Lanchow will probably be postponed so that all may attend the festivities. Look out for our next contribution – it'll be a wow. If I'm able to write it.

HOME BREW

Li Wan Fa and Lo Tze Li

Note: Jack's account of Lo Tse Li's wedding was published in the New Yorker of 19 February 1949 for which Jack received a generous fee.

Howell Jones has recently sent me this magical picture of John Peter with Jimmy, the monkey, on his shoulder. It seems that John had been a circus performer in Rangoon and may have brought Jimmy with him when he escaped the Japanese invasion of Burma and drove a truck over the Burma Road into China. Howell has also told me that as a keen lover of animals Jack nearly got into fights when he saw Chinese people mistreating them, but he finally decided John Peter could no longer keep his unquakerly monkey at the garage and Jimmy was given to a zoo. John's daughter however has passed on a different story to me, as told by her father, that Jimmy was brutally shot by the communists right in front of him.

Embezzlement, salaries and the importance of being a Quaker

By registering as conscientious objectors and joining the Friends Ambulance Unit, conscientious objectors excluded themselves from the benefits available to the military such as a regular salary, allowances for dependents, a post service gratuity, a pension and long term assistance with attributable illness and injury. In addition the stigma of being a 'conshie' could even make finding jobs more difficult. What mattered to them though was to 'go anywhere and do anything', (GADA, was a slogan of the FAU), and not to ask for any reward, except knowing they were being of service to their fellows.

In the open letter that follows, Jack continues an ongoing debate in the Chronicle, defending these original 'hair-shirt' principles of the China Convoy against the growing expectation of newly recruited post-war relief workers that they should be paid a professional salary. He also opens a rare debate about the interesting mix of Friends and others within the Unit.

Jack himself had been an 'attender' though not a member of The Religious Society of Friends in the thirties, but rarely if ever does he refer to his own personal beliefs in his writings. While he is open and frank in creating a public persona for himself on paper, he was in fact a very private person and did not wear his beliefs, such as they were, on his sleeve. At times in his writings he seems pretty sceptical about China missionaries and in his book, *Daughters of an Ancient Race* he described how he saw through his father's ferocious and puritanical Christianity at an early age, causing a serious conflict between them. Nonetheless he was deeply imbued with the Christian ethic in wanting to be of service to his fellow human beings and to promote international understanding.

What is striking about the China Convoy is that despite a broad mix of members, of Friends and non-Friends, believers and non-believers, through mutual respect, good team work and a consultative rather than hierarchical style of management, harmonious relations were generally maintained despite challenging working conditions. Their commitment to non-violence as conscientious objectors was their core value, though an acceptance of divergent views on other matters is exemplified by the Chronicle's editors printing Jack's punchy open letter that now follows. What's more, they later printed Jack's outrageous story of his hemorrhoidechtomy, written by him for the Chronicle in verse, prose and Lincolnshire dialect! Was it wise though of Jack to cross swords in this letter with Dr Heath Thompson, whose scalpel he was soon to confront?

A hint of acrimony... money again and married women

FSU Chronicle Number 22, 30 August 1947

MORE IN ANGER THAN IN SORROW
(An Open Reply to Heath Thompson's Open Letter to me.)

Dear Heath:
I regret to see so many of the Chronicle's pages devoted to polemics these days. Still more do I regret to find myself involved in the arguments. But when an Open Letter is addressed to one in the columns of a semi-public journal, common courtesy (not to mention an instinctive resort to self-defense), requires that one should reply if possible. So here goes with apologies to the rest of the Unit for being such a bore...

West China members [ie at the Chungking transport depot] DO NOT augment their pocket-money by transferring relief monies to their own pockets, - and I very much doubt whether the members of other sections do so either. You have now made the allegation that members do so twice in the Chronicle, Heath, and I think it is high time that you brought up some evidence to prove your point. That nobody in the Unit takes your charge very seriously is proved by the fact that so far I have been the only member to "rush into print" to refute what you say.

Salaries: I respectfully submit, Heath, that three of the lowest tricks a debater can descend to are 1. isolating certain of the other chap's phrases from their contexts... [He continues at length to point 3.!]

Well, let us drop to your level of argument. I quite agree with you and Spencer [Coxe]...

1. that the FSU, if it is going to be a permanent relief body, will require one or two permanent or semi-permanent projects as its backbone: I myself hope to be a long-term worker in some such project.

2. that not all the long-term workers will be bachelors, quaint or otherwise – (though I must say I think this is probably unfortunate), and 3. I agree that even a relief worker is worthy of his hire...

You say that "having married people in the Unit creates problems that Pool is not much of an answer to" – why? [Private income of members was 'pooled' and shared with everyone else.] I cannot for the life of me understand why a married couple needs more spending money than two single people. Everybody who has lived in lodgings knows that it is a lot cheaper for two people to live together than it is for them to live separately: you pool your resources and the money goes much further. Why should it be different when two people of opposite sexes start living together? I am quite sure that if the Unit pays all of a married couple's living expenses, as it does a single person's, they ought to get along comfortably on Pool in China, especially at the rates at which it is being paid these days.

Bunny and Heath Thompson

No doubt you will bring up the subject of families at this point: but I doubt whether this is relevant. When a woman member has a baby she ceases to be a relief worker – she can't do two jobs at once – and in my opinion she ought not to be out here. I subscribe to the old-fashioned belief that a Married Woman's Place is not a Hostel but her own home. At the same time I believe with my bachelor's idealism, that it should be possible for an exceptional woman to have a baby, do relief work, live in a Hostel happily with other members, and abide by the rules of the organization to which she belongs, and though I myself do not propose to burden myself – or the Unit – with a wife, it is possible that if I met a woman who bade fair to develop all these qualities, my hormones, (which, with such faultless taste, you have brought to public notice along with those of Bob McClure), would spontaneously emerge from the refrigerator. I am quite certain that no foreign girl however would meet the above conditions: it would take an easy-going and uninhibited Chinese girl, the sort that has babies without bother and is used to living with gangs of people without theorizing about community living, to make a success of married life in a Unit hostel.

JACK JONES

Piling on the pressure – Jack's operation

A little more than three months later Jack got his come-uppance for confronting surgeon, Heath Thompson, just at the time his hemorrhoids needed taking down to size. The FAU in Chungking often used the services of the Canadian Mission Hospital in the hills of the south bank when its staff were sick. Dr Stewart Allen, its superintendant and principal surgeon, was chairman of the Medical Committee of the International Relief Committee, for whom the Unit distributed medical supplies, but unfortunately his relationship with Jack was somewhat strained, Jack describing him as his 'arch-enemy'. With regard to his hemorrhoids Jack was thus between a rock and a hard place, chosing instead to fly down to Hankow where he was operated on by Dr Heath Thompson, a young New Zealander, at the Union Hospital run by the London Missionary Society.

The Union Hospital, Hankow

The operation over, he no doubt had too much time on his hands, so he sat (or more likely lay) on a hospital bed and composed his, 'Haemorrhoidectomy – An Anal-ytic drama in three parts'. This was published in the Chronicle (Number 57, 13 December 1947), of which the following verses are a mercifully brief sample. This 'drama', in verse, prose and Lincolnshire dialect, is noteworthy at least for including what is probably the very first use in written English of the vernacular expression, 'gob smacked'.

They stretched me on an ironing board
With rubber wheels equipped.
A brown-eyed nurse piped "Teng-i-ha"
As to my side she tripped…

"O.K." she cooed, "he's had it now,
Forth to the abattoir."
They wheeled me down the corridor
To Heath – my old bête noire;
His grin was grisly for to see:
"Ha, victim, here you are."

Weddings, floods, and an exceptionally pretty nurse

FSU Chronicle Number 21, 23 August 1947

FARTHEST WEST

I am sorry I haven't got around to telling you about the double wedding before this. At this late date it is sufficient to say that everything went off without a hitch, unless the fact that I always bowed at the wrong time and in the wrong directions can be counted as hitches. After Tulip's wedding I had a tiresome time with Gerard [Walmesley], who would insist that he had drunk me under the table, though I am still fairly certain I wasn't under the table. The next day I was able to go to Lo Tse Li's wedding [a story to be told by Jack in the New Yorker], and play my part in the wedding with my usual dignity and grace; Gerard, however, did not turn up to this affair, and I had an even more tiresome time with him that evening, when I tried to prove that his absence from the second feast was relevant to our argument the previous evening, and proved something or other.

Both the happy bridegrooms dashed off on the earliest available convoys, and as is usual in such cases the new wives were raised to the status of the other wives, and given the freedom of our clinic: both have been in to ask questions which task my knowledge of Chinese and Jeanette's knowledge of Physiology (or what not), and one of them, I regret to say, is already having to make weekly visits to hospital. Well, that's life, as Kirby used to say.

Gerard Walmesley, Tulip and Bernard Smith on their 4,000 kilometer round trip to Shantan, July and August 1946

To turn to business matters, wheels in West China have ceased to turn this last week. This is not due to shortage of petrol, tyres, or cash, but to the state of the roads. Gerard was the first to come to rest. He made a fast and very well documented trip, all the way to Shantan, got a return cargo for Chengtu, and was all set to be back within the month. Then came a telegram from Tienshui, 1200 kilos away: BRIDGE OUT MINIMUM TWO WEEKS. The next day came a telegram from Mark, who was on his way to Lanchow with three trucks: ROAD AWASH NECK DEEP TWELVE KILOS HENCE SEND CORACLES. This was sent

from Santai, less than 400 kilos away. We were now quite prepared to hear what disaster had befallen George at Paochi with four trucks, and sure enough the next day we got a cable which on being translated said: BRIDGE OUT AT PAOCHI SEND TWO MILLION. At this point I gave up the ghost and went to hospital.

Next day Mike and Jeanette turned up with two more telegrams, one more from Mark, now at Mienyang 50 kilos further on from his last position: WATERED DOWN INDEFINITELY: the other from the remaining convoy, John Peter's, also Lanchow-bound: SEND COMPLETE REAR AXLE WITH HALF SHAFTS WITH [Mark] JONES CONVOY FLOODS PERMITTING. Goaded beyond bearing we sent the following reply to John: JONES CONVOY LEFT TEN DAYS AGO MIND YOU DON'T GET YOUR FEET WET JACK or words to that effect. (I am writing this in Shanghai [there for meetings with the IRC], far from my references, and my memory is not what it was in my young days). As far as I can see three of our convoys will soon be based at Tienshui, one north of the wash-out and two south of it. [Mark's photo album has pictures captioned, 'washed-out bridge, Wei River near Tienshui... total convoy time lost: 6 weeks (3 x 2 weeks)' and 'the bridge that cost another fortnight:Mienyang'.]

Meanwhile the boys in the yard are having a quiet time booting and bolting tyres. This temporary set-back is a blow, as if the trucks had been able to keep going we should have just about finished our programme on the specified dead-line, September 30th – at least the last convoy would have gone out by then, though maybe they wouldn't have all got back by that date. Now the ARC supplies will last into October [American Red Cross].

Above you will see it hinted – with a brave smile – that I have been in hospital. Great concern and sorrow was felt by all West China – but especially me – when my temperature began to act like a flying saucer. Jeanette said Roy Lucas shouldn't be allowed to write such letters about me and Mike said that if I didn't climb half way down peoples' throats when looking for signs of diphtheria I should be all right. They waited until I was better, then they took me to [the Catholic] hospital. Four nurses then set about making me comfortable and, boy, was I hard to please. I developed what I thought was a neat bit of strategy: whenever a nurse suggested something I didn't want to do, I said, "Pu tung!" [don't know]; this worked until they dug up a Cantonese speaking nurse who spoke English as well as I do. Our worthy editor suggests that I ought to have started talking in French at this point, but, as I reminded him, there are limits to a mere Transport Director's duplicity. [Jack did get a C for French at school though!]

Howell Jones and a black and yellow striped CNRRA jeep, Kaifeng

The first two mornings I was bathed by an exceptionally pretty little nurse, a native of Chungking, whose lingering and luxurious way with a hot towel did me a world of good: in fact it did me so much good that on the third day I put the nurse in bed and gave her a bath. Shortly afterwards I was discharged.

Jeanette, David, Mike and Sam, who thought they had got rid of me for six weeks (for we thought I was starting typhoid), were not prepared for this speedy return and they promptly booked me a seat on the next plane to Shanghai, and here I am. Ostensibly I have time for important conferences with the IRC, etc, etc, but so far I have done nothing but interview the Editor on his bed of sickness, or be interviewed by him on my bed of rest. Then, last night, old Howell Jones blew in from Kaifeng… The first thing he said was, "God, if I'd known you were here, I'd have brought another crate of beer with me." He still remembers, you see, the austerity of his life in West China.

HOME BREW

RIVER CROSSINGS

It is hard now to appreciate how absolutely China was divided by its rivers and how their capricious behaviour would either allow the distribution of medical supplies to their destination or else frustrate the herculean efforts of the FAU. There were of course some fine ancient bridges and with the coming era of motor transport a few new roads with properly engineered culverts and bridges had recently been built. However, river crossings were generally ferries or perhaps temporary dry season structures that would be impassable or swept away as the seasons changed. Every crossing, even the best of bridges, was subject to violent weather and arbitrary acts of God. The Yangtse itself which, according to Jack, rose and fell with the seasons 'like a contralto's bosom', created an obstinate and fickle barrier to travel northwards. From the south bank at Hai Tang Chi there was a passenger ferry and a vehicle ferry and their running or non-running impacted fundamentally on the lives and work of the FAU. Their quip that when crossing to Chungking they were 'going overseas' was more truthful than exaggeration. If armies were passing or when vehicles were dropped into the drink, the truck queues were measured sometimes not in hours but in days. The truck ferry was nothing more than a low decked barge with a small tug boat that lay lashed alongside it and which struggled out into the current, always headed directly upstream but crabbing downstream towards Shanghai. Five metres forwards through the water and one over the ground perhaps, it was a titanic struggle of puny man against nature. The river had created the city and its strategic position high up on the cliffs, to which clung a massively swollen population of refugees from the Japanese invaders. Likewise the life of the foreshores, of temporary stalls, shacks and sampans with the constant churning of its struggling population was vivid and vibrant and a constant fascination for Jack, always the sensitive observer of teeming humanity.

4 TIN MINES, SLAVE LABOUR AND AN ANTI-MALARIA PROJECT – MAY 1948

The story of Jack's anti-malaria project can be gleaned from news letter articles received from the AFSC archives in Philadelphia and from a long article by Jack that I found in the archives of the Bangkok Post. This is what seems to have happened in the early part of 1948.

In 1947 at its annual staff meeting, the FSU had considered a request from the Church of Christ in China (CCC) based in Kunming, Yunnan, and the local authorities in Shihping, a small town south of Kunming, asking for help to deal with an outbreak of a particularly virulent strain of malaria. As Jack was the West China Director and as he got bored sitting at his desk in Chungking he agreed to travel to Shihping to assess the feasibility of the project. Meanwhile a potential team of medical and other staff was lined up and ready to travel as soon as the project could be given the go ahead.

On Sunday 17 April 1948 Jack handed over running of the transport operation in Chungking to Peter Verrall, and left Chungking by truck, arriving in Kunming the following Thursday. The story of the journey, including being held up at gun point by Nationalist soldiers, appears below. On Monday 26 April he took the Yunnan-Indochina railway southwards, arriving at Kienshui late the next day, an exciting journey which he describes in the piece that follows.

In those days Kienshui was a fair bit further than the back of beyond and it was a major expedition to get there. Over sixty years later I arrived by bus in this pleasant small town, now known as Jianshui, with plenty of time to eat in its vibrant night market, having flown into Kunming from Bangkok that same day. The world has certainly shrunk and, despite its mountains and its vastness, so has China.

Beaten up by Nationalist soldiers

FSU Chronicle Number 56, 1 May 1948

WEST CHINA: Jack Jones has once again proved himself the Editor's Best Friend by providing the following account of his recent trip to Kunming from Chungking: [The trip over 1150 kilometres of appalling road was to do the feasibility study for the proposed anti-malaria project in Shiping.]

'....Actually got away [from the Chungking garage] at 10:30[pm] and trundled along in fine style until my steering seized up. After that we trundled some more until Chi Hsu Lin's generator burnt out. Then some more until my lights failed. A gremlin seemed to have got into the circuit, and I eventually had to drive by the light of the moon to the nearest village. Here we fed on two eggs each and no rice, as an army of over a thousand men had got billeted into the village about two hours before we arrived. Came the dawn, and on the next big mountain my radiator boiled and I discovered that it was emulating the contraptions that John Peter rigs up in every section he goes to. Having had this repaired at Tungtse, we bowled along without further mishap for 240 kilos; then Chi Hsu Lin drove across the suspension bridge at Wukiang too fast, and incurred the ire of the guards; after numerous apologies and much wagging of the Assyrian beard in the Egyptian wind (I quote Louis MacNeice) we put up in Wukiang for the night. The next 105 kilos to Kweiyang were soon covered next morning, in fact we hit Kweiyang at 10 a.m. As Chi Hsu Lin hadn't seen his wife for ten months, and as she is a bonny lass, and as I am a very benevolent sort of despot, I said we couldn't

Chinese soldiers eating, Yunnan province

possibly leave Kweiyang that day, so we spent the rest of the day in Kweiyang, feasting with ex-employee Tien Lo Chien, with Roger Arnold at the YMCA, and with the Litherlands at the CIM [China Inland Mission], and then with Tien Lo Chien again in the small hours of the morning. Came another dawn, and a broken spring after 68 kilos. We quickly attached a piece of wood and a piece of string in the approved Chinese style and attacked the mountains. It was market day at Huang Kuo Hsu and I stopped to admire the Miaos as well as the stupendous waterfalls, which are fuller of water than I have ever seen them before, and a grand sight. [In Howell Jones' words, the falls were 'the mid-morning stop before lunch in Anshun', and are now in the guide books as Huangguoshu, 31 miles SW of Anshun.]

Forty kilos later, on the crest of a long mountain climb, we were just letting our engine cool down when an ambulance drew up at our rear. It was Doc Carlson seven days out of Hankow [apparently a malaria specialist on his way to appraise the same project]. He had a massive load, and had done remarkably well to get so far in so short a time. For the rest of that day it was a tortoise and hare business; Carlson would pass us, and later we would find him with a burst tire, or stuck in the mud, or fuelling up, or stuck in the mud again; we always helped him out, and finally we ran into Annan twenty minutes ahead of him, in pouring rain and over foul roads. The next day he was off before us, and we didn't see him again. The rest of that day over the endless mountains, was superb but spoiled by the frontier guards, who guard all the steep pitches where the truck is doing about one mile an hour in bottom, and hold you up and demand baksheesh for protecting you from the bandits. That night we stopped early in Pingyi, to

The falls taken by Nellie Bonsall in 1996

avoid a fierce thunderstorm which broke about half an hour after. The next morning we had our only real trouble. An officer had asked for a lift, and I had firmly but courteously refused, as usual. [As a pacifist organisation, there was a fundamental objection to carrying soldiers.] We finished fuelling up and took off. Less than half a mile outside the village we were held up by twelve soldiers drawn up in battle array with levelled guns.

As soon as we stopped they made a beeline for Chi Hsu Lin, tried to drag him out of the cab, and when that failed began clubbing and butting him with their rifles. I tried to intervene, but was pushed away and kept where I was by two soldiers with levelled guns. So I went to look for my hu chao [travel permit]. Meanwhile, one soldier removed the bayonet from his gun and jabbed Chi Hsu Lin repeatedly with the muzzle, badly hurting his arms and ribs.

A column of Nationalist soldiers

I found my hu chao, and returned just as the officer I had refused to give the lift to appeared. He was in a towering rage, as it is unthinkable for a company commander to be refused a lift. I was polite and conciliatory, chiefly for Chi Hsu Lin's sake, and in the end we got away with the officer and three guards [on board], after I had asked the officer, as an officer, to order some other officers to get off the trucks - they had taken advantage of the fracas to make themselves comfortable. We drove on twenty kilos; as usual Chi Hsu Lin stopped to make sure I was following. He was all smiles when I condoled with him. "Mei yu kuan hsi. Hsien tsai t'a shih wo-ti peng yu. T'a ko-chi to hen." [Don't worry. Now he's my friend. He's very polite.] When the officer eventually got out he and Chi Hsu Lin shook hands warmly. The officer wanted to shake hands with me too, but I told him I would not shake hands with a man who set twelve armed men onto one unarmed driver and allowed them to beat the driver up. I also told him I wanted half a million for fares and damages to Chi Hsu Lin. The officer then began to tell a hard luck story, saying that he had been commanded to report at Chanyi and he had to obey, and ours were the only trucks in Pingyi this morning, (which was true); so I read him another little lecture, and then drove off. I was fuming of course, but it is a case, as Chi Hsu Lin says, of "mei yu pan fa"; you can't do anything about the bastards. I think that this is the first time one of our drivers has actually been beaten up; the officer said it was all right for me as a foreigner to refuse to take him, but for a Chinese driver to do so was insufferable. After this we reached Kunming without further incident.

Yesterday morning I had a brief talk with Clark [regional director of the Church of Christ in China which had requested the project] and Carlson, and I spent the rest of the day unloading. As I had fifteen different shipments, and as you aren't allowed to drive a truck in the city between 8 a.m. and 6 p.m., this was a hell of a job, and I was lucky to be able to borrow Ken's jeep and trailer [FAU member, Ken Cross], and, for part of the time, Ken too. And last night I went to dinner with the Carlsons. I like the man more and more; he's certainly the Unit type; I've seen him on his back in the mud fixing chains, and I think I would trust him to fix anything anywhere.

Clark, Carlson and I were to have set off for Shihping today, but Clark's tu tsu is pu hao and the trip has been put off till Monday. [Bowel problems!] We had hoped to see the big man of the Shihping district here in Kunming, but he left for Shihping early yesterday morning. Actually however, it won't do any harm if we have our look round first.

There's not much yet that I can say about the (malaria) project. It is quite clear however that Carlson is very interested and willing to work with us. He thinks the project could be run without a Unit doctor and with himself in a supervisory capacity, visiting the team at regular intervals. Ken on the other hand is convinced we need a full-time Unit doctor. But I cannot say anything definite until I have seen for myself. I hope to send you a report in ten day's time.'

Kunming pagoda and FAU truck

Chin Bi Lu, Kunming

Yunnan... Jack writes from Kienshui

FSU Chronicle Number 57, 8 May 1948

Clark, Carlson and I left Kunming Monday morning at 8:30. [In his later Bangkok Post article of 1977 Jack says he took the train with Dr. Clark, regional director of the the Church of Christ in China, the superintendant of the the Church of Christ in China hospital in Kaiyuan and a 'world renowned malariologist'.]

It occurs to me that I shall have to bang out a pretty comprehensive itinerary for the team. The journey takes days and the finding of missions and ticket offices, etc. is quite complicated. We left from the station near the East Gate, which is in easy walking distance from the Huei Tien Hospital. We booked to K'ai yuan (second class – fare, 922.000 [yuan]).

The train, which runs on a small gauge, and is so small that when you inspect the locomotive you instinctively look for the key to wind it up with, was not by any means crowded, and by comparison with trains in the east, remarkably comfortable and punctual. For the first fifty kilos you climb, eventually achieving a height of 8000 feet; at this point you have reached what the National Geographic Mag. calls "an airline distance" from Kunming of about 15 kilos. You then plunge down a spectacular precipice to a beautiful lake which lies among superb mountains. From this point on to K'ai yuan the train runs almost continuously on a shelf on some towering mountainside, with often a sheer drop into a boiling torrent – first the headwaters of the East River, then the headwaters of the Pearl River, which finally gets down to Canton. As you descend, the vegetation, etc. changes before your eyes, and soon you are in tropical jungle: bougainvilleas and what Clark calls "high-biscus" at every station and kapok trees, cotton trees, banana palms, rhododendrons, orchids, and many another gorgeous flower and blossom I cannot recognize. One place I recall in particular is Chiao Chia Tu, (the Chiao family fort), a wild station on a mountain top, with a romantic trail crossing the ford below and winding

up into bare mountains, and Miao and Annamese people [Chinese hill tribe and Vietnamese] on the station trying to sell you spectacular pheasants with tail feathers three feet long and marked like snakes. One bird, 120,000 [yuan], if you're interested. The train appears to run through three gorges, each wilder than the last; these are separated by short plains. Often monkeys are to be seen in the trees or walking on all fours along the edge of the river, some with babies clinging to their midriffs; and there are a thousand other things to be seen.

At one point I saw one train of about ten goods-vans in three tunnels simultaneously; a few seconds later it was over one bridge and in two of the tunnels simultaneously. There are about 150 of these tunnels, and as the engine burns an especially sulphurous sort of fuel, they are a severe strain on the nose and eyes. But this is the only drawback to a magnificent ride.

K'ai yuan was reached dead on time at 6:35 p.m. It is a very attractive small town in a magnificent setting of mountains. We were met by Mr. Koonradt, who knows many an old FAU-er. He led us to the Mission, which has just become established in a huge building, the owner of which now languishes in clink for dealing in opium. Shortly after a wonderful sunset I went to bed, in preparation for the morrow.

Came the dawn, but long before that we were up, for the train leaves on the next stage soon after 6 a.m. We booked to Pi Che Ch'ai, at a cost of 68,500. There's no trouble about class distinctions on this train: you all get in with the pigs and chickens, and a p'ou kai is a luxury seat. You climb for about three hours through more fine mountain country. The best mountains, the Go Chiu range [Gejiu], 9000 feet, (where 5% of the world's tin is mined) are on your right; but don't bother if you are on the wrong side of the train; they will be there for three hours after you leave Pi Che Ch'ai, - on your left. [Pi Che Ch'ai is on the southerly railway towards Hanoi where a branch line turns north westwards to Kianshui and Shihping.]

At Pi Che Ch'ai you leap from the train and make a dash for the ticket office, (which is under the big sign with the station's name on it). Here you stand in a well-organized queue, the organization being provided by gun-butts wielded by railway guards. Tickets to Kienshui cost, now, 222,000. For this trifling outlay you are privileged to ride on the most fascinating railway I have ever encountered. The gauge is two feet. The trains come straight from the brain and pen of Emmet in Punch. [The cartoonist, Frederick Emett, 1906-1990.] The engines are marvels, overhanging the wheels by about two feet on each side; they have ten driving wheels, to which are affixed prodigiously large counter-balance-weights; what they lack in size they make up in the number of domes – three – and the size of the whistle, which causes landslides in the gorges, and terrifies the jungle-birds in distant Thailand: every time they use that whistle they have to stop the train to get up steam again. The railway is owned and run by the great business moguls of the district, chiefly tin-mine operators. They used to have 24 locomotives, 6 are left. The rest have been cannibalized. For three years they were unable to obtain engine grease, which explains the high mortality amongst the bearings.

As we were taking petrol up to the hospital at Kienshui, somebody had to ride in the guards van – this is a railway regulation: - to prevent the guards from smoking in the vicinity of the drums; I volunteered for this chore, and rode for the rest of the day in comfort on a bag of rice, with plenty of room for my legs, while the others were smothered in chickens, people, babies, piglets, sugar-cane and dirty bundles containing God knows what. My companions were two armed guards and two Annamese women. The latter I found very interesting for several reasons, for one thing one of them was very good-looking. Also their knowledge of Chinese was equal to mine, so that we could all stutter more satisfactorily than to the guards. At first I was rather sorry for the older of the two: her teeth were all blackened and she seemed to be spitting blood: later I realized she was chewing betel-nut. Both girls disappeared at stations, returning with a smile as the train got under way: I realised that they had omitted the formality of buying tickets. Twice they were caught and questioned: they then said that they were

guarding some luggage for some men at whose name the guards were visibly impressed. "What is the luggage?" the guards would ask. "Don't know," the girls replied; "but it is for so-and-so." They had actually one beaten up old sack, which looked as if it contained shavings or screwed-up paper. Anyhow, they won the day, and got right through to Kienshui.

At Kienshui the entire hospital staff was on the station to meet us. There are five foreign ladies here, including Dr. MacKenzie. The hospital superintendent, Dr. Cheng, appears to be a very fine young chap and will accompany us to Shiping today. You will be interested to hear that I had my usual salutary effect on the pregnant: Mrs. Ransome took one look at me yesterday morning, and had her third – a girl – in the Hospital during the night. Both Dr. Cheng and Dr. Fang here were under Ken Cross at Cheeloo. [The one-time Shantung Christian University.]

Yesterday we made a round of important officials, but all were out. They have all gone to Men Sze [Mengzi], which it appears was raided by bandits last week. A large body of troops has been sent there. I have seen a letter however from all the big bugs of the district asking for somebody to come in and help stem the malaria epidemic. We are pretty sure of a welcome from the gentry anyway. The Chu Yuan's secretary was most cordial, and told us the chief breeding places of the mosquitoes were the puddles which the peasants make when they throw away the water they have used in making tou-fu!

"My hand aches and a louse becomes McBain's…." Sorry, but please tell the latter his generator was going like hell during the delivery last night. One of the most pathetic cases in the Hospital right now is a woman with three bullet holes in her hip and thigh. Someone was ill in the house and someone else let off a gun to scare the devils away…..There are several cases of bullet-wounds and stabbings. The town however is quiet and clean and it also contains the third largest Confucian temple in China, an impressive assemblage of buildings, with some good gates, etc. The weather is just heavenly, Kunming-like….I can't write more now, but I will write my full official report as soon as I get back from Shihping, and after a further talk with Drs. Carlson, McKenzie and Chang.

Yours as ever,
Jack.

Arriving by train in Shihping

Taking the train on to Shihping, the party was met at the station 'by a posse of local dignitaries in trilby hats and ankle-length blue gowns and by the romantic light of the carbide lamps', to be borne away in sedan chairs by women bearers, as described by Jack in his Bangkok Post article of 1977.

On my own visit to Shihping in 2010 I was able to find and photograph the railway station built by the French as part of their penetration into Yunnan from Indo-China.

At Shihping (1 May)

We have had a wonderful reception and in spite of the fact that all the chief people are away combating bandits we have accomplished much.

There is no doubt in my mind that the [malaria] epidemic was as serious as alleged last year. The district is frightened of a repetition this year. The position at the moment is this: at the Boys Middle School, where they have 400 students, between 20 and 30 were away from school today because of malignant malaria. One boy died last week.

According to Dr. Li 80% of the population have enlarged spleens [a symptom of malaria].

The disease is worse in the villages than in the city. The villages are all dotted around the lake, whose edges are shallow and swampy and ideal breeding sites for mosquitoes. There are not many anopheles [mosquitoes] now, due to wind; they begin to increase in June, after the rains; and they and the disease multiply until the climax is reached in the autumn. There seems little doubt that there will be another epidemic this year. The doctors – Carlson, MacKenzie, Chang, Fang – all agree on this.

Consequently I have gone ahead and inspected premises. I was shown five and finally selected the Li Family's Ancestral Shrine. This building is in the centre of the city, is clean and well-built, with stone floors downstairs and wooden ones upstairs. It contains at present six large rooms, the smallest 15 feet by 15, and four verandahs, each 35 feet by 12, and each easily convertible into 3 rooms, making 12 in all. There are also two courtyards half roofed-in which would make store-rooms, a large courtyard and a garden. We can have this free of charge for as long as we want, but IT IS ESSENTIAL TO GET OUR PEOPLE IN QUICK, as the military might take it otherwise. We have also been offered separate rooms for clinics at the West and East gates – the chief ones – and the middle school for boys. The Head of the latter wanted me to lecture on malaria control on the spot!

We feel here that the best plan would be to get the team flown to Kunming at once. The Kienshui hospital has plenty of atabrin [an anti-malarial drug developed in the thirties]. This should be used in a blitz in the villages at once, a prophylactic blitz – there is a 100% incidence of the disease in some of them. Meanwhile the Li Shrine should be prepared for an HQ with living quarters, lab., examination room, etc.

Leave the rest to...

Your loving grandfather,

Jack

The malaria project goes ahead

The team consisted of John Woodall and Jenifer Woodall, (a doctor and nurse), Jean Liu Lung-Chien, (who later married Peter Verrall, with whom she was to live in Nova Scotia and Princeton, NJ, where Peter gained his PhD), Wong Hsiao Hsin (or Wang Hsiao Hsin), who was finishing his secondment at the Shantan Bailie School, and Roger Way an American, (at the time of writing living with other FAU stalwarts in Foxdale Village, Pennsylvania, a Quaker directed retirement community), who extended his two year contract to take part in the project.

The Woodalls and Roger Way travelled from Shanghai to the south bank garage at Chungking towards the end of May where they pitched in to help with the work in the clinic. Mike Frankton reports in the Chronicle that after John Woodall had left, having 'examined all our neurotic employees and their wives', he is appalled at the prospect of coping alone, and that the clinic is now so tidy he can't find anything. Peter Verrall then abandoned his desk there and drove the team, including Jean Liu down to Kunming where they were met by Jack, Hsiao Hsin arriving separately by air. The plan was then to leave by train for Shihping on 31 May.

In the meantime Jack had made a visit to the tin mines where he was appalled at the conditions in which child labour was being used underground as bonded slaves. His article in the Chronicle entitled, 'The Yunnan Tin Mines', apparently was first written as a long letter to Spencer Coxe, an influential FAU 'cheese' in Shanghai, hoping to prick his conscience. Either Coxe or someone else seems to have sent the letter to the press which had some adverse consequences for Jack, as will be seen.

Jean Liu

FSU Chronicle Number 60, 29 May 1948

THE YUNNAN TIN MINES

...Shihping is a bower of bliss compared with Ko Chiu [Gejiu, known as 'tin city']. Of course the malaria is serious and if our team can help to prevent it from spreading they will be doing a really well-worth job. But the plight of the 40,000 boys in the private mines is infinitely worse than that of the people of Shihping. The latter live in a pleasant town, they are fairly well off, (some really rich, because they exploit the boy-labour), they are able to live normal lives and usually reach middle age if not a ripe old age. The boys in the mines are lucky if they live till twenty, or rather, unlucky.

I shall have to skip my impressions of Ko Chiu, the wildest town I have been in since the Lolo towns of Fulin and Luku in Sikang, (over 200 unsolved murders within the walls last year; not bad for a population of roughly 40,000). I must skip the government mine, which we explored thoroughly, being over 700 feet down for three hours. It must be sufficient to say that the government mine appears to be very efficiently run and I should think it is in fact one of the most efficient industrial concerns in China. It shows that the tin can be mined at an enormous profit without using boys. Somebody told us the mine made a profit of 70%, but this was not confirmed.

After sleeping at the govt mine (at a height of 8,500 feet, and after a hard day, including a 10 mile walk all up-hill and about 4 miles underground) we were provided with extra guards (making four, all armed with rifles and revolvers) and went off to look at the private mines. The first we came to had an entrance three feet square. The shaft went down at an angle of about 60 degrees, getting narrower as it descended. As we were peering in, surrounded by the guards, we heard stertorous breathing way down the shaft and soon saw the glimmer of a carbide lamp. Soon, pausing often to lean gasping against the wall of the shaft, a scarecrow of a lad appeared. He was so thin that he reminded me of Phiz's drawings of Smike. [Cartoonist, Hablot K. Browne.]

He was naked except for a few rags which were red with rust --- for there is much low-grade iron in these parts --- and he was soaking wet, partly with sweat, partly with the water that runs in all these mines. Over his bony shoulder he carried two bags of ore, one at his back and the other hanging before him; in the front part of the front one his carbide lamp was placed. He emerged from the opening and without straightening up from his crouched position went about ten yards away and sank down on the ground, gasping pitifully. He had a ghastly pallor under the smeared rust on his cheekbones and his pale brown pupil-less eyes were those of a heavy opium-smoker. He was suspicious of us and not willing to answer questions. He said he was nineteen years old and didn't know how long he had been in the mines. He made three trips to the face every shift and a shift lasted "all day". In a few seconds he got up and moved away… still without straightening up. It was with nasty shock that I realised that he couldn't. He was permanently bent in the posture in which he crawls through the underground tunnels. Some of the other lads that were emerging from that shaft were similarly deformed, others had thighs like a ballet-dancer's, the muscles have slipped round to the side, I suppose as a result of constant crouching. All the lads in this mine appeared to be in their late teens, and all were obvious opium-smokers. They have to be to last that long: apparently opium makes the work bearable.

We looked into the stone building which is home to these lads. It was a stone building, completely bare except for a few rags scattered on the earth floor. On these rags two boys were lying, ill. Both had horrible ulcers on their legs which they said had started from cuts long ago. The boys are always ill, always take a long time to get well – if they do get well – because of malnutrition, overwork, and the opium. I did not see any opium paraphernalia in this dormitory – or prison – but we could not fail to see the heavy bars at the window and heavy padlocks on the doors. The boys are imprisoned at night – at some mines they are said still to be chained, though we did not see any evidence of this. But there are roughly a thousand mines, and we only saw three, all close to the "road". This mine anyway was not typical, in that lads almost full-grown were used. We went to see a more typical one.

I had already noticed a huge slag heap spilling over a small col between two mountains, a great heap of grey shale over and round which long lines of little boys were crawling and climbing, looking like red ants in their scanty, rusty rags.

When I got up to this slag heap I was horrified to find that the majority of these boys were about the size of Terry Hoskins – just tiny kids. The oldest appeared to be about twelve or thirteen. It was terrible to see them edging their way along dangerous, insecure paths to where they could dump their ore; it was worse still to hear them, their gasping, wheezing breath. The harm done to these small boys by heavy work, bad air, and poor food is immense and usually in a few years fatal. But boys this size have to be used, say the owners, because only they are small enough to get through the underground passages.

We climbed up to the top of the slag-heap and had a surprise. The mouth of the mine was forty feet below us, at the bottom of a huge hole in the slag. The slag had in fact just been thrown up in a heap all around the entrance. The general slope is very steep, and the slag looks very insecure; a heavy rain might dislodge the whole lot, and bottle up the mine entrance. If it did so, a thousand little boys would be suffocated before help could reach them.

This is the mine that employs the most boys and has the biggest output. A constant stream of them was appearing at the entrance, pausing to catch a bit of breath, and then climbing wearily, with frequent stops, up the steep slope to the top of the slag, where we were. Another stream was going down on their way into the mine; it was pathetic rather than otherwise to see them stop for a minute at the entrance and blow out each other's lights in fun, and tussle with each other as small boys will. But the boy I remember best was one who later told us he was ten years old, and came from Chaotung. He was particularly small and still had more of the baby than the man in him. You could hear him breathing heavily when he first emerged from the shaft, forty feet below. He came up very slowly, pausing three or four times because he was so weak. He paused again about twelve feet from the top. By bad luck one of the guards dislodged a lump of limestone weighing three or four pounds. The stone went straight for the boy as if it was aimed in spite and struck him on one dirty bare ankle. The boy gave a cry of pain and bent and clutched his ankle. The stone went bouncing on and disappeared into the mine. The small boy looked up and cursed the soldier. Blood began to ooze between his fingers and the pain got worse. It was more than he could bear. Two bigger boys, coming up with their loads, found him in their way and shouted to him to get a move on. As he began to toil upwards, the tears were streaming down his face. He reached the crest, and squatted down, crying to himself, with no hope of comfort. He wiped the back of his hand across his face, leaving a smear of rust. It looked like blood. He was so small and completely lonely that the tears came to my own eyes, and come to them again as I write this, and I'm no cry baby, Spencer. [This article was thus apparently written as a letter to Spencer Coxe in Shanghai and then published in the Chronicle.]

Mr. Clark reported these things to the Generalissimo [Chiang Kai-shek] some time ago and as a result the Generalissimo sent down a directive that social welfare and hospital work was to be begun on behalf of the boys and a tax levied on the mine-owners to pay for this. The CCC [Church of Christ in China] was asked to go in and start work but of course they refused to do so under these conditions, which would have made their position untenable. Murder is an everyday occurrence up there and anyone who goes in to help the boys must go independently and not try and compel the owners, or the boys, to do anything. As a matter of fact, probably as a result of the Generalissimo's directive, the WSS are established at the only temple up there. [The Weishengshu or National Health Authority.] This temple is called the Rat Temple, and it commemorates some rats who according to legend fed a boy who got stuck in the mines and kept him alive. (Most are just left to die, unless they happen to be blocking an important passage). We visited this temple, and met a chap who was introduced as doctor, but said he wasn't, and he didn't look like one either. He said there were two male nurses, but they were away. I don't think anything was being done there. The usual YPHA story.

The CCC is now in touch with an American doctor who has done social welfare work in a mining area for many years. But there is little hope that he will go to this place. The difficulties and dangers of work in the area are enormous. The mine owners won't want you: they know they are in the wrong; some of them have to take a bodyguard of twenty armed men on the rare occasions when they visit their own mines. The boys won't want you at first: they are suspicious and superstitious, they don't trust anybody, they have been ill-treated all their lives, and they won't understand a relief worker's motives. In any case they wouldn't be allowed to visit him, for they work all day, and are locked up in stone forts at nightfall. They have their own comforts – opium and homosexuality. They are worse than any problem children; fights to the death are common; these often occur underground. Recently the boys in one mine heard the sounds of a tunnel being dug towards theirs and waited with guns for the boys of the other mine to break into their shaft. (This often happens as the passages twist and undulate all over the place). Several boys were killed on this occasion before it was realised that the intruders belonged to the same mine, and had happened to work back to the same vein… Besides all this the area is very scattered, and being on the top of the Ko Chiu range, at 9,000 ft. plus, it is bleak in the extreme.

Short-term work might be able to achieve something in the way of relief of direct suffering but what is requited is a man who will devote his life to the district. The man would have to be a superman who could stand unutterable solitude and the constant danger of a bullet in his back. He would have to have a wonderful personality to be able to attract and win the confidence of the boys without getting himself into hot water with the owners. The only real solution of the problem is of course even more radical than that. The Govt mine shows that tin mines can be mechanised and run without boy-labour. But the present private mines cannot be mechanised, owing to the extreme smallness of the galleries. Maybe nationalisation of the mines might help, but I can't see that happening. The mine-owners – those rich, cultivated, charming men who invited us to Shihp'ing to save their home-town from being decimated by malaria – are rich and powerful, and more than most Chinese they seem to band together for their common good; witness the Ko Pi Shih railway, built and owned and run by them all for their mutual benefit, and the anti-malaria committee. I do not know what we could do, but nobody can see those boys in the mines and not try to do something for them. I hope you can do something with this letter which may ultimately help those boys.

JACK JONES

End note: Jack's letter causes ripples across the world

A long article by Jack called, '*The poor "little red ants" of China*', about child labour in the tin mines, appeared in the Bangkok Post just twenty nine years later on 29 May 1977. In this article he suggests that the Shihping anti-malaria project had been requested by the authorities there mainly because mosquitoes 'feed on the rich' as well as the poor. Meanwhile in the mines the poor little red ants whose exploitation made these same mine owners and merchants of Shihping wealthy were dying in droves.

Jack then says in the article that he wrote a letter to a friend in Shanghai, presumably Spencer Coxe, and, 'The silly ass sent it to the North China Daily before I got out of Yunnan, who published it'. Back in Kunming, he recounts, he was sent for by the Governor of Yunnan who, 'in a blistering fury', told him to be in his truck and out of Kunming by the next day. The article was then spotted and republished in the Manchester Guardian, causing an international storm. The Kuomintang government then became involved and passed regulations that workers must be aged at least sixteen to work in the tin mines. Jack concludes that though the law would have been totally ignored, the real resolution of the problem came two years later when the communists closed down all private tin mines, retaining only the publicly owned mines which were adequately mechanised.

A further melodramatic thrust of Jack's Bangkok Post article is that while he was down the tin mine an attempt was made on his life by releasing a runaway ore truck down the dark gallery in which he was walking alone, which made a great ending for the story.

Shihping today is well known for its production of tofu. The elimination of water puddles produced when making tofu might have been the key to eradicating malarial mosquitoes, though in fact prophylaxis and treatment in the clinic was the project's objective.

The team thus arrived in Shiping at the beginning of June 1948 and sometime soon after that Jack returned to Chungking, having apparently crossed swords with the Governor. In August there was an earthquake in Shiping and by September, with no malaria epidemic apparent, the number of patients was dropping off. It was therefore concluded that the project should close in October.

Kutsing city wall

5 'STAR OF THE ORIENT'–THE LOVELY ACTRESS, MRS CMS – SEPTEMBER 1948

Brevity was never one of Jack's greatest virtues as a writer and I can imagine his sense of escape as he joyfully belted the typewriter keys in the heat and humidity of the Chungking summer flowing freely. In five parts, the following article is particularly self-indulgent but its story of a theatrical performance in the next village put on by Chang Min Sang, one of the FAU drivers, and his lovely wife has hardly a dull sentence. A shorter version later appeared in the August 1949 issue of Holiday, the magazine of the Automobile Association of America and again as a chapter in, "*Daughters of an Ancient Race*", Jack bitterly resenting the editor's deletions.

Though I have found two pictures with Chang Min Sang in them, the employees' wives only seem to appear in wedding photos, so Mrs CMS (with whom Howell tells me Jack was besotted) has escaped the camera. In her honour, however, there now follows many a thousand words.

FSU Chronicle Number 77, Shanghai, September 15, 1948

'STAR OF THE ORIENT'

(A story in 3 parts by Jack Jones)

Yesterday afternoon, as sunny a Saturday afternoon as ever was, we were leading a healthy open-air life in deckchairs on the verandah when Chang Min Sang approached and said, in view of the fact that the river was so high that we should be prevented this weekend from crossing it and throwing ourselves with our usual abandon into the glittering social whirl of life on the North Bank, perhaps we could honour him by indulging in the humbler pleasures of a visit to his theatre at Lo Chia Pa, which, as every schoolboy knows, is on "our" side of the Yangtse. Thinking of (1) the shrieking and unintelligible talkies, (2) the chocolate-coated ice-cream without chocolate coats, (because

Chang Min Sang

the chocolate-coating part of the machinery has broken down), and (3) the inhibition-ridden tea with milk and missionaries, which constitute the social whirl in Chungking; and comparing these pleasures with those of the Chinese theatre, where one gets (1) shrieking and unintelligibility in excelsis, (2) sunflower seeds instead of ices, and (3) tea with chrysanthemums in it instead of milk – (and no inhibitions whatever) - we decided that life might have something good in store for us after all, and, graciously thanking Chang Min Sang for his kind invitation, we signified that we should be at the doors of the theatre by eight o'clock.

Accordingly at a quarter past seven we all put on shirts and shoes and set off for Lo Chia Pa. (In case you have a fantastic picture on your mind, and one injurious to our modesty, I must point out that we already had our shorts on). As we passed through the first village, Ssu Kung Li, we noticed that our employees and their families were conspicuous by their absence; in fact the only one in view was Old Tobacco, who is convalescing after malaria and was lying in a deck chair, fanning himself and minding the baby. The story-teller at Wang Wen Pei's tea-shop was rapping on his desk to catch the attention of a meagre audience consisting entirely of strangers, whilst the rival tea-shop further down the road had such a spare attendance that its two sing-song girls had given up song-singing in their nasal sing-song, and were stretched in wicker chaise-longues with relaxed limbs and (no doubt) throats. Clearly a large part of the population had gone to seek its pleasures in pastures new.

Shortly, as we came round the hairpin bend onto the brink of the Yangtse valley, and looked down over the knotted mountain ranges and the glimmering rice fields to the smudge of yellow haze which overhung the river, a complete stranger called out to us, "Ah, you foreigners also are going to see the show, eh?" and in a flash I saw that all the lines of the declining road and the hilltops were running down to meet and culminate in the theatre, every winding path with its load of idlers in single file was leading that way, the whole landscape was concentrated on that one spot: Chang Min Sang's theatre, this breathless Saturday night, was the hub of the universe. Later with our long foreign legs we overtook groups of our employees lounging downwards, fanning themselves as they walked; a few yards ahead of each group went its women and children, like sheep and lambs driven through the gathering dusk. Hardly anyone we knew was missing; the Kung I Chou Hu Tuei [FAU people] seemed to have been invited en bloc to the show.

British patriots may question my veracity, but to me Lo Chia Pa looked just like Piccadilly, only better. The same massed electric lights, without the tasteless electric signs. The same muddle of vehicles, but rickshaws instead of taxis. The same amazing mob with its multitudinous legs like bent scythe-handles swinging, and its multitudinous heads, each with that black hole in front, out of which all the noise comes. Light and shadows wriggling all over everyone like seething maggots. And then suddenly Chang Min Sang appeared before us, his teeth shining in the especially formal and expansive smile which he reserves for occasions when he is host....

II

Chang Min Sang, (hereinafter referred to as CMS for short) is one of our most dashing drivers. There have been occasions when he has been a bit too dashing. Once he dashed into a muleteer, killing him. Once he dashed over the edge on a perfectly straight bit of road; it was Boxing Day, too, and the voices of those who had to turn out with packs and tow-ropes to the rescue were thick with emotion. Once he dashed into an army jeep, thereby entangling us in red tape for days. His life reads like a boy's adventure story. Goodness knows how many times he has been banditted. He was with Henry Liu when the Chi-an convoy was ambushed; with Mike and me when we had it [and were captured by bandits] at So P'ing Shan. For some hours that day he and I were tied together with the same length of rope. Besides being a dashing man of action, CMS is no mean talker; indeed, it was largely his polite, persuasive, persistent, perpetual talking which got us out of the bandit's hands; they just couldn't stand it any longer. This faculty for talking himself out of trouble offsets his faculty for getting into it; one day he has you exasperated, the next you are dazzled by his tact and brilliance. Many a time I have felt like sacking him, but he has weathered every storm.

His private life seems to have been as full of dash as his professional one. Any man could come as a penniless refugee from distant Anhwei and fall in love with a famous actress in Chungking. Such a man seldom gets beyond applauding extra heartily from the front row of the gallery. CMS went further than that. He got himself a job in the theatre. He made himself known to the actress. She was a lovely creature, the adopted daughter of the manager, who had bought her for a few dollars on the street and kicked and beaten her through her teens to stardom. He talked to her in that persuasive, persistent way of his, every sentence ending with an "ah", either sharp, or enquiring, or tender, or jocular, or harsh; there is an amazing subtlety and variety in the range of CMS's "ah's". The actress could no more withstand his eloquence than later the bandits could. She eloped with him. She eloped with CMS, thus plunging the manager and all his family into bankruptcy and ruin. The lovers fled to Kweiyang, where eventually CMS joined the Unit as a driver.

For three whole years (I am told) they remained in love with each other. Mrs. CMS was supremely happy, though her husband was a poor man, and they often went cold and hungry. (This was before they found the Unit, of course). Mrs. CMS said she didn't miss the glamour of her old life or notice the hardship of the new; love made the present beautiful. But gradually the novelty began to wear off, as it wears off even the most dashing husbands. She began to pine for the drums and violins, the thunders of applause when as many as three people forget themselves and start to clap all together, as sometimes happens in Chinese theatres. She even recalled with regret her adopted father; he had kicked and beaten her it was true, but he also had made her a celebrity, and she had repaid him by ruining him. I remember when he came to Kweiyang to plead with her to return to the theatre. Shortly afterwards we all removed to Chungking, (not cause and effect; the Unit was closing down in Kweiyang anyway) and shortly after that Mrs. CMS resumed her theatrical career, working at the family theatre, which had now opened up in Cheng Yang Kai [in Chungking city].

By this time I had got to know Mrs. CMS well. There were three reasons for this, all connected with our clinic. First of all she had a cough, which she said was TB and I said was too many cigarettes. Then her younger daughter, a tiny child as pretty as a doll, had a persistent eruption of sores on her legs and back which I always was treating. Thirdly, Mrs. CMS recently had a severe attack of mastitis, during which I had been in constant attendance. (See FAU News letter No. ??? for an interesting and authoritative account of this case.) [The question marks in the brackets are in the original Chronicle.] I appreciated Mrs. CMS warmly. She had a grace of carriage which is not often attained by Chinese women; with her dark brown skin, her strangely sleepy eyes, her large un-Chinese mouth, she seemed more like a Balinese woman than a daughter of Han. Often I imagined her sweeping onto the opera stage in gorgeous stately garments, her eyes asleep in a face painted to a dead-white mask, her slim agile hands garnished with rings and long false fingernails and contorted in the preposterous but pleasing gestures of the stylised dance. I longed to see her on the stage. And the first time I was invited to do so I went expecting to be dumbfounded by her grace and beauty.

I was dumbfounded all right. She shot out from the wings on a one-wheel bicycle.

Now I know Mrs. CMS better still. I know what to expect of her. I know that she can do anything any mortal ever did on a one-wheel bicycle, and because she is a genius in her line I place her with Myra Hess and Sappho and Rita Hayworth and the other women, few as they are, who are perfect at their jobs. I know further that she can walk the tight-rope, do cartwheels and the splits, strike ballerina poses while standing on various portions of another girl's anatomy, sing love songs and bawdy comic songs, and dance with so much grace that she makes all the other girls look like embarrassed elephants. I know that she is an inexhaustible mine of farcical plots and situations and could be one of the world's leading comedy dramatists if only she could write. I know that she is theatre to her fingertips, and that she will make me enjoy any show I see, if only she appears in it. But I am not an uncritical fan. I admit she has limitations. There are spots on this sun, as on every other; have I not seen her return to the gutter in a fit of temper, and drive her husband from her door, screaming obscenities like a Billingsgate fishwife? But this is not the place to discourse on her manners. It is time to go in to the theatre.

(Continued next week in FSU Chronicle 78, October 2, 1948.)

III

The usual self-important nonentity was making the usual fuss at the pay box because they wouldn't let him in free, but we brushed by him in all the pride of complementary tickets and were promptly knocked backwards by the unbelievable stench which usually knocks you backwards just inside the entrance to a Chinese theatre: that stench which has the whole soul of China in it. Only temporarily deterred, we then sagged towards our seats.

The theatre at Lo Chia Pa resembles that in Regent's Park insofar as it is open-air. But there the resemblance ends. This Lo Chia Pa theatre is in fact a disused truck-yard. On one side are the backs of the tea-shops which line the street; on the other is a hundred foot high cliff, on which a large crowd of non-paying spectators is already assembled, very precariously, and in every stage of dishabille down to the complete nudity of several infants. No sumptuously upholstered chairs receive us but rows of remarkably narrow benches placed on either side of narrow tables. If you are on a bench on the stage-ward side of the table, you have something to lean against while you watch the show, but you have to turn round to get a drink of tea; if you are behind the table you can drink without making a corkscrew of yourself but you have nothing to lean against. You can't even lean on the table, for there is no room for your tea, your seeds, half a dozen babies, three or four piles of airing nappies, and your elbows. Indeed, there is scarcely room for you in the theatre at all; numbers are painted on the tables, and one person is supposed to sit at each number; no allowance is made for the extra fat man at the end, nor for the lady who has brought in half a dozen sucklings on one ticket and is therefore incapable of confining herself to the number assigned to her; and peas in their pods have the wide open spaces all around them compared with you on your bench by the time it has received its full complement of patrons. Still, the seat has cost only 200,000, you get the tea thrown in, and what Chinese ever worried about personal comfort? As long as there's room to spit everything's fine.

All eyes are fixed on the curtains in front, as though everybody expected them to rise at the appointed time. Nothing of course is more unlikely. Stretched on the curtains is a pink silk banner with a green border. We are surprised to see the Chinese characters for the FAU inscribed on this. It is explained to us that the other characters are very polite and say that it is hoped that we shall not find the show disappointing. I look at the solid phalanx of our boys in the front rows and I sincerely hope it won't be. Every one of them – except Li Wan Fa, who is like Kipling's 'Cat Who Walked by Himself' – has sunk five million into this venture, and they will be expecting something for their money.

Chang Min Sang comes up to see if we are comfortable – "but of course, of course" – and is prevailed upon to outline the finances of the business. This is the fourth night the theatre has been operating. It gives a show at night, at eight. (How blandly he told us this, with his wristwatch pointing to 8:25!) The night before they had taken thirty-four million. Twenty percent of the takings have to be paid, immediately after the show each night, to the village headman and a few other dignitaries, in return for which the headman guarantees protection if anything happens. It costs fourteen million a day to feed the cast and staff. That leaves about thirteen million for all other expenses, such as costumes, lights, and tea for the customers. It didn't seem likely that we should lose CMS's services as a driver yet, I thought, doing mental arithmetic.

While CMS was still giving us this information we suddenly were startled by the braying of an ass. With a thrill of anticipation we realized that it was a trumpet and that perhaps the show was about to begin. But after a few exploratory bars of Sousa march the donkey died and ten minutes later sporadic bursts of ironic clapping failed to resuscitate it. By nine o'clock we had given up hope that anything would happen that night and we were wondering how much longer we must wait before we could withdraw without discourtesy. This is the point you always reach sooner or later in a Chinese theatre, the point of exasperation; but just as you all start getting up from your seats, the curtains go up, and you have to sit down again, looking foolish. This process is what is known in military strategy as "softening up the enemy"; the management cleverly gets you so bored with Nothing that you will be pleased with Just Anything, and so the show can't possibly fail.

And so, suddenly without any warning at all, the curtains jerked up and revealed to us four ladies of various shapes, sizes and ages going through something like – but not very like – a Goldwyn girl routine. They were dancing without any musical accompaniment, and another odd thing was that they seemed to have started the dance long before the curtain went up; as though they thought their part of the business was to dance; whether visible or not was not their affair; it was up to the stage manager to raise the curtain if he wanted to. Maybe, I thought, half the program has already been performed behind closed curtains, and that's why those people up there on the cliff, who can see over them, have been so interested in the stage all this time! Meanwhile, the girls continued to hop and skip in a silence only broken by a hoarse voice calling to the donkey that the show was on and that it was time for him to bray. Suddenly he brayed, throwing all the girls out of gear, but they quickly recovered themselves; and as we watched and listened it dawned upon us that the dance was done to a popular number of our Sunday School days – "Shall We Gather At The River?" – so suitable, as everyone will admit, for chorins [sic] to do their chores to.

The one on the extreme left, I was explaining to Peter, the crushed looking one with the turned up nose, is the wife who always gets the black eyes, and the bold and beefy hussy next to her, now lightly embracing that slender waist with a Junoesque arm, is the other wife, the one who hands out the said black eyes. The gorgeous animal next to her, I said to Peter, you will recognize, and everybody who ever has been connected with West China transport would recognize her too; she is as pretty as a kitten and as sweet as Turkish delight, and she is Mrs. CMS's sister. Finally, the one on the far right, the one with lovely tawny skin and the sleepy eyes..... "I know, I know, I know," says Peter; "It's Mrs. CMS herself, and by the way you seem to have made a good job of it that time she had mastitis." "Her legs are also worthy of study," I rejoin, and it is instructive to notice the easy grace of her movements; while the others are throwing themselves about and making themselves puff, she covers just as much ground and duplicates all their actions without fuss; she seems to do everything in slow motion, yet she is in perfect time with the others – well, nearly perfect. In this ability of hers to do with unhurried ease what others only do with effort she resembles several other dancers such as Margo Fonteyn, Tatiana Riabouchinska, Alicia Markova and Sally Gilmour – in short, she has a touch of genius in her dancing…", I am saying, when suddenly without warning, and to the obvious surprise of the dancers, who haven't nearly finished yet, the curtain falls and the donkey gives up in the middle of a particular flat hee-haw. Everybody has a sip of tea and picks up a free handful of sunflower seeds.

After this the turns come thick and fast, with only ten minute intervals between them. I never have been able to understand why there are such long intervals in a Chinese variety theatre. Obviously there is feverish activity behind the lowered curtains. Men are rushing about, shouting at each other, dragging heavy objects across the boards; the curtains are bellied out by many a miniature tornado caused by human beings in rapid motion, elbows and bottoms momentarily mould them to strange contours, a wildly agitated face is thrust between them to gaze in despair at the audience briefly, then whipped back so suddenly that one conjectures that the owner has been kicked in the rear by a distracted stage hand… and what is the final result? The curtain at last goes up on exactly the same scene as before – an absolutely empty stage and a thin plain backdrop. I used to think that perhaps the stage was also the dressing room, and that the girls were changing their costumes, and some colour seemed to be lent to this theory last night, when I noticed that the whole of the non-paying audience on the cliff seemed to be even more absorbed in what was going forward on the stage between scenes than during them; but the theory broke down during the third turn of the evening, when Mrs. CMS and her sister were doing their famous boy-meets-girl act, Mrs. CMS in white shirt and blue slacks, and her sister in a flowered frock; for while they danced and sang, the shadows of the other two girls, obviously behind the thin white backdrop, were thrown large upon it, pulling this down over their heads, and that up over their hips and them shaking their heads and fluffing up their hair at the back – all this in huge silhouette on the backdrop, and somehow of such compelling interest that it diverted my attention from Mrs. CMS for several seconds… so I still don't know what is going on on the stage between acts, but whatever it is, it's pretty engrossing to those who can see.

IV

Progams at CMS theatres always are divided into three parts, like Gaul. First, Les Girls, dancing and singing as a troupe, in solos, in duets, in trios, and in a variety of fetching costumes, all industriously sown on the FAU treadle sowing machine we still keep in "Jeanette's room". (Mrs. CMS, that amazing woman, makes all the costumes, too.)

Reluctantly I must admit that she comes nearer to a Baranova than a Schiaparelli. [Irina Baranova, 1919-2008, was a Russian ballet dancer and Elsa Schiaparelli, 1890-1972, an Italian fashion designer.] Some of her ideas are really rather weird: for instance, why was her sister looking extra-ordinarily pretty in spangled blouse and ballerina skirt allowed to appear in shorts that were too, too Chinese, (and moreover had one leg red and the other black?)

After Les Girls, drama. Finally as climax, the Thrills – the tight rope or trick cycling or conjuring tricks. The ritual is fixed inexorably like that of High Mass and woe betide any innovator who dared meddle with the tradition.

Of the three parts of the program, the part I liked best is the second part, the drama. The first part is just crude; frankly, it brings home to you the fact that the antics of chorus girls are merely exhibitionist and therefore obscene; they turn their bodies about like trumpets to catch the light, forgetting that a trumpet is not beautiful in itself but only becomes so when it is used by an artist to express his emotions in music. Even Mrs. CMS herself, if she did but know, is a more pleasing object to the eye as she crouches over the washtub in an old sack of a blue gown than when she turns and twists her body to catch the light, even though her twists and turns are done with a considerable and saving grace. For over her washtub she is expressing something (albeit unconsciously) – her concern for the family perhaps; but dancing on the stage she doesn't know what she is supposed to be doing. She is not interpreting the music, because she could go through the same routine without any music at all; she isn't doing it to amuse herself, because obviously she is bored; she has no idea of arousing concupiscent ideas in men's minds, because she is too Chinese and therefore essentially modest. As far as I can see she just dances because it is the thing to do. It's part of the game. Her attitude to her one-wheel bicycle is quite different – that's something she enjoys doing – and when we come to drama I think we have found the department of the theatre in which her genius finds its highest expression. I now have seen five plays produced and invented by Mrs. CMS, and I can honestly say that any dramatist would be proud to have invented five plays as good as hers. And Mrs. CMS invents a new one every week like a Chinese Lope de Vega. [Spanish playwright and poet, 1562-1635, 'one of the most prolific authors in the history of literature'.]

Her approach to comedy is basically that of the Restoration dramatists at home. She takes half a dozen strongly marked types or characters that are familiar the world over: the figaro, the henpecked husband, the self-important minor official, the fool who is not so much of a fool as he looks, the nonentity who pretends to be somebody (in one play he described himself as a CNAC pilot) and so on, and she thrusts them into a situation which seems feasible enough in the first scene, but has in it the grains of farcical development. The play is built up in half a dozen short scenes and moves swiftly towards the denouement. The speed of the action is quite remarkable when you consider the snail's pace at which Oriental drama usually moves. Once I saw a murder drama made up by Mrs. CMS. It was as swift and exciting as a Hitchcock film. Moreover, unlike most murder dramas, it never got out of touch with real life. It is in this department – the introduction of the telling realistic detail – that Mrs. CMS's plays excel.

Consider this scene. The villain, having murdered his servant, is skulking in a poor fan-t'ien [eating place]. The fan-t'ien keeper, a garrulous man, confides his troubles in him, but the villain is too preoccupied with his own affairs to take much notice. His fear and preoccupation are clearly conveyed by his disjointed answers and the fan-t'ien keeper's surprise at them. Then what the villain fears happens. The detective comes in. A tense dialogue ensues during which it becomes clear to the detective that here is his man and to the villain that he is recognized. They come to blows and in the middle of the melee a couple of comic policemen who have been confusing the issue and arresting the wrong persons throughout the play rush on and arrest the detective. They are sure they have the right man for he has some evidence in his pocket with which he had been confronting the villain. Luckily the detective manages to throw suspicion on the villain and they detain him, too. Just at his moment Mrs. CMS, handsomely dressed in a sumptuous fur coat, dashes in through the door and asks breathlessly for the mao fang [latrine]. She is directed and disappears in great haste. The villain slips out after her while the police are binding the detective. When they find the villain has disappeared they are furious, yet when he slips back disguised as a woman in the fur coat they do not recognize him. In fact they ask him if he has seen himself. Meanwhile the gagged detective is struggling to free himself from his bonds. The villain slips out and immediately Mrs. CMS runs on, minus the coat. She is still smoothing down her skirt and she is fuming. When the police ask her what is the matter she says it is a nice thing when a lady has the squitters and goes into a mao fang and hangs her coat up on the door and a so-and-so of a man comes in and sneaks her coat when she is in such a position she can do nothing about it.

The whole scene, being packed with action and humor and acted with much vigour, was very good theatre, and I submit that the mind which conceived the lady with the fur coat and the squitters was that of a great comic dramatist.

Wil Jenkins, Arch McMillan, Duncan Wood, and Michael Harris in a fan tien

And only a good dramatist would have made the woman vent her wrath on the already-discomfited detective on the assumption that he was the fan-t'ien keeper. Mrs. CMS is a modern Rabelais, and I only wish she could write. As it is, her art is as ephemeral as ice-cream.

(Concluded in FSU Chronicle 79, October 9, 1948.)
Last night the play was one of her (Mrs. CMS') slighter efforts. It concerned an orphan girl who asked the public notary to find a husband for her. The first scene was full of comedy, the girl moderately nymphomaniac but anxious to appear a lady of refinement, the notary sizing her up as he grinds ink, adroitly hinting that a well-oiled palm can accomplish more than a dry one, finally, when he has bled the girl as much as is politic, hitching up the sleeve of his gown and writing the "Husband wanted" ad.... Two prospective bridegrooms apply, one an impecunious scholar who is only interested if the girl has money, the other a ne'er-do-well and fop. Each makes a good impression at first but makes a false move and is rejected. They decide to revenge themselves on the girl for their disappointment. Meeting a dirty and uncouth coolie who is selling flowers they dress him up in fine clothes and give him a quick lesson in etiquette: "A gentleman never sits on a stool when talking to a lady. He sits on the table smoking a cigarette and swinging his leg." When this male Galatea has taken shape he is presented at the notary's as an applicant for the lady's hand. Of course, the notary sees through him at once, but the girl, dazzled by his good looks, his fine clothes, his elegant manners, ("he studied in America, that's why he acts so strange") falls in love with him at once, marries him and takes him home.

The last scene occurs at their home immediately after the wedding. The girl wants to buy some flowers to decorate the home and is surprised to find the bridegroom so knowledgeable about what varieties are in bloom, etc. She goes out while the fop and the scholar congratulate the bridegroom on his success, point out to him that he owes it all to them, and try to extract some of his newly-won fortune from him. While they are still importuning him the wife returns and having first tartly said that she thought he could have got rid of his friends by now, she starts to arrange the flowers in an old mao tai bottle. "How much did you give for those flowers?" asks her husband. She tells him and he howls with anger. "You have been rooked", he shouts, "Yesterday I was selling them on the streets for half that price."

The curtain falls, as it so often falls in Mrs. CMS's plays, on the spectacle of an incensed wife belabouring her husband and his men friends with a t'iao pole. [A pole for carrying loads across the shoulders.] And the whole audience roars with laughter because it is so true to life and yet so much funnier than real life seems to be – which is the impression always made on an audience by a good comedy. As I have said, this was one of Mrs. CMS's slighter efforts, but the ingredients which make her plays so good, - the clear cut, well-contrasted characters, the well-knit plot, the witty "business" and the spicy dialogue, (which of course goes over my head but keeps the audience in a constant chuckle) were all to the fore.

Her methods are very simple. She first of all explains the whole plot thoroughly to the cast, working it out scene by scene and working up every bit of business with the actors concerned. When all is plotted and fixed they rehearse. Three rehearsals are sufficient, usually. Then they go on and play it. The actors embroider the parts Mrs. CMS has created for them, but I am told that she is constantly suggesting little improvements to them throughout. Naturally such plays have a spontaneity and freshness which is seldom achieved in the west, where woe betide the man who ad-libs or who is not word-perfect or who blinks his eyes twice in the actual performance if the producer has told him at rehearsals that once is enough! There is much to be said for a sketch; as many an artist has found out to his surprise, it is often better than the laboriously finished picture.

V.

And now we have bowed down at the altar of sex and been cleansed by purifying laughter. Complete darkness has fallen and a million stars have swung low to see the show. The glow of the footlights is flung upwards into the night, it covers the theatre like a tent of transparent gold, through which the stars look down like diamonds or Scandinavian eyes. Everywhere fans are wagging back and forth, moth's wings in the reflected light. The cliff is like a choir of angels, for everyone is in white, the men with white singlets and long white trousers, the women mostly with scant white vests worn outside their k'u-tzu. The k'ai-shui man [hot water seller] has put up the enormous kettle with which he has been regularly replenishing our tea-cups; he is now collecting the tea-cups in a wicker basket. The woman in front of me, literally just under my nose turns round for a final swig of tea; her frock is open in front and her vest rolled up; a drop of milk still clings like a pearl to one teat, though her engorged baby boy, curled in her lap in the attitude and state in which he was born, has been sleeping for ten minutes or more. I catch the eyes of Mrs. Chang Wu Leng regarding me and I throw her the sop of one of my rare smiles. She laughs and says something to Mrs. Lo Tse Li. Mrs. Lo Tse Li, Mrs. Wang Wen Pei and Mrs. Wang Chien all turn round and laugh at me. I throw them one smile each, carefully measured smiles, a good broad one for each of the Mesdames Wang, a less expansive one for Mrs. Lo Tze Li, who is a little bitch in my opinion. Three or four husbands turn round and regard me with raised eyebrows.

I straighten my face and would look at my program if I had one. It is a serious crime to smile at a married woman in China… but not nearly so serious as smiling at an unmarried one. Then the curtain goes up and diverts the attention of the husbands and the beady eyes of the stars from me and my embarrassment.

A small girl is flying round and round the stage on a one-wheel bicycle. She is a skinny little girl, the daughter of Mrs. CMS's brother by his larger wife. She has the dark skin and the lucky horse-shoe underlip of her aunt. She continues to circle the stage at great speed and with a dead-pan face until a shout from the wings tells her to stop. She goes off and Mrs. CMS comes on. Mrs. CMS is transformed. It is not only that she is attired in a loose silk blouse and shorts which fit her like a glove. She circles the stage two or three times, her blouse fluttering as she rushes through the air, her long wavy tresses of jet black hair streaming behind her. Gone is her sleepy expression; her eyes are sparkling, her face is flushed and happy. Suddenly she comes up to the footlights at full speed and stops dead with her arms outstretched, perfectly balanced on the one-wheel, then charges backwards and stops dead again, within an inch of the black back-cloth. Then with a laugh she is off and swooping round the stage again. It is impossible to explain all the tricks she does. But the last of course is the best.

Somebody hands her an air-rifle and the stands at the edge of the stage, right, holding a small gong at arm's length. Mrs. CMS on her one-wheel bicycle turns small circles at furious speed, left. She loads the gun as she rides, puts it to her shoulder, takes aim at the gong. The first time she misses and laughs aloud. Again she loads the gun while in full flight, again takes aim while flying round and round in tiny circles. This time she finds the mark, the gong swings violently as the pellet hits, a musical chime is released and floats out over the theatre. Mrs. CMS leaps off her machine and with bike in one hand, rifle in the other, bows to us all. The great mane of hair comes tumbling over her head and falls before her, almost sweeping over the floor. With a toss of her head she flings it back again, and goes off, springy and slim, a gallant figure. And immediately her brother takes over.

His is an apparently normal bike with two wheels, but when he stands in the middle of the stage and swings it around him with one hand on the saddle, he can make the front wheel and handlebars rotate like a top. Then he vaults into the saddle. He does one lap of the fifteen foot square stage in that conventional attitude, but that is all. For the next five minutes he rides the bike in every conceivable manner except the orthodox one. Impossible to describe his agility. To anyone familiar with Chinese cyclists he appears to be a miracle. (It will be recalled that in the Olympic games the Chinese cyclist was so amazed at completing the course without mishap that he fell off after crossing the line for no reason whatever, unless it was sheer surprise, and was carried off unconscious on a stretcher, and never heard of again). For five minutes this hero continues to give as polished an exhibition of trick riding as I have ever seen, even at the Finsbury Park Empire, where I used to have a regular sixpennorth of the gallery on Saturday nights in the winter, and saw all the marvels of my age in the early thirties. The audience watches spellbound. Like Americans I think the Chinese are always more readily bewitched by virtuosity than by art. But the climax is still to come.

Enter the cyclist's two wives bearing three ordinary fan-t'ien stools apiece. They pile them up in two piles close together, one pile being at right angles to the other. ("I see some reckless foolishness is about to be indulged in," says Peter.) When the two piles have passed certain tests of their rigidity the two wives squat down beside them to hold them steady.

It is instructive to see them, the big swaggering wife who plays the handsome bully on the stage and in real life, the little sullen rather pretty wife whom one has often heard sobbing her heart out for hours on end, thus combining to assist their lord and master to put on his great piece de resistance. Soon he lifts his bicycle and stands it on the two piles of stools, which are placed like a capital T, which is towards the audience. Balancing it carefully, he stands on one pedal. He maintains his balance by allowing the front wheel to move an inch or two to the right or left; if it went much further it would run off the stool altogether and he would come down in a fine tangle of bike and stools, probably maiming the small wife in the process. (One feels that the bigger one would have the good luck to get out of the way).

Now slowly he lowers himself to a squatting position on the pedal and with infinite difficulty, the front wheel jerking backwards and forwards along the top of the front stool, he begins to thrust his head under the cross-bar. It is an awful struggle to get his head through, a struggle which holds all watchers breathless. The small wife has dropped her head on the thin arms with which she is holding the front pile of stools steady; it looks as if she is praying, praying that the trick will succeed. At last his head is through; cautiously one hand comes off the handlebars, follows his head through the frame, reaches blindly up for the handlebar again. The hand gropes and jerks foolishly; people begin to laugh, but there is anxiety in their laughter; the front wheel moves dangerously far to one side and back again.

Suddenly the hand closes on what it seeks. It is easier now. The rest of his body follows through the frame; then one leg arrives and is placed on the pedal; then at last the other leg, and he strikes a triumphant pose, standing on one leg on the far side of the bike from which he started. There is a light spatter of applause which in China amounts to an ovation. One hopes that he will descend from his perch satisfied, and rest on his laurels. But he hasn't finished yet. He intends to subject our nerves to an even more violent strain.

Carefully he lowers himself to a squatting position on one pedal again and begins to repeat the trick backwards. The sweat is pouring from his face. He has an even fiercer struggle to get his head under the cross-bar. The gropings of his hand are more prolonged and almost frantic; the bike wobbles so violently that he comes within an inch of disaster; his hand is raised jerkily again and again like that of a drowning man. There is something ludicrous about that fumbling, desperate though it is; impressive; and one sympathizes with the laughter, though unable to join in. Suddenly he has snatched what he was seeking. The trick is as good as over. With a sinuous movement he snakes the rest of his body through the frame and strikes an Eros pose on one pedal again. There is nothing stagey about his smile; he is genuinely pleased with his achievement. "That is all for tonight, please come again", he cries, and then he leaps lightly to the stage, catching the bike as it falls after him. The three-course meal has been served: part one, Les Girls; part two, the play; part three, the thrill. The show is over.

We rise from our stools and make for the narrow wicket. (We know just where to hold our noses now.) The press in the narrow gateway is pretty severe. For a few minutes we are firmly wedged in by a mass of struggling, sweating bodies, unable to ply our limbs free; borne along by the gigantic forces of China. I see the heads of Mike and Peter floating on that tide of humanity like flotsam. It seems symbolic: our bodies are engulfed in China, but our heads still ride above it, detached and alien. Then we are through and standing on our own feet again.

A rickshaw man like a bandit importunes us; a few late pedlars are folding up their stalls; a man is waving a flaming piece of paper to scare the devils from his front door for the night. Soon we are clear of the village. The first range [of mountains] stands up black against the sky where the moon is rising. The light of the moon reaches up over the horizon and sets fire to a scrap of cloud which burns like a white flame. The stars seem to have withdrawn; now that the show is over, they are bored with the Earth. Our feet kick up white dust like steam as we tackle the hill. The cicadas and the frogs are making an immense din.

"God", says Peter, "what a lovely night. And what a bloody crude show that was, wasn't it?"

Note: Mike and Peter who were with Jack at the show must have been Mike Frankton and Peter Verrall. Peter Mason, a later recruit, had not yet arrived in Chungking at that time.

FAU
FAU
FAU
FAU

F.A
F.A.U. 63

FUEL CONVOYS TO THE FAR NORTH WEST

The Japanese invasion meant that supplies of fuel could no longer be brought in from Burma over the Burma Road and so most FAU trucks were converted to run on charcoal gas. Petrol and oil in small quantities could then only be obtained from Lanchow and the Suchow oil wells in the far north west and convoys of trucks laden with oil drums ran from late 1943 through to 1945, at which time fuel became available from the American army. Paul Cope's sketch map, 'Fuel Convoys to Suchow' which appears at the beginning of this book shows the huge distances to be covered. The journey of several months was one of the great challenges for the men to confront and was fondly remembered despite the hardship. The trucks were piled high with five gallon drums and they inevitably faced extreme temperatures. Petrol was essential to get the charcoal burners started in the morning so these hazardous convoys had to get through.

Photos were often taken before departure and we see George Kan and Peter Verrall (above) sitting with their team of drivers. Owen Jackson stands in front of his Dodge (above right) while Gerard Walmesley, Bernard Smith and their men (left) pose by their truck before setting off to the north west. Not one but two photographers recorded the moment a truck loaded high with empty oil drums emerged from the Kutsing depot (far left). Out in the Gobi Desert it was sometimes many degrees below freezing and Parry Jones (top left) is seen holding off the cold with his sheepskin coat, hat and pipe. Six trucks stand in the yard at Lanchow (far left) but it's still a long road to be covered if the final destination is Suchow itself. Finally, a series of tiny prints collected by John Simpson then suggest the excitement of departure and the lonely tribulations of these convoys far out into the deserts of the north west.

6 LIFE IN WEST CHINA AS THE COMMUNISTS ADVANCE – APRIL TO SEPTEMBER 1949

Nanking is 'liberated' and so is Shanghai

Crucial news of the inexorable communist advance appeared in the FSU Chronicle in April and again in August 1949. While mail was still being delivered between areas controlled by the Nationalists and the communists, Jack in West China, still under Nationalist control, was becoming increasingly cut off. He made few references to these seismic events in what he wrote and he and his men just got on with the job as best they could. However, by this time feeling jaded, Jack was talking of handing over to someone else, having been working in China for three and a half years without a break and as the big cheese for West China for almost three. The following tells the breaking news as it was reported at the time.

FSU Chronicle Number 96, Shanghai, 30 April 1949

NEWS!

The Communist armies entered the capital city of Nanking last Saturday, April 23rd, at 3:41 a.m., and thus the Shanghai HQ becomes out of communication with another Unit Section. According to all the reports we have been able to receive, the changeover was orderly and without fighting in the city. No direct word has been received from the Nanking team since their liberation but last Saturday we learned through UNICEF that all were well. There are six Unit members in Nanking at the present time – PHYLLIDA THORNTON, ENA HADFIELD, ELIZABETH FILE, WANG HSIAO HSIN, ROY MASON and JAMES YANG.

As of today, all is quiet on the Shanghai front – as quiet as usual, that is. The Premier has promised that Shanghai will be defended at all costs and from the recent preparations throughout the Kiangwan Area, it would seem that he means to keep his promise.

FSU Chronicle Number 97, Shanghai, 6 August 1949

SHANGHAI

Liberation of Shanghai brought renewed activity to the headquarters staff after a brief lull while fighting was going on in and around the City. During previous months we had only been in regular communication with West China and the Home Committees, but then we were again able to contact sections which had been isolated. Cable service was restored the first day of total occupation by the PLA [Peoples' Liberation Army]. Riding bicycles downtown to send the first messages, we passed in front of the Hongkew Garrison Headquarters [in the Honkou area of Shanghai] which was strewn with destroyed vehicles and the paraphernalia of the army which had taken flight two days previously. At the cable office there were dozens of people, like ourselves, who were sending word to friends in areas to the north. After months of uncertainty and very brief word from Hong Kong which led us to believe that much of the Unit program in Chungmou had been forced to close down, it was very reassuring to know that we were close to getting the full story, good or bad.

Information other than cables, came in more slowly than we had hoped, as mail service was held up by breaks in the railways but gradually reports came in from the various sections. They had faced many problems during the months of separation but none of them had been as overwhelming as we had been led to expect. It very quickly became apparent that a visit by one of the headquarters staff to the field was needed to get a clearer understanding of the problems workers were meeting and to discuss the program and policy. One week after liberation we made our initial visits to [the new communist] officials in an attempt to arrange this trip. But it was only after six weeks of extended negotiations that a travel permit was issued to myself for a month's journey to the North. At the same time we tried to get permission for new workers and representatives for Staff Meeting to go North, but so far these efforts have failed. On July 26, Joseph Yu and I started on our trip after several official delays which caused us to wonder if we would be able to get away at all and for a little more than a month I have escaped from the office routine!

From our Chairman.

Meanwhile in Chungking they're getting nervous...

Despite the communist advance, the FSU was extremely reluctant to give up trying to help China in some way. The AFSC in Philadelphia was continuing to recruit new volunteers who were arriving in Hong Kong and, after some delays, were flown in to Chungking in the last months of 1949 shortly before the communists arrived. While they had the courage to face an uncertain future in China, the American authorities had been warning since April that their citizens might become trapped both by the closure of routes and the refusal of exit permits.

Extract from a letter: Jack Jones in Chungking to Spencer Coxe at the AFSC China desk in Philadelphia dated 8th August 1949.

MacGeary, the US Consul, has today sent me in a double registered envelope the following message:

"Dear Jack, Don Moore informs us that the FAU is expecting a number of additions to the local organization [at the South bank garage], some of whom will be American citizens. Will you please call this notice to their attention and urge them to register with the Consulate as soon as possible after their arrival? Sincerely yours, Stan, etc.

The notice runs as follows:

TO ALL AMERICAN CITIZENS IN THE CHUNGKING CONSULAR DISTRICT

Reference is made to the statement issued by this office on April 25, 1949, warning American citizens residing in this consular district who were not prepared to remain under possibly hazardous conditions that they should plan at once to move to places of safety. In view of hostilities in southern China and the likelihood that hostilities may result in the cutting off of the means of egress from the consular district, this warning is now being repeated in order that American citizens in affected areas may give the most serious consideration to the advisability of evacuation at this time. In this connection Americans are advised to utilize existing transportation facilities while they are still available.

In this regard attention is called to the fact that the Chinese Communist authorities have this far, in areas under their control, demonstrated in many cases an inability or unwillingness to afford adequate protection to foreigners or to safeguard their individual liberties, particularly in connection with arrest, detention, trial, and mob action. Moreover, no satisfactory procedure has thus far been afforded foreigners wishing to secure permits for exit from China or even for travel between points in Communist controlled China. Signed, etc.

Note: Communist soldiers finally reached the Chungking south bank garage on 30 November 1949, heralded by the sound of shots being fired as Jack and his colleagues worked in the new clinic there. They were perhaps lucky to suffer no more than minor damage as not far away in the hills of the south bank, a large group of missionaries doing language studies at the mission home of the China Inland Mission found themselves in the middle of a serious fire fight between the departing Nationalist soldiers and the incoming communists and were confronted with their first corpses. The incident is described in *China:The Reluctant Exodus* by Phyllis Thompson.

Chaff on the wind... as the old order changes

The following news items, circulated in uncertain times as the communists advanced towards Chungking, indicate that the Unit has contracted and now has fewer foreign members, perhaps a third of earlier numbers. Travel restrictions have become a major impediment and new recruits cannot get the necessary permissions to enter China. It seems that Jack now has little time or inclination to write for the news letter which, with so many political and communication difficulties, now comes out less frequently. The editor of a new 'Overseas Chronicle' which was produced in Philadelphia for distribution outside China, therefore culled newsworthy paragraphs from the business reports and letters that Jack had written to headquarters. Fortunately Jack's business style is chatty and personal and reads well for a wider readership. Following an introduction by the editor in Philadelphia, extracts from Jack's letters appear below in the order they were printed in this, the first Overseas Chronicle to be issued.

Overseas Chronicle One, 28 September 1949

NEWS OF THE UNIT

By way of introduction to the following reports from West China, Hong Kong and Shanghai, a few words and statistics about the Unit as a whole might be helpful. The last personnel disposition list (July) reveals a Unit of 47 members in China, including 20 Chinese, 13 Americans, 11 British, two New Zealanders, one German and one Canadian. Only West China transport [at Chungking], and possibly Curwen and Archer at Santan remain unliberated. The Chungmou Project as formerly known [rehabilitation of a village in Honan], is now gone; the Nanking team, having finished its work has disbanded, and meanwhile a new project [working with refugees at the North Point Relief camp] is taking shape in Hong Kong, to absorb the energies of new members until they can get into China itself.

The good times at Chungmou

North Point Relief Camp, Hong Kong 1949

The Unit, from what we gather by cable, occasional letter, and telephone, is insecure about the present and perplexed about the future. The new government has not gone out of its way to cooperate with foreigners, and the Unit is no exception. Indifference rather than hostility is inferred. The main practical difficulty is regarding travel. No foreign Unit member, old or new, has been allowed to enter Communist territory since early April. Even permission to travel about within the Liberated Areas has been difficult to obtain. These restrictions have prevented replacement and reinforcement of foreign membership, and have impeded efficient use of what Unit members there are.

And now for some first hand reports from Chungking, being excerpts of letters from Jack Jones.

Transport: (24 August 1949) The Garage is a hive of industry these days. At the moment our trucks are on the way to, at, or returning from Kweiyang, Tzeliutsing, Pei P'ei and Chengtu. Two leave for Chaotung tomorrow, a perilous business [presumably owing to bandits] but I've got three good chaps on the job. On Monday I took Leonard Walker [a Quaker missionary] to Tungliang in Celery Stalks [the battered old jeep]. He had money and didn't want to go by ordinary truck or bus, and when he agreed to my price, eighty silver dollars, off I went. She has a new engine in and I had to go slow. We left Chungking in sunshine but on the top of Koloshan the water was four inches deep and coming down like a waterfall, we all got soaked and I could hardly see to drive. Just at this point the distributor had to pack up of course. At Pishan [68 kilometres north of Chungking] we found we had shed a spring shackle. At ninety kilos we found our exhaust pipe was loose and coming adrift and when we finally pulled up at Tungliang we were steaming like a Puffing Billy; a radiator hose had gone… Next morning we mended the radiator hose and set off [home] in teeming rain again. As I floated downhill I saw a six-by [a six wheeled truck] shouldering its way up through the rain and I put on my brakes. Down went my feet to the boards and pumping failed to find anything. A couple of quick gear changes and the help of the mud brought us up in just the right number of yards to prevent a catastrophe and getting out to investigate we found that the exhaust pipe waggling about had fractured the brake line. So I did 50 kilos without any brakes and then we came to a repair shop. It poured all day but all the same it was a good trip, a nice break. I liked it so much that tomorrow I am going to Chengtu…

(6 September 1949) I had one wild night in Chengtu (apart from the feast, which was more than just wild). On the wild night I went out with a beautiful Russian spy and bought her ice cream. It turned out she thought I was a JCRR man [Joint Committee for Rural Rehabilitation] earning about 10,000 US a year. When she found out the facts

George Kan unloading FAU medplies, the gift of the Canadian Red Cross

of the case the shining admiration in her eyes, which I had thought was inspired by my beard, (which must, I thought, have brought back tender memories to her [of bearded Russians?!]), went out like a doused bulb; I suppose she couldn't afford to waste the current. It was a disappointing evening, but the ice cream was good.....

(14 September 1949) At the beginning of the year we had about seventy tons of IRC [International Relief Committee] medical supplies in our godowns to be allocated and distributed. During that month ECA supplies [from the American funded 'Economic Co-operation Administration'] began to arrive [presumably by air] and we had all the trucks struggling to get about 400 tons of medical supplies and pesticides up to our godowns from [across] the river. The struggle was due to the imminence of New Year, the scarcity of cash to pay coolies, the wreck of one sampan, the bogging down of trucks in the river bed, and the fact that the stuff always arrived [at the airfield] fifty tons at a time, usually just before dark, and usually on a Saturday or a Sunday. After delays due to uncertainty as to whether we were to do the distribution, and then a delay due to our having to wait for an ECA team to arrive here, and then a delay due to the fact that the ECA couldn't pay us and the IRC in Shanghai were cut off, we finally got cracking on distribution. In May a further 200 tons of medicine were air-lifted in from ECA Canton and we had a fleet of trucks buzzing around trying to contact the planes which arrived in batches of nine or ten at unexpected intervals, disgorged their cargoes, and left them out in the monsoon rains (which we caught good and proper this year).

At last this 200 tons was safely put to bed in godowns in Pei P'ei. Meanwhile we were distributing stuff as fast as we could get it out. Kilometre tonnages during the year compare well with other years.

By the end of August all the first 400 tons of ECA supplies was distributed except for about 30 tons for the northwest which will probably be reallocated [because of 'regime change'], and about 30 tons of pesticides that beneficiary organizations apparently won't take as a gift. These supplies are still in our godowns, together with 30 tons of IRC supplies. The IRC has had to take a back seat for the last three months, but we expect to send all their Kunming supplies, four truckloads, next week. In this connection it should be remembered that the Kunming road was "out" owing to warlords and bandits for several months; it cleared and we sent in a five-truck convoy; then it was closed again; and we now hear it is open again. So with the Chaotung and northwest routes; we bung in trucks when we hear the going is good and so far they have always just got through, except for George [Kan]. (And the rest of his convoy made it all right, too). Chi Hsu Lin is the champion; twice he has slipped through contending armies in the north and now he is safely back in Kweiyang from Chaotung, which twice this year has been held by "rebel" armies for weeks on end.

Of course there is no ECA now – everything has been handed to JCRR - So with JCRR relief supplies, we move them and we don't take it off our ECA money, but off the JCRR in cash…. Meanwhile JCRR HQ in Chengtu have asked me to run their Motor Pool, as they can't do it themselves, having no mechanics and the craziest drivers

This American agency donated essential funding for the China Convoy

Tony Renolds badging a Dodge

'Okeford Fitzpaine' inside the Kutsing depot. c.1945

'Anne Boleyn'

that ever worked for any organization. They pay us 3,500 silver dollars per month for the privilege of having Sam [Yen] there and three of our drivers and three of our mechanics with tools, we buying spare parts and they providing fuel. This pan fa began as of Sept. 1st and barring accidents should last as long as we do. It is true to say that ever since the IRC ceased to support us we have been better off than ever before.... [As further documents below will show, Jack was keeping the Unit afloat by selling his services to this other agency.]

A word should be said about our Dodges. You knew and loved them in your youth, Douglas [Turner]. (You were a cruel lover too, sometimes). The fleet is now greatly decimated. The thirty three have come down to fifteen – we still have number 17 on the books, but George has 57 and 125 has been cannibalised until it consists now of a chassis propped against the wall under the boys' hostel. In spite of the hard wear and tear, the trucks are still in good condition and look more presentable than most on these roads. Leonard Walker [the Quaker missionary] in Tungliang still recognizes them as they come over the crest of the hill three kilos away and gets to the city gate in time to stop them. He says he never makes a mistake – they are the only tidy trucks on the roads. Some of the metal is getting tired now and we seem to be for ever riveting cracked chassises, but some of the old names remain, Okeford Fitzpaine, Fatima, Ngiao, etc. A recent development, following the opening of a mission at Ssu Kung Li, was the appearance of Faith, Hope and Charity – Feng Ah Fu is Hope, Faith has gone to Chengtu, but Charity begins at home, and she is the yard... [Some of the members had learned to drive on milk trucks at Okeford Fitzpaine in Dorset, while a 1941 Chevrolet, the first to have her head machined down to raise the compression ratio on conversion to charcoal gas, was accordingly named 'Anne Boleyn'.]

Chaff: (Excerpts of a letter from Jack Jones, 16 July 1949)
New recruits are welcome to come here and the more the merrier. Is it true that Rita Hayworth has joined the Unit and is anxious to come out here? Rumours to that effect continue to circulate in Chungking, and I have got a room emptied ready to receive her the day she arrives… During the last few weeks there has been a wholesale clear-out of the less desirable missionaries. They have toddled off to Java and Manila and India where it is slightly safer to save souls for the Lord at the present day and have dropped a whole lot of projects which they had only just started in the last eighteen months or so when they came here from other parts of China that were getting dangerous. There is plenty we could do in West China – nay, in Chungking, if we wanted to.

(14 September 1949) Amongst the dogs there is nothing but tragedy to report; Cuthbert was shot, Phoebe [the matriarch], Hsiao Pien and Ta Pien were run over; Betsy died, Pooch was shot but recovered with expert nursing. Hsiao Pien also had been shot through the shoulder and had to wear a splint for three weeks. We have now only Pooch, Stinker, the handsome Bully, and two almost full-grown pups of Phoebe's last litter, Wee-wee and Piddly. These are both females so the future outlook is bright…

(18 August 1949) Refugees [from the communist advance] are pouring in here by the truckload. Last night we collected a couple, Messrs. Joe Stepanek and Solly Solomon from Shaoyang. They arrived in a jeep and trailer, accompanied by a Father Pius, who once made me drive my truck till midnight much against my will, but then put everything right by producing a dish of several dozen eggs done in some Hungarian fashion that made them simply delicious.

The Nationalists had demanded the forty AIS trucks in the Shaoyang compound [Agricultural and Industrial Services], saying if you don't give them to us we'll bomb them to hell. The AIS said bomb away and next day a couple of Mosquitoes came over and did so. Both Stepanek and Solly were slightly injured and very much shaken and they left within twenty four hours. They expect to be working on new AIS projects in Szechuan for a few weeks… [In 1948 the Nationalists acquired 300 De Havilland Mosquitoes built in Canada, supplied to aid the war against the communists.]

7 | NEW RECRUITS, NEW PROJECTS AS JACK CRIES FOR HELP – JULY TO OCTOBER 1949

Even though the old order is changing and the future very uncertain, Jack now writes long letters to Spencer Coxe in Philadelphia proposing new projects and plans. These run to many pages and give an inside flavour of how difficult it was with poor communications and bosses scattered across the oceans to push plans through to fruition. They do however sharply exemplify the many nightmarish problems of running the transport unit in China. As the communist armies approached, incoming funding from America was drying up and Jack was under instructions to close the transport operation. With other agencies such as JCRR closing but medical supplies still in storage and arriving, he felt strongly that there was important distribution work remained to be done. He was going to hold on as long as he could despite all the difficulties, his health in consequence coming under strain.

Though they are business letters in difficult times, it is perhaps surprising that Jack continues to write in his usual jokey manner as if writing to an old friend about a good holiday. It reflects the collegial and non-hierarchical style by which the Unit was run, but it still makes one wonder if Jack drove them mad at times.

In spite of his many problems with the transport section and despite his half-hearted pleas for somebody to relieve him or give him some time off, the main theme in his letters is the search for new medical projects in West China. With 'free China' getting ever smaller, this was the only region that could receive the mainly American recruits who were arriving in Hong Kong.

In the light of history, it now seems surprising they ever thought that an American based unit in particular could continue to work under the communists, let alone to expand, but first impressions of the new regime were good. Similarly the China Inland Mission had also decided not to withdraw and in 1949 actually recruited and deployed forty nine new missionaries into China.

One possible plan was that Jack should hand over his job as transport director and run a new project rebuilding a remote leprosy hospital called Stonegateway which had been destroyed in an earthquake, but it wasn't to be.

In the face of financial stringency and political uncertainty, Spencer Coxe, who was on the China Desk of the Foreign Service Section at the AFSC in Philadelphia, pushed Jack to wind down the transport operation but Jack dug his heels in and bombarded him with letters, deadly serious in substance but still peppered with personal detail and amusing anecdote.

More painful were Jack's mysterious references scattered in the letters that follow to a certain Miss Tzu or 'Zoo', a secretary or accounts clerk, for whom he had a frustrated passion. At the same time she was also the object of desire of one Jim Moorhouse, an FSU member who allegedly was getting divorced, with Miss Tzu in his sights. Jack watched their affair with anguish, though he still lived in hope even when she was transferred to work in Chengdu.

One of Jack's recently discovered lost stories called, 'The Forty Five Bends', is possibly based on this entanglement. The narrator who transparently is Jack, in competition with one 'Beevers', has the hots for a pretty Chinese employee. This he lays on with a trowel as follows. 'Assigned Chien-fan as my private secretary. Irresistibly attracted at once by her beauty and repose, with all the thousands of years of culture behind it. (Myfanwy always smelled of milk, the Grimsby wenches of fish). My first tentative approaches and her cool rebuffs.... Chien'fan losing patience and getting herself transferred to the accounts department. The weeks of frustration, I in my small corner, she cool, aloof, indifferent, bent over her ledgers. And then her sudden, inexplicable relenting.'

View from the Kweiyang depot; note the two hills on the extreme right

Here the story turns perhaps to fiction or farce. At the staff dance Beevers is drunk and disorderly, Jack's alter ego grabs the girl in the dark and Beevers' blood ends up on his fist. At the end of the story, to maximise Jack's guilt, she ends up dead, shot by bandits on the Forty Five Bends, a tragic chain of events that was all his stupid fault.

Her possible real life prototype however apparently ended up more happily. The FAU's members' list for 1954 shows Tsou Ling-hwa, (possibly pronounced 'Zoo'), and 'otherwise known as Dora Ch'au', as having an address in Vaud, Switzerland and she may later have settled in Hong Kong.

This identification is curiously corroborated as there is circumstantial evidence that Jack admired a girl called Dora, in one significant respect at least. A topographical feature of the countryside around the Kweiyang depot where Jack first met Bernard Llewellyn is a series of regular, steep and perfectly conical hills. Both men were keen hill walkers and in 1957 Jack inscribed and gave to Bernard a copy of his newly published Bangkok novel. In it he wrote, 'Recalling all those happy times when we have met and paused awhile between the breasts of Dora'.

Though Dora may not have been Jack's 1949 passion, her special qualities were also much admired other than by hill walkers. As one FAU man wrote to another similarly smitten, 'She's still as attractive as ever from the neck downwards and her hair is glorious'. What's more, only a few months ago Dora gave me a truly ravishing smile from some grainy footage viewed at London's Imperial War Museum, so I do wonder what became of her in the years that followed.

More conventionally, the Shanghai wedding photo of Spencer Coxe to Elize Marie de Miranda of Paramaibo, Surinam, appeared in the FSU Chronicle in April 1947. Half a century later in 1996 they both joined a China Convoy reunion visiting all the old haunts in China and in 2014 I exchanged email messages with Elize and spoke to one of her sons. It was he who has recently mailed to me three of Jack's lost China stories found among his father's papers, including 'The Forty Five Bends'.

Recalling all those happy times when we have met, and paused awhile, between the Breasts of Dora and the back streets of Bangkok.

Jack.

April 29 1957

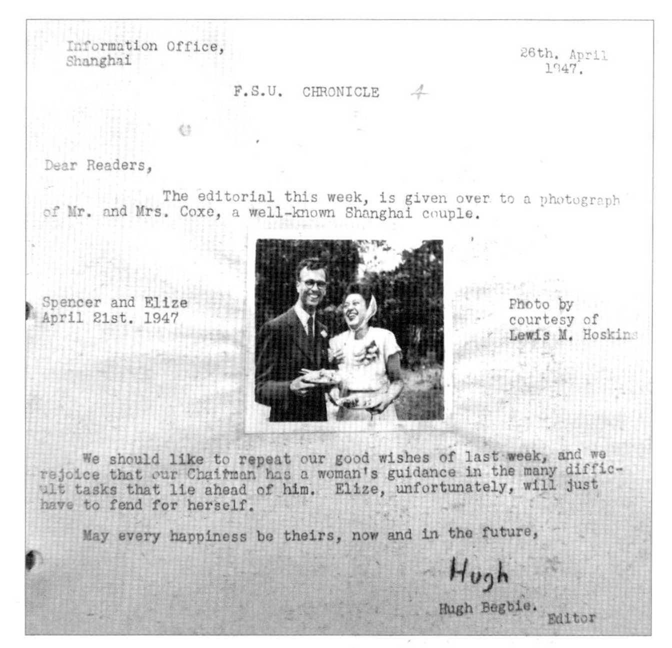

Information Office,
Shanghai

26th. April
1947.

F.S.U. CHRONICLE 4

Dear Readers,

The editorial this week, is given over to a photograph of Mr. and Mrs. Coxe, a well-known Shanghai couple.

Spencer and Elize
April 21st. 1947

Photo by
courtesy of
Lewis M. Hoskins

We should like to repeat our good wishes of last week, and we rejoice that our Chairman has a woman's guidance in the many difficult tasks that lie ahead of him. Elize, unfortunately, will just have to fend for herself.

May every happiness be theirs, now and in the future,

Hugh

Hugh Begbie. Editor

Sundry letters to the AFSC in Philadelphia

JC-2

IRC Chungking garage

July 16, 1949

Spencer Coxe

AFSC, Philadelphia, USA

Dear Spencer,

The prospect of being sucked into bureaucracy is a dismal one, brightened only by two rays of sunshine: (1) at least I may get an occasional letter from somebody: (2) the letter when it comes will be from you. I don't want to gush about it, but I do like receiving letters from you, particularly.

So far my mail this week, and this is Saturday, has consisted of one ancient copy of the Motor Cycle and a mysterious little package which after prolonged research in our laboratory was presumed to be a portion of my sister's wedding cake, very much the worse for the journey through tropic climes. We ate it, so as not to offend its feelings, and kept it down with a stiff peg of whiskey, presented by an admirer in the ECA. [Jack's sister, Gwenneth, born in September 1914 fifteen months after Jack, married Brian Langford on 16 April 1949. Jack's father officiated as minister at his own church, Lower Clapton Congregational Church, north London. For Jack, despite the jocularity, some well-travelled cake three months old must have been small recompense for missing this family event.]

TRAVEL The route by air from Hongkong to Chungking is still open, and indeed Pete Mason will be taking it tomorrow, in the reverse direction. [Peter has recently attended the China Convoy reunions in London and I see him from time to time at his home in Arundel.] New recruits are welcome to come here and the more the merrier...

As for travel to Honan – (1) I have no idea yet how it could be affected from here. I don't know where the line is at the moment. The last man who tried to get from West China into Communist territory was Hugh Elliott, who started to walk from

Shantan. [While teaching at the Shantan Bailie School.] You will have heard what happened to him, I expect; he was in clink until the Nationalists granted an amnesty to all political prisoners in Nanking, where he was. I've no doubt something could be arranged, and I have inklings where it could be done from, but – (2). Why send more people to Honan? From hints in letters we gather that the Honan project [rehabilitating the devastated village of Chungmou] has all but folded... Owing to the fact that we get no papers and seldom have power to work the radio we get almost no news of China (or the rest of the world) and you probably know more about the possibilities of getting people to our team in Nanking from say Canton than I do... If you insisted on sending people across the line we could have a smack at it from here, of course.

Doug Turner weighs a child at Chungmou

WEST CHINA PROJECT This sounds to me a sensibler pan fa and one that given funds could easily put into operation... There is plenty we could do in West China – nay, in Chungking, if we wanted to. Further notes on projects below.

RECRUITS AS SKETCHED Four of the recruits, Waldie, White, Mosescu, and Saunderson, could all be absorbed by the garage straight away, since all have engineering experience and/or interests. Now I know you don't want to give me too many men here but what I mean is that while waiting in Chungking to go elsewhere they could climb into overalls, (or take everything off except their shorts this weather) and get cracking right in this yard. Pete Mason leaves tomorrow, Dennis [Frone] has been offered a job with BUAC [British United Aid to China] and leaves any time, and I am the sole representative of the white race in this dump when they have gone. The world will be the richer for my isolation, seeing that I am writing a novel in the evenings, with a fan in one hand and a bottle of salichiu in the other, frantically hitting the keys of my typewriter with the end of my nose; at least this is my explanation of why my nose is turning red at the end. But what we want round this place is some more of The Race, and particularly driver mechanics. We have NO foreign convoy leaders now.

FLEDA JONES [A prospective recruit and qualified lab. technician.] How many more ruddy Joneses? And what is the meaning of this Americanism, plenty on the ball? I can understand "on the ball," meaning, where the ball is, there the player is, ready to smite it with hand, foot, racket, bat, stick or what-all; but "plenty on the ball" suggests a really Beefy Hockey-Girl. NB, are you becoming so Chinese in outlook that you have difficulty pronouncing "R"?... [Not Freda!] A lab. technician could be made use of in any number of places in W. China. She would probably have to be on her own unless the doctor, Mostym (should be Mostyn, a Welsh name?) came out too, in which case some of the medical projects suggested below could be started up._

POSSIBLE WEST CHINA PROJECTS 1) Stonegateway. It just fell thru because I couldn't possibly get away. I'm still keen to go there when I have either wound this job up or handed over to some competent person. I made a pathetic effort to get away at the end of last month – sent in my resignation [to the IRC, his nominal employer]. It was eagerly accepted by Stuart Allen [chairman of the IRC's medical committee and doctor at the Canadian Mission Hospital], who hates my guts, not without reason, and more regretfully accepted by the rest of the IRC Medical Committee, four of whom rang me up to see whether I could alter my decision. Then 50-word cables began to pour in from London requesting Frone to go to Hongkong as BUAC man. I think Frone will go, though he will doubtless spend another two weeks dithering. I never knew anyone so chronically and consistently incapable of making a decision. He is like a whole Friend's Business Meeting trying to decide whether it ought to open the window or not. If Frone goes, I have perforce to stay put... What the hell has this got to do with Stonegateway? Anyway, I am sure there is a still a job there for us, if we can get there. Reports were that Chaotung has been captured; later reports were that these reports were exaggerated; but I haven't heard anything from that region for a month...

You ask why the ECA doesn't use commercial trucks [but pays Jack to transport their medical supplies]. The answer is, for the same reason that the missions don't use them if they can help it. Night after night I go to bed burning with shame over inefficiency and delay and whatnot; but we deliver the goods quicker and more safely than any other organisation in the West. This isn't boasting, it's just facts. The ECA used commercial trucks on local haulage a bit and lost stuff. The CIM sent a truckload to Chengtu and it took five weeks to get there – we take two days. Butler, the man who was here set off for Kweiyang three weeks ago; he had done 120 kilos in two days when our Kunming convoy overtook him; he went on our convoy and got to Kweiyang four days before his original truck got there. The ECA reckon they can trust us and when I doubled their rate not long ago they agreed to pay the extra without a murmur – they said it was worth it to know we were taking the stuff.

IMPORTANT All the things you assume in your letter that I know I don't know. We have had no news for weeks. Why does administration require an extra man? If I can run this place practically single handed year in year out the mob in Shanghai ought to be able to manage the Unit. It certainly wouldn't hurt them to work two hours extra per day – they have always worked extremely short hours there, I think. And it's not half as hot and humid as here, either... A weekly Newsletter would be very acceptable; even a monthly one would be more than we get now.

Yor-hors, Jack.

P.S. Walter Illsley has also just dropped in. He says Anthony Curwen came off a motorbike in Lanchow a few days ago and fractured his skull. Don't know how bad he is. – J.

Note: The son of Canon Curwen of Haslemere, Sussex, Anthony Curwen survived his accident and in 1965 became a fellow in Modern Chinese History at the School of Oriental and African Studies, London.

As to the possible Stone Gateway project, this was the leprosy hospital in a remote Miao village set up in 1900 by an English missionary, Samuel Pollard. Getting there would have necessitated a long and arduous journey many hundreds of tortuous miles to the south west. A photo essay at *www.shimenkan.org/en/cammie/smk/* describes the route from Guiyang (Kweiyang) as being six hours by train to Zhaotung (Chaotung), then one hour by bus to Zhongshui, followed by three to six hours by SUV or truck to Stone Gateway. How much more difficult it would have been in 1949, though it would not have fazed a China Convoy transport man..

JC — 3

IRC Chunk Garage
August 3, 1949

Spencer Coxe
AFSC, Philadelphia, US.

Dear Spencer,

I sent thee late a cable brief for which the Post Office wanted to charge me 75 silver dollars, enough to pay our three highest paid employees their half-month's wages, so we sent it at a cheaper rate and I hope it reaches you sometime. I put in a plea for funds and if you are going to expect us to start up some projects here, or even send you many more cables, will you please send us some US cheques, for amounts up to 200 US dollars. Bigger than that they are difficult to negotiate. As before, I live on the edge of bankruptcy perpetually, and never know one payday where the next payday's wages are coming from. By a lucky fluke or a brilliant sustained argument lasting two hours, I got 1,600 dollars out of JCRR last week, enough to pay wages on Saturday and send off the Chengtu convoy. Now I am broke and prospectless until I have another brainwave.

I strove to make my cable clear and I hope I succeeded. By the way, I have not sent a cable to Shanghai as for one thing it is impossible and for another it would be too expensive. I hope you can keep them informed of what goes on.

I will now give you a bit more dope on possible projects… [He writes several more pages on this topic.]

JCRR [Joint Committee for Rural Reconstruction] have offered me a job as their Transport Director in Chengtu. They first asked us to run their transport for them; I was agreeable while their HQ was here, now it is moving to Chengtu it is all off. It would have been a contract job and would have solved half of our financial worries. They now want to fly me to Chengtu and back so that I can get them organised and so they can work on me some more to get me to join them. This touching belief of people in WC that

Mike Frankton pays wages in times of hyper-inflation

because I run the IRC Transport I know something about running trucks always gives me a good laugh. Actually I don't know the lower upper t'gains'l [top gallant sail] on the foremast from the lower upper staysail on the mizzen. Or whatever.

George [Kan], at Lanchow last Wednesday, is expected home from Tihua [Urumchi] anytime now. Sam [Yen] got back from Kunming after twice escaping banditry by a few lucky minutes. Other trucks got it. He is getting ready to go back there again with the last Kunming convoy. We have had five trucks loaded for Chengtu for two weeks. They were waiting for the river to go down and the thousands of army trucks to get out of the way. It's a curious state of affairs at the river now; hundreds of trucks are running away from Paochi and crossing to the south; and hundreds of trucks are running away from Canton and crossing to the north. Commercial trucks wait for days while our brave defenders occupy every ferry in both directions. I was going to take these trucks to Chengtu, but the departure at very short notice of Miss Ancestors [Miss Tzu, the accounts clerk] condemned me to this place for another spell. Somebody has to

Unloading trucks, Chungking

stop here to answer the frantic telegrams from [British FSU member, Jim] Moorhouse, who has divorced his wife by now, I believe, only to find the co-respondent [Miss Tzu] slipping from his clammy grasp. While I thought she was still going to marry old Jim I treated her as an accountant, honest I did; when she told All, I did a bit of good for myself, but as she often said, weeping hot salt tears into my beard, it's too late. Why do I keep reverting to that sordid business.

The trucks left yesterday for Chengtu, and got as far as the ferry, to find that a truck there had fallen off the ramps and was upside down in the river, a frequent occurrence, and one which stopped the ferry for a day this time. They crossed this morning. They have a bloke with them, a missionary by the name of David Day. David Day first offended me by saying that I looked like my father, for whom he pretends to have an intense admiration; after further talk, when I found he had been dogging me about the world all his life, I asked him what school he went to. My premonition was correct. He started at the school just after I left, which is the probable explanation of why he became a missionary. He is a reasonable one, however, though pretty hard on a Dodge gearbox. He drinks salichiu as long as it is referred to as a fruit juice, and he doesn't attempt to convert me until he is well on with his second glass, by which time I am at the bottom of my third and in fit condition to demolish any doctrine that is proposed to me... All this and prickly heat too.

One thing that has cheered me is the news that you, my loved one, are coming to China again. And look here, Coxe, if you don't ruddy well pay a visit to Chungking this time...... Hoping to see you again very soon....

Yorhors,

Jack Jones, Transport Director.

Note: Jack was at school at Trinity County School, Wood Green, North London, a prestigious Christian foundation, his father being a local Congregational minister. David Day, mentioned by Jack, also apparently went to the same school. By chance he was with the China Inland Mission in Chungking and he was later imprisoned by the communists for resisting a physical attack at their mission home in the hills of the south bank.

JC/4 IRC Chungking Garage

Spencer Coxe, August 8, 1949

AFSC Philadelphia, Penn. US.

Dear Spencer, (or successor, legatee, or relique),

… Do you want any more publicity stuff? I have just written an account of the last piece of midwifery I did, when the tinsmith's wife had her baby at about twenty minutes notice, about a fortnight ago. I don't know what sort of magazine would be likely to publish it; it is a subject after my own heart and I let myself go on it. I also have an account of selling an engine and the long bargaining in silver, notes, pen p'iao of two different kinds, GY [Gold Yuan], gold bars, the final agreement to exchange two tyres, and the descent through Goodyears, Michelins, Sieberlings, Kellys, Firestones (made in India or US) until I am beaten down to a pair of Goodrich 10-plies. This one is a bit technical, containing as it does the argument as whether the engine is to have its flywheel housing or not, and what other accessories are included. It might strike the great American public as humorous, though to me and the dealers it is all deadly serious and we spend hours and hours in conclave and drink gallons of tea over the negotiations.

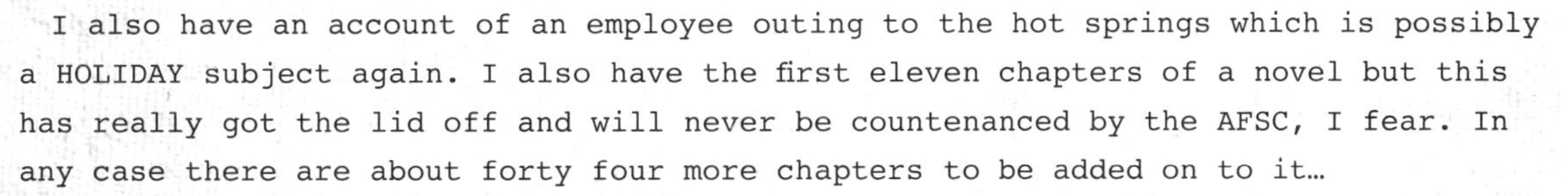

I also have an account of an employee outing to the hot springs which is possibly a HOLIDAY subject again. I also have the first eleven chapters of a novel but this has really got the lid off and will never be countenanced by the AFSC, I fear. In any case there are about forty four more chapters to be added on to it…

Yours,

Jack Jones

Note: Remarkably this article just referred to surfaced from among Spencer Coxe's papers in 2014. Called, 'Miss Lo' it poignantly describes Jack's 'brief encounter' at the hot springs with a former patient, looking very fetching in red dress and dark glasses. *Holiday* was the magazine of the American Automobile Association in which he'd already published his article about Mrs CMS and her theatre performance.

JC-5

IRC Chungking Garage
August 18, 1949

Spencer Coxe (or whoever)
AFSC China Desk
Philadelphia

Dear Spencer,

…Gosh, how I need a holiday. I have had to take this letter out of the typewriter four times. [Hence the photo image this editor has to work from is partly illegible!] The last time I put it back, instead of putting both of the page twos in, I put your copy of page two backed by your copy of page one, and proceeded to produce what archaeologist call, I believe, a palimpsest. So you will have to be content with a carbon of page one and if ever I want to refer to page one I shall have to decipher the palimpsest.

Last month I was cheated of a trip to Chengtu by the sudden and unexpected departure of Miss Zoo [Tzu]. Last week I was cheated of a trip to Kweiyang, my home from home in China, because I was expecting dramatic developments not only from Philadelphia, but also from Hongkong, to which place, now a divorcee, Jim Moorhouse has returned. This coming weekend I am planning to drive Leonard Walker back to Tungliang in the jeep; it is only 100 kilos to the place and surely to goodness I shall be able to get that far. I haven't laid one night abroad since returning from Staff Meeting in Shanghai last November 3rd.

I hope that you will send us information about the Staff Meeting which has been held in Chungmou recently. It would indeed be a charming gesture if AFSC could send us TIME or some such publication regularly. Every thunderstorm puts our power out of action for three or four weeks, and the minute that the transformer is restored to health, there is another storm. We haven't had any radio for well over one month now, and of course no newspapers of any sort. Dennis sent us the New Statesman and Nation for August 8!!!!! yesterday; it is my favourite periodical, but of course it confines itself to the news; and much of the stuff in it is quite pointless to us because we don't know the facts that are being commented on. TIME is also quite incomprehensible to us at times, but now we have Waldie [a new recruit from Canada] here to translate for us...

This week the British Consul has come into line with the American one and advised all who can to git [leave] while the going is good. All the men in two of the missions here have gone, leaving in each case a few old ladies to face the music; these old girls have been here for about thirty years each, they consider China their home, and they know if they go now they may never get back again; so they are staying put. The CIM [China Inland Missions] are all staying, I believe; there are about 400 of them in this area (spread over several provinces, of course). The Catholic Hospital plans to go, I understand. Don't know about the Canadians.

As for the Unit preserving a stiff upper lip, etc etc etc

Yours as ever,
Jack Jones.

IRC Chungking Garage, August 24, 1949
[Received stamp] Sep 6 1949
JC/6

Don Warrington
Foreign Service Section
Philadelphia, 7,
Penn., USA.

Dear Don,

…THE AGENDA for Staff Meeting reached me yesterday. A letter from Bert King [an FSU staff member in Shanghai] arrived today. Dated July 20th, it is the first communication we have had for over a month. First intimation I had that there was a Staff Meeting fixed came in Spencer's letter which reached here ten days after Staff Meeting was finished. I see all the same blether about salaries was to come up again – and the philosophy of the Unit – I'm glad I was spared it all this time.

THE IMPORTANCE OF FINDING A SUBSTITUTE FOR JONES should never for a moment be lost sight of. Dennis wrote me yesterday to say he intends to stay with BUAC in Hongkong. [The FSU had seconded Dennis Frone to British United Aid to China.] He makes a reference to his conscience, which he says is bothered about leaving me in the soup here, but the BUAC job is just what he wants. He says he is going to talk to Spencer about my plight. I have been talking to Spencer about it myself on and off for years, it seems, and I have come to the conclusion that talking to Spencer, usually a rewarding experience, is on this subject about as unfruitful as talking could be. Of course I realize the difficulties of replacing me, etc. It looks as though the Reuman bird [poor Dorothy!] will be popped straight into a typewriter walloping job in Hongkong... Whoever does come should overlap with me at least a couple of months, and two months is a long time these days, when I am revolving a lot of plans for Jones personally. No doubt this will all come to grief but I am making efforts to see they don't this time…

I liked it so much [his disastrous drive in the jeep to Tungliang!] that tomorrow I am going to Chengtu. JCRR [Joint Committee for Rural Rehabilitation] have asked me to run their fleet for them with our men. I said if we can have complete control, including purchase of spares and fuel etc. on a contract basis, it's a deal. They agreed. Maybe Council will mutter that's not been minuted by us but I haven't finished my commitments yet and I've got to get dough somehow. Next week all being well, if I can raise the dough for the fare, I'm going to Hongkong. [He didn't go.] The excuse is to see Spencer, and I certainly hope he will be there, as long as he doesn't occupy too much of my time. But I'm very much hoping to see A.N. Other, too. [The lovely Miss Tzu?]

With which cryptic remark ENDIT.

Yours as ever,
Jack Jones.

Chengtu, Miss Tzu, and Jack gets sick

JC/7

IRC Chungking Garage
Sept. 6, 1949

Spencer Coxe
Philadelphia

Dear Coxe,

I returned from Chengtu yesterday and buried under mountains of correspondence I found CJ/5. Which reminds me I ought to put a ref. no. at the top of this letter. Excuse me a moment…

They have a new idea in medical supplies distribution. Justly asserting that if you give stuff to the WSS [the Weishengshu or National Health Administration] it is sold in the big city where the WSS hangs out, they are sending a standard shipment to each hsien [county or administrative district] in Yunnan, Kweichou and Szechuan – to one much advertised individual, not the hsien chang [district head], in each hsien. They say, "yes, these goods marked not to be sold are still sold" but they are sold in the hsien under their system and the lao pei hsing [ordinary people] get a chance to buy them. They then pressed me to take on the job of distribution. There's blokes there earning US 8,000.00 per annum who do beggar all [sic] but sit on their backsides fanning themselves and they ask me at 7.50 a month to do all that. They say money is no object – "just ask what you want, we know it costs 20 cents US per lb. to buy your way through bandit areas." There are about 300 hsien in the area, most of them miles off any road. They seemed quite peeved when I backed out, reiterated that money was no object ("and we know you need money") and plied me with the old whisky again. Fortunately I am good at being plied with whisky and keep my head when all about me are losing theirs and giving blate the fame [a Spoonerism], so they still don't know how to get the stuff distributed. Some of their program stinks but they are doing a certain amount of good in these parts. I expect a rebuke from Philadelphia for mixing myself up with them; I only hope the crime is so heinous that you promptly send a replacement for me. I have got to the point where I think it would be better to be recalled in disgrace than never to be recalled at all.

A word or two on my trip [by jeep to Chengtu]. I left at 1.30 last Saturday week having planned to leave at the break of dawn. Apart from breaking the third leaf of the front spring we pushed along without mishap until 8.30 p.m. when we ran into Langchung. We spent the night on tables in a fan tien into

which we had driven the jeep. Any idea we had that the tables would be less bug-ridden than beds, and any ideas the scientists have about the efficiency of DDT, were proved to be erroneous in a few minutes. [It was possibly from these bites, that Jack got the scrub typhus that nearly killed him.] A gang of drunken soldiers playing the finger game kept me awake, with the help of the bugs, till two, and from then on I found that the tables I was on formed a rodent grove of Astarte [the goddess of love and fertility] and a hell of an orgy was going on for the rest of the night over and under and all round me. Usually I resent being booted out of an inn at dawn but that time I felt like a prisoner escaping from the condemned cell when they final dropped the front of the shop out and set up the tou chang tables. We bowled along through the pure air of dawn, scratching ourselves at frequent intervals, until we reached the ferry at Pei Wen Chen. Coming off this my gear lever jammed in second. We finally had to take the top off the box with the result that we got the lever into neutral, but the gears were still in second. So we pushed on to Neichang, unable to get into first or third or reverse, but always prone to jump out of second the moment the foot was lifted from the accelerator.

In Neichang we realized it was a case of mei yu pan fa [no other solution] unless we dropped out the gearbox, so I decided to push on the 300 kilos to Chengtu in second. It was then noon; we reached Chengtu at 8 p.m., having coasted down all the hills in true Chinese style to keep up our average and having just teetered over the top of the mountain without having to chock. [On a steep hill the old charcoal gas trucks used to run out of power and stop. A chock was then put under the rear wheels to stop it running backwards.] We blew a front tyre while descending one hill at about 40 mph but by superb driving the wizard at the wheel, (me), kept all four wheels on the road. We were rewarded by a glimpse of the snow mountains of Tibet from the top of the mountain just outside Chengtu: they are only visible about three or four times a year and they are superb in the sunset, a fantastic height above the Chengtu plain.

We had the gearbox to bits in Chengtu and found a small ball bearing had jumped out of place and had jammed one of the sliders. After this the return journey was tame, except for the first 100 kilos being through mud several inches deep, which led to some lively skidding, which made Mrs. Sam, passenger, gasp once or twice. (And me.) Incidentally our average from Chengtu to Pei Wen Chen, with all gears available, was slightly below our average in the other direction, with only one. The scenery was superb throughout and as the rice harvest was being gathered in it was all very picturesque, and I enjoyed it no end. I am very easily pleased. My chief impression of the trip is of the peace and serenity of Chengtu compared with this place – it is a town of beauty and culture – even the soldiers are polite – the climate is bearable – the Campus is in all respects a pleasant place; what spare time I had was spent with Miss Mickey, perhaps the leading authority on Miao folk; it so happens that I have seen one or two things she hasn't; including a whole tribe she has never heard of, in the Ko Chiu area [that Jack must have encountered when on his anti-malaria mission in Yunnan]...

ENTERTAINMENT Holiday [the magazine of the Automobile Association of America that published his article] certainly treated me much better than the New Yorker did. On the whole I think their cuts judicious, though any cuts of course destroy the perfect symmetry and balance, etc etc – and one or two of them seem to destroy the sense. With regard to the illustrations I can never understand

WCUU, Chengdu, Feb 43, building a new medical wing, the attic windows on the right being the FAU hostel

The same Chengdu campus in 2013

why it is better art to put a bicep on the back of the arm and a calf on the front of shin, but the drawings have good decorative value, and the one of the trumpeter is very good indeed. One criticism, which I level against all drawings of China: the costumes are coastal and especially Peiping ones. Anyone dressed like the majority of people in those pictures would expire from heat exhaustion in Chungking. In wintertime the Water Carrier's daughter wears five gowns, three jerseys, two undervests, two pairs of long trousers and a pair of underpants; in summer she wears one gown and the underpants and a pair of sandals, and the top of the gown is practically always open down to her navel. Once in Mass Observation mood I tried to make a list of the exposed female bosoms I saw from my truck: "Number of women with one breast exposed, such and such a date, so many; number of women with two breasts exposed so and so; number of women with three…" and so on. The numbers were surprisingly high, though I had to watch the road at least half the time I was doing my observations. The object of these remarks is to prove to you that everyone in the crowd scene is wearing too much.

Love,

Jack.

Note: Mass Observation was a social survey movement begun at the end of the thirties which required ordinary people to write their observations of life around them. Jack was a contributor when he was working in the sugar beet fields of Lincolnshire, though sadly what he wrote appears to be lost from the archives at Sussex University. By chance, he much later came to write the Bangkok Post obituary of Tom Harrisson, one of Mass Observation's founders, who was killed together with his wife in a road accident in Thailand in 1976.

SC/8

IRC Chungking Garage
Sept. 16, 1949

Spencer Coxe
AFSC, Philadelphia, USA

Dear Spencer,

… FINANCE As I haven't had time to do a financial statement for the two months since Miss Tsu [the delectable accountant] left I don't know exactly how much it is costing to run the garage these days. I know my half-monthly turnover is always between 3,000 and 4,000 dollars (silver) but this includes suspense items such as floats and contra floats, FSU cables, and business connected with half a dozen things like Jim [Moorhouse] and Miss Tsu which aren't strictly IRC business. [That's a wry joke!]

I have now got the decks cleared for action and next week I am going to contrive a mammoth statement covering these two months. From that I shall be able to deduce how much it costs to run the garage and also our FSU members' maintenance. Results will be communicated to you in due course. We haven't bought fuel or tyres recently but of course I know the silver value of the fuel and tyres the ECA advanced us. Actually the garage is just paying its way now - just. After paying wages yesterday I still have 1,000 silver dollars in the safe – this is a record after payday. I think the damned river has done us out of some profitable business this week: our trucks were ordered out to distribute JCRR seeds and pesticides but the damn river came up and while our trucks sit in the queue this side of the river, commercial trucks on that side are doing the job. Can't be helped and why shouldn't the commercial trucks do it anyway? Because we want the dough to continue distributing medical supplies, that's why.

PERIODICALS. TIME'S news is better than no news…

TRAVEL As explained in my last, there is no need to abandon the idea of sending recruits [from Hong Kong] on the erroneous assumption that because the CNAC have failed us we have no air service. The sky is alive with planes, at least half a dozen a day, and the only places they can possibly come from now are Canton and Hongkong (and Chengtu and Hsichang, which hardly count). A letter from Dennis Frone today says that David White is in Hongkong and raring to come here. He is alleged to be interested in Transport with a capital T. He would suit us to a T in that case. Especially now that Waldie is likely to be hors de combat for a while.

TYCOS PHYGOMETER [A Sphygmomanometer, a device for reading blood pressure.] I'm sure you haven't spelt this right, Spencer. Anyway, it is in Hongkong together with most of Waldie's tungshi. Or perhaps it is here lurking in some godown. Between them Waldie and Mason made a balls up of getting the stuff here and as you know it is fatal to get separated from your tungshi in this country. CMC makes frequent unfructuous (I quote) efforts to find out where the stuff is; at last we have got a weighbill and we might find out soon. If I ever hear anything about this item I'll let you know... [Jack had a high opinion of Chou Ming Cheng in every way except his English.]

COXE Excuses excuses excuses. Men have gone on their knees all the way from Wadi Walla to Mecca. Two youths drove in reverse all the way from New York to San Francisco, or vice versa. Leander swam the Hellespont and was a Hero to his Hero. I myself when really determined to go to some place or other have been known to walk even. You could come [to visit Chungking] if you would, and would heaven you would.

BUMPH The wads of bumph were read by me and digested. It is nice to think there will soon be a new section on the scene. I hope they soon get their shoulders up against a good heavy wheel and one worth turning. I regret the cancellation of Saunderson, [a potential recruit] still without knowing anything about him. It must be the name.

ENCLOSED, if I can finish typing it this weekend, you will find my latest journalistic work. I think it probable that if you want to publish it you will have to start a magazine specially to carry it but if it is unprintable I hope it will do for that small coterie of my admirers you so flatteringly write about. I myself am an admirer of one Coxe (as all reasonable critics I divorce the man from his work of course, and I am here referring to his works) and of one Meager, who, after a meteoric rise to fame etc etc. retired into the obscurity of conjugality and must now apparently be conjugated in the past imperfect. [Great wordplay, Jack! Tony Meager, just married in the USA, was later to be Jack's most loyal friend and colleague at Unicef in Bangkok.] Can Shakespeare no longer live and write again amongst the millions of typewriters at twenty south twelfth street? Are there no rats in Philadelphia for Meager to hunt? Often I turn to a tattered old file which contains a rich vein of literature, the old Chronicle and Newsletter files. It's a pity nothing is being added to them now. [Presumably conditions were too challenging to produce and distribute regular news letters.]

Yours as ever, and sweating like hell, because the autumn tiger is here.

Jack Jones

Sept. 21. Not enclosed. Jones has malaria with suspected complications. Just off to Catholic Hospital to be admitted. [Handwritten note.]

The Catholic Hospital, Chungking

A letter faintly written in pencil.

[Received stamp] Oct. 17 1949
JC/9-A

Sept 29th [1949]
Cath. Hosp. Ckg

Dear Scoxe,

Excuse the homely pencil and the pages torn from the exercise book. Your pen pal is in Hosp. recovering from scrub typhus. I think I got it on our verandah, as I remember when I got the [tic] bites that Doc Cochin [Dr Marcel Couchin of the French Catholic Hospital] puts the blame on. Stuart Allen [doctor at the Canadian Mission Hospital] reckons I got it at that lousy fan tien in Lungch'ang.

It's uncommon here; it is more common up there. Anyway I had a high-temp. and a howling yowling headache for over a week. Now I am normal and can sleep and eat again. Life is just wonderful. [In *Daughters of an Ancient Race* Jack also describes his near death experience with typhus, a disease which killed at least two other FAU members.]

It has been: 'Let's Be Kind to Jones' week in Ckg. Everybody has been to see me, from employees and their families, spare parts dealers, JCRR cheeses, Mrs. MacCork and the Yihs, up to my arch enemy Stuart Allen, who has just spent an hour with me, during which there was an affecting reconciliation. The damn bedroom is like a Kuang Sun Yuan shop with all the oranges, biscuits, pears, sweets (trans. candies) [Coxe is of course a Yank], pisspots etc. I forgot to mention that Shell Co. and the British Vice-Consul [Edward Mitchell] also arrived one afternoon bearing a huge bundle of motoring papers. I love the way these things are in these magazines. "On the 33rd lap Stropsky overturned at 120 mph. The beautifully turned out Alfa Romeo was unfortunately seriously damaged. Stropsky succumbed to his injuries." One always hears the unspoken comment — "serves the blighter right for damaging such a car."

When I was sick unto death I sent a cable to Frone [Dennis Frone in Hong Kong] as follows: "PLEASE INFORM PHILADELPHIA LONDON WALDIE PROGRESSING SATISFACTORILY JONES IN CHKHOSPITAL SCRUB TYPHUS SEND WHITE SOONEST." I had hoped White, who I know is yearning to come here, would be aboard the St. Paul which came in last night; but apparently that was too soon. That God-damned plane! We have had a truck loaded with Hsichang stuff for one month! Four times the plane has been in and not taken it. This time they said the permit to land at Hsichang had expired. [The Lutheran World Federation operated a C47 plane called St Paul which crashed on 11 February 1949. This was replaced by St Paul II, another C47 bought in Manila the next month.]

Douglas C47 St Paul II

About recruits. Why don't you tell us something about them? Why do we have to find out from Frone that Fleda approxes less to Lana Turner [the white Hollywood actress] than to Marian Anderson? [The black American contralto.] In the old days you used to get a thin piece of yellow paper about each recruit, closely-typed with his name, age, next of kin, appearance, experience, background and a long list of dubious-looking academic distinctions. What was wrong with that idea?

… Dr. Cochin has just looked in and shouted: "I forrbid you to worrrk!!" I must just tell you this however. The Frone reaction to my cable has been to come [to

Chungking to help out] in person! Hart wouldn't let White come. Who is this blighter Hart? Why has he such a hell of a big say in Unit affairs? [Robert Hart, ex-UNRRA, Kaifeng, was working in Hong Kong setting up the Fish and Vegetable Wholesale Marketing Organisation. He also acted informally as agent for the FSU there.]

All the three recruits now in Hkg. want to come here. There they are working in a refugee camp [North Point Relief Camp] which gets adequate supervision – including medical – from the British authorities. Here in Ckg. is poverty and disease such as you never saw in Central China, Spencer. If you don't want to go in for any of the schemes I have mooted – what about an FSU Hospital in the empty godowns at 4½ kilos? [Over the bamboo fence beyond Jack's garage.] I have often thought of it when turning away from the clinic people I couldn't possibly help. It would be a good bit of work and we'd all be on the same "compound" – if you can call it that; all the bamboo fences have blown down again.

I asked Frone about joining the [Transport] Unit. He's "seriously considering it".

Yours,

Jack.

Jack pleads for repatriation funds from his hospital bed

Another pencilled letter written in hospital to Spencer Coxe, though Jack is not too sure of the date.

JC/9B
[Received stamp] Oct 17, 1949

Catholic Hospital
Oct. 3 (?) 1949

Dear Spencer, (thou gem-like flame), [quoted from Walter Pater.]

I don't know how you expect to get my reply by the 12th Oct., when your CJ/8 only reached me this morning (Monday); but I still endeavour to reply straight away.

Incidentally I have just got up for the first time after two weeks and two days on my back. The last week has been an exceedingly pleasant holiday, similar to the one I had in Hankow a couple of years ago [having a haemorrhoidectomy], but not so perfect. These are the only "holidays" I have had in four years. But for my piles and scrub typhus, I should be completely worn out by now.

To business.

(1) JCRR [Joint Committee for Rural Reconstruction] is now paying for West China Transport. This is a typical Coxian sweeping statement. Without JCRR support we should flop, but much of our income still derives from double-crossing other organisations (Consulates, missions, etc), and from return cargoes. With the improvement of war news in these parts, trade in the second-hand-car and return cargo departments has picked up; while in Hosp. I have sold one truck for eleven oz. of gold and two cars @ 10% commission. I leave no stone unturned, no avenue unexplored, and car dealers consider me a tough nut, and send me flowers when I am in Hospital. [Jack was selling cars on commission for fleeing missionaries.]

(2) J.J. is tired of being TD [transport director]. This is the impression I have striven to give, though it could be truer to say that JJ is tired of being a Lone Wolf with ALL the responsibility on his own graying shoulders. Waldie was a disappointment for that reason. As Stuart says, he is "strangely immature". [Waldie, the new recruit is in hospital and Stuart Allen is his doctor.] Now the Frone has returned [to Chungking], obviously a bit conscious stricken, (he lays part of the blame for my collapse at his own door); and things may be easier.

(3) I am glad indeed to hear that the IRC still has that US 2,500.00 [for staff severance pay/repatriations].

(4) So am I in favour of selling equipment, and I am doing it! But you people at home don't realise how hard it is to sell transport equipment in Ckg. Over 1,000 trucks are laid up in the city. Dealers only want a couple of crankshafts and a set of pistons at a time. To get money for value you have to dicker at least two weeks over each item. We could never make much on sale of equipment.

(5) Actual tonnages [of medical supplies] in our godowns:

IRC: 27 tons [International Relief Committee]
ECA: 30 tons [Economic Cooperation Administration]
CIC: 6 tons [Chinese Industrial Cooperatives]

The situation in the north is easing and I am sending trucks to Hanchung this week. I also hope to send the remaining IRC Kunming supplies this week (circa 8 tons). Most of the ECA stuff is being re-allocated and we shall be able to distribute it. Don't forget that the IRC committed us to this chore.

Now for answers to your specific questions:

(a) Does the IRC still exist? Your guess is as good as mine. TSO and YS seem still to be working part time and in an honorary capacity. [Dr TS Outerbridge was medical director, later to be President of the Bermuda branch of the BMA, and YS Djang was executive secretary.] I have had one letter from TSO since S'hai fell. Dennis and Mrs. MacCork [apparently a nickname for Christine Mclaughlin, both of them employed by the IRC] have received some backpay, so I think the IRC MUST still exist. At least the IRC Medical Committee (W. China) is still very much alive under the able (and inescapable) Chairmanship of S. Allen.

(b) At our present rate, and with the major changes in the political picture, we could finish [distributing the medical supplies in the godowns] by Xmas.

(c) The "repatriation reserve" of US $ 2,500 is for paying off the employees. Each member is entitled to repatriation up to a certain limit, with a bonus for length of service. I have worked out an elaborate scheme which ensures that everyone gets a fair deal on this scheme; the IRC Standing C'mttee approved the scheme, (a big improvement on the old FAU one) and voted the 2,500 U.S. which would have covered it at that time.

I also think the "transmittal difficulties" are an IRC ruse to hang on to the money. I hope you will send it in the form of cheques, (checks, sorry), and have it credited to FSU a/c's by IRC. At the bitter end after sale of trucks etc we may be able to refund it.

Comments on Coxe's conclusions:

(1) I would not be greatly surprised at anything in China including a re-opening of the NW. If this happened we would have work for 6 months. If not, for 3 months.

(2) IRC may not be defunct, and our obligation to them has always been scant in my eyes. I consider if we have an obligation it is to the Hospitals in W. China. Wherever the drugs come from they look to the FAU (so-called) to distribute them. W.China without <u>some</u> FAU transport is inconceivable. Because of your upbringing, Spencer, - the fact that you were never in the West – you don't and can't realise just what the FAU (working in cooperation with the IRC, and at odd times with the WSS, ARC, ECA) means to West China. I am very strongly opposed to the complete closing down of transport. Now that they have no medical supplies coming in, the IRC Committee in Ckg has set up a purchasing agency: they buy

drugs here on order from the hospitals. There will always be work to do...

(3) Just why is the JCRR a stench in the nostrils? Time was, about a year ago, when sunshine came out of Jimmy Yen's a--e and his Mass Education movement [which, with American money, was transformed into JCRR,] was said to be wonderful. Todd Almighty is moving mountains for them in Sze. (literally) and I find that far from stinking, much of their program is a good thing. It is going to benefit the community if they get time to finish it. [Oliver J. Todd was chief of the irrigation engineering division of JCRR and author of, "*The China That I Knew*", 1973.]

(4) FAU transport is better known, - in China – than any other FSU work. People (missionaries, doctors and such) often say to me, "long after your malaria projects and your other flyaway projects are forgotten FAU transport will be remembered; it is the one unique FAU contribution which is unquestionably useful and irreplaceable." I agree with this view and I believe that we are so well known and have such a good reputation that we could survive the changeover [of regimes] and continue to function.

(5) Don't imagine that my release from the project would kill it. It has more vitality than that.

Do you realise, O Prince of Coxe, that with the exception of the new blacksmith not one of our employees has been with us less than three years? That the whole 47 of them are welded into one team that works, each member in perfect harmony with his fellows? That with the departure of all our foreigners and the temporary loss of George [Kan, who had been unable to return from a convoy because of fighting], we have found in the rank and file of the drivers men with all the necessary FAU qualities to handle convoys on dangerous roads – caution, resourcefulness, boldness, and mechanical ingenuity? You have here a very fine instrument for relief work, forged and tempered during nine years of hardship and adventure. It would be ridiculous to break that tool to pieces unless quite convinced there was no place for it in W. China.

We have an obligation to the boys - and all their dependants too – do you ever think of that? It is difficult for anybody to get jobs these days, once he has lost his present job. Now they are all one big family together. From memory [in my hospital bed] I compile this list of men and their dependants:

1. Storekeeper. An alleged wife in Kweiyang.

A page from Mark Jones' China album

2. Chief Mechanic. Wife, child, mother, wife expecting.
3. Engine fitter. Crippled wife, 2 children, wife's brother.
4. Lo Tse Li. Wife, child, mother-in-law. [whose wedding was featured in Jack's story in the New Yorker.]
5. Ling Cheng Wen. Wife, child, mother-in-law.
6. Wang An Ch'ang. Wife, 2 children, sister, 2 brothers, dissolute old father.
7. Sugar Bean. Wife, 4 children, mother, mother-in-law.
8. Chu Hu. Wife (blind).
9. Chen Chi An. Alleged wife in Kutsing.
10. Hsia Wu Ch'u. Wife, 2 children, orphaned relatives (2).
11. Chief tinsmith. Has had at least 4 wives I know of. Present wife has 2 kids.

Mother-in-law.

12. Blacksmith. Wife, 4 children, odd relatives.

13. Welder. Wife, mother, younger brother, widowed sister-in-law with 2 children.

14. Turner. Invalid wife. ["The Turner's Wife" is a chapter in, "*Daughters of an Ancient Race*".]

15. 2nd tinsmith. Wife, 3 children, mother.

16. Striker. Wife, 2 babies, ancient grandmother.

17. Electrician. Wife, baby, mother-in-law.

18. Carpenter. Alleged wife and family (never seen).

19. Apprentice. Single.

20. Apprentice. Wife, mother and father, also in-laws.

21. Apprentice. Wife.

22. Apprentice. Wife, 2 children, 3rd expected, 2 unmarried sisters, widowed mother and aunt.

23-27. Apprentices. Single.

28. Drivers: Chang Ming Sang. Wife, 3 kids, invalid mother, odd relatives. ['Mrs CMS' is another chapter in *Daughters of an Ancient Race.*]

29. Chang Wu Leng: wife, 2 kids, 3rd expected, mother.

30. Chi Hsu Lin. Wife, 2 kids.

31. Chen Wei Ling. Wife, child (adopted).

32. Feng Ah Fu. Alleged family. Never seen.

33. Tulip. Wife and relatives. Child died recently.

34. Old Tobacco. Present wife has two kids. Refugee family of 4 living with him.

35. P'ang tzu. Wife, 5 kids.

36. Lao Wang. Wife, two children.

37. Coolies, etc. Boys' Cook. Wife, baby, mother-in-law.

38. Fuel coolie. Wife, 2 kids. 3rd kid born last night in this hospital.

39. Watchman. Family in Kweiyang.

40. Coolie(1). Wife, child, parents, wife expecting.

41. Coolie(2). Wife, 2 children, out-of-work brother.

42. Coolie(3). Wife, child.

43. Our Cook. Wife, 5 children, parents on both sides.

44. Laundryman, TB wife, 2 kids.

45. Tableboy 2 sons, 2 daughters.

46. P'eng Pei Pei. [Their rotund female cook.] 2 daughters, grandson.

Peng Pei Pei, the cook

I make this come to just under 200 people, counting unborn babies, (all due this month except one) and not counting all the odd relatives who sponge on them and also come to the clinic.

Sorry to bore you. I've plenty of time in hospital.

Finally, "let's sell the trucks and get out." You said your letter might be fatuous, and that sentence is. It took 2 months to sell up and close down [the former depot at] Kweiyang and we sent 12 truck loads of stuff to Chungking. Kweiyang was a small place compared with this. Closing down will take a fairly large staff at least several weeks. You, like Frank [Miles] before he came here, have absolutely no conception of the sheer size of this project. You think it is just another HM&G. [Honan Machine Shop and Garage.] I wish to God you could come and see the place.

John Hsu hasn't showed up. He is probably right about the origin of the fire [in Chungking city]. I have only heard one person blame it all entirely on the wind – an unusual natural phenomena in Ckg, where it hardly ever blows, except just before a storm.

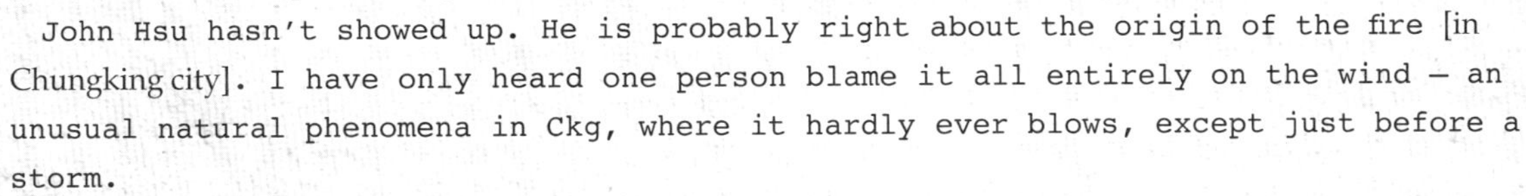

All the SM bumph [staff meeting papers] arrived this morning. God help us! It was nice to see our clinic getting "official" recognition from the Medical Director, it is the joy of my life. The fuelkeeper's wife walked into my room yesterday and said: "The doctor says I'm going to have my baby tonight; what do you think?" Sister Mafalda [of the Catholic Hospital] was in here and she laughed like hell.

While in hospital I have written a fable entitled The Wolf and Farmer Whittlestick. I'll send you a copy soon. It came to me just after they had given me two enemas (both unsuccessful) – not often I get a complete idea like that. Perhaps green soap is inspiring.

I can't make out about SM's amendment to the rule governing my earnings [from published articles]: can I do it again or not? I thought it was OK as long as I didn't touch the money while in China…

I never meant to write this much.

Yours, hopefully,

Jack.

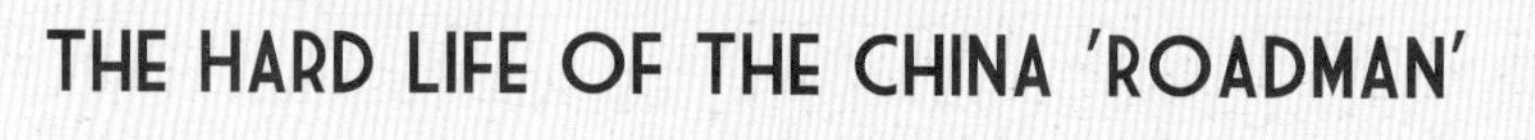

THE HARD LIFE OF THE CHINA 'ROADMAN'

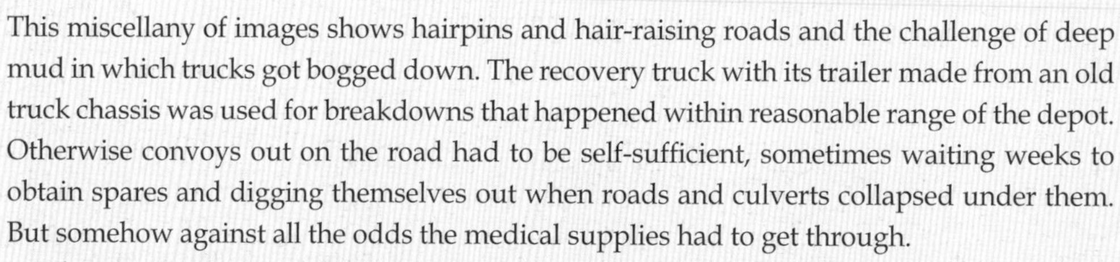

This miscellany of images shows hairpins and hair-raising roads and the challenge of deep mud in which trucks got bogged down. The recovery truck with its trailer made from an old truck chassis was used for breakdowns that happened within reasonable range of the depot. Otherwise convoys out on the road had to be self-sufficient, sometimes waiting weeks to obtain spares and digging themselves out when roads and culverts collapsed under them. But somehow against all the odds the medical supplies had to get through.

What they had to deal with was overloaded, worn out trucks, short of spares, constantly breaking down and tyres bursting all day long. They endured drafty cabs that were desperately hot and humid or else freezing cold, unpadded seats and hard springs and potholes that jarred the back and kidneys. There were hold ups when bridges were down, land slides, torrential rain and feeble wipers, brakes constantly failing. There were hold ups when papers and permits didn't satisfy, when soldiers demanded a ride, life-threatening hold ups by bandits, squalid inns and tics that kill with typhus when you stopped at night. And China had no real road system, certainly none that were sealed. Rough tracks, muddy and washed out or raising clouds of choking dust were normal, impossible hairpins up the mountains, the truck crawling at walking pace if at all, thousands of kilometres to go for weeks and months at a time and on board medical supplies that were desperately needed to save lives.

F.A.U.
FAU 112
F.A.U.

Jack pencils a welcome letter to the three new recruits

This letter of welcome, again written in pencil, was mailed to Hong Kong, typed up and given to the recruits working there in the refugee relief camp and waiting for clearance to enter China. Any of them reading of the problems and dangers that Jack describes might have wanted to run a mile, but they all willingly left the safety of British Hong Kong for distant Chunking where invasion by the communist armies and war and chaos were imminent.

Jack refers again to JCRR, the well-funded successor to Jimmy Yen's Mass Education Movement which worked in rural reconstruction. To earn money for his Unit, Jack's staff are now running JCRR's transport pool in Chengtu.

Dorothy Reuman, Dr Mary Mostyn, Howell Jones, Fleda Jones, Mark Shaw,
North Point Relief Camp, Hong Kong, Oct 1949

To David White, Fleda Jones, Elizabeth (Mary) Mostyn

Hong Kong

Catholic Hospital
Chungking
October 7, 1949

Dear Folks,

As the old man of the west I ought to have written to you long before this, extending the glad hand of welcome, with a lot of good advice, - (I have a particularly fine line of advice; people take it and promptly find themselves in a hell of a mess) - and all that rot. But first I went to Chengtu and fixed up a deal with JCRR whereby transport will be able to continue while Spencer weeps: - he thinks JCRR stinks though a year ago he thought Jimmy Yen and his mass education movement (the same thing) just wonderful. Then, probably on the journey to or from Chengtu I got scrub typhus, and for the last 15 days I have been languishing in this Catholic hospital, being potted by the Franciscan sisters by day and walked over by cockroaches two inches long (and correspondingly fat) at night. These are my excuses for not having written before, and my first bit of advice to you, children, is this: keep up with your injections! I hadn't had any for two years or more; hence the first germ I met bowled me over completely, and gave me the grandfather of all headaches, which lasted seven days and nights, during which time four sorts of sedatives failed to put me to sleep even for two or three minutes. Having a continuous sore head for 180 hours on end is not much of a joke... [To further encourage them, Jack then tells them that his latest recruit, Bob Waldie is ill in the other hospital and that he hopes to send him back to Hong Kong to convalesce.]

Vast masses of bumf have descended on my defenceless head while I have been here. (Staff Meeting always produces enough paper to keep the little box in our maufang [latrine] supplied for months)... a letter has come from Frank Miles, [the FSU chairman in Shanghai] written as recently as Sept. 22, in which he says, "I believe you have seven members in the section if Dave White is counted in"... elsewhere he assumes that you are already here. These facts lead me to believe that old Dispense-with-Soxe and Bob Hart [in Hong Kong] are being unreasonable in keeping you hawg-tied (to use a Coxe-ism) in Hong Kong; you David at least have the green light for Chungking. And by God we need you. [The FSU in Shanghai was being cautious in committing more recruits to the Chungking project.]

Chou Min Cheng and Sam Yen

Our position is at present this. Waldie is sick. George Kan has been cut off by the Coms. and is at present "seconded" as you might say to the CIC Baillie School at Shantan, 2188 kilometres to the NW. [He later managed to rejoin the Unit in Shanghai.] Sam Yen is permanently in Chengtu, running the JCRR Motor Pool. This leaves John Peter, Chou Min Cheng and me. JP is Garage Manager. CMC is buyer, interpreter, seller, liason man with the officials and part-time accountant. I am a broken reed. Frone is here and giving me some support, chiefly moral. [Why does he always poke fun at poor Dennis!] When you think that when I first came here, 4 years ago, we had 50 foreigners in transport (running only twice as many trucks but four widely scattered garages instead of one) it makes you realise just how tough the going is now. Fortunately every one of our [local] drivers has been with us for at least four years and they have become so imbued with Unit traditions that we can send them off on their own on difficult and dangerous assignments, knowing that they won't sell the cargoes of petrol or do us over too badly over return cargoes; and so far except for George, they have always got home alright. But there are two dangerous trips that must be made immediately – three trucks to Kunming (hazard bandits), two trucks to Hanchung (hazard: completely undisciplined Nationalist Forces). It is almost essential that we have a foreigner to go along with this second convoy. Why have we to go? John and I are both tied here, and owing to our inflammable tempers are not the best men to go, and be k'e-ch'i to completely undisciplined soldiers anyway. Waldie is too sick and perhaps too immature to handle such situations as might conceivably arise. (We had three trucks commandeered on this road three months ago, and had a big job getting them back, even with British Consulate aid). Frank Miles is promising us Chris Evans, (an old West China transport hand, almost worshipped by the boys) – sometime. Chris can't get here for months. You, Dave, could get here in a few days.

Now for you girls. As soon as Coxe mooted the idea of sending seven recruits here I looked up jobs for all of you. The response to date is as follows:

(1) Labourers Hospital, Chungking: Mostyn, Jones, one handyman, [or]

(2) West China Union University, Chengtu: Mostyn, Jones, both Reumans, handy man if suitably qualified

(3) Chaotung Methodist Hospital: Mostyn, Jones, handyman

(4) Catholic Hospital, Chungking: Jones

(5) Jack Jones's projected hospital for Women and Children at Ssu Kung Li Pan: Jones (Fleda), Mostyn, Jones (Jack), plus.

Let us take a look at these projects. (1) The Labourers Hospital is the only one in Chungking (theoretically) which provides free treatment for working-class people. It used to be supported by the big industrial concerns here, but they have now withdrawn their support, and it is practically defunct. It has a good site and buildings in the city and many mission and philanthropic bodies would like to get it going again, and would support it to some extent. They would, however, prefer a male doctor, as the clientele is almost entirely male. No doubt Elizabeth, we could fix you up with an Eton crop [a short hair style] and a false moustache.

(2) WCUU, [West China Union University] Chengtu. There used to be 150 foreigners on the campus, but more than half have now gone home. The hospital is undoubtedly the biggest and probably the best in West China. The Campus is a lovely place; an all out team could easily be absorbed. It's not, however, the Unit's type of project: the hospital is functioning normally. The Unit habit is of course to go into a wreck, get it running, and then "devolve" it on to someone else. "Devolve" is the Unit watchword. [Elizabeth (Mary) ultimately ended up at WCUU.]

(3) Chaotung Methodist Hospital. I originally wrote asking if we could rebuild Stonegateway Leprosarium, which was shaken down in an earthquake. The Meths [Methodists] replied that they had abandoned the leprosarium owing to local unrest but they would welcome a team of three in their well-established hospital at Chaotung, 16 miles away. No doubt, they said, if the team came the leprosarium could be restarted in time. The Unit has already sanctioned the leprosarium project at the last Staff Meeting but one.

(4) Cath. Hosp. Chungking. Sister Mafalda wants Fleda very badly she says. The

Unit is however opposed to putting single persons into jobs on their own. I don't mean single persons as opposed to married ones; I mean the Unit believes in sections of more than one person…

(5) JJ's Hospital for Women and Kids. As you may know, I run a clinic at the Garage. Attendance fluctuates seasonally; usually we see 30 people a day when busy (not counting those we turn away because they are too ill, not ill enough, have no conceivable claim on our attentions, come when we are busy etc). The proportion of patients seen is as follows: Females 55%, Children 35%, Males 10%. These queer percentages may be due to the fact that I have a great, though undeserved reputation for my knowledge of minor female complaints; mastitis is very common, too copious milk supplies are checked and too meagre ones stepped up; difficult periods are miraculously made easy etc. Also I have been lucky with a number of confinements. My successes with kids have not been so spectacular, chiefly because I only give them castor oil or cough mixture or both. Well, that's an over-simplification but anyway.

Nobody who lives in West China can fail to be impressed and disturbed (a) by the amount of physical suffering and (b) the disproportionate amount of physical suffering endured by women. Much of this is due to neglect and lack of hygiene, much too frequent indulgence in child birth coupled with malnutrition; much to lack of exercise, lack of interest, VD, malaria, dysentery, scabies, trachoma, etc. The kids are usually healthy, except for malaria and boils and bad ears and bad eyes and snuffles, until they are weaned (at 2 or 3 years, according to when the next kid comes); then they go through a very dangerous period due to the inability to digest rice and pickles, which is what the people live on.

At the present we have four large and lofty go-downs empty. They were built to house 400 tons of medical supplies and could easily accommodate 20 patients per godown. These godowns are next to the garage in a large yard rented by us [from the National Resources Commission]. The nearest hospitals are at T'u Ch'iao, (14 kilos away by road; a Govt social welfare venture, looks excellent, treatment standards not known); the Canadian Mission Hospital 8 kms. away and very inaccessible (takes two and a half hours to reach), and the Cath. Hosp. (across the river; 2 hours at least.)

FAU trucks at the National Resources Commission yard next to the south bank depot through the bamboo fence

Every time I go into those godowns I think what a damn fine hospital they would make. Of course the tile roofs blow off in storms and the mud walls collapse at a touch, but they are big, dry, and cool in summers, and the builder is always on the compound anyway.

What would you think to the idea of starting up a hospital right on the garage doorstep? I think the emphasis should be on free treatment for the poor class and kids. Soldiers will naturally come and be a hell of a nuisance. Can't blame them; such is the treatment they receive that many go off their heads, and many die of ailments that could be cured in a couple of days with the right drugs. There would probably be opposition from the local quacks and midwives; they hate my guts anyway. But it would be wonderful not to have to say to a poor country woman (as I did the day I came here), "Your bladder is leaking into your vagina because you had a bad time with that baby, and you must go to the hospital for an operation" — knowing that she can't pay the hua k'erh fare [sedan chair or litter] to the hospital, let alone pay for the operation.....

I seem to have spent a disproportionate amount of space on my pet idea but you must forgive an old man inclined to maunder on and on, dribbling into his beard the while. Swift reactions to this letter would lead to swift reactions in Philadelphia, London, Shanghai and other places where they talk (and talk and talk). It might even lead to swift actions in Chungking. At least you would be in China. You would probably find our place and our company intolerably rough; but gosh, you've only signed on for two years, haven't you?

Beg pardon for writing in pencil.... Sister Mafalda has just told me I have to stay here another week. I got a touch of squitters yesterday and everyone got excited. But I hope to be out this weekend.

All the best to you all,

signed Jack.

More letters for Spencer Coxe

Handwritten again but this time in pen on nice paper.

Catholic Hospital
Oct. 14, 1949

Spencer Coxe
America

Dear Spencer,

Waldie's luggage has at last caught up with him. In Waldie's absence (he is still in the Can. Hosp.) [Canadian Mission Hospital], [Dennis] Frone has burgled it. Hence I have some classy paper to write on (worthy of you at least, mon brave). Excuse my Gallicism; after 24 days in France [Jack is in the French run Catholic Hospital] my tongue has got a constant shiver in it from rolling all those r 's round my uvula.

ME I have high hopes of getting out [of hospital] tomorrow. ("Oh, for the weengs, for the weeengs, ovver duvver"). However, I have some persistent intestinal trouble and frostbite of the bum due to having to sit so frequently on a certain aluminium hospital utensil, and they can't find any "parrasitisme" to account for it. Dr. Cochin threatens to hold me in durance vile until the responsible agent is discovered... [More about the possible Labhospital project then follows.]

INTERJECTION Dr. Cochin now thinks I have sprue. Goddam. [Defective absorption of nutrients causing diarrhea and emaciation.]

SECOND INTERJECTION Ping Yu has just come in with a very fat face - toothache. Penicillin, sulfadiazine, gargatisme....

THIRD INTERJECTION Never do a kind act to a woman. Recently I assisted three – known to John and me as Bust, Big Bust and Bloody Enormous Bust – to go to Chengtu on our trucks. They were refugee students from Peiping and hoped to get into college there. They didn't and a week later they were [back] here. Brought flowers for me and took up residence at the Garage again. Today Bust and Big Bust arrive and tell me the old tearful story, no money, no grub, no job. I have sent them to JCRR without much hope. I think they really ought to marry three of our apprentices, I can't think of any other pan fa. If they do the latter I shall expect to exercise le droit du seigneur of course. So far all I've got out of it is the flowers..._

COTTAGE HOSPITAL I'm glad Dennis has expanded the meagre data I sent you and given you a fuller idea of the layout and possibilities [for Jack's own proposed Chungking clinic]. I wrote fully to Hkg. – the first letter I have written to the new recruits – outlining all possible projects here and giving them a list of sound advice, especially to keep up to date with typhus injections. I should have written equally fullily [sic!] to you but owing to my ennui I didn't… [A discussion of the snags for this possible project follows.]

NB Dennis made some copying mistakes owing to my poor handwriting. [Dennis Frone was presumably typing up Jack's letters and circulating them.] Emphasis not on "workmen & children" but women & children. I would add to this [that we should undertake] training of village midwives and of the mothers themselves in care of themselves and their kids. An educational program, so dear to the heart of SMs [staff meetings].... Send <u>me</u> those six books on "Maternity Care" (if they are textbooks) and I could get cracking right away...

GENERAL Paper currency, printed in Ckg, has just started to depreciate. Luckily we still have silver, gold and some of your US$.... Foreign supplies are going haywire: coffee, in April, $5.00 for 20 lbs; July $11.00; yesterday, $40.00 (silver). One jeep spring today, complete, foreign, $50.00.... JCRR has reached limit of vehicles I contracted to run and asked for two extra drivers so shall soon be able to up their monthly contribution [ie ask them to pay more]..... CMC [Chou Ming Cheng] is running the garage and doing the accounts and in all things proving that he's OK for TD [transport director]. If only he could write English. But he is coming on quickly at that too. He's a damn good chap, though somewhat touchy at times. Who wouldn't be, trying to pour oil on the troubled waters that surround me perpetually.

Liberty! Fraternities! Quality!

Yours, Jack.

Chou Min Cheng and his wife

[Received stamp] 26 Oct 1949

Home again
Oct. 19, 1949

Coxe Hsien-sheng [An honorific form of address.]
America

Dear Spencer,

On my penultimate day in captivity, (the day before yesterday) I was the recipient of a cable [from you] which I can only regard as the latest example of DEMENTIA PRAECOXE [premature dementia!]; (it was unsigned). The mis-spellings cannot be laid to your account and our difficulties with telescoped words can be ascribed to our own intellectual dullness, but the fact that all three sentences were practically unintelligible must be blamed on Philadelphia alone, (Dennis and I feel). We implore you to be a little less niggardly with the dollars and so ensure that your cables make sense. As it stands the cable is a waste of money. We don't know what you mean about transport, we don't know what you mean about the project, and we don't know what you mean about Joneshaw conferring "directly".

TRANSPORT We understand that Phila, London and Shanghai are all in favour of closing down transport immediately, whether our work is completed or not. I don't want to be obstreperous, but I must point out that Chungking is not in favour of closing down immediately but when it has finished off its job properly, and if AMERENGHAI insists on the "immediately" they must send somebody here to do the closing down, because I won't have anything to do with it. I have more respect for the good name of the Unit. We have an unfinished job on our hands and if it is humanly possible we should finish it. This week we have already sent off fifteen tons of medical supplies, mostly IRC, just over 1000 kilos to the south and just under that distance to Hangchung in the North. Eight of our Chinese employees are risking their lives to distribute these supplies, (and that is no exaggeration, and they know what they are doing, and they all volunteered to go). Hundreds of people stand to benefit from these operations. Besides this we shall also be sending a truckload of medical supplies to Chengtu this week, besides delivering a lot of re-allocated ECA supplies to the Catholic Welfare people across the river. Our job is not finished, Spencer, and you should reconsider that "immediately" in the light of Turner's and Miles's most recent letters to reach me, copies of which you no doubt have. [Douglas Turner, and Frank Miles, the FSU chairman in Shanghai.]

None knew better than I when I set off for Chengtu that there would be lifted eyebrows in the home bases over what you call our tie-up with JCRR. I was at my wits ends for money to finish off our commitments to IRC, through IRC to ECA, and to the CIC and hospitals. I made it clear to JCRR that if I undertook the work I should expect to be overpaid for it, my only object in going in for it being to finance our medical distribution program. They were perfectly willing to co-operate with us on this. The agreement can be terminated at one week's notice by either party but as the bloke on the heavy receiving end I am not going to be the one to terminate that agreement. I have more sense of fair play to the JCRR and also to Sam and our boys who have worked like blacks not primarily to help JCRR but to earn

Brian Sorensen on an FAU kala azar project ambulance based in Chengchow

the money to keep transport going until our godowns are empty.

Keep your hair on, Spencer. You are having brainstorms such as over that CRM garage scheme [Canadian Relief Mission] and the UNICEF kala-azar tie-up and that business of sending seven recruits here in early Sept. and then sacking them all and then sending some of them after all in October. [Kala-azar is a mosquito borne disease that was rife at the time.]...

[Long paragraphs then follow about getting the IRC to hand over the money they were holding for repatriating all garage staff on closing the garage.]

SECOND SENTENCE RE PROJECT Did you write "preferable" or "preferably?" If the former (that's the way we got it), it means that a West China project not connected with Missions or ECA is preferable to continuation of (present understood) unit activity such as the Clinic. This interpretation hints that the Clinic is under Mission or ECA patronage, and as it isn't, and as we know you know it isn't, we assume (Dennis and I) that the word should have an adverbial ending, in which case it means that our Cottage Hospital idea is approved. If so we are glad you approve of it and we are determined to make a damn good go of it, and we think we can.

Plumping for this reading we sent the following cable to Shaw on 18th:

PRESUME UNINTELLIGIBLE COXE CABLE BEGINNING AMERENGHAI ENDING CONSIDERATION MEANS GARAGE HOSPITAL PROJECT OKAYED IF SO SEND MOSTYN JONES WHITE SOONEST IM FINE WALDIE STILL HOSPITALISED JACK [This asks Coxe to send the three new recruits in Hong Kong to Chungking. They were Dr Mary Mostyn, who had trained at the Royal Free Hospital, London and was a friend and fellow student there of future author, Han Suyin, Fleda Jones, an American lab technician and David White.]

You will see that all the faffing about suggested in the last sentence of your cable – Joneshaw consulting directly, whatever that means – Shaw notifying you of his proposals – for Shanghai's consideration - has been cut out.

(Earlier in this epistle I accuse you of acting and then stopping to think; in case you retort that I am on the road to doing the same thing I can only plead that I have been thinking all the time I have been in hospital, where I have had first rate opportunities for indulging in this unusual pastime, and I don't expect to make any withdrawals.)

The cable may surprise Mark [Shaw] as an earlier one, composed by me on the thirteenth, and saying "SEND WHITE SOONEST RESERVE MOSTYN JONES FOR WEST CHINA PROJECT' was for some reason never sent. I plan to use White in transport for a few weeks when he gets here. I have been sending for him all the time I have been in hospital but still enquiries come from Shaw, do we want him or not? We have a feeling that a whole batch of communications entrusted to St Paul [letters put on the Lutheran plane to Hong Kong] have gone astray.

Jones was discharged [from hospital] yesterday or rather he walked out when CMC [Chou Ming Cheng] turned up with the usual bevy of wives. I think [Dr] Cochin was just keeping me while he finished my copy of *"Lhasa: The Holy City"*. [This is a long, dense book of 326 pages by F. Spencer Chapman, whose later book, '*The Jungle is Neutral*' tells the story of working behind the lines against the Japanese in wartime Malaya. Could Jack have known that, like himself, Chapman had briefly mortified the flesh by working on a North Sea trawler out of Grimsby? Could they perhaps even have met each other there?]

My heart was broken as usual at having to leave one nurse with my passion undeclared; I can honestly say that no girl I have ever met before has punched holes in my posterior with such admirable technique and such an attractive smile. In my very last hour she gave me a final stab and the male nurse rallied round to give me the daily enema. Nobody knows what bug is at large in my intestines but I hope to have him in a few days with my own medication. My beard, which I have not seen for a month, has flourished like a bay tree and is worth crossing the Pacific to see, but my hair is coming out in handfuls and I am beginning to look almost as much of an intellectual as yourself. This doesn't say much however as perhaps the most intellectual looking person in the world is the second of the Three Stooges, the one that looks like a dreamy sort of Epstein. [One of this American Vaudeville act did indeed look like the sculptor, Jacob Epstein.]

This morning I took it easy, in accordance with medical instructions, reading Dennis' New Statesmen and Nation and helping Bob Edwards of IHT, Chengtu (who is now staying with us) repair an X-ray. But this afternoon I heard the call of duty, stern daughter of the Voice of God, you know [and so returned to his desk]. How I loathe that curiously misbegotten personification! It is nice to have Dennis rattling the old keys on yon side of the desk and John and everybody else happy.

A letter from Mark [Mark Shaw in Hong Kong] this morning, clearing up the Mostyn mystery. He gives Fleda full marks and Mary somewhat fewer but says she's a good girl. Her briefing in London he says was quite inadequate. Remember what I said about Waldie? [being inadequately briefed.] I suppose the recruits just can't take it in, no amount of indoctrination can prepare you for the full shock of China.

Yours, in the glad knowledge that I can never again have typhus,

Jack Jones.

Mark Shaw chairs a staff meeting, March 1948, presumably at the Friends Centre, Shanghai. Left Spencer Coxe, Dick Ruddell, query, Mark bearded, John Rue, Tim Haworth at the front

8 THE AWFUL STORY OF BOB WALDIE – AUGUST TO NOVEMBER 1949

Dr Stewart Allen,
Canadian Mission Hospital

China was in turmoil in 1949 as the communists moved south and westwards, putting in question the very future of the FAU's work there. Nonetheless, ever optimistic despite the uncertainty, recruitment of foreign staff for relief work continued, the geographical focus reverting to Jack's fiefdom in Chungking which was the last region to fall to the communists. A changing list of no fewer than seven mainly American recruits were thus apparently on their way to China, some first working for a time at the refugee relief camp at North Point in Hong Kong while the cheeses in Shanghai decided what to do with them. Jack's nightmare was that because of poor communications with FSU headquarters in China and Philadelphia he had little idea whether and when any of them might arrive.

The first to reach Chungking was Robert Waldie whose name appears repeatedly in Jack's reports and letters for reasons that will appear as the story unfolds below. The following snippets culled from the fading papers in the archives start with extracts from Jack's letters to Spencer Coxe at the AFSC China Desk in Philadelphia from July to October 1949.

For some reason Jack seems to have had a poor opinion of Dr Stuart Allen who was to operate on Waldie for appendicitis. A Canadian missionary who was at the Canadian Mission Hospital for many years, later to be arrested and imprisoned by the communists for a year, Dr. Alexander Stuart Allen was Jack's model for 'Dr Roland Hickman', a mission hospital doctor who appears as a key character in Jack's book of 1974, *Daughters of an Ancient Race.* In the book he describes him as follows; 'a bulky Britisher with a domineering manner, he had a pink fat face, gold rimmed glasses, a dark tie and a beautifully tailored brown serge suit'. In Jack's story, when one of Hickman's nurses maliciously switches the patients' medical papers, causing Hickman to perform the wrong operation on Jack's patient, 'the turner's wife', she later gets her revenge by denouncing Hickman to the communist authorities. The description in the book of the difficult access to Hickman's hospital (half a day by sedan chair) fits the hilltop position of the Canadian Hospital and in the story 'Dr Hickman' was later arrested and held for a year by the communists for causing the death by negligence of a communist general by leaving a swab in his intestines during an operation. The awful reality of Dr Allen's arrest and the story in Jack's book therefore closely coincide.

The following extracts from Jack's letters etc now pull together the events surrounding the new recruit, Robert Waldie.

RECRUITS AS SKETCHED Four of the recruits, Waldie, White, Mosescu, and Saunderson, could all be absorbed by the garage straight away, since all have engineering experience and/or interests…

WHERE'S WALDIE NOW?

Can the first recruit bring us some chocolate and if possible a crate of beer. The latter could be picked up in Hongkong. If I drink much more salichiu I shall turn into a Miao. [Jack's letter of 16 July 1949 to Spencer Coxe.]

The fabulous Waldie, whom I had come to regard as a Chimera, followed a cable announcing his arrival into Chungking last Friday evening. He then for the first time developed a Christian name, an age, and an unexpected nationality. Why didn't you tell me he wasn't American? Len Price, the British Consul, said you can bring in as many..... recruits as you please as long as they are Americans; now we find that Waldie, in spite of looking like a three card monte man from south of the border, or a dealer at a faro table, was born and bred in territory that owes allegiance to Lizzies's old man [ie King George VI… meaning Waldie is Canadian]. The ten gallon hat is a great acquisition to these parts and we are waiting for the day when Waldie lassoes his first truck. He is taking China quite calmly at the moment, having first of all dared the customs to read his private correspondence, and then sat by the river for three hours while three army trucks made several unsuccessful attempts to get up the ramps onto the ferry. Later, at supper, having fallen asleep into his soup plate (he was up at 4.30, it was then 9.30 p.m., and he hadn't eaten all day) he said, when I mentioned the river, "By the way, what is that river we crossed?" as if it [the Yangtse] was a mere ditch compared with some he'd seen back home. His tone implied, 'has it got a name, or is it too damn insignificant?'

He has now gone across the river to get his license, still wearing his ten gallon hat and his riding boots, and if there's any nonsense in the office I expect and hope that he will pull out a couple of pearl-handled six-shooters and get some action that way. It is good to get a new pard in this outfit. John and I have told them to each other so many times and we both know which anecdote the other is going to trot out next.

[From Jack's Letter of 8 August 1949 to Spencer Coxe. This paragraph was also published as a news item in the FSU Overseas Chronicle of 28 September 1949 which, in view of what happened later, was perhaps a little unfortunate.]

Waldie will go with Sam Yen on his first trip or trips to get the idea. I haven't seen Waldie drive, but he is the sort of bloke we want here, I think, on a first appraisal. If you've got any more like him send 'em quick.

It is by the way very clear that Waldie has had little or no briefing on either China or the Unit. He didn't know anything at all about the set up here. I hope people will make it clear to possible new recruits that it is both rough and lonely here, quite as rough as Chungmou; that we live entirely off the country, with no foreign amenities; that the Chinese taken in bulk hate foreigners and it is therefore politic as well as desirable on moral grounds to refrain from exhibiting a feeling of superiority. No amount of talking at home will prepare the recruit for the full shock of China (and the FAU, at least as far as this section is concerned), but I think for his own sake he should have a clearer idea of what he is coming to than Waldie had. I'm not criticizing Waldie, who is already looking for consolation in the right place, - the salichiu bottle, - but even Waldie has audibly wondered whether he will be able to last out his two years in these conditions. And he hasn't been on the road yet.

[From the same letter to Spencer Coxe of 8 August 1949.]

TIME [the American news magazine] is also quite incomprehensible to us at times, but now we have Waldie here to translate for us...

Waldie, by the way, has the right temperament for this job, and we are very pleased to have him here. He has a lot to learn as a driver, though, and we are keeping him and the people of China safe by confining him to the yard for the time being.

[Letter of 18 August 1949 to Spencer Coxe.]

I read your comments with interest and hasten to assure you that the Coxe School of Indoctrination is probably a highly efficient organisation. The Jones method, founded on Bertrand Russell, ("Let the filthy little brutes find out for themselves") has also met with signal failure so far. Waldie asks more questions, especially when I am writing or reading, than anybody else around this dump; but he apparently is unable to hear my replies, for he never profits by them. No amount of indoctrination will ever make a driver of him, even by my standards. His general knowledge is non est and he must have been a rum sort of schoolmaster. His chief contribution so far has been all the dirty stories of the Northwest frontier; with these he has wiled away many a steaming evening on the verandah, and this contribution is not to be under-rated. But John and I are hoping to discover some other gift in time.

[Letter of 6 September 1949 to Spencer Coxe.]

Last night Waldie didn't eat much supper and this morning I told him when he only ate a small bowl of puffed rice for breakfast that he would be ill if he didn't eat – you must keep eating in this hot weather, I told him. He said his stomach was feeling uneasy. At 11 a.m. he came in saying his stomach was hurting a lot and he was knocking off for the day. He had a bath and I then took his temp – exactly 100 – and enquired into his symptoms. It seemed like appendix to me from what he said so we bunged him straight off to hospital. By the time we got there, in two hours, he was in severe pain and they bunged him straight on the operation table. I have just sent you a telegram in consequence saying WALDIE ACUTE APPENDICITIS OPERATION TODAY AT CANADIAN HOSPITAL. My only reason for sending him to the latter place, where the surgical standard is now low, was that the river is up and getting him across to the Catholic Hospital would have taken half a day. But I hope and trust Stuart Allen can be trusted to remove an appendix.

[Letter of 16 September 1949 to Spencer Coxe.]

Stuart [Dr Stuart Allen] wrote me before he came to see me and I quote one part: "Respecting Mr. Waldie I had hoped that one of you would be driven to talk over his case. I did not want to bother you while ill. First may I ask how he has reacted to things since he came out [to Chungking]? Has he been a psychological problem at all? For he has been a very hard case to handle. He had a rather nasty appendix I admit but not nearly so bad as several we have had since and many before that. He just does not seem to be able to tolerate pain at all. Started immediately after the operation with the most awful bellowing which he now indulges in daily. He just opens his mouth and lets go as bad as the worst woman when she is having a baby. Consequently he throws all the nurses into a jitter and they come running round to see what they can do for him and about this he is not always happy.

"It was pretty warm during the first few days and though continually warned and having had his pyjamas buttoned up by nurses, Mrs. Allen, Miss Henderson and myself on various occasions he persisted in exposing his chest. He got a little pneumonia as a result. This brought up some blood-streaked sputum which upset him and the nurses as well who thought he was TB [tubercular]. He has had a bit of a rough time but not unduly so. Both Mrs. Allen and Miss Henderson have gone over several times daily to assist with one thing and another especially in trying to get him to eat as he got the idea eating some things was making him worse. Evidently also has some dysentery bacilli hanging around… His general physical shape is bad which is one reason for his complications. Blood was down to 58% hemoglobin when he arrived, the lowest I have seen in any foreigner in China so we are now feeding him iron tonic and vitamins…There is no getting around that he has been a most difficult case to handle…but this morning he states he had not had to do any 'bellowing' so I guess is feeling better in himself…"

There's no doubt about it, Spencer, Waldie is a psychological misfit. He hasn't been happy here and I think he would probably be happier in Hongkong. One extraordinary thing about him is that he never reads a single damn word. He has never looked our books over to see what we have nor evidently picked up a magazine. He has been working quite well in the yard on JCRR jeeps and his Chinese is improving a little.

[Letter of 29 September to Spencer Coxe.]

Waldie's luggage has at last caught up with him. In Waldie's absence (he is still in the Can. Hosp.), [Dennis] Frone has burgled it. Hence I have some classy paper to write on (worthy of you at least, mon brave)…

God knows what Waldie's [hospital] bill will be. Three patients' bills came to 290 silver dollars this week – pretty steep for people they have messed up in the past and are now trying to put right.

[Letter of 14 October 1949 to Spencer Coxe.]

Waldie is still in hospital and as he has fluid on the chest still is likely to be there for another month. He has given up smoking and seems to be full of grouses. He says when he didn't want to eat they forced it down him; now he wants to eat he can't get enough. There is another foreign doctor up there now, Ian Robb, who will look after him better than Allen, who has just been off on another jaunt and is due to go on another in a few days time.

[Letter of 19 October 1949 to Spencer Coxe.]

Overseas Chronicle Two, Shanghai, 8 November 1949

We are grieved to announce that on 26 October, ROBERT WALDIE died at the Canadian Hospital in Chungking, following an operation for an intestinal obstruction.

Robert was one of the most recent Unit members to arrive in China. He had gone immediately to Chungking to work on Transport, and after a very few weeks was taken to the hospital which acute appendicitis, in mid-September. It was his and our loss that he should die before becoming known to the Unit and growing into the fraternity that binds us together. It was his and China's loss that he did not live to render the service to which he was called. Robert was interred at the Friend's School burying ground in Chungking.

Our sympathies go out to his parents, William and Nina Waldie, of Kimberley, British Columbia.

To Mark Shaw, Hong Kong. 27 October 1949

Dear Mark,

I hope you and the rest of the good folk in Hongkong are recovering from the shock of receiving my last two cables, the one announcing that Bob [Waldie] and

I were planning to fly to Hongkong tomorrow [presumably to take Bob for further treatment or convalescence], and the next, sent less than 24 hours afterwards, announcing his death. His end came very suddenly indeed.

Herewith I am enclosing a copy of a letter written by Dennis to Bob's people. This letter gives the whole story very well indeed and I think it is a letter that his family will be grateful to receive. My reason for sending a copy to you and to Spencer is to show you how completely taken by surprise we all were here too.

I also hope to include copies for both you and Spencer of Stewart's [medical] report.

FUNERAL ARRANGEMENTS After our return from hospital yesterday morning Dennis went to see Harold Morrison, the one remaining foreign Quaker here, and a local architect. Harold lives at the Friends' School [in the hills above the south bank] in the grounds of which Pip Rivett is buried. [The FAU member who had earlier died of polio.] We thought it would be best to put Bob next to Pip if this can be arranged. Harold promised to make arrangements with F. L. Yang, Headmaster of the school, and the funeral was fixed for tomorrow afternoon.

The path from the river up to the school

Dennis then carried on to the hospital to make arrangements about purchase of a coffin and hiring coolies to carry it four miles up the mountain to Ch'ing Shui Ch'i. Here it will be put on one of our trucks and taken to Huang Kuo Ya, whence it will be carried about half a mile upwards to the burying place overlooking the valley.

I had suggested to Dennis that he ask Mr McHattie of the Canadian

Mission to conduct a short service at the graveside, but Hattie says that both [doctors] Stewart and Ian Robb are going to Chengtu that day and he would not be able to leave the hospital. This morning therefore I sent across to the CIM [China Inland Mission] to see if they could provide someone and Arnold Lea [their director] immediately promised to do this and sent us a very sympathetic note.

I have approached the British Consul here about the procedures of registering the death. Apparently as Bob was a Canadian citizen this has to be done through the Canadian Immigration officer in Hongkong. Lea has given me his address and I will write to him as soon as I have obtained a death certificate from the hospital. This afternoon Dennis has gone up to the hospital again to superintend the placing of the body in the coffin, to collect the death certificate and report, and to attend to the rest of the details at that end. It is a good job Dennis is here to do all this running about as although I am very much better [after surviving typhus] and made the eight or nine kilo circuit [to the hospital] au pied yesterday without too much trouble I am exceedingly glad that I didn't have to do it again today…

Dennis brought back the [medical] report on Bob so I will now copy this out. I am not qualified to comment on it but I am surprised about the dysentery. Bob as far as I remember never had squitters [diarrhea] while here. His complexion was always yellow but so is that of many North Americans; he never complained of tiredness or other signs of anaemia. He had no cough but was an exceedingly heavy smoker, would get through a packet of 200 Chinese fags in three days. The Sunday before he was taken ill he and John [John Peter] went out to Pei P'ei, a beauty spot about 80 kilos away, and Bob seemed to enjoy this outing and a feast with Chinese members of the JCRR very much. He always seemed cheerful, he was on excellent terms with John, and often spent his evenings with the boys in the club or with the employees in their homes, picking up Chinese quite fast. Some nights he boxed a couple of rounds with John before retiring to bed on the verandah. He had an odd streak, not reading, very slow to learn, telling improbable tales about his prowess and adventures, but he was getting into Unit ways, and the employees liked him, which is always a good sign. We miss him very much.

Yours,

Jack Jones.

Overseas Chronicle Two, 8 November 1949

ROBERT WALDIE

(From a letter from Jack Jones, October 29, 1949)

"In the morning I put up a note saying that the garage would be closed in the afternoon and the burial would take place at 3:30. I went across the river to collect the man from the CIM [China Inland Mission] and to buy a wreath, and a representative of the boys accompanied us. The usual series of misadventures took place. Bishop Bevan of the CIM had already left for our place aboard a CIM station wagon which we somehow missed. I got held up by other business in the city, then when we got to the ferry a truck slid off the ramps and had to be unloaded, which took an hour; then on its next trip both engines of the ferry failed and it drifted down to Chiao Tien Men [the main Chungking port area], and had to be rescued by a passenger ferry (steam), and ignominiously towed back. As a result we got back to the garage after 2 p.m.

"I was very pleased to find that all the employees now in the garage were in their best clothes and proposing to attend the funeral. Many of the men now on the road or at Chengtu were represented by their wives. In addition there were a few friends from the village and neighbourhood. The truck driven by John, was very heavily loaded for its trip over the First Range and I took the Bishop and some of the wives up in the jeep.

"Jeep and truck dropped their passengers in the village of Huang Kuo Ya and both vehicles proceeded to Ch'ing Shui Ch'i, where Dennis was waiting with the coffin and the ten coolies who had carried it the four miles up the mountain from the hospital. The coffin, a typical Chinese one, lacquered black without decoration, was put on the truck, the coolies climbed on, and we proceeded the two kilos back to Huang Kuo Ya.

"A vast crowd had gathered in the village and a procession was quickly formed. Two white bands, thirty yards long, were tied to the bamboo frame from which the

The path in the hills

The graves, Friends High School, Chungking

coffin was slung and our employees carried these in front of the coffin. Between the tapes four employees walked carrying four large wreaths and behind them and between the tapes walked John, Dennis, David, the Bishop, and I. Ahead of course went the fuel coolie with a never-ending supply of crackers and behind the coffin as is usual came the numerous women and children belonging to the FAU and the people of Huang Kuo Ya who were interested.

"Thus arranged we toiled up a narrow ledge on a very steep mountain side which is thickly planted with Scotch pines. Between their trunks is a magnificent view across the valley to the second range on the top of which the summer residences of the missionaries are placed. Next to Bob's grave on one side is Pip Rivett's [the FAU member who had earlier died of polio]; on the other side lies the daughter of a former English teacher at the Friend's School. The hillside is thickly carpeted with flowering bushes, ferns and brambles and in the trees overhead are numberless golden orioles, magpies, and hoopoes, with other attractive birds. I have often sat there with Horace Holder [a young missionary teacher at the school] or alone and can tell you it is a very fine place.

Wen Feng Ta, the old pagoda overlooking the Friends High School in 1996

"Owing to the steepness of the ground it was difficult to lower the coffin into the grave but the coolies managed very well indeed. As soon as the coffin was in place one of the apprentices let off an interminable string of crackers. Then Bishop Bevan mounted on a chunk of rock and called for silence. At the graveside were Harold Morrison, representing the Society of Friends; Mrs. MacLauchlin and Michael Yih of the IRC; John Peter, Dave White, Dennis Frone, Chou Ming Chen and myself, members; more than twenty employees of the FAU; about thirty wives and Chinese friends; and about a hundred spectators from the village.

"I had asked Bishop Bevan – a cousin of Chris Barber [executive secretary of the FSU and later to be chairman of Oxfam], by the way – to make the service short and simple and in view of the large number of our boys present to make it bilingual. The Bishop read a short passage from the Bible – a familiar piece ending, "O death were is thy sting,' but in my ignorance I don't know where it comes from – and then in a short Chinese address he told how Bob had first got interested in China through meeting a former Unit member, Joe Awmack, how he had come out here actuated by a spirit of service, how he had died while still very young, leaving parents and sisters

Looking down on the school and Huang Kuo Ya, 1946

to mourn him, and then he explained the meaning of the passage he had just read. To everybody's surprise there was complete and respectful silence throughout his discourse. This was followed by a short prayer in English and by a short passage from the burial service - 'dust to dust, ashes to ashes, etc.' This concluded the service.

While the grave was being filled in, the choir of the Friend's School – about forty boys and girls – unexpectedly arrived with their conductor and ranging themselves on a path about thirty or forty feet above the grave they sang an arrangement of, 'Nearer, my God, to thee' very beautifully and very movingly indeed. I can honestly say that I have never heard the Chinese sing western music better.

"When the grave was filled in – the best earth being put next to the coffin and then the great chunks of sandstone rock, which in their turn were covered with good soil – the four wreaths were set up on tripods as is usual in China at the four corners of the grave, and our employees, standing in a semi-circle around the foot of the grave, performed a brief ceremony of their own, ending with three ceremonial bows towards the grave. John then drove all our people home while the Bishop, Dennis, Mrs. Mac, Dave, Harold Morrison and I were the guests of Dr. F. L. Yang, head of the Friend's School, and his wife, Dr. Joy Hua, at a Chinese meal at their house. We didn't feel much like eating but it was very kind of them as they were in the thick of some sort of convention and exceedingly busy.

"In every way the ceremony went off well. The Chinese elements were spontaneously introduced by our boys, which obviously marked real respect and affection for Bob. Bishop Bevan, an Anglican, adapted himself to the circumstances very well and we could not have had a better man to conduct the service. Dennis made all the arrangements and I'm sure Bob's family would be grateful to him for his successful efforts.

Note: Dr Yang Fang Ling, the head master, was soon in 1951 to be imprisoned for life by the communists, accused by members of his own staff, and he died in prison in 1960.

Robert Alexander Waldie was born on 5th July 1927 and as described died on 26 October 1949 following a second operation for peritonitis aged only twenty two. From British Columbia, Canada, he had left San Francisco in May 1949 for Shanghai but following the communist liberation his ship had diverted to Japan, and he took a second ship to Hong Kong. After his journey of four months it is thus no surprise if he was somewhat tired and disorientated on arriving to the culture shock of China and meeting Jack and the boys in Chungking.

Early in 2013 I visited the Friends High School and received a warm welcome from the teachers there. I climbed the hill to look for the graves and it was as spectacular as Jack describes, but this was probably the wrong place and of the graves there was nothing to be found. However, a plan of the school since discovered in the Friends archives marks the, 'Monthly Meeting Burial Ground' and this would be the most likely focus for a future search.

The school was a beautiful and peaceful place that FAU members often visited when they could and I fully understand why.

Colin Bell, FAU chairman in Chungking and Dr Eleanor Sawdon walk the hills above the school

Teresa Hsu and others coming down the path from the hills

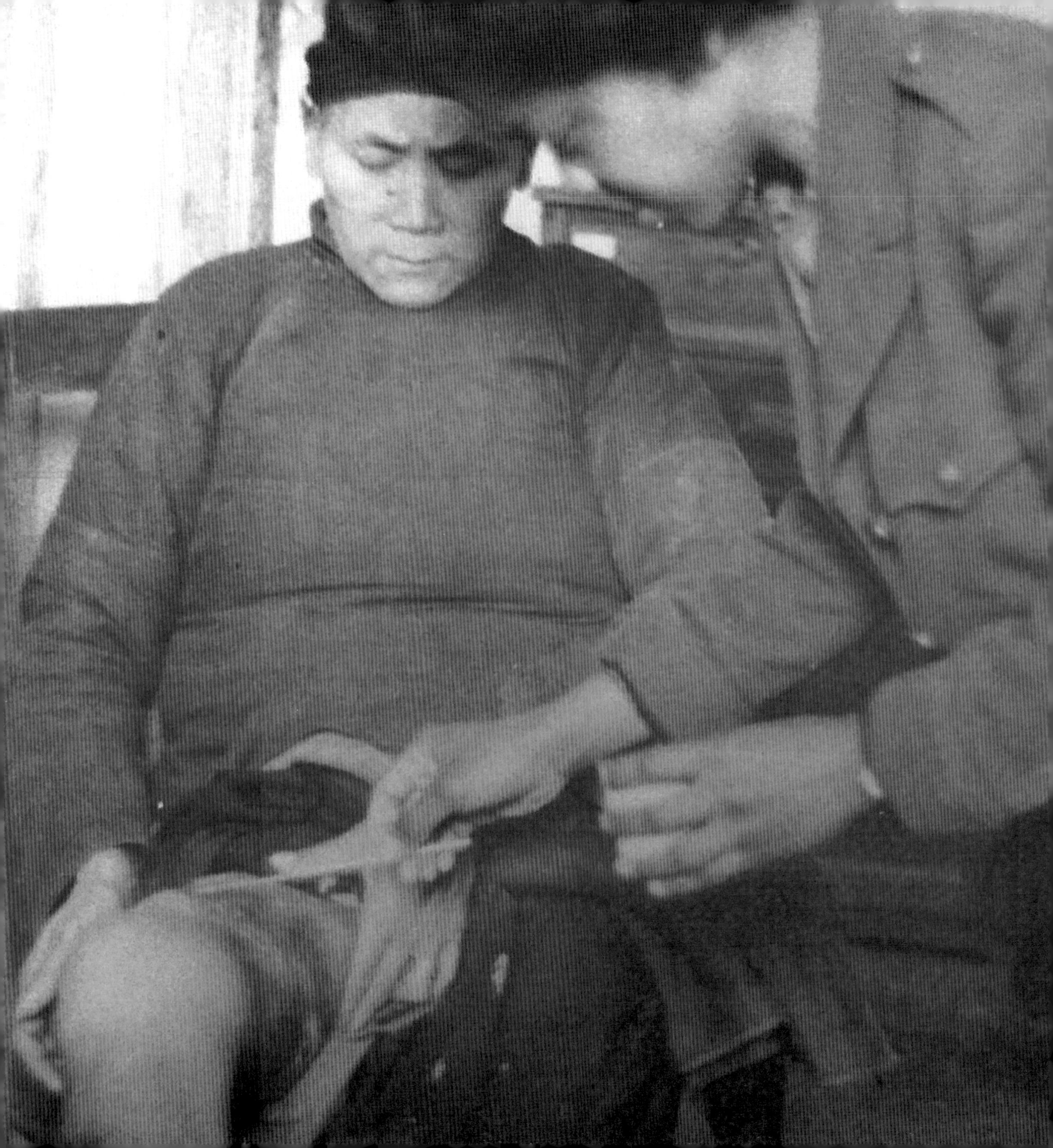

9 JACK'S NEW CLINIC AND THE STRUGGLE TO RECRUIT STAFF – NOVEMBER 1949

Jack's proposed public clinic at the south bank depot now receives formal approval from Philadelphia, thus opening up to the local populace the clinic he has always run for the employees and their families. Dennis Frone prefers his work in Hong Kong as executive secretary of BUAC (British United Aid to China) but has been helping Jack in Chungking since his battle with typhus. There are many issues to deal with, of bringing in new staff and ensuring that the clinic is adequately supplied as the communists come ever closer. On top of all this Jack desperately needs a break after four gruelling years in China, the last three as transport director.

Overseas Chronicle Two, Philadelphia, 8 November 1949

NEWS OF THE UNIT

Telephone conversations between Shanghai and Philadelphia on 24 and 25 October confirm that the Unit is still able neither to import any new members into Communist territory, nor to obtain travel permits for members already there.

Meanwhile, plans proceed apace for a new West China project to absorb the new members accumulating in Hong Kong and to give the Unit a second toehold. Shanghai has approved the assignment of Dr. Mary Mostyn, Fleda Jones and David White to Chungking, to make a hospital out of Father Jones' famed South Bank Clinic. David White is reported to have flown to Chungking on 24 October, and Dr. Mary Mostyn on 5 November for a kan-i-kan [meeting]. Presumably Fleda Jones will follow shortly if all goes well. Supplies are on hand and in our next issue we hope to announce the beginning of work...

Robert and Dorothy Reuman bound for China

The Hong Kong section has been enriched by the arrival of Dorothy and Robert Reuman. They will presumably work at the refugee camp where the Unit hostel is situated, until a more permanent assignment is made.

[Fleda Jones and the Reumans soon joined Jack's growing medical empire in Chungking. Dr Mary Mostyn had arrived there first but decided it was not the place for her and moved on to Chengtu.]

More about Dr Mary Mostyn and closing the transport unit

Jack was desperately keen to recruit a doctor for his new village clinic but when Dr Mary Mostyn arrived on the south bank, things didn't go to plan. His struggle to work out what went wrong is now set out in a long letter to Mark Shaw. Then follows below my long note about Mostyn and her interesting personal relationship with celebrated author and sinophile, Dr Han Suyin. This traces their time together as medical students in London, later as flat sharers in Kong Kong after Mostyn left China and finally when she stayed for a time at Han Suyin's marital home in Malaya.

Jack sent the following long handwritten letter to Hong Kong where it was typed up and mailed on to Shanghai, London, Philadelphia and copied back to Chungking. It survives as a very faint carbon copy in the Friends archives in Philadelphia, the typist apparently having added the introductory note in brackets.

COPY

(Note: This letter which completes the recent story of Chungking finally arrived here in Hongkong on the 28th [November], three days after the first letters, of which copies have already been made and sent.)

IRC Chungking Garage
November 15, 1949

To Mark Shaw,

Don Moore, first of ECA, and then of JCRR, having closed the ECA/JCRR office as of today, is flying out [to Hong Kong] on the 18th. This is probably our last chance of getting a letter to you. I am only sending one copy as I don't want to weigh the chap down; you said before that you would make copies and I hope that in this case you will do so.

Mary Much of what I have to say concerns this young lady [Mary Mostyn, Jack's long awaited new doctor]. As you know, she flew here on the 5th but we didn't actually contact her till the 6th, as like Dave [White] before her she accepted a lift in a private vehicle from the [out of town] airfield to the city and the said vehicle broke down eight times. Mary spent a good deal of time pushing and arrived in town late at night, having come over the mountains and hair pin bends without lights. Next morning she walked out to our place, arriving before we were up (it was Sunday). [For a young woman arriving for the first time in China alone at a military airstrip, reaching a teeming city in the dark, using the ferry next morning and then walking several miles to the garage while being constantly stared at cannot have been easy.]

All last week the pattern of her life was that she would work in the clinic till about ten o'clock and then go across the river to fix things up with the police etc. She also went to see Dr. Hua who runs a clinic at the Friends School, Stewart Allen at the Canadian Mission Hosp. and Sister Mafalda [at the Catholic Hospital]. She booked a return passage to Hongkong and sent off a cable that must have struck you as pretty daft, as she omitted to fill in the relevant dates. Then air traffic ceased practically, but there was still a chance of the Lutheran plane coming in and every day she went across with Dennis to try to contact it. She sent off another cable saying send Fleda immediately [the much hoped for new lab technician]; obviously that day she was still in favor of developing the clinic here. She made a list of pros and cons in which the cons outnumbered the pros, but she still seemed in favor of this place till yesterday a.m.

She had given us some shocks before this. Like the night when she said she proposed to fly back to Hongkong and go home till about April. We knew one of her parents was ill but the calm way in which she spoke of breaking the contract rather surprised us. She was certainly planning to go back to Hongkong and if she had done so I don't think she would have come back here.

I don't know what she expected here, but she didn't seem to cotton on to our clinic. For the first few days there were not many patients, but when the news got around that she was here people started flocking in, and today John [John Peter] and I had to cope with about forty, which took all morning for both of us. Mary seemed to be very reluctant to "have a go" with the clientele, she was obviously bored with the women and never examined them; and she quite often refused to do things for patients, saying they were obviously TB and there was nothing she could do, or that she didn't have the right medicine and equipment, or that she didn't have enough experience. John, who helped her every day as nurse and translator, was often astonished and used to come in puzzled and angry. She did the oddest things with medicine, refusing to give soldiers treatment for scabies on the grounds that our stocks of sulphur ointment were small, yet she could give someone a hundred vitamin tablets at one go, although both John and I told her never to give anybody more than three days medicine at a time, for obvious reasons. [They'd sell them.] She re-arranged the medicine cupboard, but though forgivable, John and I can't find what we want now!

Yesterday morning she once again got ready to chase the Lutheran plane and while she was waiting for the jeep I tried to get at what she really thought about things. She said the following things. (1) This was no time to start a new project here. (2) There was so much uncertainty about supplies, equipment and the attitude of the new regime to a new project that she didn't think it was worth starting up here. (3) She was conscious of her inexperience and wanted to work with more experienced people for a time. (4) She didn't think there would be enough work for Fleda.

To these points I replied as follows. It was very important that she should make her mind up soon if she feared she was going to be frustrated here, for if she hesitated much longer she could be bound to stop here for a spell. If she wanted to go back to Hongkong I might be able to arrange a passage on the JCRR plane. She said she didn't want to go to Hongkong and waste time there again, she would rather go to Chengtu. This was the first time she had mentioned this idea.

I tried to reason with her on the subject of her experience, pointing out that however inexperienced she was she was more knowledgeable than anyone for miles around, but she constantly repeated that she did not want to work on her own. She asked if we had any trucks going to Chengtu and I said no, but there might be a JCRR jeep going. She said that Chengtu had been considered as a possible FSU [Friends Service Unit] project, that I myself had said that more than 50% of the foreigners had left the [West China Union University] campus [where the hospital was], and she was sure that the right thing for her to do was to go to Chengtu. She criticized the Unit for sending out people like herself ill-equipped, without language training etc. I didn't know whether to put my foot down and say "stop here and make a go of it" or "go to Hongkong or Chengtu if you think you will be less frustrated there"; I have held all along that Mary is the doctor and if she comes here it will be her show; it is for her to decide. I have done enough of bossing doctors around in Yunnan [on the anti-malaria project] and I didn't want to say to Mary, "Do this," and then have her miserable for months.

All this discussion was perfectly friendly though I am not sure that Mary is being absolutely frank; she has been exercising the female prerogative (of changing her mind) overtime, and there must have been something to make her make it up so quickly yesterday. Possibilities: the fall of Kweiyang [to the communists], something distasteful to her in my approach to her problems, dislike of this place or of us, her failure to recognize that Mrs. Chi Hsu Lin was seriously ill (emergency op. for ectopic gestation after Mary had insisted she wasn't ill). These are surmises. Most of the time she seemed happy enough, playing patience and kan-pei – ing everybody at the feast I gave to the blokes of the Hanshung and Kunming convoys on Sunday. (They've all got back, God bless them).

To cut a long story short, Mary went across [the river] to see about the Lutheran plane and get her passport back from the police after this talk, and got an exit visa for Chengtu. This morning she got a letter of introduction from me to Dr. Leslie G. Kilborn and went across the river early with Dennis today to catch the JCRR jeep. [Kilborn was a member of a prominent medical missionary family and working at the university in Chengdu.] However, JCRR have chartered one of our trucks to go there. Tonight she is staying at the Canadian Business Agency [a missionary supplies agency, having a guest house with spectacular views overlooking the river] and tomorrow a. m. she

Views from the Canadian Business Agency, Chungking

will beat it to Chengtu with Mrs. Chang Ming Sang's husband as driver. [Mrs Chang Ming Sang's husband is Chang Ming Sang!] John and I are a bit cut up at the turn things have taken. We are both extremely keen on the hospital idea. We have decided we can't tell people we can't deal with them and we did our best with everybody who came today. John was doing most of it while I took the gynae cases (chaperoned by Mrs. Yang Chien Yeh) in an inner room. Mary never examined one but I had four really interesting ones this morning.

Jack.

Han Suyin, her lesbian lover and Jack Jones

Though her books are largely overlooked today, the author who called herself Han Suyin once had enormous prominence on the world stage as a novelist and historian of China and also as a self-appointed spokesperson and mediator for understanding between communist China and the West. A qualified doctor and polymath, she was a remarkable figure and it is sad that her death in Lausanne, Switzerland aged 95 in November 2012 attracted only a few short obituaries in the Western press. Despite her prominence as a bridge between China and a sceptical western world for several decades, the published obituaries were sparse, though happily her profession honoured her with a full obituary in the British Medical Journal of 12 January 2013.

Jack Jones was extremely well-read and he drops many literary references into his writings, but although some of Suyin's family lived in Chungking and her life intersected with his at several points, he never to my knowledge made any mention of her in what he wrote. As an aspiring writer he must have followed her career book by book and she may have influenced his work. If the flowery titles for the many books she successfully published were listed along with the elaborate names for the books Jack aspired to write but never did, it would be impossible to tell them apart. Their writing styles are sometimes similar, their fiction was invariably based on their own life experiences and curiously they both wrote in some detail about their traumatic operations for haemorrhoids. There are thus many similarities, though in contrast to Suyin, Jack was overtly and exclusively heterosexual.

Dr Mary Mostyn who Jack recruited to work at his clinic in Chungking was a close friend of Han Suyin. Together with a third friend, Cherry Heath, as from September 1944, the three women had studied medicine together at the Royal Free Hospital in London and in the early fifties, inspired by Suyin, they met up again as doctors in Hong Kong.

In 1962 Han Suyin published a novella called *Winter Love* about a lesbian affair between fellow medical students at the 'Horsham Science College' in London. On page one of the book it is 20th September 1944 and the first day of a new term. Han Suyin's female protagonist and narrator is talking with a friend about sharing a locker and is eyeing up a new and elegant student called Mara. *Winter Love* is described in a brief article on Wikipedia as an autobiographical novel about Han Suyin's acceptance of her own bisexuality.

Han Suyin also wrote an autobiography in several volumes and in the third of these, *Birdless Summer,* she wrote as follows. 'In September 1944, I entered the Hunter Street School of Medicine for women... In that first terror-stricken half hour, someone came up to me and said: 'I say, will you share my locker?' and that was Cherry Heath, who was to remain my best friend.'

As Suyin describes in some detail, she was at that time trapped in a loveless marriage with Tang Pao-huang, a Nationalist Chinese general who had been posted to London as a diplomat. *Birdless Summer* also tells us that after a major row with him, Suyin had suffered a near breakdown and moved out to stay with a friend called Margery, an older single woman. 'And now Pao tried to start a legal action against Margery,' she wrote. 'He had an uncanny knack for ferreting out gossip... there had been some rumour about... her friendship with another woman...'

In this book and elsewhere Han Suyin is very frank about her own periodic frigidity towards men. 'Though I endured the sex act, it was extremely painful, and almost unbearable', the consequence, she said, of Pao's abusive behaviour towards her. She was, she says, 'like the Ice Queen' towards both male and female, though she admits to the prevalence of lesbian friendships around her. 'During the war and afterwards with so many men away at war, in camps, in uniform, lesbianism seemed more natural than heterosexuality...'

In 1946 Pao was recalled to China for military service and in October 1947 he was killed in action. Suyin was sharing a flat with Cherry Heath just across Coram's Fields from the hospital. By the end of 1948 she had done a year as house surgeon at the Royal Free Hospital and had to decide her own future. She chose to return east to Hong Kong to be as close as possible to her beloved China and Cherry Heath and Mary Mostyn saw her off at the airport.

In Hong Kong she worked at Queen Mary Hospital, first in February 1949 with Professor Gordon King in Obstetrics and Gynecology for a year (where she failed to thrive as a surgeon), then moved to the Department of Pathology under Professor Hou Paochang, in May 1950 becoming a Casualty Officer and in February 1951 being put on the permanent staff.

During this time she had fallen in love with Ian Morrison, an England-educated Australian who, in succession to a famous father, G.E. Morrison, was a correspondent for The Times. In late summer of 1950 Ian was killed in Korea and she expressed her grief by writing the story of their love affair in the form of a novel. This was published to great acclaim and some controversy in 1952, Morrison being married with two children, under the catchy title, *A Many Splendoured Thing*. An award winning movie and a hit song then assured her fame.

When I was reading Han Suyin's fourth autobiographical volume, *My House Has Two Doors*, the name of Mary Mostyn, Jack's reluctant recruit to Chungking, caught my eye. This is how the passage goes.

'In February 1951, I [Han Suyin] became a "permanent" employee in [Hong Kong] government service and was allotted in March a government flat to share with another doctor. And as usual hazard, chance – or God – provided me with a sharer in the person of Mary Mostyn, my other friend from the Royal Free Hospital besides Cherry. I had made many entrancing bicycle excursions through the English countryside with Mary; her mother was a Yorkshire woman and fed me most wonderfully. Mary Mostyn, Cherry Heath. Both had decided to come East. I like to think there was in both of them a fundamental English romanticism, a spirit of adventure. But I think it was also my being in Hongkong that decided them. Mary had become a Quaker and was posted to China in 1949. And she had landed of all places in my own province of Szechuan, in Chengtu! But she arrived there only four months before Chengtu was liberated by the Communists. In January 1951 she became part of the exodus of missionaries from China. 'Any atrocities? was the first question she was asked (as were all missionaries) when they reached Lowu.'… Mary, Yungmei [Suyin's adoptive daughter] and I moved into the [university] flat which was luxurious with three bedrooms and two bathrooms, a living room and a verandah. Mary was provided with a job in the Medical Department…. I typed [my novel] at night and worked in Casualty by day…. Writing was now a frenzy; not solace or an opiate, but compulsion, insidious mastery of the white page waiting.'

Leonard Comber and Dr Elizabeth Tang (Han Suyin) marry

Then Suyin met Leonard Comber, a British police officer serving in Malaya who was on leave in Hong Kong and a friendship developed between them. 'I think an unplotted, well-meaning conspiracy to make me marry Leonard began', and they were married in 1952. But the marriage wasn't to last. 'For so many years, due to Pao, I had been like one dead, and then Ian had come, and I was now alive… What I did not know then was that this condition of mine, total repugnance for sex, would recur and recur, again and again. Sex would always be impossible unless there was love, a climate of love, a whole world of feeling and tenderness in which the body's act was submerged, necessary and evident. I did not think that Leonard was built that way…'

After the wedding Comber went back to his police work in Malaya taking Suyin with him. In *My House Has Two Doors* she quite casually drops the surprising fact that Mary Mostyn, her flat

Bob Reuman's shot of Lamma Island from Pokfulam, near the hospital, Hong Kong

sharer in Hong Kong, went too. 'Mary had come with Leonard and me to Malaya, and obtained a job at SATA, the Singapore Anti-Tuberculosis Association. She lived with us, and went across the Causeway to the city every day.' This was a long commute to work and the arrangement must have seemed somewhat strange at the time. The book then describes the failure of the marriage but no further mention is made of Mary.

Suyin is gracious towards Comber in describing their split up, though she is pitiless in reminding the world that he later became implicated in a horrible murder. Having lost his police career apparently because of his marriage to Suyin who was regarded as a communist sympathiser, he had moved to a new job in Singapore. Finger print evidence showed that he was having a shower in a female friend's flat while she was lying strangled in the bedroom. Suyin tells us how she then rallied to his side and took him out to lunch with her lawyer, for good measure bringing along Vincent Ratnaswamy, the new man in her life she was later to marry. Thanks to her lawyer's intervention, she claims, there was no prosecution, gratuitously adding that it simply wasn't in Leonard's character to kill someone.

Han Suyin's personal and emotional life was therefore complex and her house, it seems, had ever revolving doors. However, to the story of Jack Jones' work in China this may now seem tangential, apart from the chance intersection of these several lives. Howell Jones, Jack's friend from his Chungking garage, was studying medicine

Han Suyin, Robert Hart, Dorothy Reuman and Dr Mary Mostyn (seated)

around this time at Queen Mary Hospital where he tells me he remembers Han Suyin franticly writing her tragic novel whenever she could find the time. Mary Mostyn was back in Hong Kong when Jack arrived there in rags and tatters at the beginning of June 1951 escaping from the communist regime and it was Howell and Mary who crossed the harbour together and met him off the train in Kowloon.

A few months earlier in April 1951, Robert Reuman, the last FSU chairman, together with his wife, Dorothy, had reached Hong Kong from Shanghai and he wrote home saying, 'We have been staying here in the spacious and lovely apartment of Mary Mostyn. As a doctor at Queen Mary Hospital, HK's finest, she is provided with this superb flat enjoying a panoramic view of one side of Hong Kong harbor, and normally shares the apartment with a Eurasian woman doctor and her beautiful little girl, Yu Mei. At present, however, this doctor is recuperating elsewhere from an operation…' This of course was Han Suyin, in fact recovering from a nasty bout with that writer's complaint, piles. The Reumans were soon to meet Suyin, then known as Dr Elizabeth Tang, and Robert took photos of her with Mary, Dorothy and Bob Hart, a good friend of the FAU, relaxing on a balcony at the hospital, not long before her fame as a writer blossomed.

Whether Jack again crossed paths with Mary in Hong Kong is unimportant but if he did he could very possibly have met Suyin. By chance he was much later in Bangkok to meet her by then divorced husband. In a recent email exchange, Leon Comber, who I myself met a number of times in Hong Kong in the late seventies, told me how as director of Heinemann Books in Hong Kong in 1974 he had commissioned publication of Jack's book, *Daughters of an Ancient Race,* after meeting him by chance at the offices of the Bangkok Post.

As another irrelevant aside, I too well remember the wonderful views from those flats near the hospital, having lived in one of them for several years while lecturing at Hong Kong University. It was in mine that Bernard Llewellyn stayed with me on his visits to the region for Oxfam and first told me about the Friends Ambulance Unit China Convoy.

Returning to the trio of doctors, I have little idea what went on between them in London and Hong Kong and it is of little direct concern except perhaps in explaining Mary Mostyn's personality and behaviour. Suyin certainly had a close friendship with Cherry Heath but Cherry was soon to meet an English architect in Hong Kong and they were married and returned to London in 1952. There they went on to have three children, while Cherry, according to her husband's obituary, became 'a leading pediatrician'. With Cherry thus lost to Suyin, we now hear how Mary and Suyin later lived together both in Hong Kong and in Malaya, despite the presence of Leon.

Even if she herself was perhaps capable of playing a double game, could Suyin have been angry with Cherry for defecting to the other sex? There is an extraordinary passage in a blog article of 2007 by an English woman called Mary Mather, who has recently died aged 83. A life-long campaigner for the rights of women who herself never married, she'd known the trio of woman doctors when she was lecturing at Hong Kong University in the early fifties. Mather describes Cherry as 'tall, angular and square-shouldered', a description Howell Jones knowingly endorsed in an email to me, adding, 'for some strange reason, I recall her very large feet in open sandals'.

Writing many years later, perhaps drawing on a diary, Mather introduces her story about them as follows.

'While Dr Elizabeth Tang (Han Suyin) was writing her best-known novel *A Many Splendoured Thing* she came to my flat in the university from time to time with a chapter for me to read and comment on. In July 1951 she asked for a favour: as I had a spare bedroom, could her friend Dr. Cherry H stay with me while her flat in the hospital was being renovated. I knew that Elizabeth, Cherry and another friend, Dr. AB, [presumably Mary Mostyn] had trained together in the Royal Free Hospital in London and come out together to Hong Kong. I readily agreed. It was while Cherry was staying with me that Elizabeth designed and commissioned a tailor to create a dress for Cherry and the following incident took place.'

This was on 11 July 1951 just at the time her novel was finished and about five weeks after Jack had arrived in Hong Kong and was 'walking the Queen Mary hospital' with his old FAU friend and medical student, Howell Jones.

Cherry is in Mary Mather's flat, the tailor is fitting Cherry's dress and Suyin, 'imperious as always and ravishing in her elegant Chinese cheongsam dress, is in command'. Suffice it to say that Suyin throws a tantrum, petulantly saying that the tailor has ruined the dress, much to everyone's embarrassment. Suyin subsides into a chair and Cherry, sitting on the arm, gently puts a hand on her shoulder and in a soft caressing voice as if she were comforting a small child, tenderly says, 'Not to worry, Bun, it doesn't matter', all of this said with 'the muted gentleness of a very strong person, loving, forgiving, consoling'.

Mather is also fitted for a dress at Suyin's direction but Suyin is scathing. 'It makes you look awful, doesn't it Cherry?', to which, 'with relish', Cherry replies, 'It would suit someone I know in the hospital who has black hair and blue eyes, but it makes you look insipid.' Whether or not Mostyn had blue eyes is not recorded.

All of this was happening after Mary Mostyn had returned to Hong Kong from China but, in the light of their London experiences and the novel about a lesbian affair, the story of the three women might possibly hint at why

Dr Mostyn behaved as she did on her arrival at Jack's clinic in Chungking. Coming from a very female society in London, even if not necessarily a lesbian one, she confronted a male dominated world in Chungking where the men all lived in close proximity in a crowded bunk house. They generally fell in love with Jeanette, the Chinese hostel warden and there were often guffaws from Jack in his news letter articles about women and the complex changes of sleeping arrangements when an occasional female colleague passed their way. A group of lonely bachelors, Jack in his late thirties being older and perhaps more desperate than the others, their only solace was cuddling the puppies that Phoebe, the top dog, regularly produced for them.

As Jack had put it in his letter to Mark Shaw, was there 'something distasteful to her in my approach to her problems'? Did she have a, 'dislike of this place or of us'? From the other side, she too had not gone down well in Chungking and as Dorothy recorded in her letters home, John Peter in particular took against her, bluntly saying that if Mary was recalled to work at the clinic in Chungking, he would resign. While Mostyn did apparently consider the possibility of returning to Hong Kong, the difficulty of obtaining travel permits and flights in fact precluded the idea.

Though Jack had what he himself called 'a weakness for women', his orientation being beyond question, my ever-wise informant, Howell Jones tells me that 'Jack's sexual antennae were much too sensitive' for him to have made an inappropriate move on her in such a situation. In his view, Mary was perhaps too young and inexperienced for the very primitive situation in Chungking and understandably preferred something more structured in Chengtu. Furthermore, her doubts about the wisdom of expanding the clinic at this difficult time were soon to be justified by events.

Fleda Jones in the clinic

Having tried desperately to get a plane back to Hong Kong, she had thus taken the only other option and made the hazardous journey to Chengdu, getting totally soaked and frozen on top of a truck, in order to join Dr Kilborn at the university there. As told in *Birdless Summer*, Suyin knew Kilborn well as the 'friendly muscular man who spoke excellent Szechuanese' who in 1939 had set her up with medical work on her arrival with Pao in Chengtu. It was almost certainly she who had recommended him to Mary as a safe pair of hands who would take her in if Chungking proved impossible. Kilborn had been born into a Canadian missionary family and went to the Friends children's school in Chungking, though not himself a Quaker. In 1952 he went on to be on to be Professor of Physiology at Hong Kong University where Howell Jones did a postgraduate year as a research fellow under his supervision, remembering him with great affection.

Though Jack thus failed to retain Dr Mary Mostyn's services, his next recruit, Fleda Jones, the American lab technician, was to be successful with Jack in more ways than one. A hard-working addition to the team in the clinic, Jack fell hopelessly in love with her causing more than ripples on the pond, an uncomfortable story that is told below.

So what happened to Dr Mary Mostyn after she'd left Hong Kong with Suyin to work at the tuberculosis association in Singapore? In July 1954 the Straits Times records that Dr Mary Mostyn, a chest physician at the Royal Singapore Tuberculosis Clinic had been awarded a scholarship by the National Association for the Prevention of Tuberculosis. In 1974 a doctor of the same name was recorded as attending a respiratory tract morphology conference at the Lovelace Clinic, Albuquerque, New Mexico, USA. In 1976 while working in that same clinic, the same person swore a court affidavit supporting a damages claim, having treated an actor playing a cowboy who was dying of a chest disease caused by smoking the Marlboro cigarettes he was advertising. At this point the Google trail runs cold but Dorothy Reuman has since told me that Mary did indeed settle in New Mexico.

An unusual name with the same medical speciality, this was of course the Dr Mary Mostyn who had been so close to Han Suyin and who ran a mile on meeting Jack Jones in Chungking. It would have been difficult to trace her movements after Singapore if she had adopted a married name, though Dorothy tells me she never in fact married.

The last of the medical supplies and money worries again

Following this long digression about Han Suyin and Mary Mostyn, we return to China less than two weeks after Jack's last letter to Mark Shaw bemoaning the loss of Mary. Mary has been in China for about three weeks and is by now in Chengdu. Jack is still pondering what exactly went wrong but is now anticipating the arrival of Fleda Jones, the long promised lab technician.

The following letter was again handwritten by Jack and typed up in Hong Kong for circulation with many typos appearing. The carbon copy in the Philadelphia archives is as transcribed below, the words in round brackets apparently being inserted by the typist in Hong Kong.

COPY

IRC Chungking Garage
Nov. 21, 1949

Mark Shaw
Hongkong

Dear Mark,

Where are we now? A hell of a lot of male (sic) has come in this weekend – a letter from Crauder via Philippines on Saturday [Bob Crauder, FSU Finance Officer]; about thirty letters for Dave and Mary yesterday; and a letter from my father today. This seems to show that CAT [Civil Air Transport] is running and I am encouraged to address a letter to you. Please have the secretarial-wife that we have heard so much about copy it out and send it hither and yon as you deem necessary.

CABLES Yours telling us to expect Fleda sometime came through on the fourth day after you sent it and we promptly contacted CAT [to ask when she might arrive]. But the military have now taken over the Hai Tang Chi ferry entirely and it is extremely difficult for us to get out to the CAT office [across the river]. However, we have six trucks on yon side and also an ex UNRRA ex AIS ex JCRR jeep which we expect to be able to collect today. This will be our town runabout and if we get word in time that Fleda is coming we will endeavor to meet her with that jeep, escort her across the river and meet her with another jeep this side.

Prior to the arrival of your cable I got off one as follows: PLEASE SEND EMPLOYEES REPATRIATIONS [money for severance payments] WITH FLEDA STOP MARY JIGGERED OFF TO CHENGTU THURSDAY STOP MOORE ECA FLYING HONGKONG NINTEENTH HAS LETTERS. Don was delayed till yesterday I believe but I trust you now have this letter.

MARY She hasn't communicated with us direct but word came through JCRR that the truck reached Chengtu safely on the 18th. A rather wild letter from her arrived yesterday – posted in Hongkong before she left. She doesn't seem to be a very stable character. I shouldn't be surprised if on finding air transport resumed she wings her way straight back to you and damn us and WCUU [West China Union University].

THE TWO LETTERS I have received from home since my illness show that the whole family was thrown into distraction by the news of my serious condition. I know my family are especially prone to melodramatise these incidents but I hope that if I fall ill again people at home will not be given the impression that I am on my deathbed until I am. Average mortality including epidemics is only about 22% and it usually takes a bloke about ten days to die so the best thing is to drop the word serious during the first week of illness. Of course I can't have typhus again but if I get anything else please understate rather than overstate the seriousness of my condition.

Mary certainly left us in the lurch over the clinic and John and I were flat out all morning, John doing most of the men and kids and I doing the women (if you know what I mean), and the VD of both sexes in the inner room. I don't know how many patients John gets; I get 20 a day at least and have been forced to start a card index system. Luckily I am not so busy with transport as I was and I can spare several hours a day. We badly need someone trained though. We get some terrible cases of this and that, and some which are less terrible and some which are downright sources of pleasure; e.g. Mrs. Chang Ming Sang has got mastitis again, one of five cases now undergoing the old Jones technique. Since writing that sentence we have just had a girl brought in with threatened abortion due to malaria. Where the hell was Mary?

A local missionary who owns a command car came in yesterday and said that at last the Lord had given her a lead on what to do with the car when They [the communists] come. She is to put it into our place for the engine overhaul which I advised her to have three months ago and which the Lord then said was too expensive. We are to take our time over the overhaul as she won't need the car for several months after the visitors come. The Lord thinks the vehicle will be safer with us.... Love to all.........

(signed) Jack

cc: Shanghai, London, Philadelphia, Chungking, Shanghai conference

Mary again, Fleda Jones and the dying days of transport

This letter was typed and signed by Jack and mailed to Mark Shaw in Shanghai, Frank Miles in Hong Kong, Douglas Turner in London and Spencer Coxe in Philadelphia. Fleda Jones, the new lab technician, has just arrived in Chungking.

IRC Chungking Garage Nov. 24, 1949

Dear One and All,

Fleda got here yesterday and she's just what the doctor ordered and the morale of the section is already looking up. If you've got any more people like Mr. White and Miss Jones recruit 'em and send 'em to China because they don't expect plush seats in the mao-fangs [latrines] and they are ready and willing to do anything for the cause and they get on with the job and keep everybody happy. Thanks for sending these two people, Spencer and Mark, and thanks Frank for OK-ing their coming.

Fleda brought in so many letters and copies of letters that the sense faints picturing them but I am about to make a supreme effort to answer everything. First however I must bring you up to date.

MARY. You will all know by now that Mary got here, blew hot and cold on the clinic idea for ten days, sent off a couple of contradictory cables that had Fleda flummoxed and Mark anathematizing my name and all

David White and Shau Mei, Sam Yen's little girl

things West China, and then, when brought to bed of a fine argument of mine one wintry morning, she left me quite speechless by saying she had already got her visa for Chengtu and was going that day or the next. As father of a section that has usually come to my knees and told me too much rather than too little I was quite bowled over by this final independent action of Mary's and rightly or wrongly let her carry out her plan. In any case there was no plane connection with Hongkong and if she wanted to get out of Chungking which seemed to be the case it was better for her to go there while the going was good rather than remain frustrated and unhappy here. I don't blame Mary altogether but I cannot comprehend why she could send off such a silly cable as PROJECT DOUBTFUL SEND FLEDA SOONEST when she already had a Chengtu visa in her pocket. I am extremely glad that Fleda after cogitation decided to come here and that after 24 hours here and after spending the morning in the clinic she has decided that there is a job for her here and has made up her mind to stay put. But we have jumped to the happy ending without filling in the details since last Thursday, when Mary left; so I will retrace my steps a bit.

The day Mary left we got a cable which said, "FLEDA FLYING CAT LAIN LELAYING" [sic] and I promptly sent off a cable [asking her to bring the repatriations money.] Then the days went by and every day we saved a supper for Fleda in case she came but she never did and Monday I wrote to Mary thus:

"It appears that air contact with Hongkong has been re-established and you may want to take advantage of this. Since by leaving here you have shown that you don't approve of our cottage hospital scheme (the object of your looksee trip) it would be in order for you to go back to Hongkong. If however you have made any arrangements with Chengtu people you won't be able to do so. Also if Fleda comes in response to your cable we shall have another problem on our hands. If Fleda comes here and you do not get work in Chengtu you will have to come back here and work in the clinic; if Fleda comes here and you have got work in Chengtu we shall have to decide whether Fleda is to work in Chengtu or here; if Fleda doesn't come in it is up to you to decide whether you stay in Chengtu, return to Chungking, or go back to Hongkong, for no question of a 'section' will be involved."

Tuesday night we were informed that Fleda and a couple of rickshaws full of luggage had arrived at the Canadian Business Agency and next morning early CMC [Chou Min Cheng]

Lungmenhao some years earlier

galloped across by sampan to get her away before Rackham's bill [for accommodation] got into the millions, accompanied by me. Slipping and slithering along from Lungmenhao [after the sampan back to the south bank was swept way downstream] to Hai Tang Chi [where the road meets the ferry], Fleda said, "I can understand why Mary didn't like Chungking." In fact Fleda, while allowing that there may be something in Mary's contention that she was inexperienced, that she preferred to work under another doctor, that she thought that she was going in to kala-azar work [an FAU disease prevention project], that her father was seriously ill, and the other reasons Mary gave for not wishing to stay here, believes that basically Mary just can't rough it. She likes things to be nice, and was even dissatisfied with living conditions in Hongkong. [The hostel rooms at the North Point Relief Camp.] If that is so she couldn't have chosen a better place than Chengtu to go to. The missionaries there all live in palaces and running water is not unknown.

Today I got the following from Mary, which I have had deciphered at tremendous expense (she certainly is a typical doctor as far as her calligraphy goes) : "I arrived up here on Friday midday after 3 days of hardly de luxe travel – but great fun – the truck was loaded to capacity as there were 12 Wongs. I sat for the [??] time on a plank above the driver's cabin – very cold and very wet. Of course no one spoke English but I was fed and conducted to the mao fang at regular intervals! At the moment I'm in the thick of a truly ripe cold.

Well, to business.

1. There is plenty of work everywhere here so I start in the obstetrics gynae department at the end of the week – as soon as my bugs have left me. There is also plenty of work for Fleda if she comes to West China.

2. Money. At the moment I'm staying with the Kilborns (Dr. Leslie Kilborn. Hospital supt. WCUU – Ed.) but will be moving out to the Sewells (Bill – local quaker cheese – Ed.) at the end of the week as they are very anxious for me to be with them. [See William Sewell, *"I Stayed in China"*, George Allen & Unwin, 1966.] I will need my maintenance here – the approx costs at present standards which are unstable is 80 cents to 1 dollar gold a day. I'll also need a little extra for sundries – toilet things etc – and if my trunk doesn't reach me here - I'll have to buy clothes. (Fleda brought Mary's luggage but lost one piece en route – Ed.) So can you let me have some money fairly soon – if it is impossible to maintain here I will try and see if they can give me my maintenance.

3. Can you send me some of the Unit finance forms – as I will have to keep records of accounts.

4. William Sewell says has Dennis got some money for him – the FSC [Friends Service Council] here are very poor and are living very simply etc."

So there you have the present position chums. Mary has set up a one-man show in Chengtu. Fleda has arrived here and says she can't see any reason to move on when anyone can see with half an eye that there is plenty to do here. I honestly don't think it is worth recalling Mary from Chengtu as Dennis, John, Fleda and I all feel that she wouldn't be happy here.

THE CLINIC – NOW. We are now in the position of having enough drugs to carry on for several months, two male nurses, and a lab. tech [Dennis Frone, John Peter and Fleda].

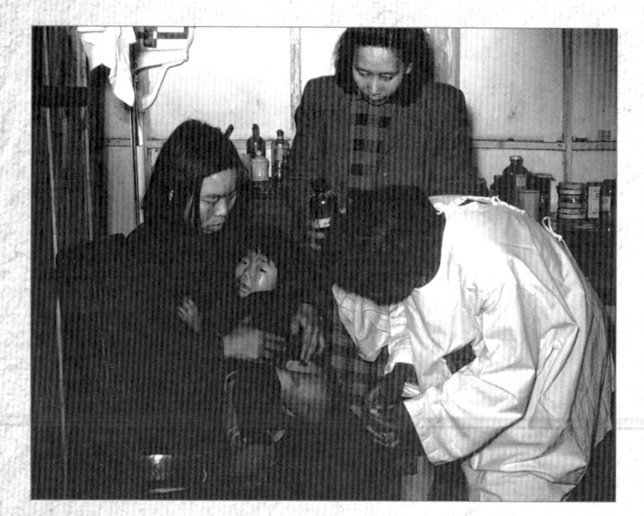

Fleda was applying dressings and giving me the benefit of her previous experience in a VD clinic this morning and she saw plenty of scope amongst this morning's patients for doing lab work too with the people we already have. With what we have and what we can get here she can hunt for worms, TB bacilli, malaria bugs and the gonococcus, she says, plus other things. She says what we have here is just right for our needs and she does not think that there is going to be any question of waste of a lab tech if she stays. But for all our sakes it would be better if we had a doctor here, especially as Miss Jones [Fleda] seems to get anxious to get rid of the locum tenens (me). She thinks I ought to go while the going is good and come back refreshed later on, and I agree. In a private letter to Mark which I have seen, Fleda stresses again and again that no doctor or nurse is going to be any good here unless he or she is willing to work under rough conditions. She seems particularly sorry that Phyllida Thornton couldn't come and thought that Phyllida would have just been the girl for the place. [Thornton had arrived in Shanghai in November 1948; FSU Chronicle 77.]

The trouble is that we now have one doctor in West China and though she is doing the Unit no good she is probably our quota. We are hearing about Chuck MacGraw – if he has plenty stuff in his [illegible]... says - but I understand that he is now working at the CIM Hospital at S'hai so Shanghai will be more reluctant than ever to part with him, I mean in this direction. We can get nurses here, Chinese, but what we want to raise us out of the amateur status is a medico. NB, Mark, when Fleda said that she didn't think Dennis would take my place in the clinic she didn't know that he is an old clinic hand from [working for the FAU in] Syria and has had more training if not more experience than I have.

TRANSPORT AND REPATRIATIONS Dave with six trucks is running the remaining ECA supplies at Pei P'ei hither and yon at Dennis's behest. Dennis blew in last night and blew out again this morning to Pei P'ei.

[David White told the story in his letters home of the anxious moments to get everything done before the communists arrived. "Transport work goes on for some unknown reason. The agencies which provide the supplies which FAU transports are withering, dying or pulling up stakes and leaving. But there still remain things to be transported and in the great haste of these agencies to close up we are called upon to distribute the last of the medical supplies. The range of our activities is being reduced all the time so most of the runs are short and take only a day or two."]

CMS [Chang Min Sang] returned from Chengtu safely yesterday and by a stroke of luck got across the river this morning. (Yesterday when we went down there we found that the ferry, tired of all the army trucks, had sunk, and CMC [Chou Min Chang] and I had to cross by sampan and passenger ferry, which now starts from a shoal of detritus from Tibet and Tsinghai in the middle of the river, the water being low)...

I suggested to Stewart Allen that it was up to the [IRC] Committee to see that our

boys got repatriations as their work is now done and he replied [by letter]: " Your letter has been received and the contents have been digested somewhat. .....I see no reason why one of our organisations should not handle these (repatriation) funds through its account and I believe that such could be quite easily arranged." He then talks about using the trucks as security and not holding the mission that handles the dough responsible for delay or non-payment. He then says that he will arrange for the committee to discuss which mission will be involved in the transaction. This will mean, Mark, that you pay gold or Hongkong dollars or what have you into the mission account in Hongkong and they shell out here in one form or other to be decided in consultation with the mission and bank. I am going to see Stewart tomorrow to get the wheels turning, as every second counts now [with the communists coming closer].

FUTURE OF TRANSPORT. TSO has cabled advising us not to sell our Ssu Kung Li godowns. [Dr T.S. Outerbridge was medical director of the IRC based in Shanghai.] Does this mean that trucks also will be needed, Stewart asks? Echo answers, does it?

One thing peeves me with Stewart's letter. In his last sentences he says "I assume that this amount is required by both foreign and Chinese to be dismissed or repatriated. Am I correct, for this amount seems a lot for the Chinese staff alone..." Doesn't it get you down, when the IRC Standing Committee approved the sum last June?

One other thing in Stewart's letter peeved me. My bill at the Cath. Hosp., including first class room and treatment and the ministrations of at least one angel (not Sister Mafalda), came to 212 dollars silver. Poor old Bob's yesterday is 839.20. [Dr Stuart Allen's bill for unsuccessfully treating Bob Waldie at the Canadian Mission Hospital.] In case you think it is all the ops. he had, that only comes to 75.00. Worst touch of all is the note at the bottom: "Please pay in silver if at all possible." We won't even be able to pay in paper this month...

WHY DO I WANT HOME LEAVE? I don't really. I'm like Greta Garbo, with a slight difference: I want to get away from it all, that's all. Seriously my nerves are in shreds and the slightest little thing gives me a fit. I am in no state to be a figurehead of a section in a crisis. Only last Saturday a damn soldier came in feeling in his hip pocket and I nearly died; he whipped out his hand and I did die. But it was a visiting card, not a gun. He was looking for Sugar Bean but I was in such a sweat I could hardly stutter out Gerbee, (which is Szechuanese for next door). I used not to be like this, and I've had my share of bayonets, swords and pistols. Do you want me to tell you about the time…? All right, all right, but you wait till I see you next time. I want to stay here and see things through but I repeat I am a danger to myself and the Unit until I get over my typhus.

If there's anything left unsaid remind me sometime.

All the best to you all,

Jack.

Note: Greta Garbo, Swedish actress, 1905-1990, is quoted as saying, 'I never said, "I want to be alone." I only said, "I want to be left alone".'

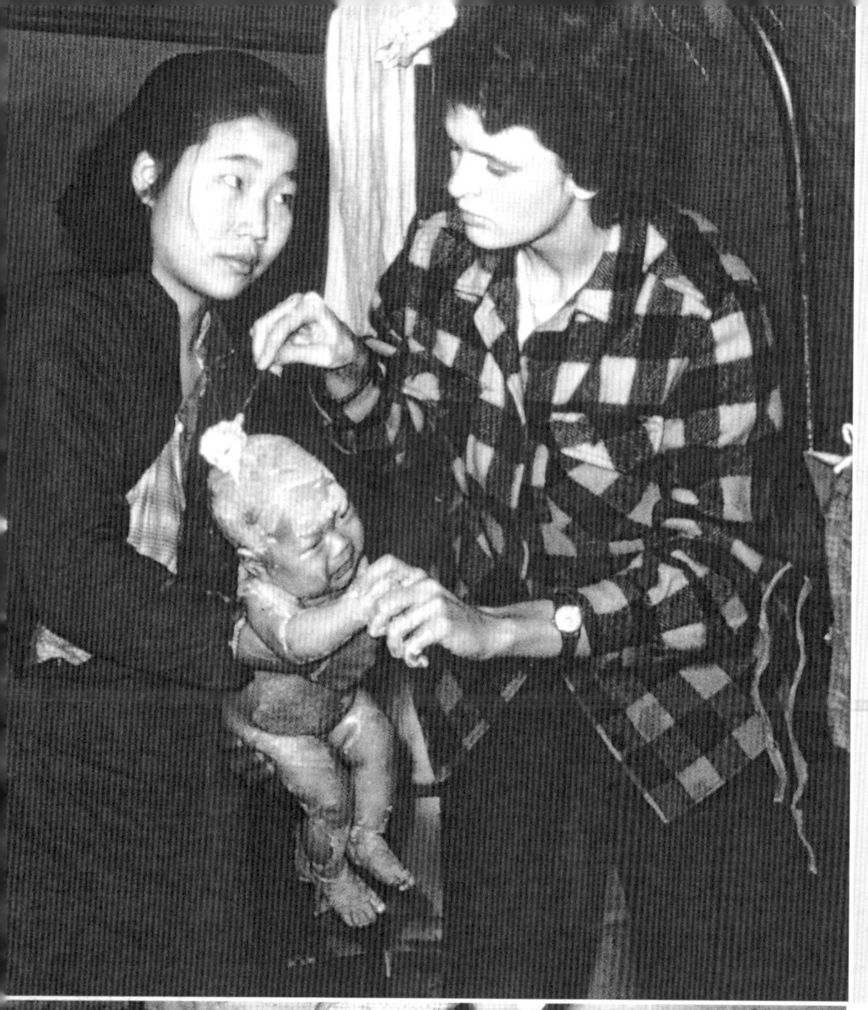

JACK'S CHUNGKING CLINIC

The pictures show Dorothy Reuman treating a child for scabies in the old truck body in which sufferers were scrubbed clean with hot water to eradicate the disease. It was a painful experience and they didn't always come back for more. The old man is sure to be suffering but he will be cured if he persists with several treatments. Fleda Jones, the lab-technician is shown in the room in which she slept and worked, while Sam Yen is anointing some boys also suffering common skin diseases. John Peter is seen treating patients, Dorothy is dealing with an again common eye problem and Fleda is seen using a breast pump, probably to alleviate mastitis or other infection.

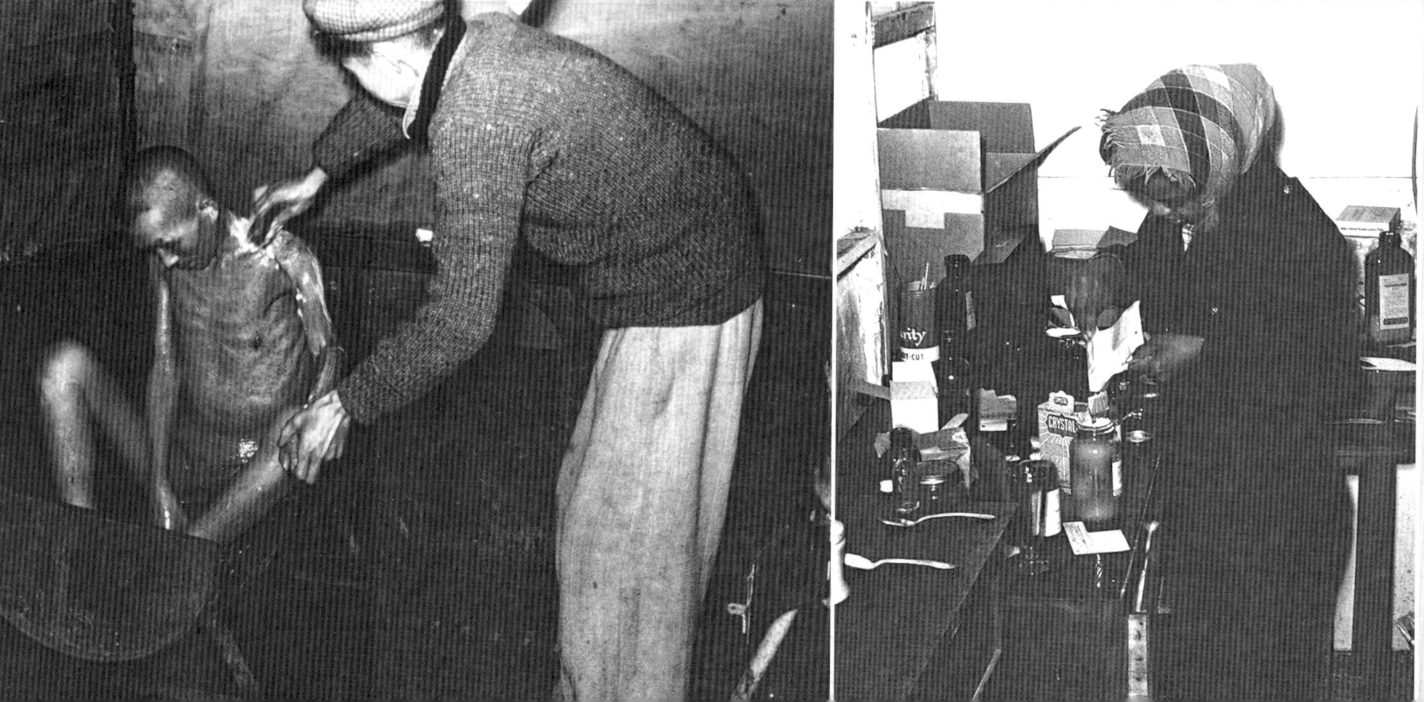

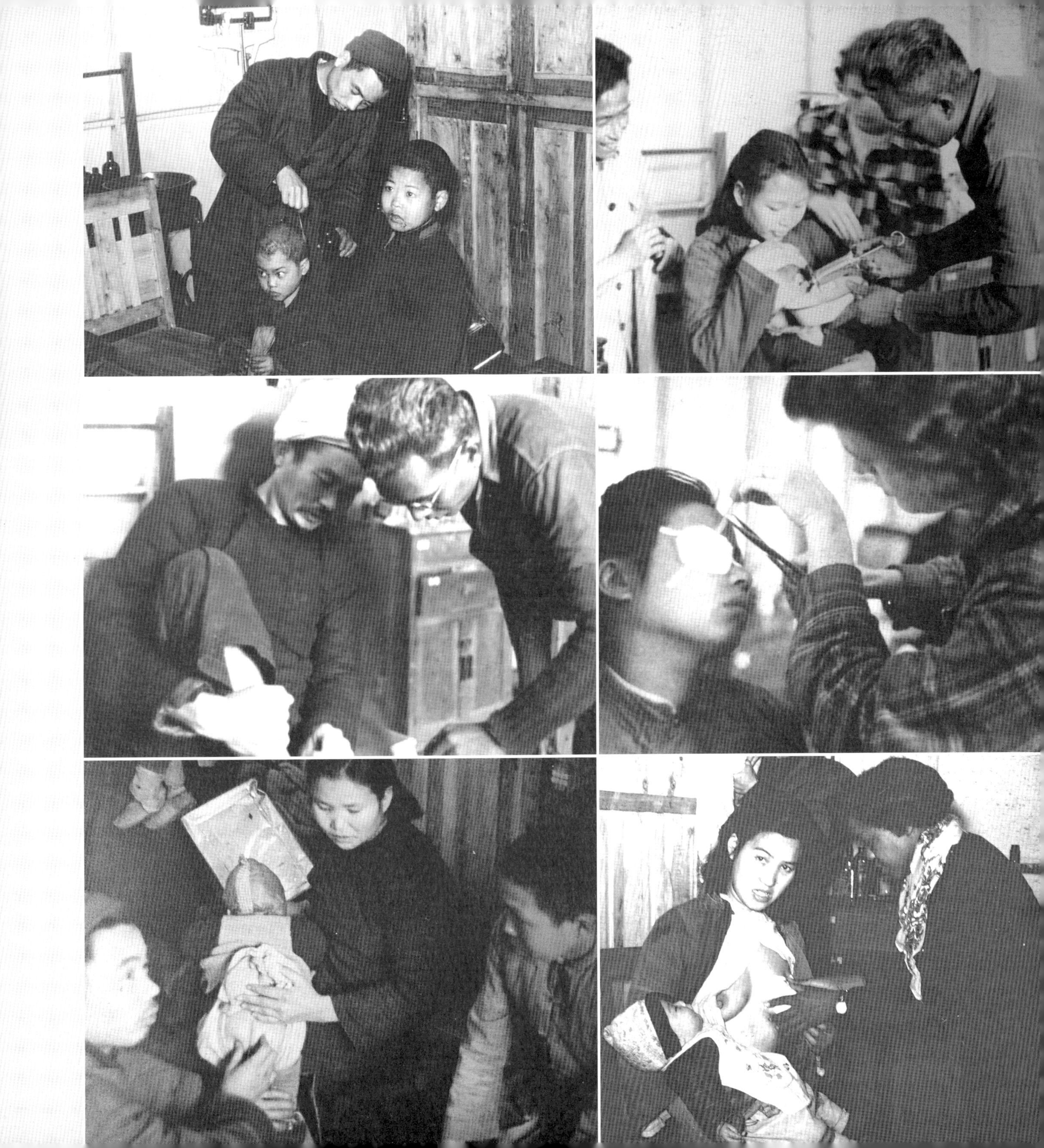

Jack's clinic is born into uncertain times

FSU Chronicle 104, Shanghai, 26 November 1949

FUTURE OF THE UNIT

It was the "Future of the Unit" which principally concerned the Council Meeting that has just been held in Shanghai. A series of informal Section Meetings, on this subject, had already been held both in Chungmou and Shanghai, and from the Minutes of those Meetings, several important facts, not available before, had become clear before Council met.

First of all it had been unanimously agreed that the Unit, as a Unit, has a future as far as Unit Members themselves are in a position to make this so. Secondly, repatriation, so far, has been confined only to Members whose contract time is finished or is overdue. Thirdly the Chungmou Hospital was neither to be closed nor devolved before next June at the earliest. Apart from all this, new medical personnel have arrived in Chungking with the object of starting a small Hospital there under the directorship of Jack Jones.

Chungmou hospital, built by the Friends

A letter to Make Sure

Jack's handwritten letter below took five weeks to arrive in Hong Kong, as Mark Shaw, who apparently typed it up there, mentions. Shaw was not to know that at the south bank depot the day after it was mailed, loud explosions and gunfire were heard and communist soldiers appeared in the garage yard. His typed version in the archives is now transcribed as follows.

This letter, postmarked Nov. 29th arrived in Hongkong on Jan. 5, 1950

COPY

Make Sure [Mark Shaw]
Hong Kong

IRC Chungking Garage
Nov. 26, 1949

Dear One,

Nobody can complain that I am keeping them short of news as no sooner have the typewriter keys cooled off after one letter that I am warming them up with another. Things keep happening and in the two days since I last wrote the following has happened.

REPATRIATIONS Fleda accompanied me on a visit to Stewart Allen yesterday and never have I felt my age more than when on the return she galloped up the final arête to the jeep leaving your erstwhile mountain chamois gasping and wheezing in the rear. [On the mountainous south bank, the Canadian Mission Hospital where Dr Allen worked was not accessible by road.] Stewart Allen proved especially tractable and readily agreed that if you can pay in the equivalent of the total repatriation funds, USD2,500 into his account, Alexander Stewart Allen with the Hong Kong and Shanghai Banking Corporation, he will give his equivalent cheques here which I can sell for whatever we can get for them and pay the boys. As a result of this I cabled you this morning:

URGENT ESSENTIAL YOU IMMEDIATELY PAY TOTAL REPATRIATION FUNDS OF TWO THOUSAND FIVE HUNDRED INTO HONGKONG SHANGHAI BANK ACCOUNT OF ALEXANDER STEWART ALLEN BORROW FROM HART IF NECESSARY REPEAT URGENT

Point about the urgency is that things are moving rapidly here. This morning most of the Szechuanese came in and asked to be repatriated at once. I told them I would

A new bamboo and thatch building in the adjoining National Resource Commission yard

be entirely happy to pay them off if I had sufficient funds and told them to wait a day or two. This dinnertime all the Ssu Kung Li boys asked if they could move into our big godowns (where the hospital was to have been) as last night several residents in the village were pressed into military service. They are willing to forego their houses to live in these old godowns and having made it clear that I could not be responsible for seeing that they weren't pressganged [as soldiers] if the pressgangers came after them I gave them permission to move. They obviously believe that solidarity is strength and good luck to them. [This move is also described in Jack's book, *Daughters of an Ancient Race*.]

Once again we had inquiries from the authorities about our fuel stocks and number of trucks this morning. The former is down to five drums or less but the number of vehicles in the yard is increasing. Sam got back yesterday with a few dollars and a weapons carrier [a six wheel American army truck] donated to us by JCRR. Old Tobacco tried to cross the river at Chu Leng Po but got bogged down in the high tide of vehicles and it will be days before he can be extricated. He went back this morning with a few rations to his truck. Miss Leininger [a missionary] has been guided by the Lord to send her command car in already for its leisurely overhaul. Except for five trucks and the UNRRA jeep which are busy on your side all our vehicles are now in the yard.

The IRC keeps on announcing that its godowns are cleared and then finding they aren't. We sent two truckloads and a weapons carrier full of beds off to the Canadian Hospital this morning. According to Mrs McCork this is positively the last but she's said that before. [This seems to be Jack's nickname for IRC employee, Christine Mclaughlin, who was probably deemed unpronounceable, especially by the Chinese.]

CELEBRATIONS Despite the tension of the times we managed to celebrate two events. At 3 p. m. on Thursday, Fleda got onto the subject of Thanksgiving dinners and after we had ascertained that pheasants would be an acceptable substitute for Turkey, and after we had ascertained that Thanksgiving Day had nothing to do with secessions or civil wars but was just a belated harvest festival, John went out and bought a brace of pheasants and Fleda gave thanks in the proper style. Yesterday [25

November] was John's birthday and he gave a feast to all the boys. The boys gave him one beautiful piece of silk, one fountain pen and one nude statue whose face John hasn't ceased admiring. We had salichiu and huang chiu and these gave John another inevitable gift at these feasts, a hangover. Mary told us Fleda didn't eat anything but she has certainly been pitching in here and she was still kan peiing [toasting] all comers after the feast was over. We kept the power on [ie the generator] and played all the old favorites and a good time was had by all. Dave got in just in time for the feast which was clever of him.

PERSONNEL With the return of Sam [Yen] and Mrs. Sam [presumably from the JCRR job in Chengdu] we have had a traffic jam in accommodation. Fleda, who was in Sam's room was moved last night into my bunk, but they moved me into the next room with John. Then David, who shares my room had to be carefully moved too; the arrival of a letter from Manila [from Leonore Perelta, his Filipina fiancée] had the expected affect and eased the job. We wondered about Dennis who also shares my room, but he didn't come home at all (he's still at [the JCRR godowns at] Pei P'ei). Today we have decided on the following movements: Mrs. MacCork, who has no urgent work to do here, to the Canadian Mission Hospital. (Stewart's recommendation, very heartily endorsed by John and me, though Mrs. MacCork did not take the bait very readily this morning and is in fact still sitting tight in the ex-Michael Yih residence next door): Sam and wife and kids into Mrs MacCork's when she has been prevailed upon to move: Fleda back into Sam's room, me back into my own bunk and Dave back into his. [Poor Christine probably didn't want to be parted from Dennis, who she eventually married in 1956.] This afternoon John, Dave and Fleda with some help are moving the clinic into the big godown we have in this yard near the gate. Reasons: the clinic is too small for its present clientele; it is felt that our expected visitors [the communists] will be charmed to see a clinic on our doorstep; Dave says all the stuff in the godown is junk and could be readily burnt anyway. Drawback to scheme; the godown has only a dirt floor, but we can get the carpenter to rectifying this on Monday.

MARY A letter from Doc Kilborn of WCUU yesterday as follows:

"About two o'clock this afternoon Mary Mostyn arrived, and for the present at least she will be staying with us. Not knowing that she was coming we had not made any arrangements in advance for her accommodation.

"She tells me she is very anxious to get some experience in obstetrical work and Dr. Gladys Cunningham who is in charge of that department of our work is quite willing to take her on in her department. So I imagine that there will be no difficulty there. I hope that her lack of knowledge of the Chinese language will not be too great a handicap. She will get along all right with our hospital house staff, all of whom have at least a fair knowledge of English. The difficulties will be with the nurses and patients. However, we shall hope that these will not be insurmountable.

You suggested that we come to some agreement as to the minimum period during which the FSU would agree to leave Dr. Mostyn here. I shall take this matter up with my colleagues, and let you know as soon as possible. Quite possibly they may wish to observe her work for a short period before coming to any decision."

Robert Reuman

Dorothy Reuman

I have written to Mary on the points she raised in her letter and mentioning how we hope to get her baggage to her. Sam gave Mary 100 silver before he left so this should keep her going for a bit. Before she left I gave her back the US dollars she had handed over to me and she had some of her pool in US too. Not much but enough for a few days anyway.

REUMANS ARRIVE I had got this far and had rushed out for another section meeting (four yesterday afternoon over moving the clinic) and had packed a missionary off to Chichiang and was just coming back when John said calmly, "The Reumans have arrived you know". For a moment I was speechless and a bit unhappy but a moment after I went around the front of the weapons carrier and met them I cheered up. In fact in one hour I had come to the conclusion that with John, Fleda, Dave, the Reumans and Dennis we have a good damn section here, (or a damn good one) and there is no need for me to stay here any longer. These people can manage. [In *"Daughters of an Ancient Race"*, Jack describes the Reumans without naming them as, 'a gigantic American ex-college football star and his pretty blonde wife, a professional cellist'. In a letter home they in turn described Jack as, 'somewhat introvertish and sensitive, possessor of a vivid English fluency and proud of a luxuriant growth of whiskers to shield his face, neck and shoulders from the winter chill'.]

If there is yet time I shall be coming out [to Hong Kong] this week. The personnel situation has certainly looked up just lately and it will be more of a wrench that I expected to leave.

Fleda got around to cervical smears yesterday. All we want is a doctor. Off my own bat I sent the following cable to ex-Unit member Philip Hsiung, now at Huei Tien [Hospital], Kunming and anxious to rejoin the Unit: BADLY NEED DOCTOR FOR FSU SOUTHBANK CLINIC WOULD YOU COME AS UNIT MEMBER WIREPLY. This is the sort of thing that a democratic Unit deliberates on for several weeks and my only excuse is that time is so short. Sam told me about Philip's interest when he came back on Friday…. Be seeing you, I hope.

Signed JACK

Nov. 29th P.S. I have decided to stay here. – J.

[A change of mind after only three days!]

Typist's comment: There is nothing to add to this letter [received in Hong Kong on 5th January five weeks after its date], as we have had no word from Jack since November, aside from the cable which the cable office assures me was sent on December 30, but which I strongly suspect was sent on November 30th…

How this letter got here is anybody's guess. Markdoddshaw

cc : Shanghai, London, Philadelphia, Chungking, Tientsin, Honan, File.

Chungking, Yangtse view

AMBUL

10 NEW LIFE UNDER THE COMMUNISTS NOVEMBER 1949 TO APRIL 1950

The Peoples Liberation Army arrives in the village

FSU Chronicle 108, January 21, 1950

EXTRACTS FROM CORRESPONDENCE

JACK JONES, Chungking, December 5th, 1949. Liberation passed off peacefully enough as far as we are concerned. We had a couple of false alarms over the weekend and all our employees not already living on our premises moved into the big godowns and camped out there. Talk about the Hongkong project – this was a real refugee camp in our very backyard. We first heard gunfire in the morning on Tuesday [29 November], just after starting the clinic. There were signs of activity all round and gunfire all that day and the next night, quite heavy, just like Guy Fawkes night. (What, have we got to explain this to you [Americans] too?) There were heavier explosions caused by [ammunition] dumps which had been mined going up and one almighty one, quite close at about 10.30 at night, broke up a bridge game and broke a number of windows. For a few moments I thought it was the V2 business all over again and I almost instinctively reached for my tin hat and stretcher but it was all right. [Jack was in London when the V2 bombing began in late 1944 and presumably worked with the FAU fire squad.] Next morning when we woke up we found Communist soldiers in our yard. [Thursday, Ist December.] Later that morning they borrowed three of our trucks and a few minutes after that an officer came in and told us our trucks were not KMT trucks and no further use would be made of them. There was no more excitement until that night at 10 when Fleda looked up and said, "Oh, what a lovely pink sky. There must be a fire somewhere." We just had time to duck when the wall by my ear came in about a foot and went back again in the old familiar way and the windows burst open over our heads and a sound of tinkling glass was heard all over the shop. This really was a bewt and blew in our bedroom wall in one place and busted several walls of godowns, etc. Nobody was hurt but we have been dealing with some dreadful casualties since. The next village down the road was completely destroyed as I saw when I was called to T'u Ch'iao the next day to see the Communist Staff Officer in this district. I must say this officer and the other Communists I have met this far have made an exceedingly good impression. The officer asked us about the Unit… We were told to carry on as usual until the political officers arrived, and this we are doing to the best of our ability.

The Frone and White [Dennis and Dave], who on Monday had set off for Pei P'ei, were meanwhile having fun and games on their own. They went to Pei P'ei loaded down to the gunwales with refugees and troops. The changeover there was peacefully made. All nationalist troops passing through were fed by the populace, then posters were stuck up to welcome the Communists, then they turned out to be more Nationalists and the posters were taken down again, then the Communists really came and they put the posters up again. Dave was asked to take Communist troops to Ch'ing Ma Kuan and as he figured that we have had to help the Nationalists before but are supposed to be neutral, he took it as an opportunity to even things up… he had no difficulty in getting a permit to leave.

Dave and Dorothy describe being liberated

David White's widow, Carol, has sent me Dave's letters home from Chungking. One of these, nine typed pages long, tells the story of clearing the JCRR godowns at Pei P'ei of the final medical supplies and it tallies precisely with Jack's account. Dave tells in detail how the town's authorities were desperate to placate and feed the fleeing Nationalist rabble and to move them on as quickly as possible before welcoming a small, polite contingent of communist soldiers. His full story of being commandeered to transport the communists, an unknowable crowd of soldiers with whom he could not communicate, was in fact a far more challenging experience than Jack makes out.

Dave's letters also describe how on the eve of the communist liberation Chungking city was waiting in terror as its occupants saw the currency collapsing and sat on the roadsides selling what little they had before evacuating in all directions to places they hoped might be safer. Ragged bands of Nationalist soldiers could be seen retreating up the road past the FAU garage towards the city, the whole place awash with fearful rumours. "On Monday", Dave wrote, "we thought [the communists] had arrived. A story circulated about a battle which had taken place less than twenty miles down the road. More than a hundred men had been killed and several civilians. Everyone naturally considered it to be a battle between the two opposing armies and that we would be liberated by the Tuesday morning. But late Monday afternoon we got the details of the incident. The fight had not involved the two armies, only the Nationalist army and the state police. It seems the soldiers were jealous of the police because they had better uniforms than the army and some small spark set the whole thing off. Before the smoke had cleared away a fully fledged battle had developed, one of the few in this war in recent months."

In a memoir of 2003 that Dorothy Reuman has sent me, she describes the actual liberation night in a way that again is more graphic than Jack's laconic newsletter version that appears above. "One evening, about three days after we arrived [in Chungking from Hong Kong], we were playing bridge, when I looked up out of the window and said, 'Oh, what a brilliant sunset!' And then we all simultaneously realized the sun doesn't set at 10:00 in

Bob Reuman's shot of 'arriving communist troops on the road outside the Unit.'

the evening! And the sound of an explosion rattled the windows. The retreating Nationalists had blown up an ammunition dump about a mile away. We later learned that they also set fire to a prison in Chungking that night, and machine gunned all of those who tried to get away; the inmates were mostly political prisoners, including young students from the university. We spent part of the night down in the garage in one of the grease pits, and heard occasional small bursts of gunfire in the distance. But nothing else happened. The next morning, the young soldiers walking along the road in front of the clinic had red Communist stars on their hats, instead of the blue KMT ones. And fewer of them had shoes, and there were fewer small horses to help carry the loads. So we were liberated. Had we come [to Chungking] later, we would never have obtained permission to enter China, but now we were inside, and it remained to be seen what we could do to be helpful and how long we could stay. The history books, of course, have a much bigger tale of liberation to tell; this was just ours."

One of Dorothy and Bob's first letters home from Chungking gave greater detail. 'We are in no danger,' they wrote for their parents' benefit, 'but we were close enough on Tuesday to hear considerable rifle and machine gun fire on several sides. Tuesday night there were six or eight big explosions, probably occasioned by Nationalists dynamiting, some across the river and some quite close. First we'd see a pink haze lighting up the nocturnal mist, then after from five to twenty five seconds a rushing, rumbling roaring sound which would shake our flimsy walls and burst open the unlatched windows. There is no danger from fragments due to the great distance and even if the concussion should blow the house down there would be no danger because the walls are only plaster stuck lightly over bamboo lath and the roof a single layer of tiles; but it gave us an eerie feeling anyhow especially the first time the windows blew open. There we were playing bridge by candle-light, the electricity having been off for some time, a brilliant flash outside, followed so much later that we had recommenced our game with a big whoosh of wind and sound which blew open the windows and tossed the candle flames into a frenzied dancing. Wednesday morning the communist troops were stationed all around, at the gate, across the valley, and on the hill tops where the Nationalists had been digging in the day before. There was no fighting around though Wednesday night, last night, the blasts continued, one rather close on this side. Jack passed through the area today and said that a mile either side of the blast was levelled with debris all over the road, apparently due to a time bomb left by the retreating Nationalists.... So far as we are concerned, I believe the war is over.'

Dorothy and Bob's earlier letters home from Hong Kong tell how without a moment's doubt they had willingly flown into this incipient war zone. Kicking their heels working at the North Point Relief Camp in Hong Kong, they were desperate for clearance from the FSU leadership to enter China. On Friday mid-day they received a cable following an FSU council meeting in Shanghai which read, APPROVE REUMANS CHUNGKING. They immediately rushed to book a flight, to pack and write their final letters home. At four on Saturday morning they woke the snoring crew of a sampan and crossed the harbour to the Kowloon side. Checking in their bags at the city terminal they rode on top of the baggage truck to the airport. They arrived in Chungking that Saturday, the second to last flight in, and the communists reached Chungking on the Tuesday. These were truly exciting times.

In one of his letters home Dave White told his family that he had been out of Chungking at the time of the liberation and first saw communist soldiers in Pei P'ei as he was clearing the JCRR godowns of the last medical supplies. He went on to say that the fleeing Nationalists when blowing up the ammunition dump, 'did not even bother to warn the 2,000 employees living on the premises. Over 300 political prisoners had been locked in huts which in turn were set on fire and then machine gunned. A little too late to do much good a guard threw the keys into the prisoners and only ten escaped. One explosion in the neighbourhood blew out our windows and caved in the wall of our hostel.'

Just by being in Chungking, David and his colleagues had thus voluntarily put themselves in harm's way, caught in the middle between two rampaging armies and dreadful things could have happened to them. As it transpired, the arrival of the communists was a welcome change from the unpredictable Nationalist soldiery. David White's letters go on to tell the same story of how Jack Jones and Chou Min Cheng had an informal interview with the new local commanding officer who courteously told them to carry on their work as before but that some soldiers mistook their trucks for government property and borrowed three of them to haul their troops, in return for a formal receipt. Hardly had the trucks been taken when an officer returned them on realising the mistake.

His letters also praise the surprisingly good conduct of the enlisted communist soldiers who were orderly, polite and friendly, keeping Dave well supplied with cigarettes when he was driving his truck for them. He also makes some perceptive comments about the inevitable need for the communists to assert China's nationhood. "I hope Pearl Buck is wrong about the communists and that they will bring to China the strong central government she needs so badly', he wrote to his family. 'I fear nationalism is a prerequisite for a desire to live on an international level. Until the peoples of the world are organised in their respective units it is unreasonable to expect them to think in terms of international brotherhood."

Writing eighteen days after the liberation by the communists, he also saw signs for optimism if only the wider world could give them positive support. "So far, our dealings with the Communists have been most encouraging and satisfactory. They are willing to get down to business and deal with the matter at hand. They treat the individual as a person and on the merits of his own story without trying to hold him up until he kicks thru with some sort of bribe. They deal with people on a first come first served basis, not according to how many cigarettes you can pass around. The Communists have a tremendous job ahead of them in China. I believe they represent a form of government which is needed here and which is applicable to a politically unconscious and immature nation. If they can hold to their ideals and bring about some of the basic changes and reforms needed in China, they can produce some important improvements in a single generation. They will need the encouragement, cooperation and understanding of the rest of the world and not the cold black shadow of fear and hate which some forces in America seem determined to cast over all Asia."

History suggests that he was correct and that the anti-communist hysteria typified by the McCarthy purges in the USA probably boosted the more extreme elements within the communist party and justified fears that China could only expect an aggressive stance from the West. With China re-emerging today as an economic super-power, his comments about the need to welcome her to the community of nations rather than to treat her with fear and suspicion now apply with equal force.

Shanghai HQ receives a cable from Chungking at last

FSU Chronicle 106, 24 December 1949

CHUNGKING

First news direct from Chungking since the Liberation of the City was received on December 15, in the following telegram:

GREETINGS PAL TROUBLE FREE LIBERATION PLEASE URGE TSO REMIT EQUIVALENT TWENTY FIVE HUNDRED BUCKS FOR EMPLOYEES REPATRIATIONS TO IRC WESTCHINA MEDICAL COMMITTEE IMMEDIATELY NO MORE MESSING ABOUT.

JACK

Note: The FAU/FSU were affiliated to and had taken over the transport work of the IRC (International Relief Committee). As time went on, funding for transport became haphazard and Jack had to work as an entrepreneur, obtaining return cargoes after a delivering relief supplies many weeks journey away, doing contract work for other agencies, selling scrap metal and so on. His despairing appeal to Dr. T.S. Outerbridge of the IRC for funds was for the cost of repatriating the Chinese employees following their redundancy as the Unit was obliged to give them severance payments to enable them to get home, many being refugees from other provinces, and to re-establish their lives. This issue became a nightmare for Jack and after the garage was finally closed, a big staff meeting at which tempers became frayed put long standing working relationships at risk. Jack was genuinely concerned for his men and their families and was distressed and made ill by tensions that were not of his own making.

Jack's 'predisposition for woman-trouble'

Born on 19 June 1913, Jack was now well into his thirty seventh year and was of course still single. His writings show that he had a keen interest in women but actual relationships and experience seem to have been in short supply. Clearly he was a loner and liked to be 'on his Jack Jones', as the Cockney rhyming slang of the time would have it. In 1978 he published an article in the Bangkok Post called, 'A Bachelor at World's End' which describes his three winters living as a young man totally alone at a cottage in the mountains at World's End, nine miles walk from Llangollen. Despite being at the end of the world and in perhaps the bleakest, remotest and most menacing place in North Wales, Jack wrote in the article, 'I have never been happier that when I was in that cottage'.

His life choices thus never seemed to be conducive to finding a mate. If like Jack you get back to your digs from your North Sea trawler smelling of fish or work long hours growing potatoes in Lincolnshire, and if, rather than swaggering around in military uniform you are shunned as a conshie, all the while struggling with the church's injunction against fornication, you inevitably diminish your chances with the girls. As he wrote in an unpublished article about China, 'Heaven blast narrow Welsh non-conformity. You think you have cast it off but the sense of sin is ingrained and you carry it through life'. At the same time, as a late starter and racked with insecurity and self-consciousness, you most likely make yourself miserable and obsess with the need to make up for lost time. Perhaps that was how it was for Jack.

In 1956 Jack wrote to his old FAU friend, Howell Jones, telling how in the first half of 1939 he'd rented a large house in Kent for a song because it was haunted and no one wanted to share it with a ghost. 'I did my writing in one bedroom and sculpture in another,' he wrote, 'and I wish I could say I'd done all the local girls in the others but I was a good boy then, and lavished all my affection on

Possibly Jack's cottage beneath the Eglwyseg Rocks at World's End

an Alsatian named Peter. God, how I regret my mis-spent youth… mis-spent in the sense that I didn't mis-spend it enough.'

In Jack's jottings in a nineteen fifties' note book, there is a brief synopsis for an autobiographical novel about life with the FAU in China in which the protagonist goes aboard ship bound for the East and loses his virginity in a first class cabin with one Mrs Stubein, a journalist. Though the novel was never written, this little cameo was not forgotten and in 1972 Jack used it in an article published in *Impact*, a weekend supplement to Bangkok's leading English language newspaper. In his autobiographical story, an old bore of a narrator sits in a Bangkok bar bemoaning a 'mis-spent' youth and tells how as a young man he left England by ship to work in China. 'Even when they mobbed me in my speedway days I remained as celibate as a monk,' Jack wrote. 'I were thirty two and bound for China before I first climbed into bed… actually it were a bunk in a first class cabin… and got self broke in by a female journalist, Mrs Stubein, divorcee or widow I never found out.'

Jack had indeed embarked eastwards from Liverpool aged thirty two on 3rd September 1945 aboard the Hall Line's 'City of Chester', all of whose passenger cabins were first class. The passenger list includes Emrys Reynolds Jones, 'ambulance worker', but disappointingly no Mrs Stubein is shown. However, a Mrs Ingrid Eleanor Papworth, a government official from Greenwich aged twenty seven, was on board and, with a surname like that, she might have attracted the roving eye of an inexperienced ambulance worker. On the other hand, Mrs Stubein could possibly have come aboard when the ship later docked en route, or been rescued even when sighted clinging to floating wreckage in the Mediterranean. More likely though, 'Mrs Stubein' was merely a silent and unrequited passion on Jack's part whose first class ship-board consummation was but a fantasy.

Once in China there was many a million women to choose from but for various reasons the fruit was either forbidden or had already been squeezed and blemished. It seems that Jack forever gazed admiringly at sweet young things but his yearnings were generally unfulfilled. Recently a packet containing three of Jack's lost China stories has been sent to me from Seattle by the son of Spencer Coxe, and two of the three are poignant stories about hopeless longings for a Chinese girl. In one story Jack is overwhelmed by his feelings for the young secretary who daily sits with him in his office. As already suggested, this could possibly be based on his craving for 'Miss Zoo' in July 1949 which he mysteriously refers to in his letters that appear above.

In the other story called, 'Miss Lo', Jack falls for a pretty young patient who he treats for an abscess on her 'chest'. He doesn't see her again but by chance on a staff jaunt by truck to the southern hot springs Miss Lo suddenly appears. She is standing there in dark glasses and a red dress. 'The tiny, slender, shapely figure, that delicate budding of a nose, those full and kindly lips revealing the usual magnificent teeth. I feel my own worn features breaking out and I sink and drown in the brown pools of her eyes'. She lets him take her arm and he foolishly climbs a cliff to cut rhododendrons for her. Then she accepts a lift home in the truck, sitting promisingly close to him in the cab, but she gets out at her village without taking the flowers and the story concludes unhappily. 'The bouquet bounces about on the floor of the cab. Some of the petals have already been knocked off'.

This story about Miss Lo also gave Jack's protagonist a chance to ruminate on his solitary predicament. 'Of course I have had my moments in China,' he wrote. 'But they are not the sort you remember with gratefulness of heart... The life of the foreign bachelor in China can be trying. Of course there are prostitutes galore. There are also three kinds of k'ai-p'an-tzu, but these are frustrating [possibly meaning secondary wives or concubines]. Chungking has Japanese style baths, where, if he is sufficiently Orientalised, he may be washed by a beauteous female attendant as prelude to a queer, exciting, costly evening. But if he desires decent feminine company the case is different. No respectable Chinese girl likes to be seen with a foreigner; she loses her good reputation immediately. Most girls who make friends are only out to exploit you. And what makes it worse is that well-educated Chinese girls, with their beauty, their poise, their good-nature, their easy-going manner, - the products of good breeding and urban refinement, - attract the western male very powerfully. Like a knight of old he lives under a spell, and the sorcerer is la belle dame sans merci – a la Chinoise.' What made it worse was that the FAU men were unpaid volunteers and therefore penniless, always a handicap even for the most perfect, gentle knight.

Also recently found in Spencer Coxe's papers is a funny but deeply depressing poem called, 'The Ballad of the Cheerless Adolescent', which portrays in rhyming doggerel the sexual awakening and disillusion of a precocious and woeful boy. When at nine he tried to kill himself, the twine round his neck breaks, leaving him alone in his world of woe. He'd lost all hope when he came to ten but the servant girl, whose name was Gwen, suddenly guessed what ailed him then and she let him into the lion's den; she ushered him into the world of men and gone he thought was all his woe.

'But now that I am turned eleven,
with a libi-dah and a libi-do,
I knew it was no makeshift heaven
between her thighs of burning snow,
But only another world of woe.'

Dated 20th June 1948 at about the time Jack was working on the malaria project in Yunnan, the poem suggests that sexual desire, even when briefly satisfied is only a source of torment and unhappiness, is only 'another world of woe'. By being in China Jack had once again put himself in a situation that was likely to deny him the closeness and reassurance of a female partner. FAU men were invariably bachelors, fated to be solitary, though a small minority did

Stan Betterton, Grace Chang Mei-ching, Stan's future sister-in-law, and Paul Matthews

find Chinese wives, often those they were working with.

In a very male environment it wasn't only sexual frustration they suffered though but a general lack of close female company, along with the constant ache of exile. They had only their fluffy puppies to cuddle and being so young must have missing their Mums and her cooking, despite all the machismo of the transport depot.

In his novel of 1956, *A Woman of Bangkok,* Jack later expressed this longing for physical contact through the thoughts of Reggie when he first spent an entire night with the dance hostess, Vilai. "Do you realize this is the first time in my twenty seven years I've actually slept with a woman – I mean, just lying down peacefully beside her with my eyes closed?... This is the climax of my life, this is peace, this is what I've been seeking, without properly knowing it, ever since I first got impatient of my mother's fondlings when I was around six or seven."

Now in China in his late thirties, Jack's solitary predicament was therefore more than serious. On this theme, Howell Jones has told me something of note, that in Chungking Jack fell hopelessly in thrall to his lab technician, Fleda Jones, but that all his hopes for a happy future together were cruelly dashed. On leaving China Fleda sailed away to do medical relief work in India, leaving Jack bereft. I have assumed Howell's recollection of this painful affair to be correct but have had no corroboration of it whatsoever, that is until now.

Another small mystery is that towards the end of 1949 Jack had suffered a near fatal attack of typhus which left him in a weakened condition, necessitating the return to Chunking of Dennis Frone to hold the fort. These events were fully told in the FAU news letters and reports, yet when Jack again became ill and was hospitalised soon afterwards in mid-January 1950 the nature of the problem never seemed to be specifically mentioned. This time Jack appears to have been in hospital and convalescing for more than two months but his illness, deliberately or otherwise, was kept obscure.

I had resigned myself to minor matters such as this remaining unresolved, but then to my surprise late in 2013 Dorothy Reuman sent me from Connecticut a bound set of photocopies of the letters she and her husband, Bob, mailed home from China, amounting to two hundred and thirty typed pages in all. These two fine correspondents can thus now add to the story of Jack and the Chungking clinic and solve these mysteries for us.

On 23 January 1950 Dorothy wrote home as follows about the goings on at the Chungking clinic.

'After a month and a half of dogging Fleda's footsteps, with what success we don't know, Jack suddenly became discouraged, about life in general, I guess, and about a week ago took some barbitol [barbiturate sleeping pills] late one evening. All the fellows were quick enough that he came out of it all right, with some first aid and emergency injections that we fortunately had in the clinic. He much needed a rest and although we hoped that when we came [to work at the clinic] he would be able to get away, he couldn't make it, and with all the uncertainty of the garage and the change-over tie-ups and delays, he just evidently couldn't see the way through. His recovery from an October siege with typhus was not yet complete, either. It really knocked us all for a wallop, but he's doing well over at the hospital, and will, we hope, be able to get his vacation now. When Fleda is over at the hospital, I work in the back room…'

Bob's letter in the same envelope adds… 'Dorothy has told you the big news of the section here and the sad situation with regard to Jack so I don't need to enlarge on it. Jack is well past the physical crisis now and we hope his psyche will not be too violently upset. It must be a devastating experience to attempt suicide and then to have to look in the face a few days later those who you left and who so ungraciously and ignominiously foiled the plan, poked a tube in your stomach, pumped water in both ends, and needles into various spots. It's a sad experience and a bitter blow to the unit. One interesting sideline is that an essential element in curing barbiturate poisoning is the injection at frequent intervals of strychnine, another deadly poison. I believe they said they gave Jack four times the lethal dose, though he took about ten times as much barbital as one needs to ensure slumber. We trust that this will work out satisfactorily.'

Further letters from them tell that after about two weeks at the Catholic Hospital up on the cliffs of Chungking Jack was moved to convalesce at a French Catholic home, probably several miles over the hills from Lungmenhao on the south bank where the French had a base as a retreat from the heat and chaos of the city. Bob and John Peter went to the hospital and helped him pack, crossed the river and walked with him over the steep trails, carrying his suitcase for two hours to reach the home, before hiking another four to return to the garage depot. It seems that Jack was then convalescing there for about two months, latterly returning to the depot for weekends on a number of occasions.

Dorothy's letter of 17th March 1950 makes a few concluding comments. 'Jack seems to be quite a bit better, though on his weekends here he seems to be completely infatuated with Fleda. He's planning to go home to England with one of the former Unit members with whom he's very close, just as soon as he can get permission to travel; Mike [Frankton] is in Hankow. Jack's been here since 1945, with a pretty heavy load on his shoulders most of the time. He has had a predisposition for woman-trouble, but never anything like this before; John has been with him out here most of the time and knows him pretty well. We guessed it was barbital after seeing the effects and finding some in a matchbox he had, and later Fleda's somewhat inadvertent mention of the fact that she had known that he had some and had said he intended to take it. The night watchman heard his laboured breathing and called Sam for assistance.

Fleda was one of the four of us who trained together in Philadelphia, a negress, about 29 years old or so, the lab technician of the group… She's not very easy to work with, if she makes up her mind she won't be moved; some days everything is fine, then some days she is impossible. We keep trying and will keep on trying to keep things running smoothly. Their little love affair has been quite exclusive, so it's been sort of hard to keep the section one big happy family…'

The mysteries of Jack's love affair and his 'illness' thus were interlinked and are conclusively solved by the detail and remarkable survival of the Reuman letters and their chance delivery into my hands.

It is hard to imagine though the shock when Jack's disaster was discovered in the dead of night, the panic to assess his condition, to find and administer the antidote and to rehydrate him. They then had to decide whether to put him in a jeep and rush him down to the river, to waken a sampan crew and get him across the river and to carry him some way upstream and several hundred feet up the cliff to where the Catholic Hospital brooded above the river, or whether instead to wait for the morning. Saving his life seems to have been no small achievement for a group of unqualified young people but as Bob Reuman observed in one of his letters, in such a situation you just have to do what you can.

One final tangential observation now has to be made. In *A Woman of Bangkok*, the book's anti-hero Reggie, (who like Jack is the speedway-riding son of a Christian minister), has been perfidiously rejected by his girl for writing courtly love poems but failing resolutely to ravish her. When she then falls into the more manly arms of his older brother and is made pregnant, Reggie takes an overdose of barbital, only to be rescued from the jaws of death by his loyal and vigilant landlady. Novels are often autobiographical and Jack's novel of course is no exception.

Jack walks Chungking city and sings with the communists

Again scorning the virtue of conciseness, Jack's following article rambles on at some length but it is carefully constructed and very readable. Written for his usual small audience and full of obscure references to people and places, some prior explanation is however needed.

By late 1949 Jack had long been mired in the awful process of closing the transport unit, including the financial tensions with the IRC, his partner institution, over a painful dispute with the Chinese employees about their severance payments. Jack was plainly exhausted, in mid-January 1950 taking an overdose, and the position of West China Director was passed to Dennis Frone. Jack's hospitalisation and convalescence continued through to April and so he had plenty of time to indulge in his favourite therapeutic activity, writing. After so deep a depression, we find him in manic writing mode again. In the long article below that resulted he talks of eating turnips at the 'Catholic Home for the Destitute', where he was convalescing in the hills at Szemushan on the south bank of the

Yangtse, in whose cemetery many French sailors were buried.

Jack starts his story in self-deprecatory mood, depicting himself as yesterday's man, his glory days as the transport unit's big-cheese now over. Even the dogs don't listen to him any more, though at least the newsletter editor can be tipped off to let him expound at length on paper. He thus flies off at many a tangent, taking the mickey out of American sports and pronunciation and talking irrelevantly of Daredevil Cyrillo and Rita Hayworth. (Bernard Llewellyn's son, Michael assures me that Bernard did indeed remain eternally faithful to the ethereally beautiful Rita.) After a few jokes about Wordsworth and mention of the French sailors, he makes an obscure reference to Robert Payne whose book, *'Chungking Diary'* was published in 1945. He then compares the mountains to the breasts of his employees' wives, extolling the vastness and beauty of the Chinese mountain scenery.

Chungking, steps down to the Yangtse

At last he moves on to the central part of the article, a description of Chungking city high on the cliffs above the Yangtze, the eternal hubbub of whose crowded millions could be heard even as he crossed the river. Pushed aside by a funeral procession he then climbs up the stone staircase from the river and plunges into the raucous ant heap of urban Chungking.

Next he changes tack again to give a farcical account of the repetitive treadmill of life at his south bank garage depot and clinic. For Jack, evenings are an eternal cycle

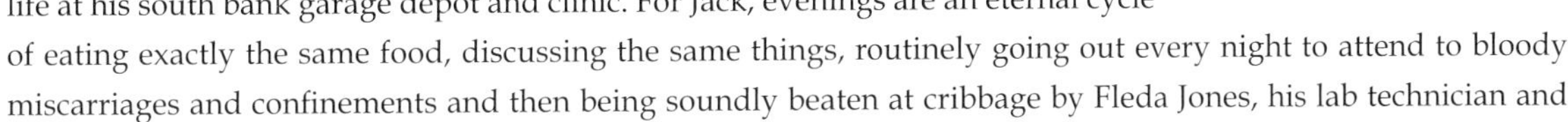

of eating exactly the same food, discussing the same things, routinely going out every night to attend to bloody miscarriages and confinements and then being soundly beaten at cribbage by Fleda Jones, his lab technician and

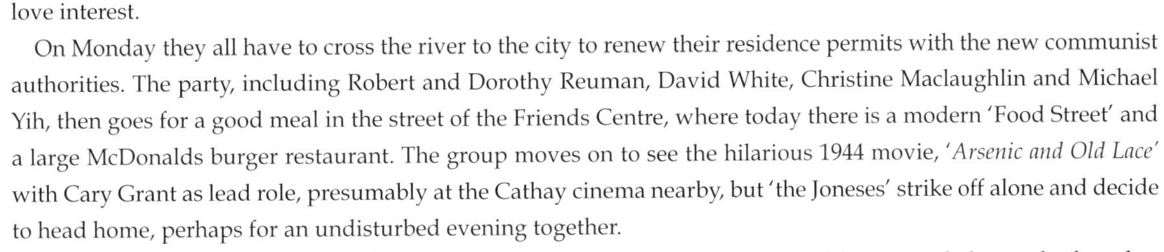

love interest.

On Monday they all have to cross the river to the city to renew their residence permits with the new communist authorities. The party, including Robert and Dorothy Reuman, David White, Christine Maclaughlin and Michael Yih, then goes for a good meal in the street of the Friends Centre, where today there is a modern 'Food Street' and a large McDonalds burger restaurant. The group moves on to see the hilarious 1944 movie, *'Arsenic and Old Lace'* with Cary Grant as lead role, presumably at the Cathay cinema nearby, but 'the Joneses' strike off alone and decide to head home, perhaps for an undisturbed evening together.

Reaching the Yangtse, Jack and Fleda find a large contingent of communist soldiers crowded onto the ferry but they are politely ushered aboard, together with four missionaries. The officer asks the foreigners to sing and the soldiers then respond, a moment of musical solidarity which later proves sadly ironic. The first to break into song is Olin Stockwell, an American Methodist minister who had first come to China in 1929 and who, with his wife, used music as an integral part of their mission. Articles in Time magazine tell how some months later in November 1950 he was imprisoned for espionage and held in solitary confinement by the communists, only being released in December 1952. His book, *With God in Red China* tells the awful story in full.

The easy way up the steps from the river

Finally on Tuesday Jack finds himself sidelined as a mere observer as Dennis Frone pays off the garage employees who are now out of work. He again crosses the river and has a nostalgic meal with Old Tobacco, one of the men he has worked with for many years. Finally he buys a bottle at Kuan Sun Yuan, a bakery and food store that still has a presence in China. Thus after so long, Jack's beloved FAU is finished. It and his long and circuitous article have come full circle as he makes his way back across the Yangtze and up the steep steps on the south bank again.

Crowds climb the Chungking steps

FSU Chronicle 115, April 22, 1950

FARTHEST WEST

One great difference between the world then and the world now is that now I can't get a word in edgeways. Time was when if I but cleared my throat a reverent silence fell around the table, a silence broken only by the sound of the pips of whatever fruit was in season bouncing off the un-Happy Dragon [a young employee]; the very dogs would interrupt their unending manoeuvres, all twenty of them, to sit with one ear up, one down and tails slowly oscillating about my knee, reminding me of my dear grandchildren at home; nor would Gerard 'Boswell' Walmesley go unnoticed as he surreptitiously drew his notebook out of his sporran, ready to put down all I said, so that posterity could hold it against me forever. But now if I but clear my throat they still go on oblivious, and if I but clear it again still they [his American colleagues] go on – about the time Jackie Robinson [the black American baseball player] kicked 323 goals in one afternoon, about how the St. Louis Archdeacons [Cardinals!] once won the Washing-up Bowl, about biscuits by which they mean rolls and about barbecues and marshmallows - 'No, not Turkish delight, Jack' – for sometimes I do get a word in, not edgeways but somehow, but it is almost always wrong… Hence, after all these months, another 'Farthest West': here at least I can talk my head off and who shall say me nay? (for a CHRONICLE editor can always be squared). And so to begin with a riddle: since Stinker's no longer a dog but a dahg, why wasn't Oscar a hahg, but a hawg? Is it just the difference between Szechuan-hua and Honan-hua? [Chinese dialects.] No doubt I could get the question answered here, if only I could get it asked. Meanwhile replies should be addressed to this Editor, not to individual contributors. [Stinker was one of the Unit's dogs while Oscar was a huge Berkshire boar imported to do as England expected in the village of Sherlitou in Honan… which fails to explain the American dialectic differences!]

Oscar, the hawg at Chung Mou

Well, it is so long since I last wrote a 'Farthest West' [the latest found in the archives being 21 February 1948] that I can't possibly recount the entire history of the intervening epoch, so I will begin at 2.16 p.m. on Friday, March 21, 1950, at which time (if the nurse's watch was correct)…, having downed the last turnip for the week (for I am lodging at a Catholic Home for the Destitute, and poverty and turnips go together in China as everywhere else in the world) – I set off to walk from Szemushan to Ssu-kung-li-pan [the south bank transport depot], from Catholicism to Quakerism, from monasticism and meditation to - well, you will see. Note that I say I set off to walk. One day I set off to ride, and then suddenly the pony set off… Interpret those dots your own way, as T. S. Eliot said. All I know is that that animal had three flat tyres, no springs, and a defective clutch; every time the muleteer, mistaking my moans of fear for inarticulate expressions of the foreigner's well-known lust for speed, twisted the creature's tail, we shot forward like Daredevil Cyrillo in his rocket car, but fortunately, (unlike Daredevil Cyrillo on one celebrated occasion) we never got stuck upside down in the course of looping the loop, because, (fortunately again), we never once looped the loop, unless I didn't notice that. Note for the newborn – Daredevil Cyrillo was later in his career to become even less famous as John Peter, and he still does somehow contrive to get his anecdotes heard, heaven knows how. But to return to our sheep. [In Jack's 1974 book, '*Daughters of an Ancient Race*' Jack repeats this story about John Peter as Daredevil Cyrillo in his rocket car, placing it in Rangoon prior to John's escape from the Japanese over the Burma Road and into the FAU.]

This paragraph will deal with scenery, of which there are large quantities between Szemushan and Ssu-kung-li-pan. Everyone who has walked the world from the Snowdon Horseshoe [in north Wales] to Shanghai Bund is aware that when Wordsworth leaned his belly against the balustrade of Westminster Bridge and trotted out the mellifluous whopper that 'Earth hath not anything to show more fair', he obviously hadn't seen a whole heap of things – Rita Hayworth's navel for instance, as Llewellyn and Norton would promptly have told him (unless they have turned fickle with the years) – and what was Wordsworth doing on the bridge at that hour of the morning anyway? Not going to work, because he has a 'competency' and didn't have to work: - Was he coming home from a party? That might explain the sonnet… Rita, one

Across the Yangtse to the hills of the south bank

feels, would have made the poet eat his words: 'Now, no more sermons from stones, honey: how about a hot little number for my next film, something like your "She stood bust high" only, well, hotter' – and Szemushan would have made him eat them too.

What are Wordsworths anyway – what for that matter are words worth – in the face of these gigantic vistas of sky and mountains and river? One feels that the French sailors (whose mortal remains lie here in such numbers that it's clear it was still dangerous to be French and a sailor even after the Battle of Trafalgar was all over) one feels that they, poor chaps, must be compensated for the misfortune of having died in foreign parts by the aesthetic pleasure of being buried in such a magnificent spot… Sentimentalism, of course: every one of them would rather have gone home… And eternally these mountains march down to the river, and eternally that kite circles between their heads; there he was wheeling when Robert Payne looked up and mistook him for an eagle and so misrepresented him in his book; there he will still be gliding, on his wide tattered wings, long after the flattery is forgotten. [In *Chungking Diary* at page 27 Robert Payne describes an eagle in solitary flight during a walk above Huang-k'o-ya in the hills of the south bank.]

It is one of those landscapes that are so immense you are daunted by them. You feel almost physically incapable of lifting your eyes to the hills. Not that the hills themselves are huge: they are Chinese; they are feminine; they dance like the jolly little waves in old Dutch seascapes. Wordsworths are fond of comparing mountains to female breasts, not always aptly; but here the comparison is a good one, and as I walk along I recognize individual shapes – Mrs. Taeng Yen Siu's, Mrs. Liu Cheng Wen's, Mrs. Hsu Kuo Ping's…

Is this the catch in the Chinese landscape – that as a whole, if only you could grasp the whole, it is sublime, but the whole is too big to grasp, so you turn to the details, the minutiae, - and find them all absurd, trivial and shabby? Is the imposing mountain made of rubbish and imposing only because it is made of so much rubbish? Doubtful, you turn your attention to recognizing birds and crops, to counting the men with buckets of nightsoil, to sniffing at beans and rape and blossoms – anything to keep your mind off the size of it, this crushing incubus of China you carry on your back all your working hours.

And if your spirit reels in the mountains, how will you fare on the stone stairs which are the streets of T'ang-chia-k'ai?

Here, if anywhere on earth, a man stands in need of his five senses. I am not being unreasonable about this: admitted that to the Chinese these soaring alleys of stone steps are only Main Street, Broadway, Skid-Row – the tame and familiar, home; admitted that Doris Wu Wilks probably finds Oxford Street more exciting than I recall it. [She had married Dr John Wilks of the FAU and accompanied him back to London.] But nevertheless after more than four years of Chinese streets – everyone will agree there's more to smell in them; and I'll swear there's more to see and hear in them too.

The entry to the town [overland from the west] is deceptively tranquil; there is a long stone causeway winding through fields of cabbages and beans; there are scattered shacks from which comes the rhythmic clacking of looms; fifteen dogs are mobbing a beggar, naked under his tattered coat and he stands calmly amongst them, wolfing rice from his broken bowl; a soldier eyes you malevolently; a crowd of women and children rush to a doorway to see the Frenchman [do they take Jack to be French?], the minute he has passed their laughter bursts out.... As I often say to______, it is wonderful to be like Joe E. Brown or Schnozzle Durante [famous long nosed American comics], to be able to go about just the way God made you and without any effort at all to set a whole nation laughing...

I hear myself correctly explained by a coolie as Kung I Chou Hu Tuei [an FAU man]: how do they do it, I wonder, thus far from my natural habitat; I suppose it is because every true Transport man always looks as if he has just been run over by his own truck. Of course, White Russians look like that too; but they also always look as if they are expecting to be run over again any minute; which makes the differential diagnosis easy... And then suddenly you are Dante in 'The Inferno'. The shops crowd in on you, the damned and the despairing... But if you were to dawdle through a thousand cantos [of that book] you couldn't absorb it all. My own method of keeping sane is to take one thing at a time. How many men carrying, well – this or that? How many cases of trachoma? [An eye disease.] How many women (because I'm still the same old Home Brew) with_____, but the Unit has changed, alas… The method smacks of Mass Observation [a social analysis movement that Jack contributed to before his China days], but the alternative is to be buried alive under an avalanche of impressions and to arrive on the river-front bemused and with a headache, unable to take in any more…

But you need all your faculties about you by the river too. Probably the New York skyline as you are dredged up out of the Atlantic is more majestic and beautiful than the Chungking skyline as you creep like an ant along the vast opposite shore; probably Somerset Maugham got it right the first time when he said the city looked like a battleship nosing into the Yangtse.

The thing that always strikes me first is not the enormous sweep of the vista but its huge muffled roar, a sound made up not by trams and trains or to any great extent by cars and their hooters, but by one million uplifted voices and two million shuffling feet, by gongs and bells and looms and hammers and crackling firewood and beggars' fiddles and snarling dogs. It is a roar I have heard nowhere else on Earth – lying in bed in London you hear something like it, but then it is all around you – here it comes from a distance, and it is overwhelming. All you can see, across half a mile of water (for the river is low and you are on the bed, more than eighty feet below the flood level reached last year) is a conglomeration of walls and rooves clinging to fantastic cliffs; here and there the rock shows through, like a beggar's body through his rags. Not a man is to be

The Yangtse from south bank, Chungking, early 1950

A funeral passes the FAU garage, May 1947

The pagoda above the school can just be seen

seen, but all this thunder of activity is produced by men. What in hell are they all doing?

Once again the mind reels before the immensity of China. You know what they are doing, but it would take a huge book to say it… Suddenly you are bawled at and you flatten yourself against a cliff in the riverbed to let a funeral go by. Sixteen men carry the black shiny coffin; before goes a youth with a lighted hurricane lamp; behind come the women in blue gowns and white headgear; there is one boy propping loganberry-red incense sticks in crevices in the rocks, another scattering spirit money; on the coffin's lid rides the doomed cock, and as he bounces past, he looks you straight in the eye, as if he sought an explanation from you. His own eye, round and foolish and shiny like a bead, is bewildered and apprehensive, as well it might be. The mourners laugh at you: is your own eye bewildered and apprehensive too?

You continue your walk, heading for a pagoda that was built seventy years ago to encourage the love of learning [which can be seen on the hills of the south bank, standing above the Friends High School beyond]. To your right, the Kialing [River] is pouring into the Yangtse; dozens of junks and sampans are jostling there, coming down sideways with the current or struggling slowly up against it; you hear the chant of the boatmen, and the shrill wails of steamboats which are also caught in the mess. How any boat ever survives you cannot imagine; perhaps the secret is that as every other boat is also being pushed around by billions of tons of water travelling at six miles an hour, they all suffer from the same disabilities and therefore start equal in the struggle…

To your left the Chinese are indulging their current passion for hoopla; and suddenly rounding a rock, you come on a beggar: down on his knees, with his behind bare, he is waving a magnificent prolapse of the bowels in your face; as an amateur

The convoy to Henan goes over the edge near the garage, 1946

doctor you are thrilled, though you can't help feeling it must be a cold way to make a living; he folds his wings and cries like a gull; Chungking vanishes, and I am back in the North Sea; just so would a mollymawk alight on the whaleback and cry, while kittiwakes gloomily circled the smokestack, trying to keep warm… [A mollyhawk is a type of albatross; Jack had once worked on a steam trawler out of Grimsby.]

Enough of this nonsense. Let's get cracking on the weekend. 5.30[pm]. We arrive garage. 5.45. Eat chops. Conversation about developers. 7.00. Film strip show in Boy's Club [the big godown]. Producer: Dr. CLARA NUTTING, (who is doing some health work through our clinic). Projection: DAVE WHITE. Commentary: SAM YEN. [Art work by Jack, who spent a lot of time working on this medical education scheme for local people.] Subject: Vaccination. Touching tale about Chinese woman who scoffed at lover's warning, caught smallpox and lost him, suffered despair, then faced by a challenging situation devoted life to vaccinating other people, finally through dedication to sense of service won love of better man who saw through her spots to the true, warm hearted, essentially beautiful woman lurking beneath… 9.00 Commercial truck goes over edge 100 yards from Garage.

Members rally round to pull it out. I go from one to the other trying to tell them this is nothing; once when I was travelling with four trucks from Chungking to Kweiyang… They are all too busy to listen. Finally I corner FLEDA JONES and say 'This is nothing. Once…' but Fleda says 'I don't want to hear it. I can't see what you guys see in your old trucks, they're too damn dangerous.' Aghast, I await the lightning flash, the stench of burning flesh. But she stands there calmly with her hands in her breeches' pockets. The blasphemy has passed unnoticed.

Saturday Sam and Mrs. Sam and two of the boys vaccinate the people. This in addition to normal clinic work. Midday: the Joneses called to confinement. Water carrier's wife. Find mother sitting on stool giving directions, next to her, on mud floor, the baby; next to the baby, also on mud floor, the afterbirth; next to afterbirth, four hens, all remarking to each other that it's much easier to lay eggs. Afternoon, John leaves for Catholic Hospital, there to attend to his extra-curricular duties of keeping the nurses happy. 5.45 Chops. Conversation about developers. 7.00 to midnight. Trying to teach Fleda to play crib. Score: 5-2 in Fleda's favour.

Dorothy Reuman, 'Mrs Sam' and her children

Sunday a.m. Fleda changes laboratory around – at least I change it under her directions. Pm Fleda changes lab back again – at least, (see above). 5.45. Eat chops. Conversation about developers. 6.50. Joneses called to a miscarriage. Lovely blood all over the place. 8.00 to midnight continue to show Fleda the 'prahper' way to play crib. She wins 6-1.

Monday Clinic closed. We all cross the river to register [with the communist authorities] for the second time. All receive six-months' residents' certificates. Magnificent lunch at Cheng Yang Kai fan t'ien, which is no longer the grease-blackened dive beloved of old but one of those posh places where they give you plates to put your po-ping on; luckily the grub hasn't altered, it is still the best in town, and the lao pan [old proprietor] is fatter than ever.

Bob, Dope [Dorothy], John, Dave, Mrs. McCork and Michael Yih [both of the IRC] elect to see 'Arsenic and Old Lace': the Joneses hear the call of home.

Find hundreds of soldiers boarding the ferry; modestly hold back; an officer says, 'But you have paid the fare; please come aboard.' (Can you imagine the KMT…!) Are joined by four missionaries who are headed for the garage on a k'an-i-k'an [a social call]. Cast off. Soldiers begin plying us with questions. They are friendly. The two chief puzzles – Fleda's beard and my complexion are satisfactorily explained. [Fleda being a black American while Jack had the beard!] Finally they ask us to sing. The other foreigners seem eager to sing. Even I (for I have been kan-pei-ing John at lunch) feel that we probably ought to sing. Suddenly Olin Stockwell lets fly with 'Carry me back' and I hear myself join in with the rest 'to old Virginny, that's where

Bob Reuman's photo of the ferry taking communist troops across the Yangtse, Chungking, early 1950

the la-la-di-dy-doh-di-da-di-do'. The army is charmed and we receive an ovation. [A minstrel song by James A Bland, 1854-1911, adapting an older traditional song. Did Jack know that old Virginny was 'where this old darkey's heart long'd to go', and how did Fleda feel singing about an emancipated slave's nostalgia for the old days of black slavery?]

We insist that they sing for us. They demur of course but a very nice officer gets up off his bundles and says, 'Now the foreigners have entertained us and we must return the courtesy. What song shall we sing?' One or two are suggested; the officer takes the first line of one of them – just like the cantor in a Welsh chapel – and off they go.

Out there in the middle of the yellow rushing Yangtse, huddled together on that little ferryboat which is struggling across from cliffs crowded with shacks to mountains covered with trees, - headed [upstream] towards Luhsien but going rapidly down towards Ichang sternwards while the water rolls up in foam and whirlpools over the hidden rocks – quite unabashed by the majesty of the setting or the amazing temerity of man who trusts himself in a shell of planks on these merciless currents – with the red stars on their caps that are pushed back from their flat brown faces and all their guns and equipment stacked around them – they sing as only the Peoples' Liberation Army can sing in China, with a power and conviction and mellow volume of masculine voices that would be moving anywhere, and is doubly moving here where it is so unexpected. I don't know how it effects the missionaries, but two of us t***e [illegible] come from singing peoples and we are at the mercy of our blood [African American and Welsh]. The boat reaches the south bank; the engine room telegraph rings; the engines slow, reverse, stop, rumble again; ropes are thrown and missed and thrown once more, but still the song goes on, nor does a man move off the boat till it is finished. Then there is a great cheer from Chinese and foreigners alike and we tumble ashore. 'I'm glad I didn't go to the movie', Fleda says, and I think her voice is a bit husky. I can't answer because I have a lump in my throat as big as one of those turnips they fed me at Szemushan... We walk home, [four and a half kilometres] chitchatting with the missionaries. 5.45. Chops again. Conversation about developers. 7.00. Miscarriage has another one or something [sic]. 8.30 – 11.00. Final effort to teach Fleda crib. She wins eight games, I don't win any. She'll never learn.

Tuesday Clinic inundated with patients. Frone paying off employees [on closure of the transport unit]. I go from one to the other saying: This is nothing, once...! Finally they can't stand it any longer. They pack me off to explain about the miscarriage at the hospital [having probably transferred a patient for further medical attention.]. The truck ferry [over the Yangtse] runs on natural gas again; there are no trucks waiting (not with the price of petrol at ten ounces of gold for a drum), we run straight on board and are kept waiting for an hour until another jeep arrives and makes the crossing worthwhile. Later

John Peter supervises the queue at the clinic

Old Tobacco and I discuss po-ping, moh-hsi-jou, onions, cold meats, and ta chin at Ch'eng Yang Kai. 'The last time', he says. 'FAU finished.' He is indeed being paid off for the fourth time. He asks the price of our jeep trailer: he is thinking of going into transport in a new way: 'horses don't eat petrol', he says. He takes me to the Kuan Sun Yuan, where I buy a bottle of wine to sustain me till next Saturday, and thence to Chiao T'ien Men, where I cross the river again. And so to Tang-chia-kai, and back through paragraphs four and three to where we started.

Jack Jones.

MAY DAY PARADE, CHUNGKING, 1950

On 8th May 1950 Bob Reuman wrote home to his family about the May Day parade. 'Monday was May First which as any good socialist knows is an important day to the workers of the world. There were big parades in town, although it is rainy and grey, and Dave and I represented the American people. It was a long affair stretching at least several miles... with a basic unit constantly reiterated of large red People's government flags, followed by posters of Mao Tse Tung and Chu Teh, Stalin and Lenin. After this a drum and cymbals played, arrayed in flashy pinks, greens, reds and yellows, using the hesitation stride and flailing arm stroke that I have described to you before. It is very impressive. After this came a cheering section, waving flags and chanting exhortations after the leader shouted a brief phrase. A most colourful display. I managed a few pictures, both colour and black and white. The latter I developed tonight and they are sharp enough but went hardly further than the heads of the spectators in front of me.'

The pictures now reproduced are from Bob's colour slides that were sent back to the USA where they could be developed.

11 CELEBRATION AND CONFLICT AS THE GARAGE IS CLOSED – MAY 1950

Jack arrived in China in 1945 just as the world conflict had ended and the Japanese invaders left China, allowing the main focus of the 'China Convoy' to move northwards into new geographical areas and to change their core activity from transporting medical supplies to relief and rehabilitation work. When the American Friends Service Committee in Philadelphia took over the FAU in mid-1946, renaming it the Friends Service Unit (FSU), Jack's transport unit was likely soon to be closed. It was repeatedly proposed that medical supplies for the hospitals should in future be moved by commercial truckers in order to free up FSU resources for other projects, but Jack fought his corner, arguing that while there were still supplies needing distribution his transport unit offered unique reliability and efficiency and he doggedly kept the unit in operation until late 1949. When the Shanghai HQ told him that it must be closed, he bluntly told them they'd have to find someone else to do the dirty work of winding it up.

As the communists approached Chungking, Jack was tired, often asking to be relieved of his post or to take a rest but, perhaps unwilling to leave Fleda, he kept working and never even took his full entitlement to local leave. This led to the life-threatening crisis in January 1950 when he finally stepped down as West China Director and Dennis Frone took the leadership.

Jack had kept the show on the road against all the odds, earning desperately needed income by operating a fleet of vehicles for JCRR in Chengtu, selling scrap and even selling vehicles on commission for departing missionaries. The transport unit was thus the achievement of his lifetime, but with the godowns emptying of medical supplies there was little more to distribute and the writing was on the wall. Closing the garage after so many years meant throwing a big party for the men and Jack was moved to write at length about the celebration and his feelings of loss.

Weighing scrap

During all this time, the problems of disposing of equipment and laying off staff were continuing, while patients still arrived daily at the clinic in droves. In a letter home at the end of April Dorothy Reuman reported that Jack was still recuperating, helping in the clinic occasionally, doing art work for Dr. Nutting's health education filmstrips and writing articles, including the one that follows. This she reports as being called, 'Imputations of Immorality' instead of 'Immortality', a nice Freudian slip. Writing was clearly the best therapy for Jack, to sit and hammer away at his old black typewriter, pouring out his emotions for the tiny circle of people who might read his story in the FSU Chronicle that follows below.

I can imagine him too with an open bottle as he typed the title to this article, mangling Wordsworth's "Intimations of Immortality from Recollections of Early Childhood." He also quotes from the First World War poet, Edward Thomas, (who by chance lived in Hampshire in the south of England close to where I am writing this now), and he mentions Louis MacNeice who he later quoted on the title page of his novel, *A Woman of Bangkok*. He was nothing if not in poetic mood.

In the long two part article that now follows, Jack swims in nostalgia and strong spirits as the men celebrate the closure of his beloved Chungking garage with a sumptuous dinner. In the second part, his description of the thrill and camaraderie of the road is one of his most evocative pieces of writing. Hidden in the archives for sixty years, rescuing this particular piece has been a near miracle as its pages are faded, the original print starved of ink and in parts only semi-legible.

Sadly the apparent good mood of the party was soon to become tarnished as within a few weeks a group of employees challenged the repatriation payments they had already been paid and demanded more money. An intractable dispute ensued that fell to Dennis Frone to resolve under the supervision and intervention of the Foreign Affairs Bureau of the new communist government. The story continues in the documents that follow this long article.

A big party as the Chungking garage finally closes down

FSU Chronicle 117, Shanghai, 20 May 1950

IMPUTATIONS OF IMMORTALITY FROM RECOLLECTIONS
OF EARLY TRANSPORT

Good Friday, 1950, [7 April] will ever be memorable to me because of the feast we had. Feasts of course are always memorable: mere mention of the word brings half a dozen to mind – the one after which Kirby spliced the main mast [not the main brace!], the one after which Frankton and I rescued a maiden from suffocation by eels and hsi-kua [watermelons!], the one after which I wanted to fight Howell over a misunderstanding about which of us was supposed to be putting the other to bed, the one which ended when a chicken-carcase caught me on the point of the jaw and Stickings simultaneously fell into a bowl of soup (as I recall it), the one after which.....

but some memories are too sacred to be divulged in public, with the libel laws the way they are. There was however that feast in Kunming at which the noted cosmopolitan and bon viveur Tony Meager delicately ate the tip of the elephant's trunk and threw the rest of the animal away, and that feast at which Mason.... (censored)......and after which Mason.....(censored again). God, what a feast that was! I remember after I had thrown Mason into a paddy-field to cool him off, and after Mason had pulled me out again... [Both Howell Jones and Peter Mason tell me they have no idea what Jack was talking about!]

But let us return to Good Friday, to the feast which remains clearest in my mind, undimmed alike by the passage of time and the fumes of alcohol.

This Good Friday was not like any of the others. Feasting is so inseparably connected in the Protestant mind with joviality and the bibbing of wine that to us "a solemn feast" sounds like a contradiction in terms. Yet to most of the people present at that feast the other night, (and every one of our paid-off employees was there, and all the members of the section), it was a solemn rather than a jolly occasion. Of course we have had farewell feasts before; one recalls the last one in Kweiyang, after which, in spite of having kan-pei'd all fifty people present, most of them several times, I shook hands with and personally thanked every employee for his help, my score being no hics, no cups, and one error only, when I called Chu Li Wu, Wu Li Chu, which I think was forgivable. And Wang An Ch'ing's farewell feast for Mike, at which Charley's daughter served the dishes over my shoulder every time, with the result that I had a stiff neck and she a severe case of mastitis next morning. And of course every Xmas the boys have thrown us a feast, and every Chinese New Year we have thrown it back, because "it's the last chance – next year there won't be any transport". We had gone through this routine so many times that we'd come to believe that the Unit was immortal, that it could neither die nor fade away. And then suddenly stacks of money and a testimonial pass across a desk in one direction and a cancelled paybook in the other, and a partnership that has lasted in some cases for ten years is dissolved, it seems, forever. Having had the sack myself once or twice in my life I know how the boys are feeling. It's like when you are looking for something in a room you don't know very well and suddenly the lights fail.

Scabies clinic to the left

The feast is timed for six o'clock, but long before the last soldier, overcome by the shock of total immersion, has been carried in a fainting condition out of the old truck body which is our scabies clinic, the yard, which erstwhile rang with the cheerful clamour of hammers on metal but now has degenerated into one great big mao-fang for the clinic patients, is taken over by the same old gang of cut-throats who have had the run of it all these years – from P'ang-tzu, the oldest employee, who has

Fleda, Dorothy and Jack can be clearly seen to the left of the group but Dennis seems to be hiding

put in ten years and put on three stone in the Unit to Chung Shao Jen, our most recent acquisition, who in ten months had succeeded in proving what I had begun to doubt---- that there are blacksmiths who can be trusted not to make things difficult for you by running away with spares, (like Ting Chieh Chong), or for themselves, by running away with an IRC employee's maid servant, like our other one. Even the two chief-troublemakers, who have threatened to bump Dennis off, are there, dressed like the rest in their Sunday-best, - clothes made out of the last lot of overalls we gave them. Group photographs are taken at the gate… Walmesley's Folly as I still call it - that gate through which so many famous men have backed to glory, (if they didn't previously back into the ditch, like G---n and W-----n on certain occasions), - and then we all repair to the verandah. [Dorothy Reuman has sent me the photo opposite, taken that day by her husband, Bob.]

Like so many of the more recent feasts, this one is held in our common room. The armchairs, brought here from Kweiyang four years ago, (in spite of General Ch'i, who sent five soldiers with fixed bayonets and a horse-cart to collect them on the pretext that the BMM [British Military Mission] had only "given" them to us so they weren't ours but his) -- these armchairs have been moved out and two extra tables moved in, together with a collection of stools, benches, boxes and tins suitable for sitting on. The Happy Dragon has laid twelve pairs of chopsticks, twelve wine cups, twelve spoons and twelve small saucers on each table, and at the centre of each, a dish of melon seeds, a dish of sticky sweets, and a packet of cigarettes. The stage is set –

The common room, facing left, Chou Min Cheng, Ted Mitchell, deputy British consul, Dave White, Charlie serving and Fleda Jones

In "*A Passage to India*" [the novel by EM Forster] a group of people enter a cave "like water being sucked down a drain" and the way the boys come into the room reminds me of that image; I don't know why: there's nothing watery about them, that's a fact; it must be the way they come tumbling through the door and then slow up as they spread amongst the tables. Humility makes the firstcomers slide into the nearest seats – all except the blacksmith's Striker (that was): he goes straight to what is obviously regarded by the rest as the table dedicated to women and foreigners and sits there grinning widely and calling upon his special friends to join him; nobody responds but he continues to sit unabashed, couchant with smile rampant. (Once I made him laugh on the other side of his face when his wife spawned and I discovered her to be a primapara [giving birth for the first time]; he had been drawing a family allowance for wife and two children and I chided him for defrauding the Unit, and asked him why the embezzled monies should not be deducted from his wages; he turned as white as a sheet and the sweat stood on his brow and he knew not what to say until I, pitying him because several other of the boys were cheating us in like style but couldn't be caught, suggested that perhaps he was still supporting his first (or Mythical) family; then with what relief he admitted that his first wife was dead but he still kept her children! Of course, the following week his two children turned out to be his wife's mother, a hypochondriacal old crone with the smelliest feet in China, as I can vouch, having had them waved under my nose every day for weeks, when they were covered with loathsome and intractable sores. The foreigner can't win in China).

I make an effort to get the foreigners dispersed amongst the Chinese in the old way but in the end only Fleda [the American lab technician] and I are not within striking distance of the Striker. On my left is George's boy, who had a Christian wedding and the most disappointing feast I ever went to. On my right is Walmesley's boy, and next to him Lo Tse Li, who is inseparably connected in my mind with truck 119, and next to him is Yang Kung Fu, who was tied to Chang Ming Sang and me for hours when the bandits got us, and next to him is Fleda, making a pretty unsuccessful effort to share a seat with Tulip.... Also at the table are Chi Hsu Lin, with the brilliant golden smile – once I had to stand by, with three bayonets in my guts, while four soldiers beat him up with the butts of their guns, at P'ing yi that was, and all because I had refused to give an officer a lift; Old Tobacco, of whom so many tales could be told; Hsiao Li, who was Verrall's boy; and Lao Wang, -- few are the people in the Unit who would believe me if I were to say that you and I, Lao Wang, once fell into the same river three times in one night when we were cold

sober, and with your truck too, for few are the people in the Unit now who remember what the ferry at Hsiangtang was like when the Japanese were running it. Few recall how five trucks crossed, one per day for five days, and all five went into the drink... But there is one in Shanghai who knows... In fact old Chris arrived in Hsiangtang a couple of days after Birdsnest and I, and found us washing up dishes in the mission kitchen; Chris was raving mad because it had taken him five days to do the trip (it had taken us fourteen); afterwards I said to the lady missionaries "Chris is here" and after a short pause one replied, "Yes, we heard him. He seemed upset." The next day a stone bridge collapsed under Chris's front wheel when he was turning round on a space three inches bigger than the truck – and he was upset again, as I very well remember, seeing that I had to build the bridge again, after Chris had driven away.
[Presumably Chris Evans, a long-serving American member.]

From HOME BREW (To be continued).

Chris and Nancy Evans, Shanghai in late 1950

FSU Chronicle No 119, Shanghai, 17 June 1950 (Continued)
Spiritually this feast may be exceptional, with so much nostalgia floating around, (a lump in every throat, a tear in every eye and gallons of spit on the floor), but gastronomically it is the same mixture as before. First come what are mant'ou [fried dough] to some, rolls to others, and biscuits to a small group who are always mixed up in nomenclature, the rolls being stuffed with ham; then follow in swift succession cold meats, hot rolled savoury pancakes, chicken and chillies, fish and chillies, chillies and beef, slabs of fat pork on a mound of sweet rice, pork and octopus stew, pork and bamboo shoots, rice cooked to resemble peanut brittle and smothered in squid and chicken, chitterlings, dried shrimps in boiled lettuce, and possibly other dishes which arrive too late in the proceedings for me to notice them. Mastication is aided by the ingurgitation of huang chiu which is the weakest tipple in these parts and the only one suitable for a feast where you may be involved in scores of kan pei's. Inured by much practice I am able to keep my head when all about me are losing theirs and, giving the stuffiness of the room the blame, I sit there smiling benevolently and only drop my chopsticks on the floor

Yen Kwan Yen (Old Tobacco) and T'ien Shur Wu (Tulip)

fifteen times. The din is pretty terrific and the noise must do something to my brain for suddenly the tables expand into four enormous solar systems in which twelve planets are revolving around four suns, or is it six, at immense distances; then suddenly each nebula collapses on itself until each table is only ascaris lumbricoides ova [eggs of the giant roundworm] seen under the microscope. Tulip [one of 'the boys'] is flying above our table flapping his golden wings like an angel in a Botticelli painting; he has the cornucopia of the goat Amalthea under his arm and indeed I feel like Zeus as he pours the creamy milk into my cup and misses; it goes all over my trousers and I groan, "my cup floweth over", and he says or appears to say, "What the hell, you'll feel all right again next week". I think he thinks I am worried because he has messed up my pants, but he ought to be worried about himself – he's drunk. Somebody calls "Ch'ang chang" and I turn to find Old Tobacco smirking at me over his uplifted cup; anyone who has had Old Tobacco smirk at them over an uplifted cup will know what this does to me. As Louis MacNeice says, I think things draw to an end......

And then suddenly it hits me right under the belt – God damn it, this is the end! Blame the huang chiu if you like – but suddenly I feel as an old broody hen feels when her chicks refuse to nestle under her any more, fly up to the perches and get twisted breastbones from starting to perch too soon and pneumonia because they aren't fully fledged. All the motherliness in my nature is suddenly intensified and of course Dave [White] was right when he got exasperated with John [John Peter] and me the other day when we were trying to decide which trucks to sell... how could we bear to part with [trucks] 67 or 112 or 115 or indeed any of them...he was justified in his jibe, "My aching foot! What is this? A sentimental truckdrivers' association?" Of course it was.

Under the grease and mud and less mentionable kinds of shit which covered the roadman there always beat a soft heart; in spite of his stern eyes and uncouth blundering ways he loved little children, trucks, his own pup, his boy, the other

boys in his convoy, and some of the employees' wives: he could, and often did, weep like a girl – usually when the tou-perh [presumably a strong spirit] went down the wrong way… Unashamedly I give rein to my sentiment…

Never more, I think to myself, the fever of departure… have the tyre pressures been checked, did I load that spare front spring? What? One of the drums is leaking already? Shall I put the female missionary in the front truck out of the dust and risk her life with So-and-so or have her in the last truck with me? God forbid! Have I got my money, my cross-river papers, my loading slips, my cargo manifests, my customs free papers, my military passes, my driving licenses, my truck licenses, my passport, my residence certificate, that letter for the Catholics at Pingpong? Why won't the idiot's truck start, has my p'u kai [cotton quilt or bed roll] been put aboard? Then you will have to push the bugger - and that reminds me I need a tow chain; and how about some extra loading boards? They say the road's washed out at Pongping. Well goodbye.....I'll be seeing you in a month with any luck.... God damn it, there's a bloody tyre gone already, before we're even out of the ****yard..."

Never again the road. How many roadmen have felt with Edward Thomas, even if they haven't been able to quote him:

I love roads:
The goddesses that dwell
Far along invisible
Are my favourite gods....

Of course there were times when we hated them – those times when soldiers more dangerous than bandits held you up with guns, times when synthetic tyres were popping like corks the livelong summer's day, times when with freezing hands you were affixing chains to wheels half buried in slush, times when your brakes failed on the mountainside....when the man in the teashop did you down over a return cargo or the official in the checking station held you up over a technicality, when the short couldn't be found or when you rounded a bend and there in the glare of the headlights were the wheels of Yeh Wei Wen's truck cocked to the skies – twenty miles and a large mountain from Sunk'an, and midnight already on you because his first gear had gone and you had been pushing him up all the steep bits since nightfall.... Yeh Wei Wen played football for China in the 1936 Olympic Games but that was the last time he drove a truck for the Unit... And yet I loved him...

And there were the good days also, many, many of them: days when after hours of refreshing slumber under the open tent of the canvas you squirmed out of your sleeping bag to dress on the bed board over the cab in the grey light of dawn; rolled up your p'u kai, descended via bonnet and wing to the road, and checked oil and fuel and tyres and springs and water; wandered off and found a stall where tou-chang [tofu] with eggs and yu-t'iao [fried fish] were to be had and gobbled down same, returned to trucks, unlocked and entered cab, handed crankshaft to Scarface, pumped accelerator the correct number of times and pulled out choke the right number of inches, so that at the first turn the engine woke up and began to hum, (a little roughly to begin with but as the oil pressure settled back from sixty towards forty and he got the phlegm off his chest, he would find his true voice, that rich baritone in which were mingled the hearty manliness of Chaliapin [the Russian opera singer], the warm humidity of Bing [Crosby] and the South Pacific friendliness of Izal toilet paper), found that all the other trucks had started too, waved to the lead man, "OK pal, take off", saw first one truck, then the next, then the next.

I obey with two puffs of blue smoke, and not a Goddamned soldier to be seen... Your moment has come; you put her into first, push down your left foot an inch and gingerly raise the other; take off the handbrake, and your truck, the best truck in the Unit, nay in the world, comes to life and rolls forward down the Road. Next second you hit the first pothole of the day just as you are about to make the first gear-change of the day and this, coupled with the fact that the engine is still being fed on colostrum [the choke's still out], results in the first bad gear-change of the day.....

Never mind, in a few minutes you will be free of the town; there will be millions of paddy fields sparkling under a sky now turned from grey to pearl, huddles of trees and crooked houses on knolls, mountains wreathed in mist in the distance; and pacing you down the white ribbon of road, with a cloud of dust pursuing it, the arse-end of 104, eating up kilos....the kilos roll under your wheels; there is a real aesthetic pleasure in driving, in taking the hairpin bends, in listening to the engine and banging through the gate – the hours fly by like kilo-stones. Thirty, forty kilos, hunger is gnawing at the bowels; not far to the next town now; more and more coolies shuffle along the sides of the road; temples and houses grow more frequent; soon you slide into the evils of ribbon development; you meander cautiously through dense crowds in tortuous streets; suddenly you see the rest of your convoy drawn up before a fan tien; you pull up behind them, shouts greet your arrival, bowls of steaming

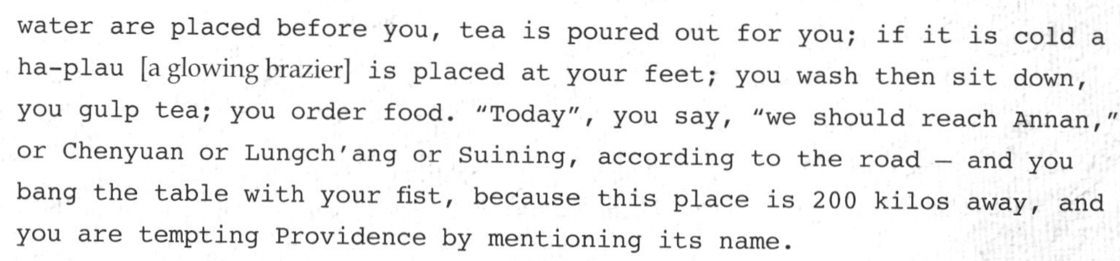

water are placed before you, tea is poured out for you; if it is cold a ha-plau [a glowing brazier] is placed at your feet; you wash then sit down, you gulp tea; you order food. "Today", you say, "we should reach Annan," or Chenyuan or Lungch'ang or Suining, according to the road – and you bang the table with your fist, because this place is 200 kilos away, and you are tempting Providence by mentioning its name.

The boys demur; they think we can reach it too but it is unwise to say so aloud, in a world so full of devils....

"Ch'ang chang, Tsai-chien" [goodbye boss]. With a start I realise that the room is almost empty. And I meant to shake hands with everyone as at Kweiyang! I rush out, (after trying three doors that aren't there), but though the verandah seems full of people, they all turn out to be Wei Fu Lin. The oldest employee – I shake his hand, I say "It's all over, Kung I Chou Hu Tuei cheng-wen-la" [the FAU is finished], and Lao Wei turns away, blinking; the fat bugger's in tears. I can't see him weep so I rush off to toast the blokes in the kitchen who are now having their own feast – the Cook, P'eng Pei Pei, the Happy Dragon, Lao Li, Charlie, and the rest; I go the round of the table; might as well be hanged for a sheep as for a lamb... It's all over, I say, it's finished, and there'll never be anything like it again. And no one understands ---

HOME BREW

A village between Kutsing & Weining

Trucks stop at a fantien

P'eng Pei Pei, the cook

Wei Fu Lin

Charlie

Note: The elusive quest for understanding

Leaning on Wei Fu Lin, probably at Kutsing

The many group photos suggest it had been a fine partnership, but who knows what long-standing tensions or resentment might have built up over time underlying the complex relations between the foreigners and their Chinese employees. Understandably nothing of this surfaces in the news letters though in his later book, *Daughters of an Ancient Race*, Jack talks of 'frequent strikes' and how on closing down the Kweiyang garage one employee, 'a thorn in my side', had screamed at him 'over some imagined injustice in my paying-off a fellow employee of his'. 'On that occasion,' he wrote, 'one solid belt in his midriff had been enough to shut him up, but he continued to take it out of me during subsequent strikes and workshop scrimmages'.

Dorothy Reuman has suggested to me by letter that I should search in the archives for a report of a serious incident that occurred in Chungking at this final party. With everyone having a good deal to drink, a dog wandered in presumably looking for scraps, and it was kicked out, beaten and possibly killed. 'When Jack remonstrated, he, too, was badly beaten. It was all very explosive', she wrote. Such tensions were now to rumble on when some of the employees challenged the amounts of their severance payments.

Dr John Wilks squatting down next to Doris Wu Wilks, moving from the Luhsien base to Honan early in 1947

Closing the garage… local staff confront their foreign bosses

Jack's Report to Staff Meeting that now follows neatly encapsulates the story of the Transport Unit in its dying days. Telling of considerable achievements in distributing medical supplies over vast distances and under impossible conditions, it is Jack's final apologia for keeping the Unit running in the face of demands for its closure. Though triumphant, it concludes with the unhappy dispute with the men over their final payments, a problem that was not of Jack's making.

The IRC in Shanghai, Jack's supposed paymasters had set aside US$2,500 in anticipation of the closure of the garage. This was to pay final bonuses and for the costs of repatriating the Chinese employees and their families to their home provinces. Many of them had come from far off looking for work, having been displaced by the Japanese or by the advancing communists, though in reality they were likely to remain living in or around Chungking. Several of the above documents show Jack desperately spending precious currency on cables begging the IRC in Shanghai to remit the money in a convertible form as soon as possible, but for reasons that were not apparent to Jack they failed to transfer it to Chungking. The dispute must have preyed on his mind at a time when he was exhausted and was a probable contributory cause of his suicide attempt. On Jack's resulting hospitalisation, Dennis Frone took over as Transport Director and was unfortunate to attract criticism for his handling of the crisis. In his supplementary report that follows Jack's, poor Dennis eats much humble pie.

As the patriarch of the south bank garage, Jack felt a strong personal responsibility to his men and their families and for the spirit and communal integrity of the Unit. It must have seemed that all his efforts had come to nothing when some of the employees then rejected the settlement already paid to them and demanded more money. His sense of failure and self-criticism surfaces at the end of this report in a style that is typical of him. However, this conflict was perhaps just the start of the Chinese people distancing themselves from all representatives of the foreigners who had dominated them for so long. While the communists seemed unsure what to do with the foreigners in their midst, at first treating them cordially, things were to get worse with the start of the Korean War in June 1950. Spencer Coxe even suggested that the communist government, 'forced the Chinese members and employees of the FSU to denounce and calumniate American Unit members in Chungking'. At the very least the men simply wanted more money for a very uncertain future and, as Dorothy Reuman commented in one of her letters home, if employees made strong demands such as this it was impossible to resist and so better to pay up and be done with it.

REPORT TO STAFF MEETING - PART 2, 31 May 1950

WEST CHINA TRANSPORT

Staff Meeting of March 1948 decided that transport should be closed by the end of the year. Staff Meeting in October 1948 re-affirmed this decision, but added that if the IRC found it impossible to get their own personnel to carry on the work, the Unit would be prepared to second one or two interested Unit members for a few months. The IRC not only failed to find replacements for us but took on extra work, and with the arrival of approximately 600 tons of relief supplies (ECA) during January 1949 our godowns were as full as they had ever been. The IRC passed out as a fund remitting body in the next month [no longer covering the Unit's outgoings] and we had to struggle along as best we could until November, when new recruits brought in a few hundred US dollars with them. We had known that given the usual conditions we could have distributed all supplies on hand by September, and our plan was to close down by the end of 1949. But the advance of the liberation armies by cutting off supply lines and causing inflation etc. added to our difficulties and the last medplies were not shifted out of our godowns until mid-November. It was still our intention to get closed down before the end of the year but liberation arrived before the repatriation funds and so transport's life was prolonged into 1950.

PERSONNEL At the time of October 1948 Staff Meeting, [foreign] personnel numbered six. To these must be added Peter Verrall, who was no longer a Unit member but on the IRC payroll. In 1948 Peter Mason, who had finished his contract with the Unit [in Honan], also joined us for six months as an IRC employee. After this the exodus began. First Mike Frankton, deluded by the latest rumours about our approaching dissolution, took a job with IHT in Hankow and left in January. Verrall left in April. George Kan went to Tihua in June and has not been seen since, though the rest of his convoy got safely home. Mason left in July, reducing our number to four, the lowest ever. The arrival of Bob Waldie in late August eased the strain, but he was taken ill in September and died the next month. As Sam Yen was by that time running a JCRR garage in Chengtu in order to earn money

Peter Mason and Peter Verrall play cards while on a langage course in Hankow

for us to finish our job, we were down to three members in Chungking. Luckily Dave White arrived from Hong Kong at the end of October. Sam got back from Chengtu a few days before liberation and at the end of the year transport strength was five – Jack Jones (Transport Director), John Peter (Garage Manager), Chou Ming Cheng (buyer, accountant, translator, etc.) and Dave and Sam, convoy leaders.

WORK DONE Various scandals at the IRC depot in the summer and autumn of 1948 seriously affected their output of medplies and for some months a good deal of commercial [trucking] work was done in order to keep the project going until the IRC stuff would be ready for delivery. In January the 600 tons of ECA supplies began to arrive and some work was done on them, but like the IRC they expected transport to function without cash and it was not until May 1949 that their payments in cash and kind set transport's wheels really turning. Financial difficulties were not the only ones and on five separate occasions convoys sneaked into and out of towns that had just been liberated from bandits (Chaotung, Kunming), or were just about to be liberated by the PLA (Lanchow, Paoki, Hanchung). Very great credit is due to the Chinese convoy leaders and drivers and boys who owing to the shortages of foreigners had to make several dangerous trips during this time. Chi Hsu Lin in particular, who had his trucks commandeered by Nationalists on one trip, and slipped into Chaotung and Kunming during short periods when the Nationalists had recovered them from the warlords and were not quite ready to lose them to the PLA, did good work, but the other convoy leaders, Lo Tse Li and Chang Ming Sang, also never refused to make any trip they were asked to undertake, however hazardous it seemed to be.

Distribution accomplished since a report was last made to Staff Meeting was as follows: [There follows a table of figures for the last two months of 1948 and 1949 up to November, showing distribution of medical and relief supplies for IRC and ECA, and transport of passengers and commercial cargoes and of fuel, oxygen cylinders and the remains of wrecked trucks. The units given are for tons transported per kilometre.]

The biggest convoy since then has been sending all the trucks across the river to get registered [with the new authorities]. They left January 19, 1950 and returned two months later. Disregarding this tremendous outing, the totals are: Nov. 1948 – Nov. 1949… Total 319,994 km/tons.

This gives an average of 24,615 km/tons per month which, in view of the facts that for the most of the period under review we were cut off from Shanghai, had no foreign convoy leaders, had great difficulty in getting tyres and fuel, had trucks held up for long periods waiting for permits and floods to be dealt with, had nine men working on a separate project in order to get money to keep the rest of it going, had to undertake a great deal of repair work in order to get cash – and in view of the fact that the roads were always being cut preventing convoys getting off for weeks at a time – may be called satisfactory.

Chief convoys during the thirteen months were: [41 convoys are listed, including 3 to Shantan, 2,188 kilometres away and one of 3,500 plus kilometres to Urumchi, Sinkiang province.]

FINANCES Although the IRC sent us occasional replenishments of our revolving fund up until February 1949, they were more or less useless, as by that time GY [Gold Yuan] had gone haywire. Towards the end it inflated at the rate of over 4,000 per cent per half-month, which meant that a remittance based on accounts that had been processed for six weeks here and in Shanghai would have been worthless even if we could have got cash on it. So we undertook several large jobs and accepted payment in rice, petrol, tyres, rope, truck canvasses, and anything else the other bloke had to offer. With the introduction of silver, things were stabilised and at the same time the ECA and the US Consulate began making substantial payments to us, the one in silver, the other in US currency. Finally we contracted to handle all ECA haulage for 8,000 gallons of fuel, 20 tyres, and 2,000 silver… All this enabled us to send IRC supplies with the ECA convoys although we were receiving no financial aid from IRC.

Usually trucks were able to get return cargoes,

Fuel drums stored under the hostel verandah

Engine testing

and good prices ruled if a city was threatened, but after the fall of Canton the economic life of the region fell to pieces and trucks frequently came home empty. Meanwhile JCRR which had been allocated all ECA supplies for redistribution and was anxious to have our trucks do all transport for them, were constantly requesting us to set up a garage for them in Chengtu, to which city they had shifted their HQ. Having made it clear that we would not do so unless we could make a lot of money out of it we set up a garage for them as of September 1st 1949 and this functioned until the end of November.

We received a monthly payment of 5,500 silver out of which we had to buy any spares they had not in stock except tyres or engines and we had to provide enough drivers and mechanics to keep up to twelve vehicles ready for action. (They had five drivers of their own too.) Sam and nine boys worked from six in the morning until late at night for two and a half months to keep this job going. Our profits from the venture were sufficient to pay all our staff their wages for half a month. JCRR on leaving donated us a weapons carrier which was a joy to us until it was taken away by the authorities in February on the grounds that as it had been JCRR property it belonged to the government not us. In July Philadelphia sent us 250 US for members' pool [for personal expenses] etc. and no other outside money was received until the new recruits brought in about 800 US in November.

CLOSING DOWN While the TD was in hospital in early October Spencer Coxe adjured him to close down transport at once. The TD's attitude was that our goal was in sight and we should finish our commitments to the IRC, and those the IRC had undertaken with the ECA, and which we had been paid for, if we humanly could. The TD wrote Coxe that if he insisted that closure should be made before the work was finished he should send someone else to do it. At the same time the TD repeated his frequent requests that the money for repatriations and paying off staff should be sent without delay. Instead agents all over the world became involved in an argument whether dollars or sterling should be used to make the payments. Finally a Hong Kong cheque arrived, but as the liberation army had also arrived it was impossible to negotiate it.

Work had come to a standstill and there was no ready money available. Sometime in January the TD called a meeting and showed the cheque to the boys as proof that we were trying to get cash for them and suggested that if we could cash the cheque we would pay their repatriations (the Chairman of the West China IRC Medical Committee [Dr Stuart Allen] had said that the money could not be used for any other purpose) and that they should live on these repatriations until such time as we got in enough money to pay their back wages and pay them off with the usual bonuses. If we couldn't cash the cheque we would all muck in together and live on boiled rice until we could raise the wind somehow. The boys agreed and morale was excellent. All except the TD's. He was taken ill again shortly after this [in mid-January 1950] and handed his job over to Dennis Frone, who will continue this report from here.

Carrying an engine to the workshop

I personally regret very much that I broke down at this juncture as the only reason for my staying on in a job that I disliked was that I had promised the boys that I would do the paying off to guarantee that they got treated exactly as they would have done under the FAU, who really, according to them, should have paid them off before it folded. I think if I had kept going much of the subsequent trouble would have been avoided. I would have handled things quite differently. Dennis and Chou Ming Chang did not want to worry me with garage affairs however, and although Dennis and Dave once walked all the way to Szemushan to ask my advice [while convalescing] they didn't act on it, though it coincided with Chou Ming Chang's. I feel personally responsible that the Unit has been let in for a much greater expenditure of money than it should have paid out and that the relations between the boys and the Unit have deteriorated so disastrously. I feel that transport had a glorious history but that it has ended up in failure, largely due to my own mistakes and weakness.

Jack Jones
Chungking, 31st May 1950.

The glory days at Kutsing, August 1945. Foreigners from front left, Lindsay Crozier, Wilf Jackson, Tony Reynolds, John Simpson, unknown, Paul Cope, Peter Rowlands, Michael Crosfield

CLOSING DOWN (Continuation) As Jack says, I [Dennis Frone] came onto the scene after he had been sick a second time – about 18th January [1950] – and tried to carry out the business of closing up the transport work in accordance with the policy agreed by the IRC and FSU. Actually I did a certain amount of work on transport in October-November 1949 when I flew back from Hong Kong after Jack had been taken ill the first time but this period has already been reported.

Since I took over, things have certainly not gone smoothly and even at the present date the termination arrangements of the 45 discharged employees have not finally been settled.

The chief difficulty with which we were faced at the time when I took over was the conversion of the "repatriation cheque"… [He explains this at some length and that the men were demanding all back payments and entitlements in full.]

Chou Min Cheng rests in the common room with the others

By 15th March 1950 however the FSU had agreed as a result of frantic telegrams and telephone conversations, to advance the requisite amount as a loan to be repaid by the IRC (this organisation being financially responsible for the garage operation). Just prior to this, meetings were held with the employees as a result of which agreement was reached on the terms of termination and the process of paying them off began on 13th March. In each case, employees received their back wages paid at current cost of living rates, two months bonus and repatriation grants according to the agreed scheme. The payments were set out individually and carefully explained by Chou Ming Cheng to each employee as he was paid off. In every case the employee accepted the money and affixed his seal to the statement. By 1st April everybody had been paid off and the customary feast was held to mark the occasion. [This was on Good Friday, 7th April, Jack's nostalgic account in the FSU Chronicle of 20 May and 17 June 1950 appearing above.]

At this, everyone sat back with a sigh of relief and we felt that we could go ahead and plan our future programme. Seven of the ex-employees were taken on again as at 1st April to help us in the hostel and clinic and a further four taken on at 21st April to undertake garage and med-mech work, making 11 in all. This time we took care to work out conditions of employment and termination with rates of pay expressed in terms of parity units at a reasonable level and on being engaged, each employee affixed his seal to the document signifying his agreement. Rates of pay were about one quarter of what they were under the old arrangement but nevertheless were still above those prevailing in most organisations in Chungking.

All went well – or reasonably well – for a month but on 1st May we were surprised to receive a set of 9 new demands signed by 28 of the ex-employees. A perusal of these would give one the impression that the employees had never been paid off… We considered that these were quite unreasonable… [Frone continues that the Foreign Affairs Bureau was then consulted, who considered the written position of both sides and advised that a further meeting with the men should be held to try to settle the outstanding issues. Extracts from the minutes of this meeting appear below.]

It is a sorry business and perhaps it can be interpreted as a most adverse comment on our work here during the last few years: we seem to have failed to get across our ideas to the employees. Instead of having a sympathetic and co-operative group ready to understand our problems and try to work out a solution for the future, we have a mercenary set of men trying to wring the last penny out of us. Maybe this is my own fault in as much as I possibly did not arrange for more meetings with them in order to discuss our problems.

However, under the conditions that prevail today when it is extremely difficult for a discharged employee to get a job elsewhere (especially where he has been employed by a foreign organisation) it is perhaps understandable that a discharged employee should be out for all they can get. Certainly, they were anxious to assure us that this dispute should be considered as a business matter and that it did not affect their relations with us, although they seem to have thought that I personally had been responsible for the trouble arising.

THE FUTURE It is most unlikely that we can continue with any transport work in the future. We still have our trucks and equipment but since there are no further medical supplies to distribute… [the transport unit therefore has to close, Frone concludes. He goes on to explain at length that to reimburse the FSU which had loaned money for repatriations, the Unit's trucks and equipment (which in fact belonged to the IRC as operator of the transport project), should be sold, if authority could be obtained from the Government. So far this authority had not been obtained. Frone then considers a number of other uses for the trucks if they could not be sold, such as passing them over to organisations such as the IHT and/or the CIC.] Some exploration has been done on the lines of a possible link up with these organisations for our future work. So far, there has been no response to our tentative approaches to these organisations.

Dennis Frone   Chungking, 1st June 1950

Jack records the chaotic proceedings of a difficult staff meeting

A staff meeting was thus called to discuss the men's demands for increased severance payments which was held at the garage late one evening. As suggested above, Jack might not have known that after many years of hard work together and despite the smiles, solidarity between the foreigners and their local employees was becoming a thing of the past. Disputes were becoming common in the missionary community, employees being urged to make things difficult for their old employees as communist xenophobia increased. As any such dispute would delay the issue of an exit permit, the slightest resentment or grievance gave an employee whose iron rice bowl had just been shattered, huge leverage against their employer. With the onset of the Korean War, America now became the hated aggressor, and with a majority of Jack's foreign staff being American, mud was bound to stick. Things were to get worse and when on 20th December 1950, the Canadian missionary, Dr Stewart Allen was called to a similar meeting with his hospital employees he was immediately imprisoned and not released for a full year, much of it in solitary confinement.

Apart from the difficulties of interpreting the two languages, the meeting was therefore acrimonious, Jack no doubt becoming increasingly tired and emotional. The minutes make for uncomfortable reading and some brief extracts from his seven page report now give the flavour of the tensions that had been building. The various employees who spoke at the meeting are not named but are shown simply as, 'Emp'.

REPORT OF MEETING BETWEEN FAU/FSU AND EMPLOYEES
May 29, 1950

29 employees present
Present for FAU: Jack Jones, Dennis Frone, D. White

J.Jones explained reason for meeting. The Foreign Affairs Bureau recommended we hold this meeting before Wed. May 31, in order to try to settle the trouble. If no agreement could be reached here it would be necessary to carry the dispute to the courts… $2,500 is the amount that had been requested from IRC last May for repatriations at that time. That is the amount they set aside for repatriations. Bonuses were to be extra.

Wang Chien hoped we wouldn't mix friendship and facts. Said he wanted true results. (Took him five minutes to say this.) Then made the following 3 points:

a. J.J. made the repatriation scheme he gave each person a certain number of points; enough to cover fares home

b. Claims Jack had another plan whereby he could get additional money if the original $2,500 was not enough to cover fares home and that this proves we were not limited to $2,500. Blamed D. Frone for changing points to make them fit in with the $2,500 available.

c. When they got their repatriation, both the number of points per man and value of each point had been changed.

J.J. FSU told Jack to shut down transport when he first came to Chungking. Staff Meeting minutes for March 1948, Oct. 1948, all state this clearly. As the FSU was threatening to close down transport the IRC took over responsibility at about the time J.J. came here, but requested the FSU to manage operations for 6 months. It was expected there would be only 3 or 4 FSU men in transport. The reason transport kept going was because there was always some work to be done and because Jack wanted to give the boys work as long as possible. In October 1949, Spencer Coxe demanded the closing of transport. Jack Jones planned to do so before liberation but the money was slow in coming through, and then Chungking was liberated and we were unable to cash the check legally after we did get it. Said he had planned to close down before liberation. When repatriation plan presented last May it was only tentative – the points at that time were not claimed to be correct as Jack did not know all the family details of each man. Points were changed when Jack obtained this information.

Garage mechanic, Chu Ho

Wang Chien Thanked J.J. for all he had done and said they all looked upon him as a friend.

J.J. Explained the basis of the repatriation plan in some detail.

Emp. Wanted to know why the points had been cut from $1.25 each as originally proposed to the $0.90 which they received. (One of the drivers said that he thought Jack was a fool for having paid him off in Kweiyang and that they had gotten too much. Ed note: Chou Ming Cheng didn't want to translate this at first and I didn't get the full sense of the statement.)

J.J. Said that if this man could say Jack was a bloody fool for paying him in Kweiyang, then it was useless to explain a plan which was designed for his own good.

Emp. Repeated request to have it explained why points had been changed.

(At this point two employees got up to leave as they said they had to attend to their truck which was down in Hai Tang Chi. Jack said if he couldn't stay for the meeting then he was wasting his time too in trying to talk the thing out with them.)

J.J. returned to the meeting. Asked why the employees hadn't raised these questions to him when he returned from [convalescing at] Sze Muo Chan every weekend during the period when the negotiations for termination payments were being made and when the boys were accepting the money.

Emp. One man claimed Jack had refused to give medical treatment to his wife on one occasion because Jack claimed he was not well.

J.J. Pointed out that while he was in hospital he had done everything possible for this man's wife…

Emp. Scheme as prepared by Jack had been agreed to by every employee. Dennis had agreed to pay accordingly. When he did pay, everything was different, number of points and value of each. [Dennis then tried to explain.]

(It was now 9.20 pm and several employees were drifting in and out of the room. Discussion centred around four employees, the rest were getting drinks of water and smoking cigarettes and walking in and out of the room.)

J.J. Went on to explain that it is possible that exchange rates might have changed enough so that $10,000 would not have covered repatriations. However, he felt that each man received enough under the plan finally used for payment to cover his fares home.

Emp. Jack's scheme all right, they agreed. They didn't want to make trouble for Jack as he had just returned from the hospital. Wanted to talk with Dennis. [At this point Dennis is subjected to an inquisition. To answer the questions he goes to get the files showing the exchange rates at which three payments for repatriations were converted. The employees threaten to go to court. They then claim that they were not given a month's notice or a Chinese New Year bonus.]

J.J. Tell them I have kept this place going 4 and a half years just to give them work. Tell Ma Ming Tsia I have kept him on not because he is a good worker, because he isn't. I kept him on so his wife could get medical treatment. I have spent hundreds of US$ on his wife. She won't cooperate and it has all been wasted and neither one of them has ever said thanks to me. Also these men must realise Dennis represents the FAU, not himself. He took over when I was sick. He didn't know all the ins and outs about this business and didn't want to trouble me with the details.

Emp. We worked here for a long time as one family. Since these other foreigners have come we haven't had much work so we couldn't work. You haven't had enough meetings with us to tell us what was going on. Seems like 8 years of friendship has been lost.

J.J. The friendship hasn't broken so far as I am concerned.

D.F I want to be friends and it isn't my fault the work had to stop.

Emp. Everything as you say, but they (these foreigners) have all broken this friendship. We can't say anything, but we just want the money. If Jack Jones wants to adjust bonus he can adjust friendship.

J.J. The Unit has changed and I'm not the boss any more...

Emp. We will drop our demand for overalls and winter coats.

Emp. Last question. We just got notice to leave in one week. (The army is taking over the compound next door where many of the former employees still live.) We hope you can help.

J.J We will do what we can. Foreigners don't have much say or influence with this government. These boys have never paid any rent for their houses over there, and at the time of liberation I told those in the village who wanted to move out here that I thought they would be safer staying in their own homes. We can't promise anything regarding the property next door but we will try to help in any way possible.

D.F. Will the boys be willing to wait on our reply to the first question (value of repatriation points) until we have contacted Shanghai?

Emp. Agreed.

[Jack's report concludes with a six point summary, including paying one month's wages in lieu of notice, a quarter month New Year bonus etc, etc and that, 'both sides will report the results of this meeting at the Foreign Affairs Bureau on Wed. May 31, 1950.']

12 JACK'S CLINIC, THE LAST OF MANY PROJECTS – MAY TO DECEMBER 1950

The Chronicle reports on life under the new regime

FSU Chronicle 117, Shanghai, 20 May 1950

Weighing a child at Chungmou

CHUNGKING Although the Chungking members are beset with quite a number of problems these days, both from within and without the Section, they seem to be handling these problems with much thought and patience. One of the difficulties is the interpretation of the FSU to the new local authorities. This situation is, in fact, an entirely different situation from any other yet faced by the Unit. Whilst the Unit personnel in Chungmou cannot exactly claim to be in a privileged position, they at least had the advantage by the time the Chinese People's Government was inaugurated of being known, accepted and understood by various Government personnel. Unfortunately there is very little that can be done or said at this time. Explanations and statements can of course be made, and naturally have to be made, but the Unit cannot truly be explained for what the Unit hopes to express through its individual members, cannot be known until it has been received, and then explanations are superfluous.

The Clinic is still much in demand, and its fame is evidently spreading. One patient suffering from worms walked 50 li to attend the clinic, and another 25 li to get his medicine. The 'Evil Eye' Clinic Annex is the busiest section and Mrs Yen is reported to be doing a 'bang-up' job there. The lack of a full-time doctor is still the main handicap, and it is to be hoped that this can be rectified in the near future.

Jack's clinic - final reports on his last project

Jack's clinic, the Friends' last new project in China designated as Medical Team 25, had a short life of little more than a year. While closing down the transport unit Jack was opening up the village clinic in the white building by the gate, setting it up in the nick of time at the end of November 1949 just before the communist troops arrived in the village. In mid-January he took an overdose and Dennis Frone was recalled from Hong Kong to take over as director while Jack convalesced. The celebratory party for the departing transport staff was held on 7 April 1950 and the meeting to reconsider their severance terms was on 29 May, so it was a busy and difficult time for all concerned.

Queueing at the new south bank clinic

It seemed remarkably optimistic that a new medical project could be launched in China under the new communist regime but as the last region not yet 'liberated', this was the only possible place to deploy the new recruits who had been waiting for the go-ahead in Hong Kong.

The clinic was not quite the 'cottage hospital' Jack had once hoped for, but after the disappointment of losing Dr Mary Mostyn when she moved on to Chengtu, he finally found and employed a Chinese doctor, as his third report below records. In the meantime, Dr Clara Nutting, a China-born medical missionary who spoke fluent Chinese was supporting the clinic with weekly visits, focussing mainly on eye problems such as trachoma. Bob Reuman in a letter home described her as a bit on the plain side but when displaying her great commitment to China with a youthful openness and humility of spirit she became 'really saintlike'. This, he wrote, was in pleasing contrast to other local missionaries, one of whom, 'has been in China umpteen years and has a mind like a muddy puddle and a voice like a New York traffic cop'.

All too soon the communist government shut down the clinic on 6 December 1950 after little more than a year, but Jack's reports suggest that much had been achieved in that time. The clinic was of course a small contribution to vast medical needs, but it has not been entirely forgotten as Jack tells some of its story in his book, *Daughters of an Ancient Race*, published much later in 1974. In this book he delights in telling us that during his time in China he delivered no fewer than 180 babies.

Extracts from three of Jack's reports now follow, enlivened by a typical smattering of quips about women which he never could resist making.

REPORT TO STAFF MEETING PART 1 26 May 1950
SOUTH BANK CLINIC, CHUNGKING (MT25)

ORIGIN AND DEVELOPMENT Transport had always run a clinic at each of its garages, a clinic which, besides ministering under our health insurance scheme to employees and their families, was always prepared to cater for a certain number of outsiders providing they were (1) obviously in a bad way (2) obviously too poor to pay for treatment elsewhere (3) had some sort of claim on us, or (4) in the case of females, were reasonably good-looking. By September 1949 the end of transport work was in sight. Our plan was to liquidate transport before liberation came. But there was a strong feeling in certain quarters that Unit work should continue in West China, the more so as the unliberated areas were the only ones in which recruits could still obtain entry. A project dear to the heart of several transport men – that hospital work should be undertaken on garage premises – was mooted abroad. The scheme proved too ambitious to get started in view of the rapid approach of the PLA, which would cut off lines of supply, so the idea was whittled down to "expansion of existing clinic." By this time four recruits, including a doctor and a lab. technician, had accumulated in Hongkong. The Transport Director was adjured to proceed to Hongkong for talks, but he thought it would be more reasonable for Mary Mostyn, the doctor, to come to Chungking for a k'an-i-k'an. On November 5th Mary arrived.

The history of the South Bank Clinic, as such, dates from the next day, for it was the next day that we threw open our doors to all comers, regardless of whether they were good-looking or not. Bad weather, the imminence of liberation, and the not unnatural feeling that there must be a catch in it somewhere kept the clientele away at first. This apparent reluctance of the lambs to come to the slaughter, coupled with the fact that there was no certainty that we would be able to obtain further supplies when the generous IRC and JCRR allocations already allotted to us had been exhausted, prompted Mary to think that it was not a good time to expand clinic work here. By the time she reached this decision we had been cut off from Hongkong and Mary therefore elected to go to the West China Union University at Chengtu where she would be able to work with trained personnel and where she felt

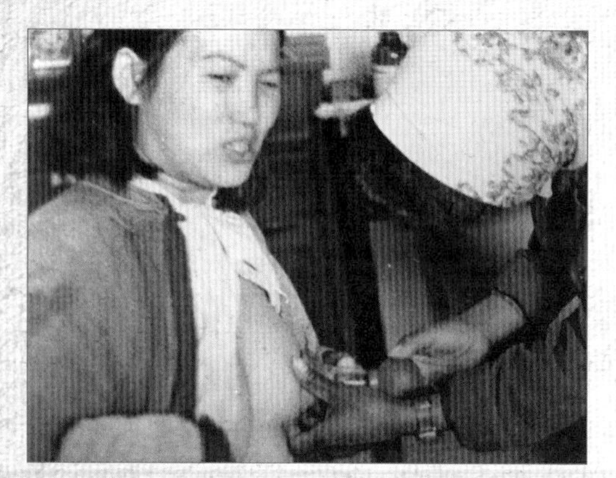

Fleda expresses milk

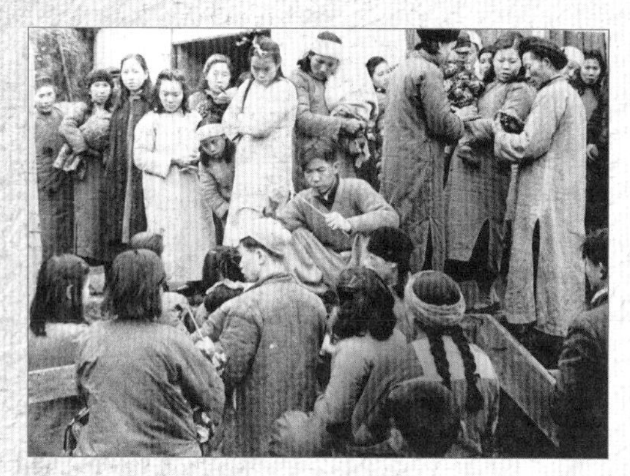

Bored crowds waiting for their turn to be seen

she would be able to do more satisfying work. She left on November 17th aboard the last Unit truck to make the trip, leaving John Peter and Jack Jones to carry on the clinic work as best as they could.

It was almost more than we could manage with the garage work as well but subsequently air contact with Hongkong was renewed and on November 24th Fleda Jones the lab. technician arrived. After spending one morning in the clinic she decided that she could be usefully occupied there and she decided to stay. A few days later the Reumans [Robert and Dorothy] arrived and three days after that liberation.

By this time there were more patrons than we could deal with in our cramped quarters and so just before liberation – in fact while we were being liberated – there we were moving [the clinic] into a large godown near the gate.

The Reumans were roped into clinic work and as the number of customers increased there was plenty of work for five people. At first the clinic was only open in the mornings and the Reumans were able to do a great deal of inventorising and so forth while Fleda did her lab. work in the afternoons; but 70 patients was the maximum that could be dealt with in one session and from January 1st onwards afternoon classes were held. Two transport employees, an ex-driver and an ex-mechanic, were taken into the clinic to hand out tickets and assist with translating and do the washing up, etc. These two chaps have proved very successful, and a third ex-transport employee, the storekeeper, was added to the clinic staff on May 7th.

OPERATION OF THE CLINIC: PERSONNEL Originally work was allocated as follows: a queue was formed, each patient was given a wooden p'ai-tzu [queueing token], and people were called in in turn. The majority went into the first room, where John, assisted by the Reumans and the Yens, dealt with abscesses, skin diseases, coughs and stomach upsets. In an inner sanctum the Joneses [Jack and Fleda] dealt with all gynae cases and anything sent through by John as doubtful.

In January Jack Jones [euphemistically] was taken ill and has only been irregular in his attendance since; the ex-mechanic assists Fleda within. The heavier schedule of clinic work meant that Fleda could not manage all the lab. work and she has been training Sam in the simpler lab. techniques; he examines all stool specimens and stains and examines GC and TB and malaria slides, though the three last are all checked by Fleda as well. In February John was taken ill [and hospitalised with bronchitis] and a heavier load fell on the shoulders of those remaining in the clinic. Fortunately Dr. Clara Nutting of UNESCO became interested in our work and began to make fairly regular visits; she did a great deal to improve the morale and increase the medical knowledge of the Unit personnel. But the lack of a resident doctor has always been keenly felt and continued efforts have been made to find one who would join us either as a member or an employee. One was supposed to begin work on May 21st, but owing to a debate about how many parity units he is worth to us he has not yet taken up office. Meanwhile Fleda is in charge of the clinic and the others working there are the Reumans, Mrs. Sam, and the three employees. John is fully engaged on medmech work in the garage, Jack is off colour again, and Sam has a full-time job in the lab.

Besides normal clinic work, a number of specialities are carried on. There is a scabies clinic, in a converted truck body, in which one of the employees scrubs and anoints the males, while Dorothy Reuman is bath attendant to the women and children. Dr. Nutting started an eye clinic, which is carried on by Mrs. Sam, assisted by yet anther chap out of the garage, who

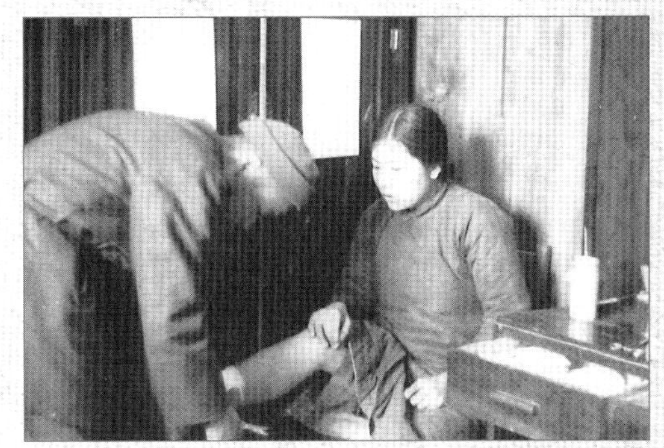

Sam Yen treats a patient

The scabies truck body by the clinic door

Mrs Sam examines a baby

puts in about three hours daily on trachoma, etc. This eye clinic deals with roughly 70 people a day. The clinic did not become heavily involved in the government's vaccination program, but as of this week we are beginning the inoculation of 2,500 people for typhoid and cholera. John and Fleda will be doing this work. We had hoped that the doctor would be here to take Fleda's place while this program is under weigh, but if he is not Jack will work at least half a day in the clinic.

The vast majority of patients seen have minor complaints with which we are well able to deal. More serious or doubtful cases are advised to go to hospital. In cases of extreme need we have paid for hospitalization, but we avoid doing so as far as possible, owing to the numerous complications of responsibility, etc. A certain number of outcalls are made, but these are usually only to employees or ex-employees or in cases where it is felt that the outing may result in improvement of relations with the military or other officials.

The government has so far displayed little interest in our clinic, either friendly or critical. Local soldiers and police have created difficulties occasionally and we have observed signs of efforts to discredit us in the eyes of the lao-pei-hsing ['old hundred names', the ordinary people]. We particularly need a doctor so that these criticisms can be silenced. We are still hopeful of getting hold of Dr. Kou, who was introduced to us through the Catholic Hospital... [There was some reluctance to employ a doctor at considerable cost but this was soon to happen.]

Liberation and more medical statistics

It was the normal practice for FAU/FSU sections to send monthly reports to headquarters in Shanghai. In his open report to the annual Staff Meeting (above) Jack said little about the arrival of the communist troops, but in his earlier monthly report, reproduced below, he felt able to give a fuller account of 'liberation', perhaps because this was a less public document. Six pages long, this report also gave greater detail than his report to the Staff Meeting, including a colourful summary of his extensive statistical tables.

His final report for June 1950 that then follows below tells of the employment at last of a properly qualified Chinese doctor, Dr Kou. In July 1950 Robert and Dorothy Reuman left Chungking by boat down the Yangtse to Shanghai where, as its final chairman, Robert was given the task of winding up the work of the FSU. The timing of the journey was to enable them to attend a crucial Staff Meeting in Shanghai and they lived in hope of being able to return to field work in Chungking, but it was not to be as desk work in Shanghai dealing with the closure was now inevitable.

SOUTH BANK CLINIC, CHUNGKING

Monthly Report, 10 March, 1950 [Received stamp] Apr 24, 1950

… It was then decided to empty the big godown by the gate in our yard and move the clinic there. The builder was busy through the weekend repairing the building. On November 26th there was a further surprise when the Reumans arrived from Hongkong. On November 28th there was a false alarm about the Communists also having arrived. On the 29th the builder was still busy in the godown. On the 30th the clinic was conducted for the last time in the old precincts. While we were working there the gun fire began. We spent all afternoon moving into our new quarters and by 06:00 p.m. the new clinic was in order. There was a big red cross on the door and a notice saying it was the FAU's Poor People's Clinic. We had supper by candle light to the music of continuous machine gun fire and explosions and next morning woke up to find Communists soldiers in the yard. The clinic had expanded just in time...

The 'big godown by the gate'

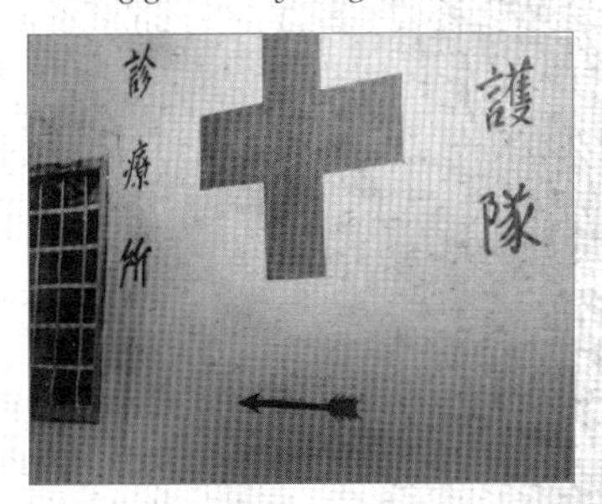

Statistics. By December 5th the clinic was sufficiently organized for us to begin to keep track of attendance…

[Daily average attendances in the first two weeks were 74 and 54 patients. As from December 19th more specific records were kept, distinguishing between men, women and children whose sex, Jack says, is difficult to determine 'owing to the multiplicity and complication of their defenses against the rigours of a Szechuan winter'. By the end of February 1950, he reports, attendances averaged just under 100 patients a day. There then follows a table of statistics of 'Diseases in Order of Popularity', nearly 40% of which are skin lesions and respiratory problems. Table III is entitled, 'Distribution of Illnesses by Sex and Size', ie men, women and children.]

From this table the intelligent reader will observe that it is more

Beggars, Honan, 1947

dangerous to be a man than a woman in the case of injuries (55% of all injuries), debility (49%), skin diseases (48%), eye complaints (47%), and skin lesions (43%). Children, though they suffer little from rheumatism (only 2% of all rheumatic attendances), sweep the board with eye complaints (77%) and enjoy about half the colds (47%), venereal disease (46%) and malaria (42%). Women, with low scores in ear complaints (9%) and injuries (17%) and moderate on skin complaints, respiratory complaints and vitamin deficiencies, have more than their fair share of gastro-intestinal troubles (40%) and rheumatism (53%), and when it comes to gynaecological diseases (100%), mastitis (100%), and pregnancies (100%), they seem to be in a class of their own.

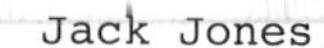

Jack Jones

SOUTH BANK CLINIC, CHINA, Report for June 3 – 30, 1950

Personnel. When Bob Reuman sent in his last report, Dr. William Kou had put in half a day at the clinic. He has now put in half a month. Since Bob and Dorothy left to attend Staff Meeting [in Shanghai] the same week that Dr. Kou took up his duties it can be said that the latter just arrived in the nick of time. Had the Reumans gone and no Dr. Kou arrived to replace them an almost intolerable strain would have been put on those that remained. As it is things go very smoothly in the clinic now and nobody is overworked or overburdened with responsibility. All new patients and many of the others are first seen by Dr Kou, who writes diagnosis and prescription on the patient's card. Treatment is then doled out in the next room by Fleda, Mrs. Sam and Chen Chi An. Chen Chi An was soon able to read the cards and Mrs. Sam is learning to read them rapidly. Lao Tsao [Chou Min Chang] is occupied full-time on the filing and Feng Ah Fu gives out tickets and does all the odd jobs. Jack Jones is first reserve in all departments, taking the place of the doctor in the consulting room, the lab technicians in the lab. or the dressers in the OPD [out patients' department] with equal facility, when called upon to do so, and in the meantime concocting hellish brews in the dispensary and reports like this.

Feng Ah Fu

Work Done. With the arrival of a new medico emphasis in the clinic work has shifted somewhat. Dr. Kou immediately realized that many of the patients are only seeking medical aid because it is free or at the worst are suffering from a stomach ache through bolting five bowls of rice in two minutes. The distribution of soda bicarb, 5 gr. t.i.d. [five grams three times a day] for 2 days shot up to dizzy heights. Careful and thorough examination of patients both as to history and physical condition (which had been undertaken before despite our inadequate knowledge of the language and of medicine) went by the board. Scabies patients were given sulph. oint and told to scrub and anoint themselves at home, - the balneal rites [bathing/scrubbing] at which Dopey [Dorothy] and Feng Ah Fu had assisted came more or less to an end – and I should say our previous efficiency on scabies, such as it was, has been greatly reduced. Lab. work came to an end except for routine stool examinations and an occasional malaria blood-slide. Gradually however the doctor is becoming more painstaking in his examinations and more venturesome in his use of the facilities at his command. While it is possible to criticize his recommendations in

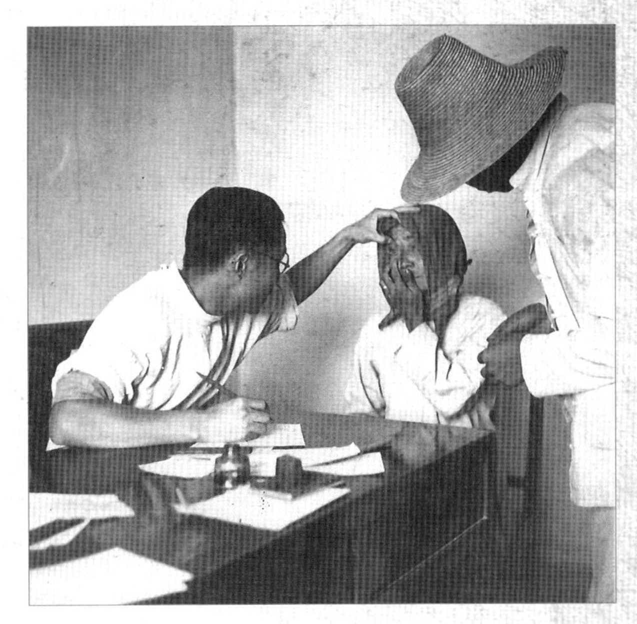

An FAU doctor at Chungmou

some instances, by and large he seems to be doing a good job and there are signs that as he settles down he will do better still. Certainly the atmosphere in the clinic has been far more peaceful and orderly since his arrival, and this is due to two factors: his ability to speak the language of the patients fluently, so that so much nervous energy isn't spent in mutual misunderstanding by patients and staff alike; and the fact that he has taken over responsibility, leaving the rest of us in the position mainly of dispensing and nursing staff. Some repeat patients, most of the skin and ulcer cases, and some others that are obviously uncomplicated, Fleda attends to, leaving the more serious cases to see the doctor; but there is no strain in attending to these and as far as the clinic staff is concerned the employment of the doctor is justified by results.

One curious result of having a doctor has been an absence of really serious cases all month. One old gentleman who took his tung oil lamp under his mosquito net when he started swatting mosquitoes used up pots of boric acid oint and yards of dressings and one small girl was so ill that she was kept on the premises all night so that she could have regular shots of penicillin, but everything else has been strictly routine. The doctor frequently asks Fleda's and sometimes my opinion, especially about female patients, and relations are good enough for us to be able to have these discussions without anyone losing face.

Sam Yen continues to help daily with the government cholera-typhoid injection drive. Considerable difficulty is being experienced in rounding up victims and all the twenty teams in this district have been told to pull their socks up. Sam's team now has three policemen detailed to it and the number of injections given shows an upward curve.

Weather during the month has been uniformly bad and there has been a decline in attendances. Gastro-intestinal complaints continue to be most popular, with coughs and colds a good second, indeed they led the field during the coldest, wettest weather. Eye cases have now fallen right back to the percentage they maintained prior to the opening of the trachoma clinic. This is partly due to the fact that another eye clinic has opened about two kilos away and partly to the fact that our clinic has cleared up the obvious effects of trachoma in a large number of cases. People are so much improved they can't see any sense in coming any more.

This feeling also accounts for the decline in the number of skin diseases, which continues; large numbers of people are now cured or much improved through attending the clinic.

End Note: Jack Jones - poet or accountant?

The mass of statistics in Jack's reports on the work of the clinic reveal a new characteristic of Jack's complex personality, namely a passion for collating information and figures. This is further indicated by an article entitled, 'The Health of the Changs' that Jack wrote and mailed to Mark Shaw in Philadelphia in the forlorn hope of getting it published. This article, recently sent to me by Spencer Coxe's's son in Seattle, consists of no fewer that ten pages of statistical tables analysing a sample of patients at the clinic by reference to sex, age and the number and nature of their complaints. As will be mentioned, the selection of this sample was quirky to say the least.

In the article Jack notes the many difficulties of record-keeping in China. The index cards cannot be stored alphabetically and so have to be arranged according to the number of brush strokes in the name's character or some other arbitrary scheme. His patients also used a variety of names and nicknames and as to their ages they were extremely vague.

The Chinese peasantry, he comments, are known as 'Old Hundred Names' and the same family names keep recurring. Confusingly more than a fifth of his patients were either Chang, Li or Wong.

Jack reports that in the six months to November 1950 his new and amateur clinic dealt with the substantial total of 9,500 patients of whom 710 were Changs, the most common family name. Jack thus took the Changs as an arbitrary sample for his statistical analysis and an impressive piece of work it is too, of possible credit towards the academic degree that his father had so aspired to for his wayward son.

Jack of course had always longed to be a poet or writer, rejecting the treadmill of formal academe and career, though unfortunately, like snowflakes in hell, jobs for poets are thin on the ground. With Jack's fascination for the orderly marshalling of numbers and statistics now revealed, the thought strikes me that he might instead have made a very formidable accountant.

Was Jack's clinic all sweetness and light?

Official reports and newsletters always aim to promote a positive view of an institution and in this respect the China Convoy's's written output was probably no different. It can be hard therefore to identify any difficulties at the south bank depot and clinic that may have been glossed over by the documents that appear in this book. Indeed there must have been many such tensions arising from intrinsic problems with the project itself and from the diverse personalities and backgrounds of the individuals involved in it.

More can potentially be learned about this from actually speaking to those who were there or by reading private letters home and the following is what I have discovered.

The three members who worked with Jack in Chungking that I have met all speak very positively about his leadership. Peter Mason clearly looked up to the older man, telling me that he was very easy to work with and that he really knew how to treat people and to get things done, such as sourcing decent whisky from the British Consulate. Howell Jones remained a close friend and admirer, keeping in touch for many years and, after Jack helped him finance his medical studies in Hong Kong, met up with him on at least one of Jack's rare visits to London. Mark Jones praised Jack's coolness under pressure and emphasised that everyone worked very effectively as a team under his leadership. The daughter of FAU member, Tony Meager, who was instrumental in helping Jack to join him at Unicef in Bangkok, also distinctly remembers her late father's admiration of Jack's exceptional skills in leading and motivation teams, especially of locally recruited staff.

The Burma Road crosses the Salween gorge, Yunnan, China

Jack's special qualities must therefore have been recognised when the job of running the transport unit from the south bank depot at Chungking was given to him in preference to other more experienced members. It was an impossibly difficult role, perhaps made more so by the collective style of democratic management which the FAU derived from key Quaker principles. At Quaker meetings there is no priest and no hierarchy, and decisions are made with everyone participating according to the sense of the meeting and without a formal vote. In a scattered organisation with poor communications a similar collective ethos based on periodic staff meetings enabled FAU members to get on with their work according to the agreed spirit, but it also must have had its limitations. The dilution of top-down leadership could have meant that control was limited and if individuals did not like what they were supposed to do, they might not actually do it at all.

Added to this, in Jack's day the FAU had reached the end of its wartime focus as a transport operation and the glory days of transport were over, causing great nostalgia amongst those who remained. The 'transport men' longed for the romance of the open road as they moped about in the garage doing mechanical work or even worse sat chained to a desk in the office. Asking them to switch to working in an untried and amateurish clinic also required another quantum leap that could not have been easy to sustain.

China was in turmoil and it must have been hard to show total commitment for a new project that was likely to be ephemeral. Dealing with the Nationalist authorities had always been a bureaucratic nightmare, and another layer of uncertainty was now interposed with new sets of rules when the communist regime took over. At the outbreak of the Korean War, suspicion of foreigners especially Americans became official policy, making it even more difficult being one in China.

Dorothy and Bob Reumans' letters home to their parents in the US always strove to reassure them that they were safe and well, though sometimes they also acted as a safety valve for private problems, revealing their view of what was going on below the surface. They told their families they were always well-fed with plentiful local produce despite post-war austerity elsewhere in the world, and that their cooking, laundry and other needs were well taken care of. Despite some frustrations they were enjoying a rich experience doing the field work they had hoped for.

Nonetheless, life at the Chungking depot was undoubtedly austere and a real challenge for new arrivals. The accommodation was cramped and the Reumans' photos show five or six people packed into a small and grubby common room. A full book-shelf of books can be seen but these had to be read before nightfall as there was rarely any electricity. Fleda's room in which she both slept and did her lab work was only accessible through Dorothy and Bob's, while the men slept in a tightly packed bunkhouse. The buildings were not old, having been built as the FAU transport depot in the early forties, but they were substandard, consisting of a light timber frame filled in with bamboo matting and mud plaster that dogs, robbers and communist explosions could easily penetrate.

Playing cards in the common room

Bob and Dorothy describe their bed as, 'a wooden frame with ropes woven across it, resting on some wooden horses, on which we spread out our sleeping bags, and covered with netting, not so much to keep out the mosquitoes but to prevent the rats which scurried across the ceiling beams from falling directly on us when they lost their footing.' Water was brought up daily by the water carrier from a flooded corner of a rice

'Washing vegetables in our drinking water pond'

field in which they also washed the vegetables. It was filtered through sand and boiled for drinking, but little if any mention is made in their letters of Bob's amoebic dysentery that was hard to shake off and caused him to lose fifty pounds in weight.

On top of all this, the climate of Chungking as one of China's 'four furnaces', is among the worst in the world. The winter is so gloomy that dogs are said to bark if the sun comes out. The cold and greyness are depressing and the rain is fine and insidious, while the inescapable mud and penetrating dampness led to chest and respiratory complaints that were hard to throw off. In addition, constant bowel and other health problems inevitably lowered morale. In summer the weather became desperately hot with high humidity that was enervating and exhausting, the small, stifling rooms unrelieved by any luxuries such as constant power for electric fans. It is thus hard to exaggerate how tough the Chungking climate was in contrast to the eternal spring of Kunming and the hill climates of the former transport depots in Kutsing and Kweiyang, adding hugely to their daily burden.

Culture shock hadn't been invented in those days but the horrors of poverty that they confronted every day in the clinic must also have been truly shocking. Bob and Dorothy keep coming back to this theme in their letters home.

'The sun very seldom peeks through the clouds, our hands are continuously cold, and the candles don't shed much light… but these are trivial inconveniences... Constantly we are reminded by the sores, the semi-nudity, the patched and tattered garments hanging from shivering shoulders… on all sides there are the unheated shacks where a slim candle provides the only extension of daylight, where fuel is so scarce that it cannot be spared from the cooking to wash the dirt and scabies from a baby's blistered body with warm water… Existence here for these people is unadorned simplicity, a round of birth, childhood, work, procreation and death, lavishly sprinkled with empty tummies, cold toes and dirty sores… And yet they smile and are grateful… and they cheerfully endure (though the kids scream) the rigours of bath and sulphur mixture as their scabies-ridden bodies smart under the sting of the penetrating medicine. Real and horrible are the sores of China that come to us day after day; bodies deeply pitted with smelly, nauseous ulcers, usually covered with a foul rag'.

Carrying a heavy load past the depot

And this was the brave version for the folks back home, saying nothing of how the constant tide of suffering they were trying to stem must have haunted their dreams.

Too many prima donnas perhaps?

If hell is other people, the greatest challenge for a group of disparate personalities thrown together in a tough predicament such as this is to work together harmoniously. The fact that they all shared the essential principle of pacifism and had a genuine desire to serve should have made things easier, but could possibly have done the exact opposite. All those coming to the FAU/FSU did so as idealistic young people with high expectations of helping mankind, but if this was not fulfilled, disappointment and disillusionment was often more damaging than indifference. Those with a Christian commitment joining a nominally Christian organisation were also sometimes disappointed by the lack of an overt Christian spirit among many of their colleagues or in the group itself. Perhaps even more crucial but mentioned less often, the essential relationships with their Chinese colleagues and employees on whom the foreigners so totally depended were nothing if not complex, perhaps much more so than they sometimes realised.

The seven foreigners serving at the south bank depot in its last years as the communists arrived at the end of 1949 were certainly an interesting and varied bunch. There were two British men, four Americans and one South African, including two Quakers, a Catholic and a Methodist, some of the rest being lapsed or sceptical, while in all there were five men and two women. In racial terms there were five white and, a rarity in China, two black. The newsletters and reports tell a lot about them all but by remarkable chance I also have the letters home of Americans, David White and Bob and Dorothy Reuman, the latter couple's consisting of over two hundred typed pages. All three were fine and perceptive writers, displaying their personal frustrations and political concerns, and they make fascinating reading. Dave focused on his own personal adventures while Bob and Dorothy were meticulous in analysing the impact on the group of the differing personalities with whom they found themselves working.

David Underhill White, an American who had recently in June 1949 graduated in agriculture from the University of Minnesota, received a very positive write-up from the Reumans. Dorothy told her parents that, 'Dave is certainly the ideal person in keeping the section as one big happy family, getting along with everyone excellently, and being liked by everyone. He's very outspoken and well-meaning, so that his words don't hurt, and yet they clear the air and move things along.'

Bob reported that, 'Dave is tiptop, as we've said before. His geniality and lively humour have more than once smoothed ruffled waters and eased the tension which sometimes gathers around the intercourse of our personalities. He is a universal fixer, filled with a practical initiative that sees what needs to be done and does it. He is adaptable, friendly, sensitive but not easily hurt. Infrequently he gets irritated, but his laugh and his jokes always save the

Dave dreaming perhaps of Leonore

day. Dave is a good friend and the kind one likes to have for a friend, and it is always fun to hike with him or to do photographic work with him. He has the best "leaven" of any of us, possibly except Dorothy, but his excellence is not of a religious sort but of a humorous approach.'

Yet for Dave being in Chungking involved a special sacrifice as on landing from the ship in Manila while on passage to China he had fallen in love with a Filipina called Leonore Perelta who he intended to marry. Waiting for up to two years before he could see her again, a separation relieved only by the occasional letter, must have been acutely painful, clouding his experience in China.

Dennis Frone, an Englishman had studied at the long established Bancroft's School in north London not too far from Jack's family home, before going on to start a career in a bank. With the accounting and management skills he had thus learned, he became an ideal executive secretary of the FSU based in Shanghai. He had earlier experience of serving in Chungking and was recalled from Hong Kong twice to take over the West China directorship when Jack had typhus and otherwise 'became sick'. Yet in all the documents he keeps a remarkably low profile and he seems to have been distinctly camera shy. Occasionally he socialised with the others, though in Bob's words, 'he is often over the hill with his lady friend, Mrs (divorced) McLaughlin', who Jack liked to call 'Mrs McCork'. Apparently an IRC employee, she and Dennis were later married in 1957, though she was sadly to die quite young.

Bob and Dorothy's first impression of Dennis was brief, describing him as 'of slight build with sandy hair. Jack succinctly sums him up,' they said, 'as a man who is so afraid of being wrong that he cannot make up his mind… an excellent phrase whether it applies to Dennis or not.'

As they got to know him better they developed a high regard for him. 'Dennis is a quiet English chap, in his thirties, very good natured and quite independent. He has been in China for quite a while, formerly with the FAU, then with the International Relief Committee, and now back with the FAU. He is an excellent executive secretary, very conscientious, hard-working and meticulous and he has more or less picked up and carried on Jack's responsibilities in an unassuming and uncomplaining fashion. In place of Jack's erratic bursts of entertaining and unilluminating literary brilliance, we now have a patient worker whose reports are accurate and timely. Repatriation was a terrific headache and while Jack blew out from underneath it, Dennis calmly shouldered it and carried it thru successfully. Dennis is no problem for he is quite unobtrusive, takes joshing in a friendly spirit and he appears never to be moody and unhappy. Perhaps essentially shy, but a fine stable chap to have around.'

For whatever reason Jack's writings sometimes teased Dennis unmercifully, though much later in his book, *Daughters of an Ancient Race*, he gave him the ultimate accolade. When describing each of his Chungking colleagues in the book he sums up Dennis as, 'a small bespectacled Englishman who had more guts and commonsense than all the rest of us put together'. Sadly by the time of its publication in 1974 Dennis had already died of a heart attack aged only fifty seven. He left a small son, born to his second wife, who at least now has been able to learn a little more from this book about the father he never knew.

JOHN PETER

John Peter deserves a host of superlatives as the longest serving member on the China Convoy, as perhaps the most versatile member in the wide range of work he could do, as probably the tallest and apparently the most photogenic of them all. Photos of him abound, including Jack Skeel's early shot of him on top of a charcoal burner poking down the fire before filling the hopper with charcoal for combustion to produce gas. The iconic photo of him painting the FAU logo onto a vehicle taken by Lindsay Crozier in Chengchow in October 1946 illustrates almost every publication about the China Convoy. A shot taken about 1942 shows him helping a patient into the mobile surgery unit in Paoshan, but it is with his friend, Jimmy the monkey, that he charms us the most, including the tiny dog-eared print that Howell Jones sent me. John had apparently performed in a circus in Rangoon and I speculate that when he escaped from the Japanese invasion over the Burma Road, Jimmy, his circus side-kick came too.

John loved nothing better than a singalong with his guitar. He can be seen in a fan tien eating rice dishes and apparently syphoning petrol in front of an admiring audience in those robust days before the constraints of 'health and safety'. Finally, as well as driver and mechanic, John was a medic, an electrician and was skilled at designing and making prosthetic limbs, his simple sketch being realised as a life-saver for this lucky individual. After leaving China in 1951 John disappeared into obscurity in Hong Kong but, as his daughter has told me, his heart remained all the time in China. His four children of course remember their father very warmly but John and his fine service to China is otherwise all but forgotten. These pages can now serve as his memorial.

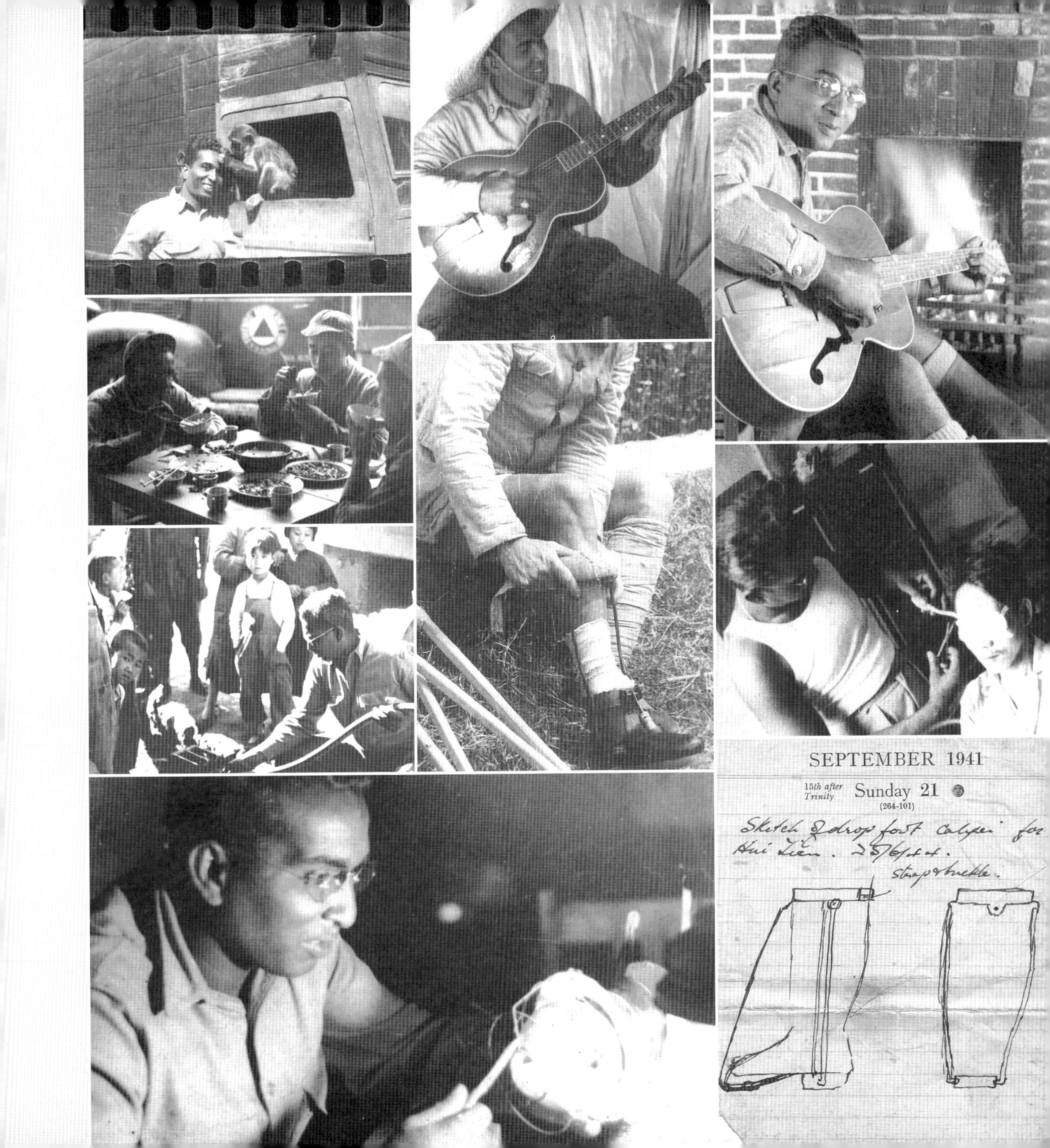
SEPTEMBER 1941
15th after Trinity
Sunday 21
(264-101)
Sketch of drop foot Caliper for
Hui Lien.
strap & buckle.

John Peter, born in Cape Town possibly of Tamil or Sikh origins and having served with the China Convoy from its very beginning, was in a much more unenviable situation. Apparently orphaned in South Africa, his daughters, who know little of where his family came from, tell me he was brought up by an 'uncle' in Rangoon and sent to a prestigious Catholic high school there. When the Japanese invaded Burma he escaped into China and the FAU and, unless they went with him, his family and friends must have been left to their fates. With the Indian colonial class disliked by the Burmese and old scores being settled, many died horribly in the jungle trying to escape on foot to India. Perhaps John did not even know what had happened to them.

In his early forties he now found himself in China with no family and nowhere to go, being, as Peter Mason has described him to me, a lost soul and effectively stateless. It would be hard to think of two less hospitable places for him to return to than South Africa and Burma. Adrift as a black man in a post-colonial world and in a vast nation with a racial superiority complex, he must have endured many slights that could have become toxic. Because of his race and his massive physique he was stared at as a freak wherever he went; he could not even escape behind a bush to relieve himself without the locals following him to take a peek. His personality and warmth shine out of the many photos of him that have survived though and Mark Jones has told me that as the first non-European he had ever met, the privilege of knowing John permanently influenced his own positive attitude to racial differences. Loyal as they were to John though, his young and relatively sheltered colleagues may not have been able to grasp his predicament and it would be surprising if he had not become bruised or brittle by so many setbacks in his life.

In the words of Gus Borgeest, a later employer, John was 'a wonderful mechanic and medical clinic attendant, a veritable artist with his hands'. He was skilled on both vehicles and medical equipment such as X Ray machines, he designed and made prosthetic limbs, he could rewire a derelict hospital, he created the hot water system for the south bank garage hostel, he was an excellent driver and convoy leader, he rose to garage manager in Chungking and he brought considerable experience to the clinic as a male nurse. Yet understandably he seems to have been unsettled, unsure of his future and as the quintessential Roadman, nostalgic for the free-wheeling days of the transport unit. As Bob put it, he is, 'morose, deprived of the romance of the road. Weekends he takes a jeep to the city and stays with his Catholic friends'.

John Peter and his hot water system. Chungking depot

More than sixty years on Dorothy Reuman remembers John as, 'a very essential member of the Chungking group'. She and Bob's initial impression of him was very positive and they maintained a genuine liking for him. 'John is a big negro chap who has a fine sympathetic nature,' Bob wrote home, ' a "jolly good" sense of humour, and capabilities along both mechanical and medical lines. He has been here for seven years and speaks Chinese with native ease.'

They also seemed to have an appreciation of his vulnerabilities. 'John is quite sensitive, evidently having been slighted often enough that he becomes sulky when he doesn't quite feel needed. After four weeks in the hospital [with bronchitis], he is now back, though as yet he has not rejoined us at the clinic except for a few minutes this morning. Fleda nipped him a couple of times, and feeling as he does that she could and should have avoided the crisis with Jack, those two sometimes are not too chummy.'

In a later letter Bob set out more of the perceived downsides to his personality. 'John I like, but John is not easy to get along with. He's a big handsome Negro chap, strong in body and opinion, grown to the forties in age but possessed of a childish streak which occasionally breaks through the genial exterior. His personality is a bit on the paradoxical side – he can be generous to a fault, he is easily touched by misery and will go out of his way to help a child or an old man, but he easily and frequently roars out in exasperated tones in the clinic at inoffensive chaps whose sole fault was to give an inconsistent answer to his question or a naïve reply. One minute he is exuberant with mirth, and the next he sulks like a little child. He is very capable with his hands, but seems to require a factotum to do his minor tasks and serve as a yes man. Quite dictatorial, though not didactic, in manner… he is sensitive and easily offended, but his reaction to offense is to draw within himself and pout. He wants to be loved and loves to be needed. Perhaps he needs constant affection most of all, but not the slavish devotion that he seems sometimes to require. His reaction to the question of getting Dr. Mostyn back was, "If she comes, I quit." It seems to be his stock answer, but John is a good chap whose virtues far outweigh his vices.'

Their bonds of friendship were sufficiently strong that even after his death in 1974 John's daughter, Magdalena, was still corresponding with the Reumans.

Robert and Dorothy Reuman themselves stand out as a remarkable couple. Committed Quakers born in China to missionary families, they were determined to live the principled life of their faith. Thus Bob refused military service as a conscientious objector in 1943, working for the duration of the war first in a camp fighting forest fires and then for two and a half years in a mental hospital. In 1948 while teaching at the University of Pennsylvania (where in 1949 he earned his PhD in philosophy) he was sentenced to a year in jail for refusing to register for the draft, serving four months in a federal penitentiary before being paroled to work under the AFSC in China. On his release from detention he and Dorothy were married and sailed for Hong Kong, their sea voyage serving as an extended honeymoon, their letters home constantly extolling their love and devotion to each other.

Dorothy and Robert's letters reveal perceptive individuals passionately concerned about the disastrous mistakes they saw their country making in its foreign policies towards China and Korea. Despite their patriotism, they saw through America's romantic view of Madame Chiang Kai Shek and the Nationalists, and thought that the new communist government could offer considerable opportunities for the peoples of China. However, when in early 1951 Bob wrote a report of nearly ten thousand words for the AFSC in Philadelphia analysing the future of foreign aid work in communist China, he sadly concluded that under present conditions there was now no place in China for the Friends.

Throughout the Reumans' time in China, long letters home flew back and forth, debating new and challenging political ideas which sometimes came close to causing offense and family rifts. Sceptical about the old school Christian missionaries he saw in China, Bob even dared tell his former China missionary parents exactly what he thought. 'The social gospel of the new [communist] regime,' he boldly wrote, 'is far more visionary and capable than that of the Christian church in China'.

Positively bursting with new ideas and idealism, with sky-high expectations for their life's union and for giving dedicated service to the suffering masses of their beloved China, arriving in Chungking was never going to be easy for them though. There they met their new leader, the tired and jaded, sometimes cynical Jack Jones, now manfully struggling to make a go of his new clinic in difficult times. While they looked forward to applying their formal learning and principles, Jack, who had missed his chance of further education, insisted they would be of little use to him until they grasped that the only thing of value in real life is practical experience. Jack who had seen it all was likely to feel threatened by their pent-up energy and motivation to change both China and his precious clinic, but it says much for all of them that they went on to work well together and to remain good friends.

Indeed when the Reumans were moved on to Shanghai to manage the final closure of all FSU operations they talk in their letters of 'our beloved Chungking' and of the real pleasure of doing field work in the real China rather than living in the artificial urban bubble of Shanghai. They had thus made a difficult experience wholly positive. They loved the Chinese countryside and particularly its people and had worked hard and with commitment on their behalf. If sometimes hurt or confused by the tensions within the Unit, their letters suggest that they did what they could to keep the show on the road and to treat any setback as a learning-experience.

Of their colleagues they seemed to have had the least easy relationship with **Fleda Jones**, in part because they felt her affair with Jack divided the Unit, she and Jack reclusively 'living their private lives' together. Bob wrote home as follows. 'Fleda is an enigma and the most difficult to get on with. She can be utterly charming and captivating if she cares to be, and she can be hell on legs if she so desires – unfortunately the latter seems to come more easily to her. Her manner is antagonistically positive and confident in a cocky way. She never doubts herself at least in public, and if you get along with her it is on such terms as she cares to dictate. Jack is her only real conquest, but he is more a slave than a lover. She seldom flares up and has excellent self-control, but usually is introvertishly drawn within her impenetrable shell. I never feel at ease with her, even when she is cordial which is not often and I feel a tension which says, careful Bob, and she may turn and snap at you in a trice.

She is like a plate of iron, strong stuff but not what you want for a friend. She is capable, I think, but her very dogmatism makes me doubt her judgment. In the clinic she is never at a loss for an answer, though none of my doctor friends would give a tinker's damn for the medical knowledge of a lab technician. The source of her ramrod temperament escapes me. It may lie in racial feelings, or in a basic feeling of insecurity. Goodness knows, both Dope and I would like to get along with her, but it is mighty hard going, and when you don't get along with her you are non gratis to Jack as well.

Here I think is the core of my feeling of incompleteness and failure, for I would like to win and I have not. Sometimes I feel that she is taking her revenge on the white race, by not allowing them to feel at ease when she is around; still, on passing contact, and often with Dave she seems to get along remarkably well. But again there's hope, for our relationship is much more cordial in the last month or so and we may surmount this obstacle yet. Pretty much so far however, our modus vivendi has been to travel our separate ways and that is no solution in a situation such as ours. But there is hope and we're trying.'

In their letters to Chungking the Reuman parents asked if the tensions within the group could be caused either by bachelor envy of Bob and Dorothy's newly married bliss or by reason of race. Dorothy replied that she thought not in either case. 'The personnel problem is not one of race or nationality, except as they may have molded the personalities of the individuals'.

Ironically back in 1947 Jack had gone public in the FAU newsletters opposing married couples in the Unit. Now he was having to work with a close-knit couple, while desperately and traumatically trying to become a part of one himself. As to John and Fleda's Indian and African origins, it is understandable if their experiences when younger and as black people in China might have affected them in some way. Confronting the attitudes of the day was perhaps far more difficult for them than we can now understand and, as a refugee from Burma, John's predicament was particularly harsh.

As to Fleda in general, what courage she must have had as a single woman, alone, petite and black, heading off to China to do relief work when civil war was raging. The one person in the clinic with any formal medical training, how was she now to assert herself working alongside a waspish Ivy League Doctor of Philosophy, the strong and experienced twenty seven year old, Robert Reuman? It is hard now to appreciate the impact that differences of gender and race had on relationships more than sixty years ago and making herself heard as an equal could have needed more than a little emphasis on her part.

It was never likely to be easy for her, though the Reumans were apparently sensitive to her positive qualities. In May 1950 Bob wrote, 'Fleda has remarkable stamina in bearing up under the weight of [work in] the clinic. She is more jovial now and chats pleasantly… Most of the time now there are only the three of us out there [in the clinic] and the constant pressure plus the July heat of these days is very wearing'.

Group dynamics are rarely easy, especially in so assorted and claustrophobic a group of expatriates as this one. As Dorothy wrote to her parents at the time, 'we're all such individuals and we just ain't orthodox'. Sixty years later in a letter to me she concluded as follows. 'There can only be so many prima donnas in any one project!'.

***

What is now most significant in the context of this book of Jack Jones' China writings is of course the Reumans' estimation of Jack himself in all his psychological complexity. They both wrote to their families about him and Bob's analysis is so incisive, whether totally correct or not, that it bears reproducing at length.

'**Jack Jones** is in many ways the most interesting person. He is in his late thirties, clad in a big beard, quite taken with China. His big failing is women – he has an almost morbid sexual interest in them all, specialises in women's cases in the clinic and in their structure and relationships in his writings, and when he falls in love, which is frequent, it is with the utmost infatuation and lack of control. He is Fleda's little dog, doing her every bidding, now as before his attempted suicide, and almost detestable in his imbecilic servility. Although it is difficult to separate him from Fleda for we have only known them together, he may be quite different by himself. Almost without doubt he has an inferiority complex which finds stability in a person of Fleda's temperament, yet this is often masked in apparent self confidence and dogmatism.

Bob's photo of Jack at the Chunking depot

He has little formal education, though he is very well read, and most of his life has been spent in menial manual labour jobs. I rather suspect that he undeservedly feels insecure on this account and he overcompensates by berating formal education; he claims from his few years of trial and error first aid work in China that he knows more about medicine than Dr. Mostyn, for example, though he would willingly extend it to include most doctors.

We had a long talk the other night in which he told me that I had too much respect for schooling and not enuf for the working man, and he adduced some shockingly irrelevant and fictitious examples… I think and hope that he is wrong here, but the point is that he has the feeling, and he is a feeling rather than a rational type in Jung's language, and I believe that it is so because he expects a man with a degree to take it seriously. He did admit that I was improving though, and he told me that once I had weathered the crisis of every intellectual, namely to learn respect for the knowledge which comes from the soil, I would make an excellent section leader or chairman of the Unit. This was flattering, both the latter part and to be classed as an intellectual, but I never have had any trouble in getting along with the men of the soil per se, indeed I have often enjoyed their company, though not always their thoughts, much more than the so-called intelligentsia.

Jack has a very great talent in the use of words and for that matter in drawing. He has done some excellent pencil sketches and he is a master of the short descriptive essay. He can write much better that I will ever be able to, for on paper he has a sense of humor which is remarkably fresh and vigorous. Unfortunately, however, there are two drawbacks here in addition to a certain literary irascibility, namely, his humor is not of the soil but of the dirt, or what could more usually be called filth. Occasionally such humor can be refreshing for its very lack of restraint, but his is so ubiquitous and so singly sordid minded that it palls on one, and even more so after knowing the writer himself.

The other fault is that his imagination is so facile that a factual account will often bear little relation to the actual occurrence if you have the chance to observe both. Yet it is not exactly false, but only misleading by innuendo.

For example, in a report of the clinic to Shanghai he says that Fleda carries all the work and responsibility of the clinic in his absence while Dorothy has "fun and games" giving baths to the scabies patients. Fleda carries no more of the responsibility than any of us and much less of the work, while "fun and games" is hardly an accurate description of the work in the scabies annex. Then too there is his negative scepticism. I have heard him compliment only one person in all the time I have known him, otherwise his remarks on people are invariably negatively critical, nor have I heard him construct positive approaches to theoretical matters, always it is to tear down what anyone else believes in.

But Jack isn't a bad sort and one could get along with him very well, I fancy, if it weren't for this Fleda infatuation and separation. Yet even that brings out his good qualities, for he is compassionate to a fault and he does innumerable small services for her. Any man that will bring warm tea and toast and goodness knows what else to a person with a slight tummy ache as he did for Fleda one night until 4 o'clock in the morning has some good in him. And he does have a great affection for the fellows in the garage and a love for China. John speaks of the devotion he showed to his work here before Fleda came and many people elsewhere speak highly of Jack so that I imagine he is quite a different person now than he was ante-Fleda, and in spite of the criticism I have made of him as a person I think that in himself he would not be an impossible person to get along with. That's part of the paradox right there: both Jack and Fleda separately aren't too bad to adjust to, but somehow when they get together they fortify the worst in each other so far as others are concerned… *But* things are looking up and our rapport is improving considerably.'

In the event, the Reumans' friendship and warmth towards Jack fully survived the experience of Chunking. It seems that after they had moved on to Shanghai, Dorothy, though chained to a typewriter in her daily work, was also spending a considerable amount of time typing up the stories that Jack had written about the FAU's work in China, intended for publication in America. Despite the excitement of his ultimate escape from China and other priorities such as family letter writing, one of the first things Jack did on arriving in Hong Kong in mid-1951 was to write a long and amusing letter to Dorothy thanking her for her help. Though the stories she typed did not apparently get published, it seems that they or some of them may be the basis for *Daughters of an Ancient Race* published much later in 1974, so her work was not entirely in vain.

A final aside is to add to my earlier suggestion that Jack's rejection by Fleda and his overdose could have inspired the similar plight of his protagonist Reggie in his novel, *A Woman of Bangkok*. Bob's description of Jack's relationship

'Virgin with child entering manger,' by ERJ

with Fleda strongly resembles Reggie's obsessive submission to Vilai, the eponymous 'woman' of the book's title. As quoted above, Bob described Jack as 'more a slave than a lover' to Fleda, as showing the 'utmost infatuation and lack of control' in 'his imbecilic servitude towards her', while debasing himself as her 'little dog', just like Reggie's subservience to Vilai..

These tough words could simply be Bob blowing off steam in his letters home, though, as observed above, there is often much of the autobiography in many novels and not least of all in Jack's.

More importantly, despite the tensions between these idealists, the clinic relieved suffering and saved lives, even if they fell short in their bid to change the world. It was a drop in the ocean of China's need, yet the good that was done is still within living memory, though only just. In the Epilogue to this book I tell how I recently visited Chongqing and amongst its teeming millions found an old lady who remembered John Peter and the FAU's clinic with gratitude. Her last surviving little brother had been dying of measles. They took him in and saved his life and, what's more, they did it for free.

PHOTOGRAPHY AND FINE OLD FACES

Amidst all the squalor of feudal China in its death throes there was much for young FAU members, immature school leavers thrown in at the deep end, to hate and fear. Yet they often developed a life-long love not just of the place but particularly of the Chinese people themselves. China was cruel and overwhelming, they were uncomfortable, scared and lonely yet somehow the Chinese people, especially the children and the serene old people, made it all worthwhile. Such positive feelings are suggested in the photographs they took of those they met in their day to day work. Conditions for photography were appalling and materials scarce, the prints poorly produced on tiny scraps of paper. Kept in scattered private collections in someone's attic, they are often faded and damaged and have few if any captions. What have survived are therefore precious and with the appointment of professional photographer, Lindsay Crozier, in the post-war period and the work of talented amateurs like Bob Reuman the quality gradually improved. Crozier loved the weathered faces of old farmers, the serious poise of the village scribe and smiling Taoist priest. A fine humanitarian, his empathy with people produced striking portraits and is apparent as he shows his camera to a fascinated child. The shots at bottom left of the children in the bamboo push cart and eating rice outside the Chungking depot are by Robert Reuman, while Crozier's shot of the mountains at Hua Shan near Xian is but one of a fine collection of dramatic landscapes taken by him.

諸峰
奇險

13 ALL'S WELL... THE FRIENDS LEAVE CHINA – MARCH 1951

The clinic closed on 6th December 1950 just over a year after its opening and the remaining Chinese members and employees departed with the trucks and equipment to the Chinese Industrial Cooperatives' Bailie School in Shandan in Kansu Province. However, though the foreigners were no longer welcome in China they were not free to leave and Jack was not able to secure an exit permit and leave Chungking until May 1951. Nothing can have been worse than the uncertainty of struggling with an unaccountable and unpredictable bureaucracy and regime and longing to move on. The final Chronicle tells the story, possibly as edited by Dorothy Reuman as one of her final tasks before she and Bob left Shanghai at the end of March 1951.

FSU Chronicle Number 125, Shanghai, March 17, 1951

FINIS

"On occasions such as these one tends very much to look back and to reflect on the contribution that we have made to China during the course of a remarkable decade, and to reflect on the consequences to us as individuals of our association with China: how some never came back, and how some came back sick, and how all who came back will always have something of China flowing in their veins."

Those words of Bill Jordan's give perhaps a proper note as the work of the Unit now comes to a close. One by one, the last members have been folding their duffle bags and knapsacks about them and stealing away into the night. The personnel lists show that there are now nine members remaining, all of

Shandan

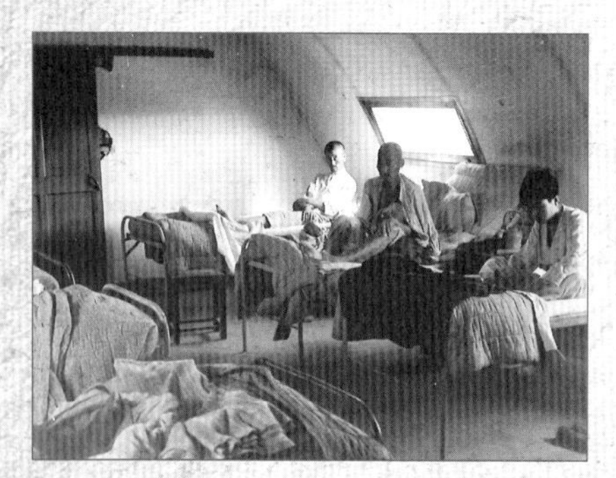

Inside a Chungmou hospital Quonset hut

them with plans for leaving in the near future. The Chungmou Hospital work was finished in November [1950], with the remaining Chinese members leaving the Unit at that time... In January Mary Mostyn and Roy Mason left their posts of secondment in Chengtu and Nanking, and are now seeking work in Hong Kong, or other points in this part of the world. [Mostyn of course became a government doctor in Hong Kong working and living with her old friend, Dr Han Suyin.] Chris Evans has remained in Hong Kong as agency representative for the Unit there... Bob and Dorothy Reuman will amble homeward. The Chinese members of the Chungking section, Chou Min Cheng, Sam Yen and Mrs. Sam left with the Bailie School Convoy at the end of January. [See below.] Remaining still in China are five foreigners of the Chungking section – Dennis Frone, Fleda Jones, Jack Jones, John Peter and Dave White. Fleda hopes to move on to work in India [she worked with refugees in Faridabad near New Delhi], and Dave plans to take unto himself a wife, the lovely Leonore of Manila. The others' plans are indefinite at the present. Courtney Archer, the last remaining former secondee, who had planned to stay on at Shantan after the Unit withdrew, has decided to take a year's leave of absence in order to help bring about more understanding of China in the rest of the world. He plans to return to China after this voyage of interpretation, to take up again his work in Shantan... [Caitriona Cameron's book records that in mid-1952 he in fact returned briefly to New Zealand to organize delegates for a Peace Conference in Beijing but on returning to the school realized that there was no longer a role for him there and finally left China in 1953.]

We can only hope that in the hearts and minds of any and all who have been members of the Unit, whether Chinese or foreign, there is some new understanding of other people and other countries; an understanding which may someday lead to a world of peace for which the Unit has striven.

CHUNGKING

After the decision of Staff Meeting to encourage [not instruct!] the Chungking section to close the clinic and close all aspects of the project, the section worked very hard to find a group which could make good use of the equipment remaining from Transport. It was finally agreed that the Chinese Industrial Cooperatives' Bailie School in

Shantan, Kansu [set up by New Zealander Rewi Alley], could take over the equipment and continue the equipment in service for the people of China. There were inevitable delays while all the authorizations from the parties concerned and from the various government departments were accumulated, but when clearance came through, things really began to move.

"The whole place is seething with activity at present, and you will not recognize parts of the Garage if you came back all of a sudden. A gang of coolies have moved down "Mary" [the generator] from her kennel onto a trailer and some of the chaps have taken down the engine to look it over as there was some talk "sabotage".

Mary the generator

They have now assembled it again and it seems to purr away quite nicely. Repairs and adjustments are being made to trucks and the students have been scraping off the FSU marks preparatory to painting on Gung Ho signs. [The popular term, gung ho, is derived from a name or slogan of the Chinese Industrial Cooperatives evoking the ethos that by working together nothing is impossible.] The main effort is in the packing and as you might expect Dave [White] is in the middle of this. Jack and Fleda [Jones] have finished inventorying and packing the QM [quartermaster's stores] and the remaining clinic supplies so we are getting on fairly well. Cupboards and drawers etc. are being used for making boxes so that the place is becoming rather bare. So far the office has not suffered many depredations – or the living room, but we expect to start on them soon. In the kitchen the cook has been making gobs and gobs of marmalade to go north [Chungking produces oranges] and the builder is repairing the wall that fell out of the QM a short while ago.

The clinic closed on December 6th, after most of the drugs were taken over by the authorities as being of doubtful origin, and with most of the personnel engaged in preparing the convoy to go north, it became impossible to continue its operation.

The final formal transfer was made on December 21st, with a book sized inventory as evidence that a momentous piece of work has been [two lines illegible] … received instructions from Peking regarding it and Cheng Hao and I were both summoned to the Foreign Affairs Bureau on the 30 January and told that the property now belonged to the Bailie School and that our responsibility had ceased. They were all set to go and so the next morning before dawn the 16 trucks set out together with the full complement of personnel. Evidently they crossed the river safely and we have heard nothing since." [These words in quotation marks may have been written by Dennis Frone, as he was the only remaining Chungking staff member, other than John Peter, not to be mentioned in it.]

The five remaining members moved their living quarters into the go-down that had been the clinic while the Bailie School students were preparing for their departure, and the only picture that has been conveyed from there since has been one of several figures curved around the drum-converted-into-a-stove which serves as fireside hearth as well as kitchen stove. The members now do their own marketing and cooking, as well as the many more duties that pertain to housekeeping. They are all awaiting the issuance of their exit permits, which are being delayed because of the inability to locate a shop which will guarantee them against any future claims which may be presented before, during, or after their departure. So far no one has been willing to accept this responsibility for the members, so that they are uncertain just when they will be leaving. Perhaps friends of the Unit may yet be favored with a Farthest West that will give the proper West China flavor to the remnant of the Friends Ambulance Unit and Friends Service Units.

A complete list of former Unit members, with their present addresses is being prepared in London by Bill Jordan. Anyone interested in having such a list may contact him at the Friends Service Council, Friends House, Euston Road, London N.W. 1, England.

The FSU 'China Convoy' is finally wound up

Though only a handful of foreign members remained, every possible way in which the Friends might continue to be of service in China was carefully considered. In a long eighteen page report to the AFSC in Philadelphia Robert Reuman, as the last chairman of the FSU, analysed the current situation and with regret concluded that foreigners were now a liability under the new regime and that withdrawal was the only option. A brief set of minutes of the last Council meeting records the final distribution of assets and the formal closure of the Unit.

FSU COUNCIL MEETING MINUTES, Meeting held March 1st, 1951, Shanghai

Present: Bob Reuman, chairman, Carol Chen, Bert King, Dorothy Reuman, co-opted.

MINUTE NO. 390. Shantan Bailie School Grant: Council approves giving a grant of ¥ 25,000,000 to the Bailie School in Shantan, Kansu, if the school is willing to accept the money.

MINUTE NO. 391. Disposition of residue funds: Council approves turning over to the Friends' Center in Shanghai whatever funds are remaining after the departure of the Headquarters' staff, with the mutual understanding and agreement of the Center and the Unit that any members of the Unit, in Shanghai or Chungking, may call upon this money until their departure.

MINUTE NO. 392. Closing of the Unit: Council recognizes the completion of the turning over of the Friends' Service Unit's major projects, and considers therefore that the Unit is officially closed.

Shanghai life, at Dr Hans Ludeke's. Left, Christine Mclaughlin, Margaret Perry, Dorothy Reuman, Chris Evans standing, Hans Ludeke, Carol Chen, Bert King, Gao Jen Di, Jack Gerson

14 WAS JACK IMPRISONED? FIVE LOST MONTHS IN FIFTY ONE

An empty time waiting for exit permits

The final FSU Chronicle of 17 March 1951 thus creates a forlorn picture of Jack and a few remaining friends sitting in the wreckage of their little empire and braving the damp chill of the Chungking winter as best they can, huddled round an improvised stove in the draughty godown where they are forced to live. With no work to do they are isolated from the recent past and from those around them because their Chinese friends and former employees can no longer be seen associating with the foreigners. Essential jobs and domestic chores have to be done but there is little else to distract from the trouble and anxiety of obtaining exit permits.

In a letter home written from Shanghai Dorothy Reuman summed up their predicament. 'They are now living in the building that was the clinic, the boys (Dennis, Dave, Jack and John) in the front part, and Fleda in the room behind. They buy all their own food and cook it, and Dave tinkers around fixing up convenience gadgets for their primitive living. They fry their food in a frying pan and boil their water in tin cans on an old stove, probably the one they rigged up last spring for the clinic out of an old gasoline drum… We learned that the convoy for the Shantan Bailie School got their load unfrozen all right, and that convoy has gone, so perhaps by now the Unit members have moved down nearer the river, as they planned to do after the convoy left. They expect the army next door to move in.'

In July of the previous year Dorothy and Robert Reuman had left Chungking, travelling down the Yangtse to Shanghai for a staff meeting and ultimately to head up the FSU and to manage its final closure. Shanghai and office work were the last thing they wanted, but at least the journey down the gorges by boat was memorable, though disappointing in that photography was forbidden.

Still with Jack in Chungking were long-time stalwart John Peter, Dave White, the energetic young American graduate in agriculture, and Dennis Frone, the Englishman who came back from Hong Kong to take over as section leader when Jack 'fell sick' and so got caught by the communist takeover. Finally there's Fleda Jones, the lab technician described by Jack in *Daughters of an Ancient Race* as, 'young, female, diminutive, pretty and black'. At this time Jack must have been grappling with the cold reality that there was no future for his relationship with Fleda, an uncomfortable situation for all of them living together cheek by jowl.

Deprived of their chosen role in China and contemplating an uncertain future in a devastated post-war world, their predicament must have been extremely trying. Jack no doubt amused himself sketching and he certainly got round to bashing his type writer again. In February 1951 Mark Shaw in Philadelphia wrote to Bob Reuman in Shanghai to say that he had received three of five of Jack's 'stories' mailed to him, possibly the ones typed by Dorothy. 'We are getting these stories typed in formal magazine form and will be doing our best to get them sold to the New Yorker and such other magazines as seem likely to have use for them,' he said. When much later in 1974 a new issue of his novel was planned, Jack wrote to his publisher, Tom Rosenthal of Martin Secker & Warburg telling him that the stories had failed to sell as the Korean War made China an inappropriate subject for upbeat stories.

There was to be a silver lining for Jack though. Some earlier ones mailed to Spencer Coxe in Philadelphia, had been sent to Bernice Baumgartner of Brandt and Brandt, an American literary agent in Park Avenue, New York. She wrote in December 1952 saying that Jack's work was 'really gifted'. 'I suspect that Mr Jones could write a very good book of his first person experiences and that is what I would dearly love to see… I cannot tell you how much I would like to see it.' When Jack later produced the first chapters of his Bangkok novel, the agent liked them. After sixteen rejections of the tattered manuscript she successfully found him a mass-market publisher, Ballantine Books of New York. *A Woman of Bangkok* was published by them in 1956, the contract, which slumbers in the archives of Princeton University, giving him an advance of $1,000 on initial royalties at 4% of the retail cover price of fifty cents. Shortly afterwards a re-edited version was issued in hard back in London as *A Sort of Beauty* by Martin Secker & Warburg, being positively reviewed across the world and thus securing Jack's reputation as a writer. And all of this was thanks to the efforts of Spencer Coxe and Mark Jones in promoting his work for him with the agent in America.

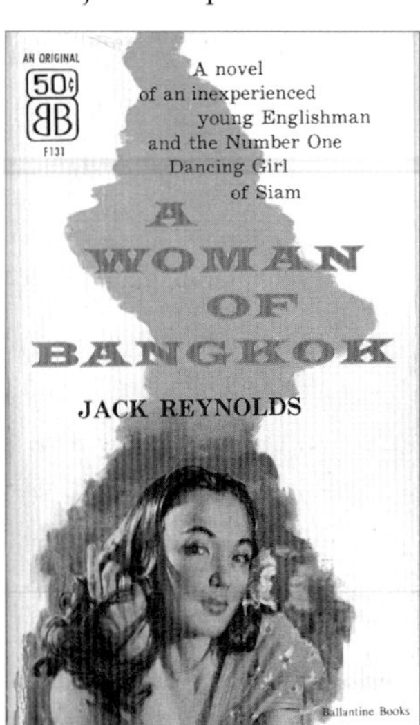

The first Ballantine edition

Back in China as previously described, closure of the clinic on 6 December 1950 was followed by frantic activity getting approvals for the handover of vehicles and equipment to the China Industrial Cooperatives, preparing detailed inventories itemising everything down to the very last detail and finally loading up the sixteen trucks. At the end of January 1951 Jack and his friends must have watched with dismay as the convoy and their Chinese friends pulled out en route to a new life at the CIC's Bailie School at Shantan in far off Kansu province, finally bringing to an end an important era in all of their lives.

In a note at the beginning of *Daughters of an Ancient Race* (1974) Jack wrote that he was asked if he too would go and teach gynaecology and obstetrics at the Shantan school, but he declined as, after years of unpaid work, he wanted a paid job and to get married and settle down. 'That may have been the biggest mistake of my life,' he concluded in the note. Courtney Archer, a New Zealand member of the FSU, did in fact stay on at the school but only until 1953, while William Sewell, the Quaker university lecturer whose book's title boasts that, *I Stayed in China*, left Chengtu via Chungking in 1952. The prospects for continued service within the communist regime would have looked pretty bleak even then, but writing his book much later in the seventies Jack was still indulging in nostalgia for a China to which he never returned.

Most immediately in Chungking, hanging over their heads was the no small matter of getting exit permits from the communist authorities and being allowed the freedom to leave China. This was to be a harrowing bureaucratic process but the exit permits eventually came through one by one, leaving a dwindling group until only Dave White and finally Dennis Frone remained China.

The work in China was done and it was time to go but getting exit permits was looking almost impossible. A confidential FSU memo of 5 February 1951 stated as follows. 'Their applications for exit permits have consistently been turned down on the grounds that they have not been able to comply with the exit guarantee regulation. This is a requirement that is being interpreted with undue harshness in Chungking and requires foreigners to obtain economic and political guarantees from local firms to testify that they are not leaving any unpaid debts and that they are "politically reliable". So far no guarantor has been found willing to commit himself to an undertaking that might force him to pay out money or suffer imprisonment at any time in the future on behalf of people who have already left the country.'

A few days later on 12 February Bob Reuman held a Council meeting in Shanghai to discuss the issue. The minutes report the possibility of approaching, 'Mr Elliott of Shell here in Shanghai', but conclude that as the response would probably be negative, it would be better to await the outcome of a British consular approach to authorities in Peking asking that the regulations be modified.

In March 1951 Dorothy Reuman wrote home to say that, 'the Chungking people are about in the same position as they were in two months ago. Fleda, John Peter and Jack Jones have all been permitted to publish their names for exit, but they have not been able to secure the guarantor, and Fleda and John's [provisional approvals] have already expired, so that they have to start over again'. Bob then adds that the only hope is that the guarantee rule, which applied solely in Chungking, be changed but that they were all resigned to staying in Chungking for another six months or even a year.

A major complication was communications as Shanghai and the AFSC in Philadelphia were having difficulty keeping in touch with Chungking. On 26 July 1951 with only the last two men remaining in Chungking, Mark Shaw, on the urging of Bob and Dorothy Reuman, wrote a memo to various AFSC worthies saying that, 'following the closing of the China Desk here in Philadelphia, someone from the Service Committee should feel it their very definite responsibility to keep in regular contact (bi-weekly) with Dave White and Dennis Frone in Chungking'. Whether the two men could actually receive letters is not recorded, though all outgoing mail from China was subject to censorship and could be stopped for arbitrary reasons.

The Reumans had no great difficulty with their exit permits and left Shanghai by train for Hong Kong, writing home from there on 29 March 1951, though who ultimately gave the guarantees for the remaining members does not appear from the archives. A Friends Service Council minute of its China Committee reported that Dennis Frone, the last member still in Chungking, 'had moved to the Mackenzie compound with the files, which [ominously] he is not allowed to destroy'. Mackenzie & Co. was a Shanghai-based shipbuilding and engineering firm which had a group of seven fine residences on the south bank at Chungking opposite the Tai Ping Men gate, so it is possible that it was they who offered the guarantees. Needless to say, exit permits were ultimately granted and the five departed one by one, a dismal affair for those left behind, especially for Dennis as the last one out.

John Peter had wanted to go with the convoy to join the Bailie School at Shandan as, after ten long years in China, he had nowhere else to go, but any request was likely to have been turned down by the authorities. He, Fleda and Jack got permits in mid-May 1951, arriving in Hong Kong on 1 June 1951. Dave White reached Hong Kong on 11 August and finally Dennis Frone on 15 September 1951. As West China director entangled in the severance disputes with the employees, one can guess why Dennis might have been last out, but it is hard to see why Dave White had so hard a time getting his permit. Dennis' plight was serious and a cutting from a London news paper reveals that his parents in Loughton were worried sick and were making representations to the Foreign Office to intervene on his behalf.

Jack seems to have written little about the difficult and empty time waiting for exit permits other than a story in *Daughters of an Ancient Race*, published more than twenty years later. This deals in fictionalised form with the torment of applying for an exit visa, though there is no mention of the requirement for guarantees. In the story, called, 'A Day in the New Chungking' he is surprisingly upbeat, crossing the river to the city, as he puts it, 'in holiday mood'. Nonetheless, it must have been a long six months from the time his beloved clinic closed in December 1950 until he finally arrived in Hong Kong to the start of a new life.

'Imprisoned in China after the communist victory'

One big question mark hangs over this period as there is a suggestion that Jack was actually imprisoned by the communists. On 2 September 1984 Jack died in Bangkok of cancer and pneumonia aged seventy one. Bernard Llewellyn, the life long friend he first met in Kweiyang, was at that time retired and writing his memoirs in England. He cut out Jack's death notice in London's Daily Telegraph of 4 September 1984 and pasted it onto the title page of his copy of *A Woman of Bangkok* below Jack's presentation inscription.

The death notice reads, 'Jack Reynolds. At Bangkok, aged 71, English writer resident in Thailand for 30 years, author of "A Woman of Bangkok" (1956) and short stories based on his China experiences. He was imprisoned in China after the communist victory in 1949.'

Jack Reynolds. At Bangkok, aged 71. English writer, resident in Thailand for 30 years; author of "Woman of Bangkok" (1956) and short stories based on his Chinese experiences. He was imprisoned in China after the Communist victory in 1949.

D Tel.
4-ix-1984

It is surprising therefore that there are no references to imprisonment in the archive material I have seen, nor in *Daughters of an Ancient Race,* which covers the time Jack lived under the communist regime. In a highly controlled communist society, travel required official permission but in the longest story in the book, 'Mistress and Maid', set early in 1950, Jack has 'temporary permits to cross the river [into the city] as often as desired during daylight hours, provided the return trip was made on the same day'. The next story, 'A Day in the New Chungking', set in about March 1951 has him happily going into Chungking at the request of the Foreign Affairs Bureau to deal with his exit permit and thoroughly enjoying the day out.

These two stories shed light on the tense situation that faced foreigners in Chungking who felt they were surrounded by spies and informers. Jack tells how a female officer from the Foreign Affairs Bureau visits his clinic to try to trap him into a false diagnosis of mastitis. With the robust help of John Peter, this poor unfortunate communist spy with a pink nipple is given short shrift and a dose of Epsom salts and, hilariously, is sent running in more ways than one.

But there is more to come concerning Jack's possible imprisonment. In March 1983, 'Living in Thailand', a Bangkok magazine published an article based on an interview with Jack by journalist, Dominic Faulder. It was called, 'Jack Reynolds, Bangkok's grand old man of letters', and was illustrated with some fine photo portraits of Jack looking bearded and craggy in old age. In the article Jack is quoted as saying that he was held in Chungking by the communists in solitary confinement under house arrest for fourteen months. Jack was hard of hearing with an incipient cancer of the inner ear and only a year and a half to live, so the reference to fourteen months probably arose from a conversation before the tape was switched on. Dominic has sent me a copy of the interview tape and the following is what Jack actually said. 'I was in isolation in one room by myself most of the time on house arrest. I could see people going by the window; some of them I knew couldn't talk to me… they'd be in trouble with the communists. I couldn't escape but I quite liked being alone after all the troubles… quite liked being all by myself except I didn't know what the end of it was going to be. I really thought I was going to be bumped off.'

Jack was certainly detained by the communists in the sense that he was not free to travel without a permit or to leave China, even if not actually imprisoned. Howell Jones, Jack's Chungking colleague and close friend told me in a recent email that, 'Jack might have been in some sort of captivity after the communists entered Chungking and I think he was captive during the trip down the Yangtze'; on which more presently. However, any detention must have been for a much shorter time than fourteen months. Given that he finally left China

Revd. Joseph Jones with Gwenneth

in May 1951, fourteen months earlier he in fact was still actively running his clinic.

Jack's supposed imprisonment must have loomed large for whoever wrote and inserted the death notice, possibly his sister, Gwenneth, who was his only close relative other than his children. So what exactly had Jack told his family about his awful last months in China?

As an author and consummate story teller, Jack was adept at weaving exotic tales around his own colourful life. Like others accused of inflating the truth in their writings (T.E. Lawrence and Hemingway for example spring to mind), nothing is more important to a writer than the story itself. As Kristiaan Inwood, a friend of Jack's in Bangkok, put it to me in an email, 'Jack was a writer to whom embellishment was second nature and his life, upon which his work was almost exclusively based, was an evolving work of art in itself. In any case, I think you would probably agree that the fantasies, exaggerations, even lies people tell can be as revealing as any truths.'

Extracting historical accuracy from Jack's autobiographical stories such as those in *Daughters of an Ancient Race* and *The Utter Shambles* is always more than challenging. In 'Mistress and Maid' for example, a female Foreign Affairs Bureau official investigating Jack's exit application reports that he, 'is believed to be a spy in the pay of western imperialists'. However, this is fictionalised and so cannot necessarily be taken at face value as a precise historical account.

In the ferment of his creative imagination, Jack could also at times be downright inaccurate when accuracy wasn't too important. For example in *Daughters of an Ancient Race* (at page 121) he says he joined the FAU in 1943 when in fact he joined in 1944. In the prefatory note to the book he pleads that he'd been doing voluntary relief work for nine years when in fact, having started his long FAU training in March 1944, it was only seven years. He also allowed the biographical note on the back of his novel to say that 'he went to China during the war for the Friends Ambulance Unit,' when in fact he'd set sail from Liverpool the day after the Japanese surrender. Such small inaccuracies bother me not one bit, but whether and how he was imprisoned by the communists is more than a minor detail.

House arrest and imprisonments under the communists were of course common and foreign residents were held on many occasions. In a letter to the AFSC in Philadelphia dated 25 January 1951 Bob Reuman wrote, 'A very common feature of the day are arrests… For example, our three foreign members leaving Chungmou [Hazell and James Lovett and John Rue] failed to make some registration or other, and were detained along with their host, Miss Sayre, for some five or six weeks. We know of the missionaries arrested in Chungking for various reasons.'

Frank Cooley of the YMCA in Chungking, a substantial institution, was held in detention for six weeks. In November 1950, Olin Stockwell, a Methodist missionary in Chungking, (the one who sang to the PLA soldiers on the ferry with Jack and Fleda), was arrested and held in prison for a full two years. Much of the time was spent in solitary confinement, followed by a period packed into an overcrowded cell. The story was told by two articles in LIFE magazine and in Stockwell's own book, *With God in Red China,* a lively and generous account which makes brief mention of the closure of FSU operations in Chungking, though nothing of Jack.

On 20 December 1950 Dr Stuart Allen, the supervisor at the Canadian Mission Hospital with whom Jack had a somewhat prickly relationship, when summoned to a meeting with his staff one evening, was subjected to a range of accusations and immediately imprisoned by the communists. Jack's fictionalisation of him in his story in *Daughters of an Ancient Race* called, 'The Turner's Wife', has 'Dr Roland Hickman' imprisoned for a year before being charged with serious medical negligence causing the death of a general. In his own book, *Trial of Faith,* Allen tells the story of his year's imprisonment, having being held guilty of misappropriating medical supplies provided by the Economic Cooperation Administration of Washington, for which he as medical director for West China of the IRC was responsible. Jack was seconded to the IRC, was a member of its medical committee and had handled and distributed some of these goods to hospitals. Having also dabbled at his clinic as a bare-faced doctor, he was thus equally or even more vulnerable to serious accusation and imprisonment.

In her autobiographical novel, *A Many Splendoured Thing,* Han Suyin mentions a young American conscientious objector who had just arrived in Hong Kong from China, who one would guess was an ex-FSU member. He had, 'been fifty-nine days in prison in China; suspected of spying'. In her book about the evacuation of the missionaries of the China Inland Mission, *China: The Reluctant Exodus,* Phyllis Thompson details many such instances, including that of David Day (who coincidentally had been at school in London with Jack) and who was imprisoned in Chungking for 'taking a firm hand with a gang of troublesome youngsters' at the mission's home in the hills of the south bank.

In her later book, *My House Has Two Doors,* Han Suyin tells the story of Marian Manly, the American medical missionary in Chengdu who had helped her write her first book, *Destination Chungking,* and who was unable to adapt to the strictures of communist rule. When her students put up a picture of Chairman Mao in her class room she then tore it down. When she refused to put it back she was reported and the public security bureau tied her hands and incarcerated her for nearly a week, a story repeated by Olin Stockwell in his book. William Sewell, the Quaker professor of Chemistry at West China Union University in Chungking who Jack knew well, mentions another similar story in his book, *I Stayed in China* and that a doctor who committed the same offence likewise was jailed.

Eric Shipton, the Himalayan explorer and mountaineer, at that time the British Consul in Kunming, was soon in 1951 to meet Jack in Chungking. He wrote in his autobiography, *That Untravelled World,* that local missionaries, 'were liable at any moment to be arrested for fictitious misdeeds and even atrocities: some doctors, for example, faced charges of murdering patients who had died under their care, even several years before.' Though Jack had no particular dislike of communism and was generally positive about the conduct of its soldiers and achievements such as controlling inflation, he was likewise at risk of being accused of such things. As the active head of a large unit and personally ministering to the ailments of many female patients, he must have trodden on many toes and could easily have been denounced. The consequences for him would have been serious and, as he said in his interview with Dominic Faulder, he feared for his life.

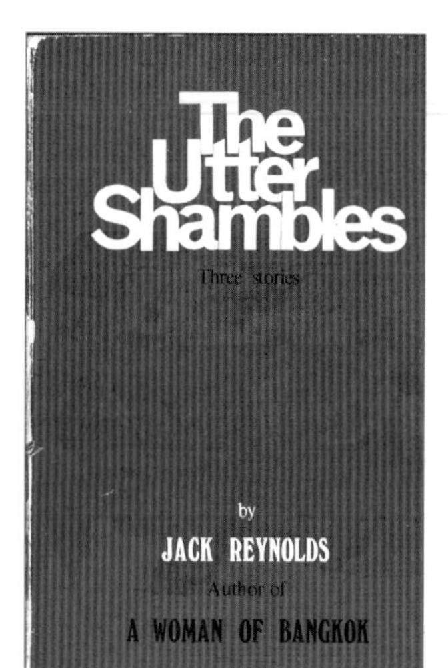

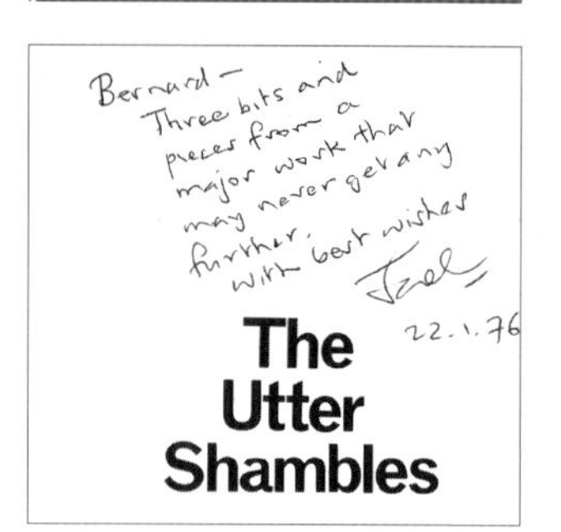

In his autobiography Shipton also describes the excesses of the peoples' kangaroo courts that sentenced many Chinese people to death. Offenders were generally local landlords, he says, who would be made to kneel in the centre of an arena where they could be accused by the onlookers of all and every misdeed possible and be slapped and kicked. 'Meanwhile the audience would be roused to a passion of indignation against the prisoner, and when at length the master of ceremonies intervened to demand the verdict of the People's Court they would howl, "Death". The unfortunate wretch would then be shot in the back of the head, his body removed and the next victim led into the arena.'

In, *My House Has Two Doors,* Han Suyin admits that starting in December 1950 and continuing through 1951 the suppression of counter-revolution through purges and executions led to many deaths and imprisonments. With extensive land reform, the execution of landlords was thus widespread. In *China: The Reluctant Exodus,* Phyllis Thompson reports that, 'on the walls of the Post Office photos were displayed of men kneeling in line on the beach of the Yangtze, hands tied behind their backs, waiting to be shot… Always there were bodies lying on the banks of the Yangtze until darkness fell, when relatives stole silently along to take them off and bury them.'

In *The Utter Shambles,* Jack's 1972 book of auto-biographical stories, his narrator sits in The Utter Shambles bar in Bangkok and relates a series of anecdotes about his long and turbulent life. He is Jack's alter ego in all except name, like Jack having been 'a trawlerman in the North Sea, a gardener in Hertfordshire, a sampler in a sugar beet factory, a captive of Miao bandits,' and what's more 'a captive of Chinese communists'. 'Ring Out the Old', the last story in this book, is set in Chungking on New Year's Day, 1952 (after Jack had left China), and in it the narrator depicts himself as being held in a single room for seven months and then being taken out and led by his guards down to the river bank. What he sees there turns his blood to ice. 'Landlords, enemies of the people being led to trial, prison or execution…. That gang is going down to the riverbed to be arraigned in the annual New Year's Day mass trial… And so am I…' The tension is powerful, but somehow the narrator survives to tell the tale, leaving behind some large question marks about Jack's own experiences.

Perhaps Jack was indeed held under some sort of house arrest as he told Dominic Faulder, but at the very least he and the others had to apply for exit visas and the communists were in no great hurry to oblige. The foreigners had to wait for permission to be allowed to apply and to advertise for claims, to fill in endless forms in Chinese and provide a guarantor as a hostage to fortune. The worst thing of all was indefinite waiting and the sense of frustration at not knowing what game was being played. As described in his book, William Sewell pleads for his friends who have loyally worked as doctors in China for many years to be allowed to leave but gets a bluff reply from the communist official. 'You think too much of the individual he explained. We must think of the people as a whole. For too long the masses have experienced the presence of the foreigner, who always claims to be right, to have special wisdom, and who had power to command. We have been shamed for too many years. We must show to everyone that the power of the men from across the ocean has been broken... Your friends will have to wait. After all, we have endured for a century. They will not have to wait as long as that.'

Sewell also explains that, 'Intent to leave the country had to be advertised in the local press: and from old servants and others arose endless claims which had to be investigated and settled, increasing the delay... all baggage had to be listed and every item repeatedly checked.' Missionaries and others, now shunned by the people in whose service they had spent many years, had nothing to do but to sit and wait, slipping into a chronic state of anxiety and depression. The bureaucracy was impenetrable and the remote possibility of unsettled claims was a major pretext for delaying the issue of permits

Eric Shipton writing of the situation in Kunming paints a very similar picture. Even getting an exit permit issued did not end the anxiety as these were sometimes issued but then cancelled at the very last moment. Shipton's permit was stamped with the required day of departure and it was obligatory for him to complete the journey to Hong Kong within one month. He was to fly first to Chungking, being allowed only fifteen pounds of luggage and was thoroughly searched before leaving and on landing. The smallest show of irritation or other small mistake could have dire consequences and he tells the story of one missionary who when asked about a can of insecticide in his luggage replied that at least it wasn't an atom bomb. He was detained for two months for ridiculing the intelligence of the Chinese people.

Jack's attitude to these strong feelings against the foreigner, made more intense by the war in Korea, was tolerant and understanding, probably a necessary mechanism for keeping his sanity. In his 1983 interview with Dominic Faulder he says that the Chinese wanted to get rid of all the missionaries, 'but that this didn't mean they were prepared to make the trip to Hong Kong easy. They were past masters of making problems for you; they'd been b...ered around by foreigners for the last two hundred years and were getting their own back... I don't blame them at all.' Likewise in his story, 'A Day in the New Chungking', he explains his relaxed attitude to the grilling given to him by the Foreign Affairs Bureau. Some foreigners, he wrote, 'have been accustomed to years of privilege and started off with an exaggerated idea of race superiority' and so find the questions pointless and impertinent. However, as a member of a Quaker unit, his reason for being in China was to promote international understanding. In his view, seemingly petty questions were in fact asked in all seriousness and had to be answered in the spirit in which they were put in order to explain any misconceptions. For example, as no Chinese would ever give away free medicines other than to his own relatives, he continued, humanitarianism being an alien concept from the communist viewpoint, members of the Unit must therefore have had ulterior motives, such as making secret maps or helping the Kuomintang.

After his tough years in China, Jack was probably now pretty good at coping with a situation such as this, though in his news letter articles he sometimes depicts himself as being a hot head in moments of confrontation or tension. Howell Jones told me on the phone from Canada that once an angry Jack had to be restrained when a soldier was being gratuitously cruel to a dog and again when the driver of a donkey was urging it on by hitting its testicles with a stick. On the other hand Mark Jones suggested to me that Jack could be remarkably cool and controlled, handling tense situations much better than many of the other men in the Unit. Over the years his role as transport director had certainly given him plenty of practice in dealing with petty bureaucrats and the new ones were perhaps not so very different, just less predictable.

Jack's escape down the Yangtse and to Hong Kong

To take up the narrative in Eric Shipton's autobiography of his journey out of China, Shipton recounts that he arrived by air in Chungking for his trip down the Yangtse to find that some 350 missionaries were already in the city and waiting for a passage downriver on a steamer. They were being despatched in batches, and with more arriving daily the congestion was not reducing. On 18 May after waiting eight days he was notified that his steamer would be leaving within an hour and then began a hectic rush through the crowded streets together with a Catholic sister to get there on time. On the same boat, also caught up in the turmoil of leaving, were Jack Jones, Fleda and John.

In Dominic Faulder's article referred to above, Jack says that 'when he was finally released and sent down the river on deck, "three to a mat" with other foreigners, they made him responsible for the group along with Eric Shipton, the famous Himalayan climber and explorer who had been the British Consul in Kunming'. In the full recording of the interview, Jack mentions that he already knew Shipton and had met Shipton's wife. She'd left Kunming earlier with the children after a similar wait in Chungking for a passage.

Shipton would have known of the FAU and its Chungking depot and might even have had previous dealings with Jack. Late in 1947 when Shipton was British consul in Kashgar, Jack's colleagues, Mark Jones and Gerard

Walmesley had used their local leave to drive through the Gobi desert and deliver to him in Tihua (Urumchi) a large 'station wagon' which they called a Cheesebox. This vehicle was a strapping six cylinder Chevrolet light truck and a page in Mark's beautifully presented album shows the two good looking young men posing with it in the yard of the Chungking depot, Mark in beret and flying goggles leaning casually on the bonnet with his foot on the front bumper. Shipton had met them on their arrival in Urumchi and a warm friendship ensued. I have seen the letters that Shipton later wrote to Mark in his spidery handwriting in which he says how much he'd enjoyed meeting them and hoping their paths would cross again. He thus had reason to be grateful to the FAU.

In his book Shipton then describes the struggle for a cabin on board the steamer and how he ended up sleeping out on deck after releasing his to a Mrs Hemingway who was causing an alarming fuss on finding herself sharing hers with a Chinese man. Early the next morning they entered the Yangtse gorges, the ship 'the size of a cross-Channel steamer' racing through the narrow channels between whirlpools and reefs and cliffs like a Himalayan valley. That evening they reached Ichang and were told to disembark. Together with about fifty missionaries they were led off by armed escorts and detained at a squalid and grossly overcrowded inn for sixteen days. The stench from the three latrines was appalling and, fed only with rice and boiled vegetables, they were very concerned about falling sick. They were also worried that if they could not complete their journey in the required month they would be turned back at the Hong Kong border. Even worse, rumours that the communists were going to invade Hong Kong, thus destroying their safe haven, added to the tense atmosphere. Jammed together in these sweaty and insanitary conditions, the discomfort and monotony were extreme. They could even hear the hoots of the steamers on the river, the inn keeper raising false hopes of departure, though they were worried he wanted to keep them there as he was grossly overcharging for their board and lodging.

At last on 4 June they embarked on a boat for Hankow, sleeping in an overcrowded hold with many Chinese passengers and fed from buckets of boiled rice.

'From Hankow, after a long struggle to get places on a train,' wrote Shipton, 'we travelled to Canton, and on the morning of June 1st, the day our permits expired, we reached the Hong Kong frontier.' Edging in a queue slowly towards the barbed wire barriers, this was the critical moment when they were thoroughly searched and examined. Luckily the examiners were not too hostile that day and at last they were out of communist China and boarding the railway to Kowloon. As Shipton concludes, 'The hills of the New Territories looked very beautiful in the evening light as, relaxed at last, I watched them glide by the window of the train to Kowloon.'

One further detail is added by Peter Steele, Shipton's biographer in his book, *Everest and Beyond*, namely that the boat they took downriver was the *Altmark*. His account of the journey is in a single paragraph and he says that Shipton arrived in Hong Kong on 1 June 1951 and then stayed in the luxury of the Peninsula Hotel. Suspecting that he had other sources, I wrote to Steele but he told me his account was taken from the autobiography and that he did not remember having anything else. As the Yangtse was within the British sphere of influence with no German vessels on the river, his reference to the *Altmark* is almost certainly incorrect.

In *My House Has Two Doors*, Han Suyin mentions that her friend, Dr Mary Mostyn, briefly Jack's colleague in Chungking, had likewise left China a few months before in January 1951 and been questioned at the Hong Kong immigration point. '"Any atrocities?" was the first question she was asked (as were all other missionaries) when they reached Lowu', the Hong Kong immigration point.

The ultimate terminus for the refugees was the Kowloon railway station where so many romantic journeys into the unknowable vastness of China had for so long begun and ended. The station with its famous clock tower, the only part that remains today, stands on the tip of the Kowloon peninsula, a final finger of the mainland pointing across the water, criss-crossed by ships and junks, to the exuberant capitalist enclave of Hong Kong island. A sight for sore eyes, Jack must have stared in disbelief at its sharp mountain peaks rising from the sea, the lower slopes crowded with buildings, and at the ceaseless vitality of the place, so very different to the unrelieved drabness of a devastated China.

The sense of relief for the exhausted refugees at the border would have been overwhelming, with many scenes of tears and emotional collapse. I can picture the physical setting well as in 1978 I took the same railway line to Guangzhou (Canton), one of the first tourists to be

The bridge to China, Lowu

My memory of Guangzhou in 1978

admitted as China at last opened its doors a crack following the Cultural Revolution. On Guangzhou's five foot ways, teeming humanity in plain white shirts or khaki drab parted to let me pass, staring at me as if an alien with a green face. Despite the greyness I warmed to the energy of the place but even after a short exile, felt relieved as I recrossed to Hong Kong at Lowu, walking the famous covered bridge over the marshes and river that forms the border. This place had been the scene of much Cold War posturing and it looked to be unchanged since the early fifties.

Back on my own side of the bamboo curtain, I saw vibrant colour again, bright clothes and lipstick, the decadent litter of Coke cans on the tracks and for me a palpable sense of home coming. I can hardly imagine how it must have been for Jack arriving as a refugee after so many years of hardship in China.

From these, my researches, I thus concluded that Jack was probably held in Ichang in the same group as Eric Shipton and that he took the train with him to Canton, arriving at the border on 1 June. During some of this time the whole party was indeed 'imprisoned', the group herded along together by soldiers, and so the statement in his death notice in the Daily Telegraph was in essence correct.

In Jack's 1983 interview, he adds a few further details to the story of his uncomfortable exit from Chungking. "When we got [down river] to Hankow [the scene of Jack's haemorrhoidectomy], of all these people who'd been years longer than me in China none had been in Hankow. I was considered to be quite a big cheese by these communists and they made me section leader in Hankow. The missionaries were very upset as they spoke better Chinese than I did. The test came when for twenty four of us altogether, somebody had to go across the river to the station to buy tickets. I collected the money and bought tickets fourth class… On the train talking to the guard we ended up in first class. We were still prisoners being escorted and they made everything difficult for us. At Hong Kong I was met by old Unit people who'd got jobs or were at university. One of them, Howell Jones, took me to the Hong Kong Hotel for some beers, me in rags and tatters, beard and straw sandals, one more out of China. He took me to the Hong Kong [University] hostel and I stayed with him in a student room, glad of some company as he'd got the hostel practically to himself and I had the room until the students came back.'

Nobody knew when a particular refugee would surface at Lowu and a Catholic priest kept up a permanent watch at the border to receive them. Perhaps somebody phoned through for Jack and left a message for Howell who would have rushed down to the Star Ferry and met him at the Kowloon railway station. Howell was studying medicine at the University and Jack apparently stayed with him in a room at his student hostel while the students were away on vacation. Jack's 'imprisonment' was well and truly over.

This was all I had gleaned about Jack's dramatic departure from China when out of the blue and with the manuscript for this book all but complete, I received a package in the mail from Dorothy Reuman in Connecticut. As well as enclosing their extensive letters home from China, it contained a veritable Holy Grail, a letter from Jack to Dorothy written on 2nd and 5th June 1951 just after his arrival in Hong Kong. Outlining his flight from China, its urgent purpose was to thank her for typing his stories in Shanghai. It thus seems a near miracle that this flimsy letter, scribbled in pencil on both sides of a piece of foolscap paper torn out of a notebook, has survived more than sixty years and is now sitting on my desk as I complete this chapter.

The letter revealed to me for the first time that John and Fleda had been issued with their exit permits and travelled with Jack in the same large party. It also confirms that Jack did indeed go all the way to Hong Kong with Eric Shipman and that they were all held under house arrest in Ichang while changing boats. It now only remains for the letter to tell the full story in Jack's own words, including a few mournful ones about his unceremonious parting from Fleda.

Hongkong
June 2 1951

Dear Dopey,
Fleda, J.P. and I hit Hongkong two days ago, after a reasonable journey, according to us, though not to the rest of our party. First class to Ichang, twelve days under house arrest there, fifth class to Hankow, a night and day of madness there, second class to Canton, the luxury of the New Asia for one day and half a night, and then a quick dash across the border. The party consisted of Eric Shipton, Everest climber and consul; his side-kick Pile; an Empire-builder's wife, permed, grey-haired, rouged, had gin and brandy in her bags (luggage I mean); two Swiss mis-

'Dear Dopey,

Fleda [Jones], J.P. [John Peter] and I hit Hongkong two days ago, after a reasonable journey according to us, though not to the rest of our party. First class [on a Yangtse river boat] to Ichang, twelve days under house arrest there, fifth class [on a larger steamer] to Hankow, a night and day of madness there, second class [train] to Canton, the luxury of

Pearl River, Canton

the New Asia [Hotel] for one day and half a night, and then [another train and] a quick dash across the border. The party consisted of Eric Shipton, Everest climber and consul; his side-kick Pile; an Empire builder's wife, permed, grey-haired, rouged, had gin and brandy in her bags (luggage I mean); two Swiss missionaries, a German baroness, English, Canadian, American, German missionaries, a French father, an Irish sister, and a French mother superior. Only mishap was losing the French father in Canton; he was being expelled from the country and they arrested him in Canton and made sure he crossed the border by escorting him to it under armed guard. In Hankow, which I knew, they sort of put me into an authoritative position, and then took no notice of me; while I was going upstairs to fetch half the party down, the other half was always going up to tell the first half to stay up. Hence these grey hairs. I looked for [your husband] Bob's maenad in the [Yangtse] Gorges, the one whose hair was floating up and down stream simultaneously, but I didn't see her. Ichang was a trial, couldn't go out, two to a room, stinking hot, bloody missionaries holding prayer meetings everywhere except the maofang [latrine]. They prayed we wouldn't have to spoil the Lord's Day by landing at Hankow on it. The Lord heard my prayer and we landed at Hankow on the Lord's Day. Best joke: on the beach at Ichang: pitch dark, stifling hot, drums, torches, howls, all the confusion and clamour of China at its wildest; and a painfully refined consular voice crying repeatedly in the night, 'Mrs Hemingway! Mrs Hemingway! Where ARE your bags?' [Your pants or trousers?] Everybody windy, John about his camera, which hadn't been sealed, Fleda about an ancient tablecloth she is fiercely attached to (it cost her a fortune), me about a drawing which had been suspected of being anti-communist by Lucy, the belle of the FAB at Ckg [the Foreign Affairs Bureau at Chungking, responsible for processing their exit permits]; but everything went through without bother. MM [Dr Mary Mostyn] and Howell [Jones] met us at Kowloon [where the train terminated], Fleda went to live with the Methodists and I haven't seen her since. JP and I are in a University hostel near enough the top of the Peak to spend most of our time in the clouds. JP is pretty ill and will have to be hospitalised. The old kidneys again, but he has pronounced ascites and oedema [fluid retention, a symptom of renal failure] and will soon be a gonner if he doesn't look out.

[Letter resumed on June 5.] John has a visa and is off to Macao to be treated by his lao peng yu, Sister Mafalda [his old friend, the former matron at the Catholic Hospital, Chungking]. Fleda leaves next day for New Delhi via Bombay [to do medical work in Faridabad], travelling first class in the most swanky boat in the harbour, the *Carthage*. Beeje [Brian Jones, ex-FAU and Unicef head in Bangkok] and Meager [Tony Meager, also ex-FAU with Unicef] have invited me onto their treponamatoses program (yaws to you) in Thailand, subject to this and that, so I expect to be sailing for Bangkok before long. Meanwhile I am walking the wards of the old Queen Mary [Hospital] with Howell, buying clothes, climbing rocks, meeting old friends, and watching the amatory procedure of the huge Japanese snails here. Do YOU know about SNAILS? You wouldn't believe!'

It's all so very Jack! How could anyone ever throw his letters away?

In Hong Kong; the beginning of the rest of Jack's life

Jack's letter to Dorothy quoted above then continues with his thanks for, 'her Herculean labours at the type writer on my behalf' in typing up five of his stories, and bewails the fact that stories numbered three and four had not been received in Philadelphia. His pre-digital agony of losing track of manuscripts was to continue and his private correspondence with Spencer Coxe in 1952 indicates that several stories, including two sent to Bill Jordan in England, were unaccounted for. One of these letters to Coxe refers to, 'a story which I wrote in the last days at Chungking and doctored and got typed up in Hong Kong'. Jack's passion for getting published was thus so strong that in the hectic few weeks spent in Hong Kong recovering from his tough years in China and making arrangements for his new life in Thailand, writing was still a priority.

Church Guest House

It's a long time ago but Howell Jones remembers that Jack stayed with him for a few days in St John's Hall, his university residence, and then moved to Church Guest House in Upper Albert Road near the Botanical Gardens, part of which still stands today. This guest house was sometimes used by FAU members when in Hong Kong and it is mentioned on the very first page of Han Suyin's novel, *A Many Splendoured Thing*. Han Suyin stayed there on her arrival from England in February 1949 and from page one onwards she paints a vivid picture of it as a refugee camp over-flowing with embittered missionaries newly ejected from China.

Dr Mary Mostyn, who had come to Chungking to work with Jack, had been a student friend of

Han Suyin and both were now working as doctors at Queen Mary Hospital. When the Reumans passed through Hong Kong on their way home in April 1951 they had stayed in the beautiful university flat that Mostyn was sharing with Han Suyin.

The further curious link with Han Suyin is that Howell, who was studying to be a doctor, knew her there and he told me the following. 'When I first met her she was the Casualty Officer at the Queen Mary Hospital in Hong Kong and used to furiously type her book during coffee and lunch breaks and at any other spare time she had. She fell in love with a journalist who was later killed in Korea and that was the source of *A Many Splendoured Thing*. Later she was in charge of a University women's hostel.' At that precise time she was dealing with her grief by obsessively writing of her own tragic love affair, the book being started in September 1950 and finished in July 1951, just at the time Jack was in Hong Kong. It is intriguing too that Jack was to go on to write his own novel which, even though not his own story, likewise was essentially an autobiographical love story.

In the 1983 interview Jack describes himself as having the time of his life in Hong Kong, as surely he must. After five and a half years amidst the poverty and deprivation of China, as transport director facing a constant barrage of insuperable problems and with his health under strain, now arriving in one of the great fleshpots of the east must have been an extraordinary time of pleasure and release. He was not entirely penniless because, although FAU members were unpaid volunteers, Roy Mason representing the FAU in Hong Kong, was able to pay him his 'personal monies'. These were possibly the fees for his articles published in Time and Holiday magazines, together with his clothing allowance and a certain amount of leave allowance for local leave he had not taken. Mason was staying in Room 410 at the European YMCA in Kowloon and using it as his office and for whatever reason, perhaps in case of a reply, that was the address Jack put at the top of his letter to Dorothy.

Howell Jones

Howell Jones has told me by email that the two of them then explored Hong Kong together and this is what he said.

Jack 'came through Hong Kong on his way to Thailand and we spent a very pleasant time together and kept in touch for many years. I went to visit him and his family in England after I returned there in 1956 but, sadly, lost touch thereafter... Jack was earning quite well in Thailand and very generously helped me keep afloat while I was in University... Yes, Jack was a very good friend to me. [Howell's Hong Kong University graduation photo is still in the Jones family album in Bangkok, with Howell's note of thanks on the back saying that without Jack's help 'all this would have been impossible'.] While he was in Hong Kong we took the ferry to Lantau Island which was devoid of anything other than farmers and fishers and a leper colony in those days. We walked the length of the island to stay overnight at a guest house run by a group of Buddhist monks. We were overcome by darkness and spent the night in the open sustained by brandy out of a ketchup bottle! Towards dawn we were awoken by the temple bell and realized that we were only a few minutes away from our destination. Anyhow we had a great day and another night staying at the guest house feeding on wonderful vegetarian food before walking back to the ferry again.'

At Po Lin monastery up in the hills of Lantau they still serve vegetarian food, now produced in vast quantities to the tourists who come to see the big Buddha.

Howell also told me that Jack and Fleda Jones, his American lab technician, became lovers but that she broke it off before leaving China, though Jack at thirty eight was more than ready to settle down and wanted something more from their relationship. In Howell's words, 'Jack told me all about it when he came to Hong Kong and he was pretty cut up at that time, really hurting.'

Jack Jones with his Unicef colleague, Mom Kraideb

Wounded though Jack may have been, it didn't apparently spoil his time in Hong Kong. In the interview with Dominic he says he found a girl there and spent time with her family. When after only about six weeks it was time to set sail he had to say goodbye and this time it was presumably he who did the dumping.

He was of course soon sailing to Bangkok and to the rest of his life. With the ideal experience and qualifications, he had quickly landed a job as transport officer with Unicef in Thailand, running a fleet of vehicles in support of their medical work in far flung parts of the country. His contacts with Brian Jones and Tony Meager, former FAU men, got him the position and within days of arrival in Hong Kong he was looking forward to confirmation that he would be working with them for Unicef based in Bangkok.

Jack eating somewhere in rural Thailand

As Jack explains in the interview, instead of a short flight to Bangkok, he had been charged with buying heavy tools for the Thai Department of Health and he was to ship these and accompany them by sea. Thus he arrived in Thailand the romantic way up the Chao Phaya River where, he says, he was met by a Unicef colleague who was the son of a Siamese prince. Mom is an honorific title for minor royal offspring and 'Mom' also shows up as a colleague of Jack's protagonist, Reggie, in *A Woman of Bangkok,* factual details as always interwoven into Jack's fiction.

In an article in the Bangkok Post of 20 February 1977, *The view from a crop-watcher's shelter*, Jack describes his first impressions on landing in Bangkok at Klong Toey dock, close to where the Bangkok Post's modern building now holds the un-indexed archives in which his extensive journalism is effectively lost. In particular, he notes, sitting outside the eating places along the way were some delectable young Thai ladies, even though the day was still young. 'Naturally I averted my eyes', he insists, but soon he would be doing the necessary research to assure authenticity for his novel, set in the sleazy dance halls of Bangkok. Written upcountry in cheap small town hotels when his Unicef work allowed him the time, the novel became a sensation on both sides of the Atlantic and gave him brief fame worldwide, while a lifetime of journalism earned him a following among readers in Bangkok. Dying in 1984, he finally disappeared from view when in 1992 his book finally went out of print in Thailand after a heroic run of thirty six years.

How thrilled he would be though to know that in 2011 a new edition of *A Woman of Bangkok* was issued by Monsoon Books of Singapore, thus extending its longevity on the book shop shelves to sixty years and counting.

When some years ago I discovered an old copy of *A Woman of Bangkok,* it was this disappearance that kindled my obsession to learn more about 'Jack Reynolds', the unknown writer who had appeared from nowhere with an accomplished novel about Thailand and then, just like me, never produced another one. Since reading the book I have learned much about his life and, most importantly, have come to discover the lost writings on his work with the Friends Ambulance Unit in China.

These news letter articles have, I hope, now been given new life and Jack should be recognised as a fine blogger of the pre-electronic age, leaving behind a unique impression of the unsung work of an obscure Quaker unit and a last glimpse of feudal China just as the new communist era was dawning.

His Chungking stories also remind us what can be achieved against all the odds when deeply held principles really matter to a group of like-minded people. Historical lessons are too readily forgotten and the message of pacifism and non-violence that Jack and his fellow workers taught by their example sadly needs many reminders today.

15 THE FAU CHINA CONVOY AND ITS AFTERMATH

So what became of Jack Jones?

Jack, Chiengmai, Thailand, 1951, 'in characteristic pose', as sent by Jack to Howell Jones

It is not the aim of this book to assess the achievements of the FAU and FSU in China in the nineteen forties. Suffice it to say that in impossibly difficult conditions their transport unit successfully distributed the majority of imported medical supplies throughout the areas open to them, thus enabling many mission and other hospitals to remain open and to continue to offer some basic services and save lives. The twenty five medical teams and other projects doing relief and rehabilitation work also made important contributions at a time of desperate need.

Though their contribution to the vast needs of China was limited, the impact of their experience on the foreign members who served there was often substantial. While it was not easy to live up to the principles of pacifism and service that motivated them, their time in China fundamentally changed the lives of many of them. **Jack Jones**, for example, never wanted to live in England again and settled permanently in Thailand in 1951.

After working in China for five and a half tough and turbulent years without a break (September 1945 to June 1951), Jack might have been more than ready to go home to take some time off and recover. But for whatever reason he pitched straight into his new Unicef job in Thailand and only flew back to London for a visit of a few months in July 1952, the Friends paying half the Bangkok to London return 'steamer' fare into his father's account by way of repatriation allowance.

One wonders how the prodigal's homecoming and reunion with his parents at their terraced Edwardian villa in north London might have gone after so many years apart, living such different lives on opposite sides of the world.

I can imagine their mixed emotions and pride at his undoubted achievements, darkened perhaps by past conflicts with his father and the prospect of losing him again. Did they say a little bitterly, 'Emrys, what about all your boxes in the attic? With you leaving us again, we can't keep your things up there forever you know.' So Jack would have sorted through his collections and treasures, throwing things out and burning the traces of his past, knowing he had no intention of returning.

ABANDONED

'Abandoned wench' — who never knew the wrench
of weighted wind on warp, nor parliament of tides,
cheep from their stone quay, seeing her away to sea
sweep, and the waves, hounds, leaping, baying at her sides.

ABDOMEN

The female breasts like swinging signs
affirm her softly generous,
but under them's a cellar to be filled,
the belly, that obscene white octopus,
spidery tentacled.

ABIDING

I saw the fields of passive night
bring forth a crop of golden grains of light,
suns that were active, therefore transient,
for energy consumes itself, is soon expent,
darkness alone is effortless, and permanent.

ABLE

Lord, hear my prayer. May all my friends concur
'Jack Jones? Ah yes. A dab, if any were,
at —' I don't care at what, at breaking hearts,
or breaking stones, or getting bulls at darts,
or even at something not the least bit clever,
or ~~merely letting off almighty farts~~.
like letting off huge farts.

On 11 September 1952 he went to see his old China friend, Bernard Llewellyn, who had recently returned from an assignment in Geneva and was staying with his parents at their home near Croydon, just south of London. The very next day Jack mailed a letter to Bernard proudly enclosing a copy of the small book of poems he had written between 1935 and 1937 and had had printed and bound in Welwyn.

'It was a real pleasure to gaze upwards into your face again yesterday,' he wrote, Bernard being about six foot four. 'I will make no comments about [the book of poems] except that as a mere beardless boy of twenty four I was proud of it'. He also enclosed with it some, 'odds and sods', consisting of twenty three precious manuscript pages of poems written between 1938 and 1940, carefully sewn together with thread at the top left corner. 'The odds and sods show me throwing off the chains a bit,' he went on. 'I wish you could see all my poems. I re-read them today, instead of going to see, "The Importance of Being Earnest". Under the stimulus of war I knocked out a few hundred that I rather appreciate now,' his letter concludes.

In those days before photocopiers Jack was thus giving to his friend probably the only manuscript copy of his later unpublished poems, Bernard being the one person who would treasure them. In consequence they are here on my desk beside me as I write this now, loaned to me by Bernard's son, Michael, together with Jack's letter and the only known copy of his book of poems.

Jack's stay in England in 1952 was short. Back east again and holding down a serious job with Unicef, he was, as he told his London publisher, finding it, 'much harder to live on a respectable wage in Thailand than I ever did as a voluntary worker in China'. He was apparently having a good time. Perhaps soon after his return from London, he was to meet Wanphen Muthikul, that rare bird, a Thai Catholic aged twenty two. Things went well and according to Jack's article published posthumously as a tribute in the Bangkok Post, in July 1953 they 'eloped' together 'for consummation of their love' to the Veterans Hotel at Lopburi, just north of Bangkok. Their first son was born in July 1954, followed in rapid succession by five more sons and a daughter, a spectacular total of seven children within ten years.

Wanphen, David and Jack in April 1955, sent by Jack to Howell Jones

Jack's job as transport manager with Unicef involved running a growing fleet of vehicles supporting the Thai Ministry of Health in its work in rural areas throughout Thailand. This required him once again to be forever driving very basic wartime jeeps for long distances over unsealed dirt roads in high temperatures and monsoon rains to all parts of the country, inspecting and maintaining the fleet. Once again he was doing battle with recalcitrant jeeps.

With his considerable medical experience and, in the words of Tony Meager, his FAU friend and Unicef colleague, being 'a genius with vehicles', Jack was perfect for the job. Nonetheless, jottings in his notebooks of the time express some frustration at finding himself not much more than a 'glorified mechanic'. Though his spare time away from home at first enabled him to complete his novel, *A Woman of Bangkok*, writer's block took hold and his career as a novelist failed to progress.

In, '*With My Back to the East*', his travel book of 1958, Bernard Llewellyn describes at length a visit to stay with Jack in Bangkok and includes an account of travelling with him by jeep upcountry to Korat. This was another happy reunion between the two, though Bernard recalls Jack's distressing failure to complete a second novel. In his book Bernard also tells how he had kept in touch with Jack by letter over the years.

' The picaresque adventures along Chinese and Thai roads which made his letters such fun to receive for the most part never found their way into print; though he was to send me in the sixties a summary of the plots and the characters around which nine separate books were to be written. But Jack could never quite settle to complete them one at a time and, in his mind, one story merged into another and he wrote and rewrote until the accumulation of material confronted him with an impossible task. Nor was the literary problem the only thing on his mind. Family life and the problem of earning a living in a country of infinite distractions held back the flowering of what seemed to me a prodigious talent.'

After his death, Bernard's son Michael found a note in Bernard's handwriting inside his inscribed copy of Jack's novel which reads as follows. 'Again and again I [Bernard] wrote the author, still living in S.E.Asia, for news of progress [with his next novel]. His reply, though deeply discouraging, has always remained in my memory. *'Recently I was crossing the river here on a punt,'* Jack wrote. *'I had the novel, almost complete, in my dispatch case. In mid-stream I stumbled and lost my balance, the case fell into the water, and a crocodile swallowed it.'"*

What was so distressing for Jack was that the door was open wide for his much longed for literary career. After the success of his novel, his agent and his London publishers, Secker & Warburg, were eagerly pressing him for his next manuscript, regarding him as a promising author to watch. In May 1959 the agent wrote to the publisher saying, 'I have had a most depressing letter from Jack Jones. He says that he is trying to get on with the book but is getting nowhere and has "absolutely no idea" when he is going to finish it, if ever. His time and energies are so completely taken up with his job and his family, that he seems to have nothing left over for writing.' The publisher wrote back rather cruelly, 'This is of course depressing but not entirely unexpected… Anyway we haven't advanced him any money on the book and we made quite a lot of money out of his previous novel, so I can bear this blow with comparative equanimity.' They and Jack were to remain disappointed and no second novel was ever submitted to them.

Jack hitting the keys at Siam Communications in Bangkok

The Unicef job in Thailand lasted until 1959, after which Jack was appointed transport officer with UNRWA in Jordan, accompanied by his growing family. When war in the Middle East came too close, the family returned to live in Bangkok and Jack eventually resigned his post in 1967. From then on he alternated his working life in Bangkok between freelance journalism and editorial work with a series of UN contracts in the Far East and Africa, the last of these being in Nigeria. The pattern of his working life was thus unsettled, a continuing battle to provide for his family, while struggling to find time to write and to cope with the demons that frustrated his longing for the literary recognition he craved so much.

Nonetheless Jack achieved local acclaim in Thailand as 'Bangkok's old man of letters', enjoying a considerable following for his many articles in the Bangkok Post on a wide range of topics, including his China experiences. On his death from cancer of the ear on 2 September 1984 aged 71 the Bangkok Post ran a full obituary and several long tributes. One of these, by his friend the distinguished film critic, Harry Rolnick, concluded that in late age Jack remained mentally a twenty five year old. 'When he was writing his travel pieces for the Post in the early seventies, his youthful recollection, vignettes, love, adoration and knowledge made him young for us forever. Like one of his admirers, Graham Greene, Jack had the talent to give us morals for our times while never ever moralizing.'

Also published in a Sunday supplement to the Post about a week after Jack's death was a long article called, 'Chiang Mai the hard way'. This describes a long and arduous drive over terrible roads in 1958 to deliver three Austin A35 pick-ups to government health authorities in the north of Thailand. Written by him shortly after the trip and languishing in his notebook for so many years, Jack, ever passionate to publish, would have been gratified that the article had at last seen the light of day.

Jack's diary or journal for 1958 also covers aspects of this delivery trip to Chiang Mai and in it Jack tells how on 1st October he handed over one of the little Austins to Valai, a pretty blushing nurse supervisor at

Jack's headstone, near Bangkok

Jack delivering an Austin to Chiang Mai

the hospital, in exchange for a worn out jeep. She was, Jack explains in his diary, very pleased with it because when driving a jeep wearing western style frocks she had to drive, as he put it, 'with her knees nipped together'. She much feared, 'an accident due to the waywardness of draperies in a breeze – an accident which looms overlarge in the female Thai mind… and perhaps in mine too.' Jack never changed, ever the wry observer!

From what I have discovered about this extraordinary life, I thus now know more fully how it was that an unknown author, 'Jack Reynolds', appeared from nowhere with an accomplished novel but never repeated the achievement and disappeared into relative obscurity. For me he was an enigma but after several years research I have now found some of the answers.

Life after China for Jack's Chungking friends

It remains now to tell the stories of what became of the last of Jack's colleagues who were with him in China after the communist liberation.

Dorothy and **Robert Reuman**, the very last recruits to enter China only days before the communists 'liberated' Chungking, moved on to work at FSU headquarters in Shanghai. In April 1951 they finally took the long train journey to Hong Kong, the next stage in their lives being as directors of a Quaker student house in Freiburg im Breisgau, Germany for a time. Their lives were to be full and rewarding, with a distinguished academic career for Robert, five children, and two further years in Germany, Robert as a Quaker International Affairs Representative working with government officials on both sides of the Berlin wall to ease tensions and resolve conflict. Dorothy became a professor of music at Colby College, Maine, and Robert died in 1997 aged 74 after many years service there as Professor of Philosophy, a much revered teacher and moral example to his students.

John Peter, sent to me by his daughter Magdalena

John Peter, the tall South African, was undoubtedly the longest serving of all the many hundreds of FAU/FSU members in China, having escaped into China as the Japanese invaded Rangoon and being ejected from China ten years later by the communists. As mentioned previously, he was born in Cape Town and, when his father died young, he was sent to live in Rangoon where he was educated at St Paul's High School, the prestigious Catholic boys school for the Anglo-Burmese and Anglo-Indian elite. It seems that he became a merchant seaman and travelled the world, worked in the motor trade in Rangoon and according to Jack, performed in a circus. After leaving China he was one of the few who left no address for the post-service listings of former members and so he effectively disappeared from view. I could not discover where he spent the rest of his life until Dorothy Reuman, my generous and ever helpful correspondent, sent me a letter written from Hong Kong in 1975 to her husband by Mary Magdalene Peter, one of John's daughters. This enabled me to focus my search and finally I made contact with Magdalene in Taiwan, her elder sister living in Australia and a brother and youngest sister still in Hong Kong.

Arriving in Hong Kong with serious kidney problems in June 1951, John immediately went to Macau for treatment. He then went to Singapore unsuccessfully looking for work making prosthetic limbs, returning to stay with the Catholic brothers in Pokfulam, teaching English for a few hours a week. Sometime following his arrival in Hong Kong he met and married a Cantonese woman called Maria. With a little daughter in tow and Magdalena aged only one month they moved to live an open air life on 'Sunshine Island', Kung Chau near Lantau, doing refugee relief work with the Quaker philanthropist, Gus Borgeest, who later won the Magsaysay Prize for the project. Borgeest described John as, 'a wonderful mechanic and medical clinic attendant, a veritable artist with his hands' and in Magdalena's words their life together on the island was free and wild and never to be forgotten.

The Peter family left the island when the project closed in about 1963 and took crowded rented accommodation in the concrete jungle of North Point on Hong Kong island. John got an engineering job with a refrigeration company but times were hard, riots broke out and there were bombs and chaos everywhere. Water supplies were often cut off which was especially trying as there was a new baby, their fourth child, to be looked after. In the summer of 1963 when baby Agnes was three, they had had more than enough of the city and John moved the family to Rennie's Mill, a steep and isolated place by the sea with a more relaxed village atmosphere where soldiers of the Kuomintang army had settled after the communist takeover of China. John got a job in a plastic toy factory while Maria took a ferry every day to her job at a medicine factory in North Point. Money was always short and the children had to be put to work at an early age in factories of any kind as soon as the schools broke up for the holidays. Hong Kong was always a tough place and it was a harsh and demanding life for all of them.

Gradually John's health began to fade. Unable to manage the climb up the hill to the bus stop he had to stop work, staying alone at home with his memories, his classical music and the BBC while the world moved on around him. In Magdalena's words, 'He was wearing out, he was tired. He wasn't that happy person he used to be… He died in the middle of the night of 4th February 1974 [aged sixty six]. It was in the middle of his sleep that he woke up with complaint of chest pain. Then he told me he was dying, asked me to be good, and died like he was going back to sleep. The night before he was still playing with Agnes and singing the song *Donna Donna* after dinner. She was not even ten… I myself believe that father's heart had been all the time in China. Like many missionaries I know, they have dedicated their whole youth to missionary work and when they are old and are sent back to whatever country they are from, they find it very difficult to adapt. Their hearts always stay back where they have worked and sacrificed. They miss that kind of life and the things they used to do.'

Fleda Jones, the American lab technician who did important work in the Chungking clinic, is shown in the post-service listings as being at Faridabad Town Hospital, India in October 1951. Apparently still with the AFSC, their records show her as having a home address at Webster Groves, Missouri, as being in California in the early fifties, while in the late fifties she is listed at an address at Riverside Drive, New York. Miraculously I have been able to trace a phone number for her still in the same building and have spoken to her there . She told me she spent the rest of her career in medical work and had never married. In her early nineties, she was keeping 'busy busy', learning Chinese and living with her photos of China and her memories.

David White, the energetic graduate in agriculture, the second to last member held in Chungking waiting for his exit permit, went on to marry Leonore Perelta, the Filipina he had met on landing from the ship in Manila and returned to the USA with her, settling in California. They had no children and sadly she died after fifteen years of marriage. In 1973 he met and married Carol with whom he had three children and, as she told me in her letter, 'thirty three rich years together'. He worked as an engineer for a big corporation, retiring in 1978 and building a home on a large plot of land where they enjoyed a self-sufficient life style, growing their own food and occasionally crossing the vast distances to visit family and to stay with the Reumans in Maine. In a most generous gesture, Carol has sent me David's letters home from Chungking which run to many pages describing how it was to be there after the communists arrived and adding much human detail to the formal records of the time.

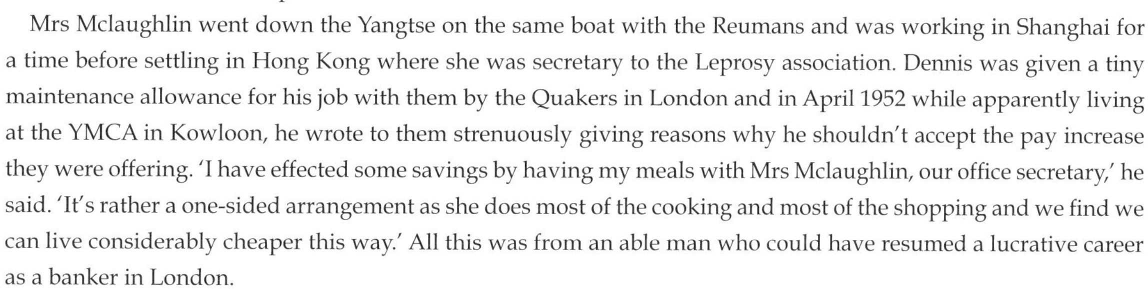

With an unusual name like **Dennis Frone,** the very last China Convoy man out of Chungking should have been the easiest to trace but he wasn't. I managed to obtain a copy of his death certificate and this showed that he had died of a heart attack in Gloucester in the south west of England in November 1973 aged only fifty seven. In desperation I wrote to the deceased's address shown on the certificate and remarkably thanks to the occupier's valiant efforts I was soon able to speak to Vera, Dennis's widow, still living in Gloucester nearby.

Dennis, arriving at last in Hong Kong on 15 September 1951 as a free man, found work there as the administrator for The Mission to Lepers' treatment centre which was moving to Hay Ling Chau, to become a thriving island project just outside Hong Kong harbour. In Chungking he'd had a special friendship with the divorced Mrs Mclaughlin, the IRC employee Jack called Mrs McCork either because she kept popping up or was totally unpronounceable for the Chinese. Dorothy Reuman tells me that she lived alone in a house up on the hill behind the Unit and that Dennis often used to visit her there.

Mrs Mclaughlin went down the Yangtse on the same boat with the Reumans and was working in Shanghai for a time before settling in Hong Kong where she was secretary to the Leprosy association. Dennis was given a tiny maintenance allowance for his job with them by the Quakers in London and in April 1952 while apparently living at the YMCA in Kowloon, he wrote to them strenuously giving reasons why he shouldn't accept the pay increase they were offering. 'I have effected some savings by having my meals with Mrs Mclaughlin, our office secretary,' he said. 'It's rather a one-sided arrangement as she does most of the cooking and most of the shopping and we find we can live considerably cheaper this way.' All this was from an able man who could have resumed a lucrative career as a banker in London.

Christine must have been the reason Dennis stayed and worked in Hong Kong as back in England in 1957 they finally were married. They had no children and Christine sadly died young. Becoming a professional photographer specialising in recording works of art, especially those of William Morris, Dennis later married his cousin Vera in 1967. They had only six years together before Dennis died suddenly, leaving a son, John, aged only two.

Nobody ever seems to have spoken ill of Dennis. He was a modest man of quiet strength and competence, liked and relied upon by everyone.

These brief sketches thus suggest lives well lived, of able people carefully selected for service with the China Convoy whose lives were hugely enriched by that experience. Joining the FAU rescued many such as Bernard Llewellyn and Tony Meager from clerical jobs of Dickensian dullness and others such as Jack from menial work that had failed to develop their wider talents. With new horizons, skills, aspirations and a network of contacts, the whole world was now their oyster and they became lawyers and doctors and excelled in a wide range of philanthropic and educational fields, settling in many parts of the Commonwealth. Indeed one former member who went on the FAU China Convoy reunion visit to China in 1996 observed that amongst their elderly party of fifteen men and six women there were several graduates of Cambridge, Oxford and Harvard, six professors, three physicians, two architects and nearly every one a writer.

The stark beauty of China itself and its desperate human needs also left a big impression on them all. Bernard Llewellyn wrote in his book, *I Left My Roots in China*, published in 1953, that there were two types of foreigner in China at that time. On the one hand many visiting westerners hated China because they never really discovered it. They often brought their own tinned food and fruit juices with them and never went beyond the 'phoney Orientalism' of the coastal cities such as Shanghai. 'But,' he concluded, 'I have met many, too, who love China in a way they cannot explain; who have discovered, even amidst the chaos of the war years, a contentment and a happiness there which they have not found anywhere else.'

The China they left behind

More troubling though is what must have happened to the vast majority of those who served with the China Convoy who were of course Chinese and who have not received due attention in this book. With their ancient country heading for years of upheaval and turmoil as the FSU was disbanded, they were to enjoy none of the privileges and opportunities of the West. As well as facing the common struggle for survival, their close association with the foreigners would have put them at considerable risk during the immediate anti-foreign purges and later the Cultural Revolution. It was hopeless for them to argue that the FAU was apolitical and altruistic and was not committed to the exploitation of China. Those who had sided with the foreigners must necessarily be counter revolutionaries and would not persuade the mob or communist struggle session to the contrary.

The Chinese who worked for the FAU included employees who did all the essential work, such as drivers, mechanics, tin smiths, carpenters, cooks and cleaners. Of these there were several hundred at the busiest times, such as the individuals Jack listed in the long letter that he pencilled from his hospital bed. This was steady employment with good wages, an iron rice bowl much valued, and many of them stayed with the Unit for years, moving from depot to depot as the focus of operations moved northwards. They were good workers and it thus seemed to the foreigners that their loyalty was genuine and that they had absorbed something of the principles of service that were the central philosophy of the FAU.

However, in 1950 as the transport unit was closed this belief was seriously shaken when a number of employees at Chungking turned on their masters, demanding better severance terms. Jack and the others were distressed at this turn of events, though it has to be seen in the light of their perilous financial situation and of their need to distance themselves from the foreigners. They were correct if they feared for the future and one wonders what became of such vibrant characters as Chang Min Sang and the lovely Mrs CMS and how they fared in the awful times to come.

The Chungking garage depot in 1946 led by Len Bonsall, in the leather jacket

Major Chiang and Henry Yu Chin-lung, Yenan, 1946

Peter Mason's 1989 photo

A small minority of Chinese in the Unit were not employees but became full FAU members after a period of associate membership. Like the Europeans they were not paid but had their expenses covered and could draw something monthly from the 'pool', having equal status with the foreign members. Of these Chinese members the FAU post-service register of 1954 lists about sixty, their addresses where known not being printed in the list to avoid them being identifiable and causing political embarrassment.

They were generally young men and women, probably Christians educated at mission schools and having functional English, who had had their university studies or careers disrupted by the Japanese invasion or by the civil war with the communists. As the foreigners struggled to grapple with the Chinese language, these Chinese members were of crucial importance as interpreters and as the essential interface both with the Chinese employees and with the extensive Chinese bureaucracies that always needed to be dealt with. Throughout the civil war and the change of regimes, a more difficult or onerous diplomatic role than this is hard to imagine and their contribution to the project was of pivotal importance.

Some of them could have been well connected within Guomintang circles, even perhaps acting as informers for the government. On the other hand one, Henry Yu, who served for a long period is reputed to have been a nephew of Chou En Lai, the communist leader. Whatever their political loyalties, all of them were marked out as being associated with the foreigners and would have had difficult times to face in the denunciations to come. A number of the women married foreigners and were able to leave China to settle abroad; Dorothy knew of eleven or twelve; but the vast majority had no such escape. What became of them can be guessed at but in most cases will never be known.

What happened to China itself and to the old haunts and work places of the FAU is easier to ascertain. In 1989 Peter Mason made a nostalgic visit to Ssu Gung Li Ban, site of the south bank depot, at Chongqing. There he found a new bridge across the Yangtse and that the dusty track that was the main route to Kweiyang had been turned into a major highway, a deep cutting into the hillside isolating the FAU depot site high up an embankment above the road. Remarkably his colour photo appears to show the end of a white building similar to the clinic still standing, though the rest of the site cannot be seen. Later in 1996 the former FAU members who went on the reunion visit to China searched hard for the depot on two occasions but were confused and frustrated in their efforts. Today the spreading countryside of hills, small farm buildings and terraced rice fields that they all knew so well has been engulfed by the expanding urban area and is now buried deep under endless ranks of modern tower blocks.

As to Chongqing city itself, in Jack's time a vermin ridden ant hill crowded with refugees barely clinging to life, there has been change in so short a period of time that would have Jack and his friends gasping in astonishment. Panoramic photographs now show the cliffs on the Yangtze as a veritable Manhattan, glittering with neon and skyscrapers, no longer the medieval city of so recent a past. One of the biggest cities in China and therefore of the world, Chongqing's urban area now has a population of perhaps seven million and if the wider municipality is included, of thirty million people. China's recent success seems remarkable in contrast to the intractable chaos of the forties from which progress and economic development looked highly improbable even to the most optimistic observer.

After their experiences in China, every FAU member must have tried to evaluate what they had achieved and how their efforts would be perceived in the longer term. What would disappoint them is that in China the FAU's story is largely unknown and forgotten.

In the nature of things the contribution of the FAU was small and while undoubtedly lives were saved and suffering was alleviated, these benefits were inevitably short term and limited in time. One of the FAU's principles was that after completing a project such as rehabilitating a war damaged hospital they should 'devolve' it to the Chinese and withdraw as soon as possible. However, apart from any such continuing benefits which were often significant, the FAU's positive contribution came to an abrupt end in 1951 when the foreigners withdrew from China.

Most important is that China has since become strong and self-reliant, though it is intriguing to note that the first three overseas directors of Oxfam,

Michael Harris and his medical team

Michael Harris with Sid Walker dresses the leg ulcer of a Chinese soldier, Paoshan

the leading British relief and development agency, had been members of the FAU China Convoy. Oxfam, which started out in the post-war period as a fund raising committee of the Oxford Quaker yearly meeting, was at first a mere collecting point for resources to support the relief work of others. The novel and ground breaking task then entrusted to these three employees was to go abroad to identify and implement longer term development projects. Thus Bernard Llewellyn, Ken Bennett and Michael Harris, all China Convoy men, successively led Oxfam's overseas development work from its inception right through to November 1984. Maggie Black wrote in her book, *Oxfam, The First Fifty Years,* that their FAU experience had given them, 'a unique grounding in the complexities of relief and welfare work in distant and unfamiliar environments'.

If Oxfam in the post-war years gained prominence and led the world of NGOs in small scale development work and as Oxfam built its strategy in part on the FAU experience in China, it is satisfying to think that the China Convoy thus had a positive influence far beyond its relatively modest scale. For example, while Oxfam was implementing the influential new idea of 'integrated development' in the early seventies, twenty five years earlier the China Convoy's experience of its Honan Area Project based on the rehabilitation of Chungmou had showed just how difficult it is to achieve this ideal.

Hong Kong, 1949, by Robert Reuman

In the late seventies and early eighties Hong Kong served as an informal regional base for Oxfam and I myself worked as a volunteer doing fund raising there, acting as host to Llewellyn and Harris and others from Oxford whenever they visited. This fund raising was highly successful, the money pouring in, and our small voluntary Oxfam group eventually grew into an NGO independent of Oxfam UK. As 'Oxfam Hong Kong', this currently does substantial development work in China and has many regional offices there, including in the very towns where the FAU had bases. The work that the FAU China Convoy began is thus being continued by Chinese people in China today with this distinct if tenuous link to the past.

16 EPILOGUE
I FINALLY VISIT CHUNGKING

Having immersed myself in Jack Jones and his FAU writings for more than four years, it became inevitable that I must fly to Chongqing to look for the places he worked in, especially Ssu Kung Li Pan, the south bank garage depot. The visit in April 2013 was made perfect by my friends, Bill and his wife, Denise Chen Yu, a professional interpreter, who made it all possible for me.

I knew I wouldn't find anything much as urban China has totally changed from decade to decade. As already mentioned, former FAU member, Peter Mason, in 1989 took a bus from the new bridge over the Yangtze and photographed what he thought was the end of the white godown building that once had been the FAU clinic.

Old FAU members visit the Friends School, 1996

In 1996 twenty one people, mostly octogenarian former FAU members, 'revisited the roads of West China', covering huge distances on poor roads in unsuitable buses to seek out their old haunts. They failed to find the Friends Centre in the city and they twice struggled to find the old garage depot site at Ssu Kung Li Pan. More happily they successfully visited the Friends High School and the Canadian Mission Hospital in the hills behind the garage, now both thriving modern institutions.

Then in April 2013 in a state of high anticipation I finally flew into Chongqing's huge and busy airport. What had once been a nightmare bus ride of many hours over steep hills, my taxi swiftly brought me into the city on fast superhighways and across a spectacular suspension bridge over the Jialing River. Chongqing city and its surroundings are Manhattan reincarnate, yet more modern and glittering even than New York. My own hostel was in a run down area off one of the last ancient ladders of steps that lead from the Yangtze River up its substantial cliffs to the city. With narrow pathways lined with crumbling stone walls and teetering houses and the occasional labourer still plying for hire, carrying loads across his shoulders on a pole, this was a rare hint of what Jack would have remembered over sixty years ago.

Chonqing, April 2013

Risking death to cross the highway at the top of my steep stairs, I discovered that the stairway had been rebuilt and continued upwards as a route to walk into town. Passing a place where a new business was celebrating its opening with a display of a new Rolls Royce, a Bentley, an Aston Martin and two Maseratis, I found the Victory Monument. Originally a wooden structure built to commemorate the death of Dr Sun Yat Sen, it had been rebuilt to celebrate the end of China's war with Japan and now stands at the crossing point of two broad pedestrian streets. I remembered a grainy monochrome picture of the Monument towering above the low commercial buildings in the streets around it. Still standing at the intersection of these two streets, but now dwarfed by skyscrapers several times its height, today it creates the focal point for a cross-shaped open pedestrian plaza. As evening fell and the lights went on, this was thronged with people enjoying the glitter of so many glamorous shops displaying every consumer luxury and designer label under the sun.

Friends Centre, Chungking under construction, 1943

It is a vibrant and exciting place, a truly dramatic piece of urban planning, and I felt elated as I turned left and walked past the site of the Cathay Cinema where the FAU men long ago had enjoyed brief escape from China's cold reality. A few minutes walk and I was in Zhengyan Jie. Here at 4 Cheng Yang Kai the FAU once had its headquarters when Chunking was the capital of the Nationalist government, fleeing as refugees from the Japanese invaders. And here in 1943 FAU stalwart, Tony Reynolds, had supervised the construction of its headquarters building, a neat L-shaped brick structure with wide verandas on both floors. Tony told his son, Peter, how this job had meant six months of standing around in the rain and mud directing the building work. Jack Jones, for his part, wrote of going to a favourite eating place in Cheng Yang Kai to enjoy a last slap up meal with Old Tobacco, one of the long serving men of the transport unit. It was an important place in their lives.

Chungking cinema

The slope of the street was recognisable from Tony's black and white photos of Cheng Yang Kai but now the eating places are McDonalds and a 'Food Street' mall which stands close to a branch of HSBC on the lower corner of the street. While there were still men putting up buildings in the rain, this time they were thirty five storeys rather than two.

On a visit by taxi to the school in the hills of the south bank, once again proudly known as the Friends High School, we arrived unannounced at the weekend but were given a warm welcome by some teachers. One of them showed me the wooded site on the hill where the headmaster's house had stood. Now nothing was left of it and, he said, they wanted to rebuild a replica but they had no pictures of it. He was genuinely shocked and delighted

Friends High School, Chongqing

when I produced for him a photo of the building taken just after its construction in 1903.

The biggest wild goose to be chased was of course to look for the south bank garage depot at Ssu Kung Li Pan, the name meaning 'four and a half foreign miles' from the river. In 1996 the visiting party of ageing FAU members had measured the four and a half kilometres from the old ferry point and ended up in front of a teachers college. 'A local friend pointed to another walled compound a couple of doors down which turned out to be a high school…' The next day they returned in pouring rain to search again. 'They were satisfied that the familiar hills once behind their garage were seen behind the teachers college' and that the school was probably on its site.

I vaguely remembered this conclusion but was sceptical about it when we got down from our taxi at Sigongli, having crossed the bridge from the city. What had been little more than a dusty track between rolling hills and paddy fields, as in Robert Reuman's fine colour photos of 1950, was now Silicon Valley itself. Here was The Economic Technology Development Zone of Chongqing, nearby many hi-tech factories and two universities. The road, now called Jingnan Avenue, is an impressive multi-lane urban highway, close by the impressive Sigongli super-highway intersection. Overhead runs a spectacular straddle beam monorail, part of the Chongqing rail transit system, this section having been opened in 2011. We found ourselves between two vast overhead stations, Sigongli, and Wugongli at the five kilometre point from the river. Around us was a glossy setting of tower blocks and an urban street with smart shops and neat granite faced pavements, all well planted with trees. Nothing of the original topography or the surrounding hills could be seen, everything hidden by tall buildings, the dips and bumps of hillock and paddy field levelled for the new road and construction work. It was going to be even more difficult for us to find the garage site than it had been in 1989 and 1996.

We had to start somewhere so we turned up a side street that climbed a slope from the main artery and which we hoped would give us a view of the hills beyond. This had the feel of a much older lane, lined with shabby blocks of flats, some built on the stone plinths of older buildings. After climbing for a few minutes between these buildings we reached a dead end where we found ourselves looking down on what we soon discovered was the campus of the Chongqing University of Education, and beyond it the hills. I had my photos of the garage with me and it was easy to believe that the peaks and the pass we were looking at were indeed the same.

As we turned to go back down again we saw a happy group of neighbours chatting together by one of the buildings. Now was my chance to ask some questions, so I bit the bullet and plunged into their midst brandishing my photos of the garage and rice fields. Denise explained everything to them and they pored over the pictures, talking nineteen to the dozen. One sixty year old said she remembered the garage premises well. After the FAU left in 1951 it had been taken over by the Peoples Liberation Army and used as an ammunition depot, she told us, finally being demolished when she was about ten, which would have been in 1963. She then promised to find us an older lady who might be able to tell us more.

She disappeared and left us for a few minutes, soon returning with Mrs Yu Zheng Yin, a strong looking eighty year old who was sat down on a chair and given Dorothy Reuman's album of colour photos of the garage and rice fields to look through. It then became apparent that in a city of fifteen million people we had found someone who not only remembered the FAU clinic but whose life had been changed by it. First of all she remembered a man who had had his leg almost hacked off by bandits. It was the clinic that had saved him. Then she recalled that it cost only four cents to register at the clinic and that all medicines were free. Her parents were landless labourers before being given land by the communists but six of her seven siblings had already died of disease. When she was about sixteen her last surviving little brother was dying of measles and the clinic took him in and treated him. During the Cultural Revolution she was criticised for praising the foreigners but she was not going to be cowed. 'Why not praise them', she said, 'as it was they who saved his life'. He is living still, she told us, and is now aged sixty eight

Mrs Yu Zheng Yin looks at Dorothy's album

Although she was sharp and alert I was a little sceptical that she might have been remembering a different clinic or that something had got confused in the telling. Then came the clinching detail. She remembered, she said, a tall, dark Indian man and a very handsome white skinned foreigner. The Indian was of course John Peter, who was totally unique and distinctive in the village. As to the European, Jack himself was heavily bearded so the contest for her favourite foreigner has to be between Bob Reuman and Dave White, both of them rugged and American.

So where was the site of the garage, we asked. The answer was a little ambivalent because we were told it was at the teachers' university or at the Chongqing 110 Middle School. Heading back down the hill and turning left on Jingnan Avenue, there immediately was the middle school. We talked our way inside and found a bright environment of running tracks and sports facilities surrounded by the tall blocks of the school. Brightly dressed children, none of them in uniform, came running up and warmly tried out their English on us. I just had to show them the photos and Denise told them the story of how somewhere here, perhaps under their classrooms, Chinese drivers and mechanics and a handful of foreigners had distributed much of China's medical supplies in the awful years of the late forties saving many lives. They were totally amazed and entranced.

The school's entrance

On returning home I found a photo of former FAU member, Nellie Bonsall (born Nellie Wee in Penang) one of the 1996 China reunion group, seen standing on this same playing field, smiling in satisfaction that they had probably found the site of their garage. Nellie, whose university education in Hong Kong had been interrupted in 1941 by the Japanese invasion, had been based at the Cheng Yang Kai headquarters in Chungking city and every week had gone out to the garage to do the accounts, there meeting Len Bonsall, the dashing garage manager.

I thus now know that we had both independently found the same site for the garage, both in 1996 and in 2013. The story of the school being built there also seems highly plausible. Next to the garage there had been the large yard and godowns used by the FAU as overspill parking for its trucks. This was owned by the KMT government's National Resources Commission and was separated from the FAU garage by only a flimsy bamboo fence. With a growing shortage of development land, these adjoining premises in army and government hands would have been an ideal site for the construction of a school, possibly also forming part of the neighbouring university campus. With the site now levelled and cut back into the rising slopes, it is impossible to guess exactly where the garage once stood, but nonetheless our wild goose had thus been glimpsed, even if not finally captured.

China Convoy nurse, Constance Pittman, born Shen Ming Chen in Nanking, China in 1929, wrote movingly of the place following her visit there in 1996 with the other elderly FAU members. 'I now realize that Ssu Kung Li Pan will always be there. We can turn off at the four and a half kilometre marker whenever we wish, to return to that place in our hearts where we will remain forever handsome and young, gay and spirited, where we will answer the call of our conscience, and give comfort and aid to China when she needs us most.'

Connie, a distinguished Professor of Endocrinology at the University of Alabama who died in 2010, would be gratified to know that the country of her birth is now strong and that its people have progressed to an extent that would have seemed impossible when she was in Chungking with the FAU almost seventy years ago. Jack too would be astounded and, I'm sure, deeply proud of what has since been achieved in his beloved China in so very short a time.

A new bridge over the Yangtse, Chongqing, 2013

APPENDICES

Glossary of Chinese Terms

Ch'ang chang	Factory/garage boss
Fan tien	Rice shop or eating place
Fa tung	Overheated
Fu ch'ang chang	Deputy factory/garage boss
Godown	Warehouse, a China coast expression of Indian derivation
Ha plau	Brazier
Hua k'erh	Sedan chair or litter
Hsi-kua	Water melon
Hsien	County or district, a small local government unit
Hsien chang	District head
Hsien sheng	Honorific greeting to one deemed senior; literally, 'Before Born'
K'an i k'an	A meeting
Kan pei	To drink a toast, literally 'dry cup'
K'e-ch'I	Impolite
Kung I Chou Hu Tuei	The Friends Ambulance Unit, sometimes transliterated as Gong Yi Jiu Hu Du, possibly referring to the Friends Service Unit
Lao pei hsing	'Old hundred names', the man in the street or peasantry
Ma chih	Horse cart
Mao fang	Latrine
Mao ping	Trouble or problem, often referring to a mechanical breakdown.
Mei yeau tien li	No electricity
Mien pao	Bread
Pen p'iao	A currency under the Nationalists
Ting hao	Quite good, fine, okay; a greeting
Pai-tzu	A token, eg with a queuing number on it
Pan fa	Way to solve a problem, repair etc
Pao mao	Broken down, literally at anchor

Pu hao tu tzes	Stomach problems
Pu hao	Not okay, as in 'a pu hao engine', ie one not working
P'u kai	Cotton quilt, bed roll
Pu tung	Don't understand
Salichou	A rice based spirit up to 50 or 60%, popular with the Miao people.
'Shui in the ch'i yu'	Water in the petrol
Sung kei ni	Give it to you
Tsai-chien	Goodbye
Tou chang with yu-tiao	Soya bean milk with dough fritters
Tu tzu	Stomach problem
Tungshi	Literally east/west, meaning things, kit or equipment
Wei kuo jen	Foreigner
Wei shih ma	Why
'Yellow fish'	Passengers hitching a lift, packed in like sardines that smell
"A chiao pole"	A lifting pole for carrying a counterbalanced load at each end carried across the shoulders.

Glossary of Abbreviations

AFSC	American Friends Service Committee, based in Philadelphia and founded in 1917 on Quaker principles as a vehicle for conscientious objectors to provide humanitarian service during and after the world conflict. As from 1946 it took over running of the London based FAU 'China Convoy' in the name of the Friends Service Council (FSU). In 1947 the AFSC was joint winner with the Friends Service Council of the Nobel Peace Prize.
AIS	Agricultural and Industrial Services, a subsidiary of CNRRA with whom FAU personnel worked in agricultural rehabilitation and distributing tools and supplies for farmers.
AMA	Army Medical Administration
ARC	American Red Cross
ATC	Air Transport Command, the American unit which flew supplies over the Hump into China.
BMM	The British Military Mission from which Jack acquired some comfortable leather chairs in Kweiyang.
BRCS	British Red Cross
BUAC	British United Aid to China. In 1942 under the leadership of Lady Elizabeth Cripps, this relief fund

for the Chinese people initially raised nearly three million Pounds. In 1946 Lady Cripps visited China, including Chungking. FAU member, Michael Harris (later overseas director of Oxfam) became its general secretary. Dennis Frone who was with Jack Jones in Chungking was seconded to BUAC in Hong Kong but twice returned to Chungking to help hold the fort when Jack fell ill, the second time taking over as transport director and being caught in China by the communist liberation. The fund in 1947 became the Sino-British Fellowship Trust.

CAT — Civil Air Transport was formed by General Claire Chennault of 'Flying Tigers' fame. Using war surplus aircraft it began airlifting supplies into war-ravaged China under contract to the Nationalist government and the CIA, including ammunition and war materials for use in the struggle against the communists. When the communists were victorious the airline decamped to Formosa, absorbing the assets of two other Chinese airlines, whose planes were impounded in Hong Kong, following protracted litigation. CAT flew covert missions during the Korean War and in support of the French in Indo-China. It was then acquired by the CIA and, as Air America, operated as America's clandestine airline during the conflict in Vietnam.

CATC — Central Air Transport Corporation, another airline of the Nationalist era.

CCC — Church of Christ in China, set up in the twenties by several Protestant denominations as an independent Chinese church to localise Christianity and to counter the appearance of foreign influence.

CBA — Canadian Business Agency, established to service Canadian and other missions in Chungking, with premises in Chungking city including a brick walled compound where the FAU could safely leave vehicles and a very nice hostel whose verandahs overlooked the river.

CGH — Church Guest House, Upper Albert Road, Hong Kong, sometimes used by FAU members, including Jack Jones when he left China. On the first page of Han Suyin's autobiographical novel, *A Many Splendoured Thing,* its author describes staying there along with many missionaries just arrived from communist China as refugees and a man who strongly resembles Robert Reuman.

CN Dollars — Chinese National dollars

CNAC — China National Aviation Corporation, staffed mainly by American pilots, was the principal airline under the Nationalists that carried passengers internally and vast quantities of crucial air freight over the Hump from India.

CIC — Chinese Industrial Co-Operatives. Promoted by New Zealander, Rewi Alley, the CIC organised refugees and others into cooperatives in China, raised money for tools and helped them market their products, sometimes selling blankets, soap and clothing to the army. Its positive attitude that anything was possible was the origin of the expression, 'gung ho', derived from a part of its name in Chinese. His Bailie School at Shuangshipu moved to Shantan owing to harassment by Nationalist soldiers and later took over the trucks and other assets of Jack's south bank transport depot and some of its staff when it finally closed in 1951.

CIM — China Inland Missions, the substantial London based protestant missionary organisation that by 1934 had 1368 missionaries scattered in 364 stations in China. When the communists were victorious it decided to remain in China with the result that when it became impossible for work to continue, the evacuation of nearly 700 missionaries presented an almost insuperable task. When Shanghai fell this operation was conducted from Chungking by its director, Arnold Lea, who also assisted Jack Jones on the death and interment of Robert Waldie.

CLARA — China Liberated Areas Relief Association, established by the communists as a counterpart agency to administer and coordinate relief supplies from UNRRA.

CMS & G — Chungmou Machine Shop and Garage, an FAU project.

CNRRA — Chinese National Relief and Rehabilitation Administration, set up in January 1945 to administer and coordinate the post-war operations in Nationalist China of UNRRA. Its work included emergency relief, returning refugees to their homes, rehabilitating the agriculture and industrial sectors and establishing a public health programme. One view is that the establishment of a distinct national entity to pursue this work was to enable the Nationalist government to take control of the substantial quantities of materials imported by UNRRA and to use them to their own purposes. With money sloshing around for well-paid foreign employees and with aid materials vulnerable to corruption and theft, Jack aimed his cynicism in one of his articles at the vast and empty polished desk in their Changsha office, while William Sewell in his book, '*I Stayed in China*', averred that CNRRA actually stood for, 'China Never Really Received Anything'.

CRACC — China Relief Agencies Clearing Committee

CRC — Chinese Red Cross with whom the FAU worked in the early days, especially at its hospital at Kweiyang. Its founder was Dr Robert Lim, an Edinburgh trained physiologist who had married a Scotswoman and served on the Western Front in the 1914-18 World War. CRC can also be the Canadian Red Cross.

ECA — The Economic Cooperation Administration was established in April 1948 under the Economic Cooperation Act which authorised the 'Marshall Plan'. Although China did not participate in the Marshall Plan, assistance was furnished to it in a similar way under other legislation. The ECA's aid and assistance work in China was later absorbed by the JCRR.

FAU — Friends Ambulance Unit, a charitable organisation set up by the Religious Society of Friends during the First World War as a channel for non-military service by conscientious objectors. Revived in the Second World War, it worked in many countries including China where, because of its core work transporting medical relief supplies, it was known as 'the China Convoy'. As essentially a war-time institution, its China work was handed over to the American AFSC in 1946.

FSC — Friends Service Council was established in 1927 as the standing committee responsible for the overseas work of the Religious Society of Friends. As it had a long-standing presence in Szechuan province, Jack Jones sometimes found himself visiting its schools and hospitals on his way to Chengtu.

FSU — Friends Service Unit, the name given by the AFSC to its unit that took over the FAU's work in China in 1946, administered from its headquarters in Philadelphia.

GADA — 'Go Anywhere, Do Anything', a declared principle of the FAU.

GY — Gold Yuan

HMS & G — Honan Machine Shop and Garage, an FAU project.

IHT — Institute of Hospital Technology, a small agency established in the 1930's based at the Union Hospital in Hankow and run by the International Relief Committee. Post-war it had strong links with the FAU/FSU, especially through a strong contingent of New Zealander members. It provided services to hospitals and training schemes for medical mechanics, physiotherapists, radiographers and laboratory technicians.

IRC — International Relief Committee, which had changed its name from the International Red Cross Committee, was a body formed by a group of mission hospitals to buy drugs abroad and distribute them within China. It also undertook to do the medical transport work of the NHA. The FAU was requested by the Chinese to work primarily in medical transport and to do this it took over the IRC base and vehicles at Kweiyang, thus doing transport work for the NHA and mission hospitals, charging on a kilometre-ton basis where possible. The relationship was complex and the FAU members working at the Chungking transport unit were seconded to the IRC, leading to many accounting difficulties in allocating costs. After the Japanese surrender the IRC was based in Shanghai, mainly staffed by foreign missionary doctors and others. With the communist take-over, it gradually imploded, failing to provide further funds to the FSU. In particular non-payment of repatriation money for Chinese employees caused considerable strife at Jack's Chungking depot when transport work was complete and they were finally laid off.

JCC — Joint China Committee in London.

JCRR	Joint Committee for Relief and Rehabilitation. James Yen, born in Szechuan in 1890, founded the Mass Education Movement and the Rural Reconstruction Movement in the twenties and in 1948 persuaded the American Congress to fund the Joint Commission on Rural Reconstruction (JCRR) which carried out land reform and educational projects. The JCRR was led by five commissioners, three of whom were Chinese, appointed by the Chinese government, and two of whom were American, appointed by the American President. During the last days of the Chinese Civil War the JCRR carried out a program of rent reduction, guarantee of tenure security, and formation of cooperatives, in addition to agronomic and irrigation programs. By one estimate, this was the largest non-communist land reform program in China before the JCRR moved to Taiwan in 1949. Jack ran a fleet of their vehicles in Chengdu for a fee to help fund continued transport work in Chungking. They had godowns eighty miles down the river at Pei P'ei from which his transport unit handled medical supplies.
KMT	The Kuomintang (Guomindang), or Chinese Nationalist Party, established in 1912 as the ruling party by Sun Yat Sen. During Jack Jones' time in China the KMT was under the leadership of Chiang Kai-shek who made his capital in Chungking during the war with Japan. In 1949 following its defeat by the communists the KMT fled to Taiwan.
LA	Liberated areas controlled by the communists
MT	Medical Team. Thus for example MT-20 was the anti-malaria project that was set up in Yunnan in 1948.
NASC	Presumably the National Airborne Service Corps which decamped to Taiwan with the Nationalists. Jack notes that he treated a lot of their employees in his clinic as he was reliant on them for vehicle spare parts.
NHA	National Health Administration, the Ministry of Health under the Nationalist government. See also WSS.
NRC	National Resources Commission which owned the yard and depot next door to the south bank garage at Ssu Kung Li Pan.
PLA	Peoples' Liberation Army
QM	Quarter Master, referring to the QM stores building or supplies.
SM	Staff Meeting
TD	Transport director
UCR	United China Relief, an American private fund for channelling assistance to Nationalist China, set up by agencies doing relief work in China in order to avoid competition in fund raising. UCR

	provided much early funding to the FAU.
UNRRA	United Nations Relief and Rehabilitation Administration, which was active in relieving victims of war mainly in 1945 and 1946 before being superseded by other UN agencies in 1947. In China it worked through CNRRA and CLARA.
USC	United Services to China, the successor to the American war-time organisation, United China Relief.
WC	West China
WCUU	West China Union University, Chengtu, now part of Sichuan University.
WSS or WSX	Weishengshu or Weishengxu, the Nationalist government's Ministry of Health, otherwise called NHA, the National Health Administration.
YMCA	Young Men's Christian Association, established in China by the Quakers among others.

Romanisation of Place Names

The left hand column shows the earlier Wade-Giles transliterations of place names as used by Jack and others writing in the nineteen forties and the right hand column shows the current or Pinyin spellings in alphabetical order.

Wade-Giles	**Pinyin**
Anhwei	Anhui
Paoki	Baoji
Peking	Beijing
Pei P'ei	Beibei
Pichieh	Bijie
Changte	Changde or Anyang
Chengtu	Chengdu
Chungking	Chongqing
Kansu	Gansu
Kwantung	Guangdong
Kwangchow (Canton)	Guangzhou
Kwangsi	Guanxi
Kweiyang	Guiyang
Kweichow	Guizhou

Hantan	Handan
Hangchow	Hangzhou
Hankow	Hankou
Hopei	Hebei
Honan	Henan
Hupeh	Hubei
K'aifeng	Kaifeng
Lanchow	Lanzhou
Kiating	Leshan
Liuchow	Liuzhou
Luhsien	Luzhou
Loyang	Luoyang
Nanking	Nanjing
Kutsing	Qujing
Shandan or Shantan	Shantan
Szechwan	Sichuan
Suchow	Suzhou or Jiuquan
Tientsin	Tianjin
Urumchi or Tihua	Urumqi
Weihwei	Weihui
Sian	Xian
Hsining	Xining
Hsuchow	Xuzhou
Yenan	Yanan
Chaotung	Zhaotung
Chengchow	Zhengzhou
Chihkiang	Zhijiang
Chungmou	Zhongmou

SELECT BIBLIOGRAPHY

About the China Convoy

Adcock, Cynthia Letts. *Revolutionary Faithfulness: The Quaker Search for a Peaceable Kingdom in China, 1939-1951.* PhD Thesis, Bryn Mawr College, Philadelphia, 1974.

Cameron, Caitriona. *Go Anywhere Do Anything: New Zealanders in the Friends Ambulance Unit in China 1945-1951.* Wellington; New Zealand Yearly Meeting of the Society of Friends, 1996.

Davies, A. Tegla. *Friends Ambulance Unit.* London; George Allen and Unwin Ltd, 1947.

Llewellyn, Bernard. *I Left My Roots in China.* London; George Allen and Unwin Ltd, 1953.

Morris, David. *China Changed My Mind.* London; Cassell & Company Ltd, 1948.

Murphey, Rhoads. *Fifty Years of China to Me: Personal Recollections of 1942-1992.* Ann Arbor, Michigan; The Association for Asian Studies, Inc., 1994.

Reynolds, Jack. *Daughters of an Ancient Race.* Hong Kong; Heinemann Educational Books (Asia) Ltd, 1974.

Simpson, John E. *Letters from China: Quaker Relief Work in Bandit Country 1944-46.* Cambridge; Ross-Evans, 2001.

Books including material on the China Convoy

Armstrong-Reid, Susan and Murray, David. *Armies of Peace: Canada and the UNRRA Years.* Toronto; University of Toronto Press, 2008.

Ayoub, Christine (Ed). *Memories of the Quaker Past, Stories of thirty-seven senior Quakers*, including memoirs by American FAU members, Bob Crauder, Mark and Mardy Shaw and Roger Way. USA. Xlibris LLC, 2014.

Jones, Dafydd. *A Life on the Road Less Travelled; the Story of Parry Jones.* Philadelphia. Infinity Publishing.com, 2008.

Scott, Munroe. *McClure: The China Years of Dr. Bob McClure, A Biography.* Toronto; Canec Publishing and Supply House, 1977.

Seagrave, Dr. Gordon S. *Burma Surgeon.* London; Victor Gollancz Ltd, 1944.

Smith, Lyn. *Pacifists in Action: The Experiences of the Friends Ambulance Unit in the Second World War.* York; William Sessions Ltd, 1998.

Other background history etc

Allen, Dr. A. Stewart. *Trial of Faith.* Ontario; The Estate of Dr. A. Stewart Allen, 1995.

Auden, W.H. and Isherwood, Christopher. *Journey to a War.* London. Faber and Faber Ltd, 1939.

Belden, Jack. *Retreat With Stilwell.* London. Cassell and Company Ltd, 1943.

Black, Maggie. *A Cause For Our Times; Oxfam, the First Fifty Years.* Oxford; Oxfam Publications, 1992.
Brown, Eugene. *The Locust Fire,* a World War Two novel of Transport Command, the American air force in China. New York. Doubleday, 1957.
Bush, Roger. *FAU: The Third Generation, Friends Ambulance Unit Post-War Service and International Service 1946-1959.* York; William Sessions Ltd, 1998.
Chiang Yee. *The Men of the Burma Road.* London; Methuen & Co Ltd, 1942.
Clegg, Arthur. *Aid China, 1937-1949; A Memoir of a Forgotten Campaign.* Beijing; New World Press, 1989 and 1997.
Crow, Carl. *The Long Road Back to China; Along the Burma Road to China's Wartime Capital in 1939.* (Paul French Ed.) Hong Kong, Earnshaw Books, 2009.
Davidson, Robert and Mason, Isaac. *Life in West China.* London; Headley Bros, 1905.
Dikotter, Frank. *The Tragedy of Liberation: A History of the Chinese Revolution, 1945-1957.* London. Bloomsbury, 2013.
Dobson, Richard P. *China Cycle.* London; Macmilland & Co Ltd, 1946.
Friburg, H. Daniel. *West China and the Burma Road.* Minneapolis; Augsburg Publishing House, 1941.
Goodall, Felicity. *Exodus Burma, The British Escape through the Jungles of Death 1942.* Stroud, Gloucestershire. The History Press, 2011.
Han Suyin. *Destination Chungking.* London. Jonathan Cape Ltd, 1942.
Han Suyin. *A Many Splendoured Thing.* London; Jonathan Cape Ltd, 1952.
Han Suyin. *Birdless Summer.* London; Jonathan Cape Ltd, 1968
Han Suyin. *My House Has Two Doors.* London; Jonathan Cape Ltd, 1980.
Hong Ying. *Daughter of the River,* a novel set on the Chungking south bank in the early Maoist era. London; Bloomsbury Publishing Plc, 1998.
Hsu, Teresa. *Love and Share, Memoirs of a Centenarian.* Singapore. Sharana Rao, 2012.
Information Office of Guiyang Municipal Government. *The International Medical Team in Guiyang,* a compilation of photos and documents about the International Medical Team for Aid to China and the Chinese Red Cross that were based in Kweiyang near the FAU depot. Guiyang. China Intercontinental Press, 2005.
Luard, Tim. *Escape from Hong Kong: Admiral Chan Chak's Christmas Day Dash, 1941.* Hong Kong; Hong Kong University Press, 2012 .
Matthews, Clifford and Cheung, Oswald. *Dispersal and Renewal, Hong Kong University During the War Years,* describing the evacuation of many of the University's staff and students to south west China, some such as Nellie Wee (Bonsall) then joining the FAU. Hong Kong. Hong Kong University Press, 1998.
Mitter, Rana. *China's War with Japan, 1937-1945. The Struggle for Survival.* London. Allen Lane, 2013.
'Pa Chin'. *Cold Nights,* a novel of Chungking under the Nationalists in 1944, a bilingual translation. Hong Kong.

Chinese University Press, 2002.
Payne, Robert. *Chungking Diary.* London. William Heinemann Ltd, 1945.
Payne, Robert. *China Awakes.* London. William Heinemann Ltd, 1947.
Rattenbury, Harold B. *China-Burma Vagabond.* London. Frederick Muller Ltd, 1946.
Reynolds, Jack. *A Woman of Bangkok.* New York. Ballantine Books Inc., 1956.
Reynolds, Jack. *A Sort of Beauty.* London. Martin Secker & Warburg Ltd, 1956. (Republished as *A Woman of Bangkok*. Pan Books Ltd, 1959, Secker & Warburg, 1974, Editions Duang Kamol, Bangkok, 1985 and Monsoon Books, Singapore, 2011.)
Reynolds, Jack. *The Utter Shambles.* Bangkok. Siam Communications Ltd, 1974
Seagrave, Sterling. *The Soong Dynasty.* New York. Harper & Row, 1986.
Sewell, William. *I Stayed in China.* London. George Allen & Unwin Ltd, 1966.
Shipton, Eric. *That Untravelled World; An Autobiography.* London. Hodder and Stoughton Ltd, 1969.
Smith, Nicol. *Burma Road. New York. Garden City Publishing Co, Inc.*
Snow, Edgar. *Red Star Over China*. New York. Random House, 1938 and 1944.
Steele, Eric. *Everest and Beyond.* London. Constable and Company Ltd, 1998.
Stockwell, Esther Beck. *Asia's Call, My Life as a Missionary in China and Singapore.* San Francisco; Stockwell Press.
Stockwell, F. Olin. *With God in Red China: The Story of Two Years in Chinese Communist Prisons*. New York; Harper & Brothers.
Thompson, Phyllis. *China: The Reluctant Exodus; The Untold Story of the Withdrawal of the China Inland Mission from China.* London. Hodder and Stoughton Ltd, 1979.
Tuchmann, Barbara W. *Sand Against the Wind, Stillwell and the American Experience in China 1911-45.* USA, Macmillan Company, 1970.
Tyzack, Charles. *Friends to China; The Davidson Brothers and the Friends' Mission to China 1886-1939.* York. William Sessions Ltd, 1988.
Tyzack, Charles. *Nearly a Chinese, A Life of Clifford Stubbs.* Sussex, England. Book Guild Publishing, 2013.
Webster, Donovan. *The Burma Road.* New York. Farrar, Strauss and Giroux, 2003.
White, Theodore, with Annalee Jacoby. *Thunder Out of China.* New York. William Morrow & Company, 1946.
Worcester, G.R.G. *The Junkman Smiles.* London. Chatto & Windus Ltd, 1959.

Further Research

Across the world families of China Convoy members have in their attic or bottom drawers fading collections of photos, papers and ephemera about their relative's experiences in China whose historical significance will be slowly forgotten and lost. By tracing the families of the men and women who feature in Jack's writings I have discovered the precious photos that appear in this book. Over the last few years I have painstakingly tried to identify faces and locations in these photographs but there are still many gaps. If you can shed light on any of these photos, especially in naming unidentified people and places or correcting any mistakes, I would very much like to hear from you.

Tony Reynolds, an especially loyal friend to China throughout his life who chronicled the work of the FAU in a number of articles

I would also be more than pleased to receive scans or original prints of any China Convoy photos that you have and while I do not need to keep the originals any new discoveries and information will be gratefully added to my digital archive.

I can be reached at **arhicks56@hotmail.com**.

Also currently progressing this research and collecting photos and information is the China Convoy reunion group which hosts a website at **www.fauchinaconvoy.org.** This site has an excellent outline history of the China Convoy. By registering as a member you can also access the members' area and read and post new information. Such was the enduring spirit of the China Convoy that a reunion is still held annually in May at Friends House, Euston Road, London, now attended mainly by the descendants of FAU members and by others with an interest like myself. The group is keen to make contact with as many such families as possible. Reunions are well attended and offspring take great pleasure in learning more of their relative's China experiences and meeting others whose family members were also there.

The China Convoy was a beacon of hope in a very dark world and its history which has not been comprehensively recorded now needs preserving by us all.

Anthony Curwen surveys erosion, Chungmou

The FAU's south bank depot